Revisiting Modern European History: 1789–1945

Revisiting Modern European History: 1789–1945

Edited by

Vandana Joshi

Pearson

Dedicated to my students, past, present and future.

Editor—Acquisitions: Kaushal Jajware
Senior Editor—Production: G. Sharmilee

ISBN 978-93-325-4110-8

First Impression, 2016
Third Impression, 2022
Fourth Impression, 2024

Published by Pearson India Education Services Pvt. Ltd, CIN: U72200TN2005PTC057128

Head Office: 1st Floor, Berger Tower, Plot No. C-001A/2, Sector 16B, Noida – 201 301,Uttar Pradesh, India.

Registered Office: Featherlite, 'The Address' 5th Floor, Survey No 203/10B, 200 Ft MMRD Road, Zamin Pallavaram, Chennai - 600044
Website: in.pearson.com; Email:companysecretary.india@pearson.com

Digitally printed in India by Trinity Academy for Corporate Training Ltd, New Delhi in the year of 2024.

Contents

Introduction

Revisiting Modern European History: 1789–1945 helps us to understand the story of modern Europe in a thematic manner. The themes chosen for this volume, namely gender, race, class and nation have been used as analytical tools that question the universality and unilinearity of the so-called progress and development that Europe achieved in the modern era. The questions posed in the volume point to the problems and perils of the progress and development based on science. Scientific advancement in the Nazi era was utilized to create a moral universe within which death factories operated day in and day out with remarkable industrial efficiency such as in Auschwitz, to annihilate entire sections of population without creating psychological disturbance and moral qualms among the murders. With impunity the executioners could execute mass killings without soiling their hands in blood and hearing the cries of the victims.

Race, gender, class and nation in the century of extremes were so muddled that we cannot find simple solutions, categorizations and gradations. That is why they form four pillars on which our understanding of power politics of modern Europe rests. Readers will find an overlap of these categories throughout the book, which only confirms the inherent interconnections. Some chapters concentrate on one concept more than the other. The first three chapters concentrate on gender, chapter four and five on race, chapters six and seven on class, while chapter eight deals with nationhood, an idea that permeates all previous categories.

The first theme of this book is gender relations. Gender as an analytical tool came to feminists and women historians in the genealogy of conceptualizing women's marginalization much after studying women as women. The chapters on gender history reflect many of the concerns that were raised in the previous volume in the chapter on European feminism. In this volume, we are shifting from women to gender as a category of analysis. This is in keeping with the way of history writing, periodization and some of the critical concerns developed historically in feminist thought. Feminists came to realize that talking about women in isolation is not very meaningful as it produced a partial and fragmented understanding of the sexual difference in society. Secondly, studying women as women, assumed that women existed as a fixed and immutable social category just as men. In other words, both men and women in this understanding were synonymous to their biological sex. Thirdly, feminists started critiquing binaries such as home/factory, private/public, production/reproduction alongside man/woman to break free from essentialist, fixed frameworks and then went on to pose fundamental challenges to philosophy of history, periodization, chronologies, social and historical transformations and so on. It made more sense to see women in relation to men. We now briefly go back in time to trace this development.

In 1990, the editors of the US-based *Journal of Women's History* suggested that feminist history was witnessing a paradigm shift. The separate spheres theory of a masculine public sphere and a feminine private sphere had outworn its usefulness and was passing its epistemological baton onto a new analytical category called gender that sought to locate women within the broader framework of their social, cultural and political relationships with men. The term gender had already started replacing women in a few pioneering studies in the 1980s, such as Denis Riley's provocative *Am I that Name? Feminism and the Category of Women in history* (1988), and Joan Wallach Scott's *Gender as a useful category of historical analysis* (1986), which claimed that a retrievable "women's history" was not possible since the very category of women was defined in essentialist terms, based on biology. They challenged the fixed characteristics associated with men and women, as these characteristics are not universal and varied across time and space. By the late 1990s gender came to acquire wider currency, which reflected in the founding of journals like *Gender and History* and a host of scholarly publications. It was agreed that studying women in history through the lens of gender made more sense. Gender, however, was redefined to refer to abstract 'representations' of the differences between men and women, a form of social relations and a set of social identities. These representations could be found through studying texts and discourses and were constantly constructed and reconstructed by powerful groups who defined what it was to be a woman or man, thus controlling the parameters of what was possible in everyday life. In this understanding experience about the past could never be captured on its own terms for it was always constructed by the language. Language in this understanding is no longer a medium of communicating thought, but a creator of 'lived experience' itself. Experience becomes a linguistic event. Language sets the terms of power, in other words, language in action, language as discourse, created reality. Some went as far as to say there is no reality outside the text. These post-structuralists upstaged language, discourse and identity at the cost of material evidence.

Women as a social category itself was splintered in the identity politics of race, region, religion, culture, sexuality, generation and so on. This theorization and deconstructive 'death of woman' has recently been attacked by practitioners of history for whom an investigation of hard, material evidence remains the key to any assertion, to deal with women as a political category and to study its agency in different times and spaces. Scholars recently are found to be talking about a spatial turn, a purported paradigm shift, which they deploy to rewrite history. Nonetheless, cultural or linguists turn has made historians ever more sensitive to and aware of silences, erasures and marginalization of those who could not stake their claims to power earlier and gender remains as ever a valid category of analysis. This way of reworking European history also allowed women's historians to put together scattered evidence in a perspective, pose new questions and look for new sources that enrich our understanding of Europe and fill many gaps in existing knowledge. Gender is the first point of departure or theoretical tool of analysis in this volume and we have set this in three most profound, epoch making ruptures of modern Europe, namely the French Revolution, the Industrial Revolution and Fascism/National Socialism.

Chapter 1 'Citizenship and Difference: The Age of Revolution' places the issue of gender in the larger context of changes brought about by the French Revolution. However, the core idea that the author examines for gender history is that of making of the nation and citizens, a process from which women were deliberately excluded. The chapter thus is an exploration of this exclusion.

While the élan of equality, liberty and fraternity triggered a series of uprisings in Europe, slave revolts in the Caribbean and intellectual stirrings elsewhere, back in revolutionary France a woman called Olympe de Gouges penned 'the Declaration of the Rights of the Woman and the Female Citizen' challenging French male revolutionaries and exhorting them to bestow the same rights upon the likes of her. Women had played a very active role in the revolution. They could be seen in protests, demonstrations and bread riots, even marching alongside the National Guard as auxiliaries. They had every reason to be as hopeful as men. Alas, that was not to be! The most radical of all, the Jacobins, banned women's revolutionary clubs and activities, dubbed them as counterrevolutionaries, guillotined a few and relegated all women to the role of domestics, of sacrificing, passive, silent homemakers, mothers and housewives. The boundaries between private and public began to firm up with the boldest statement of change in the lives of men. The middle class homebound woman was thus born in revolutionary France, nurtured in Victorian England, and turned into the ideal woman for the rest of the 'bourgeois world in the making'. Modernity did not mean the same thing for its men and women. The same fate befell the slaves in the French colonies. The land that sent universal messages of freedom, equality and fraternity had slaves and domestics at home!

This makes us acutely aware that the revolutionaries were males. Not just that, they were openly hostile to women in the public realm and wanted their ouster from politics and public sphere. For women who fought alongside men for freedom, liberty and equality it was as shocking as revealing; shocking to know how the fruits of their labour were stolen from them, revealing as the realization dawned on them that they had to fight their own battle. This fostered the birth of modern feminism.

Chapter 2 'Spaces and Places: Changing pattern of Domesticity and Work' interrogates the second marker of modernity, namely the Industrial Revolution from the point of view of the changes and shifts in the spheres of men and women. It examines how sexual difference and the related notion of separate spheres—public for men and private for women—became an organizing principal of industrialization from the late eighteenth century onwards. It insisted that all unpaid work, including women's household production was unproductive. The idea of separate spheres developed both in political and economic life in the twin revolutions: The French Revolution established the dominant political order and the Industrial Revolution set the pattern for economy and work place. The main beneficiary of this new order was the bourgeoisie, the leaders of both political and industrial revolution. Bourgeois men wanted their women to inhabit the private realm both in political and economic realms. These propertied men could afford to have dedicated domestic women as care givers of husband and children. However, gendering of work and its evaluation made certain kind of work more valuable than other. This had a huge impact on other classes as well. In the working class industrial work was conceptualized as professional, paid and masculine while household work was seen as unpaid and of less value. This created a problem for working class women and children who had to go out and work due to economic compulsions. They were neither recognized as 'real workers' nor paid the same wages as men even though their working hours and conditions were as demanding. Women industrial workers were thus discriminated in two different ways—not getting equal wages for equal work in the factories and not getting appropriate recognition for their unpaid work within the household. Even trade unionists did not pay any attention to women's concerns at the work place. They thought that women's cheap labour compromised their bargaining power. When and if bourgeois women did make an appearance in the public sphere, they did it to extend their 'feminine' influence in the harsh and brutal public realm. Early bourgeois women in public did unpaid philanthropic work. In their capacity as social workers they also engaged in sermonising women from the working class background on the virtues of motherhood, thrift, hygiene, orderliness and dedication to their family realizing little that the latter could ill afford to meet these bourgeois expectations due to limited time and resources.

Chapter 3 'Nationalization of the Female Citizenry: Nazi Germany and Fascist Italy' examines various gender related issues of Nazi Germany and fascist Italy within a comparative framework. It explores the contradictory impact of Fascism and Nazism on women. As successful mass movements both mobilized men and women alike for their cause and many would argue that women were politicized radically for the nationalist cause in their masses for the first time in history. The two regimes may appear at the first glance to be extremely right wing and conservative in prescribing maternity to women and driving them back to their home. Upon closer analysis, we notice contradictions between ideology and practice. Both initiated a lot of measures that were radical and unconventional. While they prescribed domesticity to women they simultaneously activated them in the war efforts for multiple tasking in the public sphere. They condemned women's dabbling in politics; yet, women were an important support base for these parties. Both movements in the initial stages provided enterprising women—including feminists—some autonomy on women's issues. We also observe that the two regimes, despite differences, deployed jingoism, narcissistic national pride and imperialism to erase fault lines that existed in the highly fragmented societies of interwar Europe. Gender divide was one of them. Some of the issues that the chapter examines are gender and the politics of vote, the rise and fall of early female fascists and the takeover of women's issues by male leaders and pliant women leaders, fascist gender politics of marriage and motherhood, the ruralisation campaign or the blood and soil model, gender politics in the high echelons of power, in the field of education and the job market.

The author argues that the story of marriage or motherhood was not a simple one of reassertion of conservative and patriarchal values. It was deeply connected to the population policy of the regime, which exhorted women to reproduce for the fatherland. She shows that these regimes were willing and able to go beyond bourgeois and Christian values of morality and sexuality by supporting illegitimacy, which was protected and supported by both fascist and Nazi state through agencies for mother and child welfare. In fascist Italy conventional Catholic ways of picking up abandoned children were superseded by welfare programmes initiated by the state that not just protected and supported unmarried mothers and their children but also removed stigma and gave them respect and dignity, and compelled men to acknowledge paternity of these children. In Nazi Germany, however, the idea of illegitimacy was wedded to race. Single, married or widowed women and their children of illicit alliances were divided into three categories: While the *Lebensborn* clients—both mother and child—were given a preferential treatment even though the biological parents may have been unwilling to give their name to the child, mother and child in paternity suits showed marked similarity with the preceding Weimar Republic, while mother and child who fell into the hands of the Gestapo and the judiciary due to their involvement with the prisoner of wars (POWs) were punished severely, even if they wished to legitimize their relations through matrimony. Notions such as honour, respectability, morality, freedom, patriotism and citizenship hinged on the racial purity of the alliance. This racial and exclusivist aspect of motherhood makes us keenly aware of the opportunities and perils of Nazi 'welfare maternalism', which persecuted Jewish, Polish, Gypsy, Russian and other mothers and infants. The historiographical section at the end takes up the question of women's roles and responsibilities in Nazi Germany by placing them in the paradigm of victim and perpetrator and questions the neat ideological framework which feminists have used to evaluate women's roles and responsibilities.

The second important analytical tool used in the volume is race, a category that created a vertical divide among the European peoples. History of Nazi Germany would tell us that this divide was not created to subordinate the 'lower races' and exploit them—as happens in any traditional hierarchical division—but in annihilating them altogether. Racial discrimination helps us understand the process of marginalization in modern European history in a different way than gender though both race and gender raise fundamental doubts about Europe being a fulcrum of progress and universalism. Both in their own way make us acutely aware of how difference was conceptualized in modern Europe biologically, psychologically and pseudo-scientifically to give it an essentialist dimension. Race ideology of white Europeans, led by the western, white, middle class, imperialist men, but followed by their womenfolk as well, defined the rest of the people such as Gypsies, Jews, Blacks and others in essentialist manner, created stereotypes and passed value judgements about their abilities and behaviours in order to created hatred for them in their societies. Chapter IV and V look at race as a defining feature of modernity which, combined with the emergence of nation states, proved to be dangerous for those who did not fit into homogenized national communities. While gender history makes us aware that in the modern era sharp distinctions were made between private and public as women's and men's territory, respectively, the ideas of race gave difference a new dimension and history as a struggle of different and competing races. Race ideology saw its apogee in the form of state doctrine in Nazi Germany. Unprecedented brutalities and an unimaginable form of death were 'invented' in death factories of Auschwitz, Sobibor, Chelmno, Treblinka, Belzek and Majdanek for a whole range of civilians declared enemies of an 'imagined people's community'. This racial community could only thrive on other's ashes. We only have to set German women against ethnic and racial minorities like Jews and Gypsies to realize the import of this race ideology, even though the Nazis may have been deeply anti-feminist in their thinking, the mass of German women took pride in Hitler's achievements and a large number of women willingly collaborated in the murderous politics of Nazis against the minorities. Simple categorization of women as victims cannot be accepted in this context when seen from the perspective of genocidal violence.

Chapter 4 'Race and Nation: an Intellectual History' argues that differences that were earlier understood to be part of religion, region or culture and could be resolved through conversion or long-term assimilation received the tag of race as a scientific and therefore superior way of explaining difference. Difference thus became immutable, fixed and non-alterable. Both these categories deeply corroded the Enlightenment principals of equality and freedom as basic human rights. In fact, race and gender as exclusivist strands proceeded alongside the egalitarian ethos of the Enlightenment. They were, so to say, two sides of the same coin. Human worth was evaluated in a complex and highly differentiated matrix, which reserved accolade, heroism and virtues for some while consigning others to lifelong condemnation, stigmas and shame and eventually elimination during the various twentieth-century genocides.

The author traces the intellectual roots of modern genocides to the Enlightenment, French Revolution, American Revolution and Romanticism.

He starts by interrogating the progressive legacy of the Enlightenment by rereading the ideas of Enlightenment thinkers such as Hobbes, Locke and Montesquieu regarding Blacks and other non-Whites and thus questions the universal intent of these celebrated radical visionaries.

The Enlightenment legacy released contradictory impulses—liberating for some, and confining and exclusivist for others. Its urge to understand man led to the development of new disciplines like psychology and anthropology. These disciplines deployed the much acclaimed scientific methods of classification and categorization to humans along racial lines, which were fitted into pre-existing cultural and ethical notions of beauty and aesthetics. These racial constructs were then used to justify imperialist expansion in non-European territories by the conquering white, middle class professionals. The triumphant, gallant man of the Romantics was not a hero standing alone in a void, argues the author, but an embodiment of collective aspirations and desires of a nation or race.

Thus, the novelty of modern genocides lay in the categorization of populations, their surveillance and control through modern central bureaucracies. The selection of some civilian groups for deportations or death in Nazi Germany was an effort to create a utopian, homogenized, pure stock of people. These methods are considered revolutionary in their aims, radical in their social engineering projects and ruthless in their pursuit of utopias.

This re-reading of the big intellectual and political stirrings has brought us closer to the recent tradition of feminist history writing which critiques the male politics of exclusion. As 'male-stream' historian the author and others like him have been far more receptive than conventional male historians to the feminist critique of exclusion. They have enriched this discourse by including Blacks, Jews, Asians and colonized natives or murdered and deported groups of marginalized nationalities within Europe. This understanding demonstrates that the apparently progressive milestones of modernity such as liberalism, democracy, socialism, communism and nationalism are applicable to only specific types of people, who established their supremacy over the others.

This intellectual history traces the rise and growth of anti-Semitism, racism and eugenics as complementary thoughts developed by thinkers such as Gobineau, Galton, Darwin, Chamberlain and Marr. The author does not stop at that. In fact his chapter is not only just a prelude to the next chapter on Nazism—that sees the culmination of racism, eugenics and anti-Semitism as state doctrines—but also engages with other themes of the volume such as gender, nation and empire and shows how stronger nations invariably used masculinity, eugenics and race to justify their dominance over the 'others' inside and outside the national frontiers.

Chapter 5, 'The Apogee of Racism: Nazi Germany 1933–45' considers racism as the most important feature of Nazi Germany. It argues that when it came to the question of survival or extinction, it was race that mattered in Nazi Germany. Indeed, a communist or a socialist was a serious enemy and was condemned to suffer but he or she could change his or her politics and survive. A Jew or a Gypsy could not change his or her race and could not survive no matter what their politics was. The Nazi era makes us realize that all kinds of marginalization and othering were not at par, as one could be more dangerous than the other.

In spite of this core assertion, the chapter deals with Nazi Germany in its totality. The author does not believe in the inevitability of the Holocaust, but follows the rise and growth of Nazism from a fringe ideology to a dominant philosophy and practice of a murderous regime. She argues that Nazism was a product of interwar crisis. The chapter explains why it was in Nazi Germany that race hatred experienced its apogee in spite of the fact that it was far more liberal than any other country in the pre-war era. What was its connection with modern political and intellectual life? How did such an advanced civilization fall prey to the murderous brutalities of the Nazis without much protest? The author does not see a direct connection between Hitler's *Mein Kampf* and the Final Solution, but takes a twisted road to Auschwitz by extensively dealing with the difficulties faced by the Germans after the First World War, which made them succumb to Hitler's clever rhetoric and politics. However, Hitler's myth is placed in its socio-political context to show both continuities and change in the politics of hate. Hitler displayed virulent hatred of the Jews in front of an anti-Semitic lower middle class crowd, but downplayed his anti-Semitism when faced with high-heeled sections of society. The Holocaust came as the 'Final Solution' not as the first step in the path of the longest hatred. The dynamics of rise and growth of Nazism is understood in the volatile politics of anxiety of the interwar era. The chapter provides an extensive coverage of the Weimar Republic, a context within which the rise of Nazism is placed. It then offers a quick survey of the political narrative of increasing popularity of Hitler, his early life, electoral achievements, ascendancy to power and internal and external policy successes in the peaceful years. War and the Holocaust are then treated as twin sides of the Nazi world view, which had racism, anti-Semitism, eugenics and *Lebensraum* at its core. The chapter traces the various stages of the persecution of the Jews, Gypsies and other racial aliens in different stages of the Third Reich. It argues that the onset of war ultimately removed all hurdles and inhibitions in the way of mass killings that were encountered by Hitler's professional and foot soldier of the Holocaust. The author also problematizes the intricate intertwining of race and class in the face of war and the Holocaust. She argues that it would be simplistic to assume that the German working class was as a victim of Nazi capitalist imperialism as most German workers became soldiers while a large work force of salve labour—POW and forced workers from the conquered territories—was deployed in hazardous munitions factories and other harsh jobs, while German worker turned soldier enriched himself and his family through plunder. Families of German soldiers regularly received packets from the occupied territories containing plundered commodities robbed from the Jews, Poles and others. Nazi Germany also presented an enigma to us concerning the near absence of organized protest against the regime until the very end. It is surprising given the fact that German social democrats were the forerunners of evolutionary democratic socialism and had a majority in the parliament on the eve of WWI. They had presented the most formidable challenge at the grass root level to the Nazis along with the communists. Apart from doing parliamentary and street politics they had developed a network of cultural, educational and recreational organization, which covered the entire lifespan of their followers from the cradle to the grave. Where did they vanish once the Nazis took over? This poses more fundamental questions regarding how we look at workers and their politics. Is it to be seen alone in the context of work, factory and trade unionism, or can we find places outside of work situations, e.g., home, leisure, socialization and so on through which workers' reactions could be read? The author has tried to introduce some of these elements while assessing workers in a context where racism and hyper-nationalism trumped class. In general, what applies to gender as a category of analysis applies to class too. It is seen as far more fragmented along racial, ethnic, regional, national and generational lines. Class-centred discourse in the political language is seen not as monolith but a multi-layered lived reality, whose meaning is fraught and contested. The author goes into these complexities to understand why there was an absence of protest and larger-scale compliance even among the workers. The chapter takes up controversies related to issues of the economic crisis and the collapse of Weimar Germany within those sections themselves, while the last section is exclusively devoted to major historiographical trends on Nazi Germany.

The third analytical tool is the time-tested concept of class, a category which has been almost synonymous with social change and political agency for many generations of Marxists. However, Marx was not alone in writing and fighting about the plight of the working class and the need for their emancipation. Thinkers from varied material and intellectual backgrounds and tradition worried about the misery of workers and suggested ways of transforming society and establishing an egalitarian society free of exploitation. **Chapter 6** 'In Pursuit of Social Justice: Modern European Socialism, 1850–1940' examines the origins, theories, development and impact of modern socialism in Europe between the mid-nineteenth and mid-twentieth centuries. While socialism itself was not a new ideology, having its roots in utopian thought stretching back to the ancient world, modern socialism embodied the specific conditions of industrializing and urbanizing Europe in the nineteenth century. It appealed to a new and rapidly growing segment of the population—the proletariat, or working class—increasingly dissatisfied with their precarious existence, difficult working and living conditions, and lack of political representation. Socialism also provided an alternative to other ideologies of the time, particularly liberalism that had failed to deliver on its promises of social justice. Modern socialism thus appealed to the generally disenfranchised working class, promising to transform their lives and society according to universal principles of human values and justice.

Throughout, the chapter attempts to highlight the diversity of opinion and approach within the socialist movement. It discusses a variety of utopian socialist thinkers whose ideas provided the background for the development of modern socialism as envisioned by Karl Marx. It also notes the ways that Marx's ideas were supported, challenged and reinterpreted according to the context of the time and place. The discussion of modern socialism focuses in particular on two issues that helped to make the ideology unique. First, the author examines the national vs. international orientation of the ideology. Modern socialism developed within the context of the individual nation state and its practitioners adapted it to suit their particular needs and concerns. At the same time, however, modern socialism had an inherently international orientation that stressed common human values and the necessity of worldwide unity among the proletariat for the successful achievement of the socialist society. Indeed, the international component made socialism unique among political movements in Europe at the time. To illustrate this issue, the chapter examines both national and international developments within the socialist movement. It highlights the establishment of a socialist political party, the Social Democratic Party, in Germany not only as the most active and influential national socialist organization in Europe, but it also charts the emergence of socialist parties in France, Great Britain, Belgium, Scandinavia, Spain and Italy, among others. In addition, the chapter examines the establishment of the socialist movement's international organization, the International, in its various iterations, seeking to explain the role played by internationalism within the socialist movement.

Second, the chapter discusses the different paths socialists took to achieve their ideal vision of a socialist society. Most European countries embraced gradualism. They chose to work within existing political structures and institutions to enact socialist policies and eventually to transform society according to the socialist model. Others chose violent revolution, arguing that only by destroying the old order completely could the new one emerge. Russia's revolutions provide the primary example of the implementation of the revolutionary approach, and these events are examined in detail. The success of the Russian revolutions and the impatience among some socialists for change created a divide within the socialist movement between social democrats who advocated for the gradual approach and communists who clamoured for revolution. The tensions among these trends—national vs. international and gradualism vs. revolution—created diversity within the socialist movement that enabled it to adapt effectively to changing circumstances. These tensions, however, also led to disagreements and internal discord that socialism's opponents, fearing its calls for radical change and the revolutionary potential of the working class, used effectively against them, thus undermining the unity and coherence of the socialist movement.

Overall, the chapter stresses the importance of modern socialism as a political ideology in the late nineteenth and early twentieth centuries. By providing an alternative to the established political leadership—conservative, catholic and liberal—and by promising a vision of a just society, modern socialism gained considerable support and influence throughout Europe. It emerged within a context of modernization and industrialization, and capitalized on expanding political rights to gain the backing of the working class. Yet, it also reflected a diversity of political opinion, making it adaptable to different national contexts and conditions and at the same time it attempted to advance an internationally oriented agenda. Modern socialism's unique attributes helped it to survive challenges and threats to its existence, and contributed to make it an integral element of modern European political ideology.

The emergence of class society was coterminous with the process of industrialization. Therefore the ideological origin of socialism that aimed to achieve the emancipation of the working class has been set in the material context of industrialization in **Chapter 7:** 'Industrialization and the Rise of Modern Class Society.' Industrialization brought about revolutionary changes in Europe and radically transformed its relationship with the rest of the world. Till the beginning of the eighteenth century, Europe was one power—economic and political—among many others in the world. Economically, it was not noticeably superior compared to several countries in Asia, particularly China and India; however, some even argue that it was actually inferior. However, by the end of the nineteenth century, it had far surpassed all other regions of the world economically, except North America which experienced similar changes. Politically, it held the rest of the world in its thrall directly or indirectly controlling them. In this chapter, we begin by outlining the broad features of modern industrialization, followed by the background leading to relatively rapid industrialization. The chapter traces the development of industrialization in selected European countries such as Britain, France, Germany and Russia. This survey highlights peculiarities of each nation while comparing them at the same time. This section therefore has both overlaps and specificities of each context. The chapter then goes on to analyse the impact of industrialization on European society in broad strokes and concentrates on the emergence of modern class in the process. Although some debates have been taken up in the course of the chapter, a separate section would with historiography exclusively.

Chapter 8 'Nationalism: Triumphs and Challenges in the Long Nineteenth Century and Beyond' examines another universal hope—nationhood for each—that modern Europe raised. This proved to be as exclusive as it was inclusive. The emerging nation-states invariably had peoples of different nationalities trapped within homogenizing societies struggling to break free. Each nation in the making during late nineteenth and early twentieth-century Europe had its own trajectory, often making its minority feel like 'a people without nation', increasingly so as nationhood got wedded to the ideas of a unique culture, language, ethnicity and indeed race. The aggressive nationalism of interwar era, which came riding on the shoulders of the Versailles Treaty, abetted these exclusionary spirits and sentiments. Almost the entire Europe fell to right wing dictators who helped Hitler's regime in killing Jews, Gypsies and a host of others condemned as 'internal enemies' in the name of purifying its body politic of 'contaminating races'. Nationalism that was associated with popular sovereignty in nineteenth century came under the cloud of exclusionary politics in early twentieth century.

The chapter takes a long view of nationalism to trace its rise and growth from the late eighteenth century when its first seeds were planted in the dramatic events and rhetoric of the French Revolution. As the eighteenth century ended, monarchy—the traditional and time-tested form of government and state—was on shakier ground. Though 'restored' in the second decade of the nineteenth century, the restoration could and would never be complete and by the mid-nineteenth century the power of nationalist ideology, linked to reformists and liberals, in Europe was clear. The latter half of the nineteenth century ushered in the 'heyday' of nationalist development and was the period of intense nationalist and state-making activity in many regions of Europe.

The chapter addresses these important contexts and transition moments in nationalism, beginning with the French Revolution. Focusing on the most significant legacies of the French Revolution as it connects to the birth and ascendance of nationalism on the European continent the chapter uses the French Revolution as a jumping off point, as well as a frame of reference for an exploration of nationalism in Europe.

Moving chronologically from the French Revolution, the chapter addresses the legacy of Napoleon on the development of nationalist rhetoric and nation-state administration in early nineteenth-century Europe. Whether ending traditional privileges of the noble class or insisting on uniform law codes, creating administrative departments and expanding bureaucracies, Napoleon's legacy vis-à-vis the trappings or practicalities of the modern nation state are evident throughout the nineteenth-century world. His defeat on the continent did not mean the end of the workings of the modern state but simply a transformation. The wave of (mostly failed) revolutions that swept through Europe in the 1830s and 1840s will also provide some context for understanding the development of mass politics, the impact on nationalism, the demands of new citizens and the concerns and responses by those in power.

Nationalism had many different forms and permutations and unfolded differently in different countries and regions. This chapter addresses four national histories in detail. Italy's Risorgimento (1815–1870) is considered, especially the different forms of nationalism that were voiced over the course of Italy's transformation from a place of independent kingdoms and duchies to a single united Italy. The power of the 'Young Italy' movement as well as the forms of nationalism advocated by personalities such as Guiseppe Mazzini and Guiseppe Garibaldi are also addressed.

The case of Germany's transformation to a unified nation-state provides another lens into the forms and specifics of nationalist rhetoric and practicalities. Under Prussian leadership, and through conflict with many other countries, Germany rose throughout the course of the nineteenth century to be a powerful nation. By 1871, under Prussian domination, Germany had achieved unification and had altered the power dynamics of continental Europe. The specific manipulations of the dominating Prussian ideology (and specifically Bismarck) are examined as an important dynamic in emergent German nationalism.

While national identity may still be a complicated concept and not homogenous in Italy and Germany, they do not have the on-going (or at least, very recent) points of contention that we observe in the case of Irish and Balkan nationalism. Turning to these two examples illustrates the fact that while the nineteenth and early twentieth century was the 'height' of nationalist endeavours it did not mean that all national questions were neatly tied up by the post-World War Two era. The on-going conflicts over national sovereignty and identity in Ireland and the Balkans plead the case for the continued power, and conflict, over ideas of the nations—who does it truly represent and it what ways?

Further, all of these 'mini-histories' (whether the French Revolution, Italy, Germany, Ireland or the Balkans) provide an opportunity to discuss the connected strands of nationalism—not only in rhetoric and process, but also in symbols and practicalities (the flag, language, etc.).

It is no surprise, given its import and locus of contention, that nationalism has been the topic of intense theoretical debate. Since almost the first modern use of the word nation there have been historians, political theorists and philosophers who have tried to address and understand the complicated dynamics of nationalist ideology and to understand the reasons the very concept of a nation has had such broad appeal. Beginning with Renan in the nineteenth century and focusing on more recent theorists such as Benedict Anderson, Eric Hobsbawm and Ernst Gellner, the chapter provides an overview of the theoretical work on nationalism.

Nationalism, as the chapter argues, has had a huge impact in creating the accepted structures of global relationships. While in its history nationalism is being told in this chapter as a nineteenth-century story it has an impact well beyond that—both in time and space. Indeed, as we consider the present day, for all the discussion of a post-national world, we still inhabit a globe that is structured according to the nineteenth-century ideas of the nation as the most legitimate and recognized representation of people and states.

In sum, the volume aims to show that gender, race, class and nation are some cracks on the universal and ever-evolving skin of European history, which have developed into gorges and cliffs in recent years. Curious and well-equipped historians have descended with innovative methodologies into these cracks and have come up with most rewarding results. They have fundamentally altered our understanding of Europe. The narrative today is more fractured and fragmented, less homogenous and universalising yet, as a field of inquiry much more promising for future generation of researchers.

The volume hopes to showcase in an accessible manner some of this cutting edge scholarship in the areas outlined above, which I hope, would inspire teachers, and gently guide graduates and undergraduates alike into this variegated field of enquiry.

Acknowledgements

A grant from the Humboldt Foundation and a visiting professorship at the Humboldt University offered the most suitable academic environment to complete the project. The University Grants Commission gave me a minor research grant, which partially fulfilled the requirements of the project. Dr Hemlata Reddy fostered my research and writing as always, and Sri Venkateswara College provided the infrastructural support during the early stages.

I thank the contributors for their hard work and sincerity. I enjoyed working with them and look forward to another such opportunity. All of them, as well as those whose reprints have been included in this volume share with me the credit of bringing this project into fruition. However, each author bears the responsibility for the views expressed in their chapters.

The entire team wishes to thank editorial team at Pearson Education for working with great enthusiasm. I would like to thank Praveen Dev for encouraging me to publish this volume with Pearson Education.

Thank you Michael, Nadja, Georg, Melitta, Frank, Sadia, Hanni, Bettina, Heike, Anandita, Ajay, Nirbaadh and Unmukt for being a source of delight, distraction and inspiration.

Chapter 1 and 2: Reprinted and Reproduced from Gendering European history 1780 – 1920, Barbara Caine and Glenda Sulga, Continuum (London, New York), 2000.

Chapter 4: WEITZ, ERIC D.; A CENTURY OF GENOCIDE. © 2003 Princeton University Press Reprinted by permission of Princeton University Press.

List of Contributors

Barbara Caine is Professor and Head of School of Philosophical and Historical Inquiry at the University of Sydney. She is the author of Biography and History (2010, Gordonsville: Palgrave Macmillan) and *Bombay to Bloomsbury: A Biography of the Strachey Family* (2005, Oxford: Oxford University Press).

Vandana Joshi is Associate Professor at the department of History, Sri Venkateswara College, University of Delhi. She has been an Alexander von Humboldt fellow and a visiting professor at the Humboldt University. She has published internationally acclaimed works on gender, sexuality, war and Nazi Germany. Her dissertation won the Fraenkel Prize in Contemporary History and was published as *Gender and Power in the Third Reich: Female Denouncers and the Gestapo 1933–45* by Palgrave in 2003. She edited *Themes in Modern European History: Social Movements and Cultural Currents 1789–1945* with Orient Blackswan in 2010.

Eric D. Weitz is Dean of Humanities and Arts and Distinguished Professor of History at The City College of New York. His major publications include *Weimar Germany: Promise and Tragedy* (2007), *A Century of Genocide: Utopias of Race and Nation* (2003), and *Creating German Communism, 1890-1990* (*1997*), all with Princeton University Press.

Sharon A Kowalsky is Associate Professor of History at Texas A&M University-Commerce. She received her Ph.D. in History from the University of North Carolina at Chapel Hill in 2004. Her research focuses on issues and norms of proper behavior in the Russian Revolutionary period and she has written extensively about female crime. Her book *Deviant Women: Female Crime and Criminology in Revolutionary Russia, 1880–1930* won the Southern Conference on Slavic Studies (SCSS) best book prize for 2012.

Daniella Sarnoff is a Director at the Social Science Research Council in New York. Sarnoff holds a Ph.D. in European History and has taught at Xavier University, Fordham University, and New York University. Her work focuses on extremist politics in Europe, the interwar years in France, gender ideology, and the intersections of culture and politics.

Vijaya Rajni is Associate Professor of Economics in the College of Vocational Studies, Delhi University. Her research interests are Economic History and Agricultural Economics. Her publications include *Casual Labour Contracts of Agricultural Labourers in East and West Uttar Pradesh* (Economic and Political Weekly).

Shashi Bhushan Upadhyay is Professor of History, Indira Gandhi National Open University, New Delhi. His areas of interest are Labour History, Dalit and Literary Studies. His publications include *Existence, Identity and Mobilization: The Cotton Millworkers of Bombay, 1890–1919* (2004), and two (co-edited) volumes *Dalit Assertion in Society, Literature and History* (2010) and *School Education, Pluralism and Marginality: Comparative Perspectives* (2012).

1 Citizenship and Difference: The Age of Revolution

—*Barbara Caine*

In the century and a half prior to the French Revolution, intellectuals and philosophers across Europe had discussed a number of social questions which became the focus of political activity during the revolution. The nature and merits of monarchy, the importance of equality before the law, the possibility or desirability of a republic, the basis of political participation and the meaning of the nation had been of central concern in the Enlightenment and were debated in Britain, in some of the German and Italian states, and in the Habsburg Empire as well as in France. In a similar way, questions about the meaning and implications of the physical and mental differences between men and women were discussed in a range of different fields: in educational thought, in medical and scientific debates, in the writings of jurists and political philosophers as well as in literature and in social thought. Much of this discussion centred on the relationship between women's bodies and their conventional social roles, and between masculinity, military capacity and citizenship.

What had been largely an intellectual matter until 1789 became a major political issue from the start of the French Revolution? Women participated in some of the most dramatic events of the French Revolution from 1789 onwards. Some women insisted that they be allowed the right of citizens to bear arms in defence of the Republic which the revolution had brought into being. However, the new ideas about sexual difference which emerged in the course of the eighteenth century were linked directly to the question of citizenship. In the eyes of the revolutionary governments, it was clear that the rights of citizens to participate in political debate, to vote and to bear arms were intended only for men. As Lynn Hunt and Joan Landes have shown, the political symbols and the new political language which emerged in the French Revolution emphasized the close connection between masculinity and citizenship by designating the political sphere as masculine and insisting that women devote themselves to the private sphere of family and home (Hunt, 1984; Landes, 1988). For the men who led the revolution, as for their conservative opponents, the very idea of women participating in political activity and demanding new legal and political rights brought with it the threat of sexual promiscuity and the undermining of family life. Thus while the French Revolution of 1789 brought the birth of modern politics and introduced the modern European idea of the political individual and the citizen, it emphatically designated the masculinity of that citizen.

The precise impact of the French Revolution on women has long been the source of historical discussion and debate. The unprecedented level of activity and involvement of the women of Paris in revolutionary events, accompanied by the first formal demands for political rights and citizenship for women, have made the French Revolution into the central event of the emergence of modern feminism. Those women who protested angrily at their exclusion from the political realm and who demanded rights for women brought into being modern feminism with its central demand that women be granted their full recognition as citizens (Landes, 1988; Caine, 1997).

The participation of women in the early stages of the French Revolution had to some extent been anticipated by the involvement of women in the intellectual life of the eighteenth century. Enlightenment debates took place in salons organized by women. Moreover, increasing numbers of women were also beginning to write and to publish their work—albeit often under male pseudonyms. The genre of novel, which was becoming increasingly popular in Britain and France in the eighteenth and early nineteenth centuries, provided a literary genre suited to urban experience and domestic life and in which women could excel. However, women were also becoming prominent as poets, historians, essayists and as literary and cultural theorists and critics. The phenomenon of the woman writer was itself the subject of social comment, and women's literary pretensions sometimes aroused the same hostility as their political involvement. By the end of the French Revolution, and the beginning of the nineteenth century, a new literary and cultural movement, Romanticism, emphasized the close connection between masculinity and creative power with its insistence that the genius was always a man—albeit a man with feminine sensibilities.

In this chapter we begin by examining the Enlightenment debate about sexual difference and the ways in which some philosophers argued that the possession of reason, which naturally entitled people to certain rights, was a quality only applicable to men. We then look at the role and participation of women in the French Revolution, at the attempts made by women to demand political rights and citizenship and at the reasons why those rights were denied to them. In the process, we explore the ways in which the idea of citizenship was connected with masculinity. We also look at the impact on women of the legal codes established by Napoleon in France and adopted in many other European countries. Finally we look at the emergence of women writers, at the ways in which women demanded the right to participate in literary debates and through literature in political and social issues. We also explore the ways in which the questions about gender and sexual difference which were central to the political arena in the late eighteenth and early nineteenth centuries also shaped contemporary literature and culture.

SEXUAL DIFFERENCE AND THE ENLIGHTENMENT

Many historians have commented on the discrepancy between the critical and questioning approach which the Enlightenment philosophers of the eighteenth century took to questions of government, religion and social institutions, on the one hand, and their acceptance and even endorsement of the prevailing inferior status of women, on the other. In France, in particular, there was much play with the idea of 'light', especially the light of natural reason, which alone could lead man to the perfection of knowledge and human wisdom. However, this light rarely shone on either the situation of women or on prevailing beliefs about them. On the contrary, women, like the benighted savages to be found outside Western Europe, tended to be seen as lacking in that innate reason which was the basis of natural rights. Lacking the qualities which made social reform possible, women were regarded as obstacles to progress and reform rather than as requiring reform or assistance in their own process of enlightenment.

While some see this omission of women from the Enlightenment reform agenda as essentially an oversight, others see it as fundamental to the Enlightenment understanding and idealization of reason. The philosopher Genevieve Lloyd (1984), for example, has argued strongly that the idea of a 'man of reason' points to the conceptual link that was being made between masculinity and reason both in the eighteenth century and before. From the earliest writings in Western philosophy, reason, masculinity, truth and intellect have been contrasted to sensuality, femininity, error and emotion. This contrast had particular importance in the Enlightenment when reason came to be seen as the highest human quality which brought with it an entitlement to legal and political rights. Thus the 'man of reason' became the central focus for discussion of political rights and of citizenship. Lloyd's argument has been extended and endorsed by a number of recent historians who have pointed to the extensive interest in elaborating the differences between the sexes throughout the eighteenth century. Medical and scientific texts addressed in great detail questions about the precise anatomical and physiological differences between the sexes (Jordanova, 1990). This medical literature complemented the discussion of sexual difference evident in works concerned with education and morality. Looking at a range of these medical and scientific texts, Thomas Laqueur has argued that the seventeenth and eighteenth centuries saw the development of a new model of sexual difference. Ideas about sexual difference up until this time had been dominated by the views of classical Greek writers for whom women lacked any essential elements of their own, but were seen as smaller and lesser versions of men. In accordance with the ideas of the fifth-century Greek philosopher Galen—ideas which were reformulated during the Renaissance—women were imperfect men who lacked the heat and the energy which produced men's perfect form and their physical strength. In this model of sexual difference, the similarities between men and women extended even to their reproductive structures. Thus, as Galen put it, 'all parts that men have, women have too... the difference between them lies in one thing... that in women the parts are within the body whereas in men they are outside' (Laqueur, 1990). Galen drew up careful diagrams of the male and female body with identical organs showing one as the analogue of the other. Female ovaries were equivalent to the testicles, whereas the womb was the penis turned inside out. This is a model, Laqueur insists, in which there was really only one sex—the male. Women were lesser men rather than constituting a distinct or different sex.

By contrast, in the course of the seventeenth and eighteenth centuries, a new model of sexual difference came to the fore. Men and women came to be seen as completely different from, and even opposite to, each other. For the first time, medical texts began to include a female skeleton as well as a male one. They emphasized the broader pelvis, the narrower shoulders and the smaller head, of the female, rather than assuming that a male skeleton served equally well for both men and women (Scheibinger, 1989). The distinctive nature of male and female bodies was emphasized through the introduction of new sexual terms, including 'vagina' and 'vulva', to label the various parts of the female reproductive system. This need for a new language to describe bodily differences was accompanied by an increasing interest in bodies and an emphasis on their importance in the making of sexual difference. Scientific and medical texts devoted much attention to demonstrating the extent of this difference in every element of the human body, including the emotions, the hair and the finger nails. As Laqueur points out, this new model placed much greater emphasis on bodies and bodily difference than had been the case in earlier centuries.

For much of the eighteenth century, both models of sexual difference co-existed, but increasingly the new model which stressed difference predominated. It meshed neatly with a range of arguments about the importance of the nuclear family and the home and of the need to differentiate the activities of men and women and to locate them socially in different places. Perhaps the most influential and widely read text which spelled out the social and political implications of this new approach to sexual difference was Rousseau's *Émile* (first published in 1762). Although prohibited by the censors because of its religious comments, *Émile* was an immensely popular book in France and also in England and the German states. The popularity of Rousseau's text undoubtedly owed much to the way in which it laid out a new and child-centred approach to education in which the child's curiosity was the main driving force, while its physical and mental development determined the educational programme. At a time when increasing attention was being paid to children and to the need for them to be nurtured and cared for within a nuclear family, this educational ideal, which centred on an individual tutor taking complete charge of a child and working to ensure that its education encompassed physical, moral and intellectual development, harmonized well with the ideals and aims of a growing middle class. The education Rousseau laid out for his eponymous hero, Émile, seemed designed to ensure that Émile was not only able and competent, but also a model son, husband, father and citizen.

Émile's education, as Rousseau made absolutely clear, was entirely sex-specific. The education Rousseau described for Émile emphasized the development of reason, and was completely different from the education he prescribed for 'Sophie', Émile's mate and the subject of the final chapter of *Émile*. Over hundreds of pages Rousseau detailed how the development of reason and judgement in a boy needed to be stimulated, Émile would learn to endure hardship, to explore the natural world, to develop physical strength and control, to exercise his own judgement and independence and to live according to his own values and beliefs. Sophie's education was dealt with much more briefly in a separate chapter in which Rousseau explained how every aspect of her education was to be the opposite of Émile's. Whereas Émile was to be free, Sophie was to be confined—even tied to a chair and forced to play with dolls. Whereas he was to develop intellectual independence, she was taught to submit her judgement to others and to follow the dictates of the world around her. Whereas he was encouraged to think highly of himself and to display his talents, she had to learn that modesty was the most important quality a woman could possess. In his discussion of sexual difference, Rousseau made a complex play on the idea of 'nature'. Émile's education was to be 'natural', geared to allowing him to develop reasoning powers, undertaken as much as possible in the open air and the countryside, organized around his own nature, and helping him to understand and even master the natural world. Sophie, too, was to be educated according to 'nature'. However, in her case, Rousseau shifted the emphasis of education, so that rather than her own desires, it is the nature of the world she will inhabit and the roles she will have to play as wife and mother that come to the fore.

Rousseau's ideas about the different education needed by Sophie and Émile were closely integrated into his ideas about the nature of society and of the political order. The establishment of an orderly domestic and familial life was, in his view, not only important in itself but also integral to the establishment and maintenance of civic order and virtue. Looking towards a new political order in which men would participate as active citizens, exercising political rights and carrying out a range of civic tasks, Rousseau stressed that Émile's education had to prepare him for the interrelated roles of husband, citizen and father. Sophie, by contrast, required training in submission and domesticity to make her into a dutiful and obedient wife and mother. Women, in Rousseau's view, lacked any ethical sense and hence could not be guided by their own reason. They had rather to be guided by public opinion and the dictates of men.

Rousseau's ideas were extremely influential not only in France and Britain, but also elsewhere in Europe. His insistence on the importance of women's confinement to the home, and his argument that this was both natural and conducive to morality and to civic order, provided a new form of validation of the legal situation, which prevailed in a number of countries, whereby women were completely subordinated to the rule of their husbands. In Britain, for example, in marriage husband and wife became one person in law. 'That is', as Sir William Blackstone explained in his *Commentaries on the Laws of England*, 'the very being, or legal existence of the woman is suspended during the marriage, or at least is incorporated and consolidated into that of her husband: under whose wing, protection and cover, she performs everything' (Blackstone, 1753 cited in Hill, 1987: p. 112). This meant that married women could hold no property—on the contrary, they were themselves the property of their husbands. The husband owned his wife's body and was entitled to any sexual or domestic services he desired. He also owned any children they might have. Married women could not inherit property, which, like any money they might earn, belonged to their husbands. Similarly they could not enter into contracts or sue or be sued without their husband also being involved. Blackstone, sharing Rousseau's sense that this legal status suited women's nature, saw this institution of 'coverture' as ensuring the protection of women and indeed as making them especially favoured. In a similar way, the German philosopher Immanuel Kant depicted women and men as having completely opposite characteristics, arguing that these differences provided the basis for marital laws which gave men the power to rule women (Hull, 1996).

The increasing emphasis on sexual difference in the eighteenth century was accompanied by a growing sense of the importance of male sexual energy and activity as a central feature of the male political subject. For Kant (as for his influential student and fellow philosopher, Johannes Gottlieb Fichte in the early nineteenth century) the male sexual drive was closely associated with the impulse to independence, autonomy and freedom. Hence ideas about women's sexual passivity underlay the view that they were unsuited to political rights and full citizenship. Some historians have argued that this insistence on the connection between sexual and political activity was the consequence of an apparent increase in sexual activity, both within and outside marriage, and with a new sense of the importance and imperative nature of sexual desire in the eighteenth century (Abelove, 1989; Laqueur, 1992). This in turn brought a belief that the freedom to indulge sexual desire was a male prerogative, not available to women or children. For Rousseau, it was the power of male sexual desire which necessitated the domestic seclusion of women. Male sexuality, in his view, was a potentially subversive and destructive force that needed to be contained within marriage and in the home. Seeing this issue only in heterosexual terms, Rousseau argued that the only possible way to ensure political and social order was to completely exclude women from the public realm. The presence of women in the public world would, he argued, distract men and lead to promiscuity. By contrast, the confinement of women to the home would withdraw them from the promiscuous gaze of men, and thereby keep women chaste, and by confining male sexual activity to monogamous family life, masculine behaviour would be reformed.

In recent years, historical writing on the Enlightenment has extended beyond discussions of the ideas of prominent philosophers and interest in political, legal and social reform to explore the institutional frameworks in which the new ideas associated with the Enlightenment were expressed and debated. The development of public opinion and public debates through salons and coffee houses and through the extension of publishing and of the press has thus been widely explored. Much of this new work has pointed to the role of women in the Enlightenment. Although French salon women have been most extensively researched, it was not in France alone that salon women were prominent (Goodman, 1994). In many European cities in the late eighteenth and early nineteenth centuries, salons were a central feature of intellectual and literary debate. In Berlin and Moscow, as much as in London, women played a prominent role in them. The specific form and purpose of salons differed quite markedly from one country to another: thus in Berlin, salons run by prominent Jewish women provided a way for Jewish and gentile intellectuals and businessmen to meet. In Moscow and St Petersburg, salons played an integral part in the development of Russian as a literary language. As Joan Scott (1996) has argued, salons and the women who ran them fostered the growth of critical and dissenting opinion in France, particularly the growth of opposition to absolutism. Activist and reformist women became involved in journals, such as the *Journal des Dames (The Ladies Journal)*, which anticipated the political demands made by women during the French Revolution.

As Rousseau's ideas gained European currency in the second half of the eighteenth century, and his belief in the complementarity and the differences between men and women became widely accepted, the participation of women in salons in France became the subject of debate and controversy. Rousseau himself was deeply hostile to the participation of women in any sphere of life outside the home and wrote at length of the evils attending women's involvement in salons. Intellectual life and the capacity to explore and debate scientific and social ideas were, in his view, compromised by the presence of women. If women were excluded from salons, men would be 'exempted from having to lower their ideas to the range of women and to clothe reason in gallantry' and could 'devote themselves to grave and serious discourse without fear of ridicule' (Wertheim, 1995: pp. 46–50). While some intellectuals and writers associated with the Enlightenment in France, like Diderot, rejected this view and insisted that the presence of women made it necessary to discuss the driest subjects with clarity and charm, others sided with Rousseau in accepting that masculine debate was necessary, especially for the development of scientific ideas and approaches. And indeed in the second half of the eighteenth century, more and more men's discussion groups and circles excluded women. In the process, the ideas that rational thought and science were specifically masculine pursuits and that femininity was more closely connected to stories and to poetry were also coming to be accepted.

Opposition to the participation of women in salons had a moral as well as an intellectual basis. A number of prominent salon women had sexual liaisons with the intellectual leaders who regularly attended their weekly 'evenings at home'. These women became particular targets of Rousseau's hostility and he attacked them for neglecting their family duties, for their sexual and moral corruption and for their polluting of masculine intellectual debate. Rousseau was not isolated in these views. Increasingly in the second half of the eighteenth century, the charge of sexual promiscuity was levelled against any women who participated in political life. This hostility reached a peak in France in the years leading up to the revolution of 1789 in attacks on the Queen, Marie Antoinette. A host of pornographic pamphlets and cartoons suggested that she was not only dishonest and corrupt, but also sexually voracious, indulging both in lesbian affairs and in incest with her son (Hunt, 1992). These caricatures were circulated widely in Britain as well as in France. Thus by the late 1780s, there was widespread agreement with Rousseau that women's involvement or even appearance in the public world of politics or political debate was immoral and indecent.

THE FRENCH REVOLUTION

Historians have found many different ways of setting out a chronology of the French Revolution. Questions of gender have become an increasingly important means of distinguishing between the early optimism and sense of new opportunities evident in the revolution between 1789 and 1793, and the more radical republican phase of the revolution instigated after that time. From 1793, women's claims were increasingly questioned, and their activities restricted until finally, with the assumption of power by Napoleon, women were definitively denied political rights, adult status or any recognition as citizens.

For many contemporary commentators, one of the most unsettling aspects of the early stages of the French Revolution was the very public participation of women. The English writer and political theorist, Edmund Burke, for example, viewed the march to Versailles to bring the King back to Paris, led by the market women of Paris in October 1789, as an appalling episode. He was indignant at the way the royal family was forced to return to Paris, 'moved along, amidst the horrid yells, and shrilling screams, and frantic dances and infamous contumelies, and all the unutterable abominations of the furies of hell, in the abused shape of the vilest of women' (Burke, 1965 [1790]: p. 85). Burke's depiction of working women points to his support for monarchy and his belief that political activity ought to be the prerogative of educated men. His vision of the market women as harridans illustrates his worst fears about the consequences of drastic social and political change provoked by the challenge to the King's authority. As Joan Landes has shown, even in the more positive depiction of the women of Paris, in the many cartoons and drawings in which they carry liberty trees, or heads on pikes and walk beside, or ride with soldiers, it is implied that women have 'strong sexual and martial appetites' (Landes, 1992: p. 20). Some of the women are depicted as engaging in sexual activities with soldiers and all of them appear disordered in their dress.

Direct involvement in local and community activities by Parisian working women was not new. Women had always played a major role in managing the family budget and hence in monitoring food prices. Throughout the eighteenth century, working women all over France had been very active in riots and protests over rising prices. Their responsibility for the well-being of their families had also meant that they had to become aware of and adept at dealing with the growing centralized administration which had emerged in the eighteenth century. Women had dealt with taxes, police and courts and with public works. Parisian women also had a long-standing involvement in other local and community concerns: many women had been closely involved with the Church and had participated in the debates and disputes between Jansenists and Jesuits which had preceded the expulsion of the Jesuits in 1773.

In the years before 1789, there had been no conflict or opposition between working women's home, community and economic roles. Throughout the eighteenth century, it was generally recognized that women's responsibility for their families and for the well-being of their community automatically made the question of prices and the need to find a way to resolve the food crisis their concern. In the course of 1789, particularly in Paris, even questions about food and prices began to take on a more explicitly political cast. When the growing financial crisis of the late 1780s made it necessary for the King to summon the Estates General, the group whose assent he had to have in order to raise new taxes, this event generated a vast amount of public discussion. The meeting of the Estates General in 1789, the insistence by the Third Estate (the commoners, and all those not included within the estates of the nobility and the clergy) that it embodied the Nation, and the publication of the Declaration of the Rights of Man and the Citizen in July 1789, brought a widespread new interest in politics and a new sense of the connection between the struggles of daily life and the need for the Third Estate to be heard on the political stage. This combination of political issues and immediate economic concerns was very clear in the march of Parisian women on Versailles: the marchers were spurred on by the high price of bread in the capital. They intended to bring the King back to ensure that he did his duty as a ruler by regulating prices and overseeing conditions within Paris. Thus the march connected demands for food with a sense of the political obligations of the ruler, and of justice and moral order.

The women of Paris followed up the march to Versailles by participating in a number of other political activities, often alongside men. From 1789 onwards, women began to join radical and republican clubs, and participated in their debates. Women made up the crowds demanding a referendum on the King's fate in July 1791. By 1791 too, working women in Paris were involved in their own separate activities. They continued to engage in direct action. When in 1792 the price of sugar had risen beyond what they could afford to pay, working women seized sugar supplies from merchants. At the same time, women protested to the Jacobin clubs about food hoarders and those who artificially caused the price of food to rise, and sought the death penalty for speculators and hoarders. In 1793, the women who established the Society of Republican Revolutionary Women demanded a comprehensive programme of protective and repressive measures to ensure the safety of the people. And in seeking to demonstrate their support for the Republic, they urged that all women should be required to wear the tricolour cockade in public.

As many recent historians have shown, while the 1789 Declaration of the Rights of Man and the Citizen was apparently an inclusive document, it was imbued with a very particular idea of the meaning of the term 'man'. Women were not included in the rights being claimed any more than were black men or Jews. Rousseau's very influential ideas on sexual difference made it seem obvious to many that women should not be accorded the rights of men. However, his views were not universally accepted. The first suggestion of women's entitlement to political rights and citizenship was made in 1790 in the *Journal of the Society of 1789*. In his essay 'On the Admission of Women to the Rights of Citizenship', Marquis de Condorcet, a philosopher and a liberal aristocrat, argued that the rights of men 'result simply from the fact that they are sentient beings, capable of acquiring moral ideas and of reasoning concerning these ideas. Women, having these same qualities, must necessarily possess equal rights' (Landes, 1988: pp. 114–18). Condorcet's ideas were not taken up in any significant way by the influential Constituent Assembly which had promoted the Declaration of Rights, but the Assembly did nonetheless move immediately to deal with some questions about women's legal rights. In 1790, a legislation was introduced which made divorce easier and removed earlier restrictions on women's inheritance rights. As Lyn Hunt has argued, this legislation did seek to bring a measure of greater equality into the family. Just as the king had been stripped of despotic powers, so many of those actively involved in the early stages of the Revolution sought to remove the immense powers of husbands and fathers. 'After having made man free and happy in public life', argued one Deputy in the Constituent Assembly in 1790, 'it remains for us to assure his liberty and his happiness in private life. You know that under the Old Regime the tyranny of parents was often as terrible as the despotism of ministers; often the prisons of state became family prisons. It is suitable therefore to draw up, after the declaration of rights of man and citizen, a declaration, so to speak of the rights of spouses, of father, of sons, of parents, and so on' (Hunt, 1992: p. 17).

In the years 1790–93, a number of legislative changes was introduced in regard to family life which unquestionably benefited women. The attack on the power of the Catholic Church, the introduction of civil marriage and of divorce gave women considerably more rights within marriage as well as the right to end it. The establishment of a new Family Court in 1790 and the legislation in 1792 permitting divorce in the event of a complete breakdown in marriage made a very considerable shift away from the authoritarian family structure of the old regime and towards a new and more egalitarian one. The concern among revolutionary legislators to curb the powers of husbands and fathers also benefited women and girls in terms of inheritance. In March 1793, the National Convention declared equal inheritance of all in equal line of succession, and in November 1793, it also extended this equal right of inheritance to illegitimate children upon proof of paternity. The debates surrounding the Constitution of 1791 prompted a series of pamphlets and treatises on women's rights, the best known of which are Olympe De Gouges' *Declaration of the Rights of Woman and the Citizen* in France (1791) and Mary Wollstonecraft's *Vindication of the Rights of Woman* in England (1792). Olympe De Gouges was a playwright, pamphleteer and sometime courtesan who argued for the representation of women as citizens throughout the early stages of the French Revolution. Her *Declaration of the Rights of Woman and the Citizen* paralleled the Declaration of the Rights of Man in its structure and form. It demanded all the rights and freedoms conferred on men for women, adding new demands which centred on women's need to be free of domestic tyranny. De Gouges put forward a new idea of the meaning of citizen, which included women as well as men, and insisted that the rights of the citizen needed to encompass not only the individual's political participation and activities, but also his or her personal and domestic lives and activities. She insisted that women needed some of these new rights in order to protect themselves against sexual exploitation. The right to 'the free communication of ideas and opinions' was important, she argued, because it would enable women to name the father of their child or children, and to demand shared responsibility in relation to those children. As Joan Scott has pointed out, by demanding the freedom for women to indicate the paternity of their children, De Gouges called attention to the fact that men were sexual as well as rational beings, and that women might need protection from men's sexual transgression (Scott, 1996: pp. 42–6).

The exclusion of women from many of the rights extended to men in France in the period 1789–92 also gave rise to feminist demands in other countries. Mary Wollstonecraft's *Vindication of the Rights of Woman*, still widely regarded as the founding text of Anglo-American feminism was written in England in a few weeks of furious activity in 1792. Wollstonecraft had been a passionate supporter of the French Revolution, which she thought of as the harbinger of a liberal and democratic society. However, when she saw that girls were excluded from the plan for compulsory schooling being laid down for boys in France, she was appalled. Wollstonecraft insisted that by denying women rights, and arguing that they were seeking to protect women and to secure their happiness, the men of the French Constituent Assembly were following the model of all the tyrants they ostensibly deplored. Like Condorcet and De Gouges, Wollstonecraft argued that women, like men, were rational creatures, and she set out at length the fundamental rights which ensued from this premise. Wollstonecraft did not deny the importance of sexual difference indeed she accepted that men and women would exercise their rights in different ways and that they would have different duties. However, in her view, bodily differences occurred alongside significant intellectual similarities and it was the fact that men and women shared the capacity for reason that was most important. Recognition of women as rational beings, she insisted, also required rethinking conventional ideas about women's conduct and moral qualities, taking as the first principle that there was only one standard of human virtue and that it must be the same for men and women. Wollstonecraft particularly criticized the gendering of qualities, for example questioning the ways in which the term 'modesty' was used to refer in the case of men to 'that soberness of mind which teaches a man not to think more highly of himself than he ought to think' and, in the case of women, only to sexual demeanour.

Alongside her discussion of moral questions, Wollstonecraft also argued for the institutional and legal changes which followed from the recognition of women's rationality and moral autonomy: the need for an education which was based on rational principles and which combined intellectual training with useful skills; the need for an end to the sexual double standard; the need for reform of marriage and for the admission of women to a range of fields of study and of paid employment, which would allow them to be economically independent. Wollstonecraft specified the study of medicine and of business as possible professional pursuits, and politics and history for their intellectual and moral improvement. For Wollstonecraft, as for De Gouges, the question about women's precise rights and duties, and the actual meaning of citizenship for women, were complex and sometimes confusing issues. Both Wollstonecraft and De Gouges sought to demand rights for women on the basis of their capacity for reason, and to establish the nature of sexual difference and of the kind of sexed citizenship which accompanied women's domestic and maternal duties. Hence, while protesting against the ways in which women were seen to possess only a limited range of qualities and were restricted to particular fields, they in turn emphasized maternity and women's maternal duty as the basis of their claim to political rights, legal independence and full citizenship.

During the early part of the 1790s, as women's organizations defended the right of women to participate directly in political debates and in the defence of France, women's rights were passionately demanded both in theory and practice. In 1793 in Paris, these demands and debates were stifled. This was a year of considerable economic hardship and suffering, and one in which tensions among different women's groups came to the fore. There were internal divisions within the Society of Republican Revolutionary Women, as some turned against their former leader, Claire Lecombe, accusing her of immoral conduct. There were also tensions between the Society, which sought to insist that women wear the revolutionary cockade to emphasize their patriotism, and many of the market women of Paris, who resented this interference in their lives. The market women filed a protest against the Republican Revolutionary Women. On October 30, 1793 (8 Brumaire in the revolutionary calendar), the growing hostility of the National Convention to women's political participation was manifested in its closure of the Society of Republican Revolutionary Women. Shortly after this, all women's clubs and societies were prohibited.

The prohibition of women's clubs was advocated by a prominent member of the Committee of General Security, André Amar, who echoed Rousseau in his insistence that the harmony of society required the observance of the natural sexual division of labour. 'Each sex', he insisted, 'is called to the type of occupation that is proper for it; its action is circumscribed within this circle from which it cannot escape' (Procter, 1990: p. 162). The functions of women are 'to prepare children's minds and hearts for public virtue, to direct them early in life towards the good, to elevate their souls, to educate them in the political cult of liberty... to make virtue loved.' Morality, nature and even the fate of the Republic, he argued, all depended upon women fulfilling these duties. Making quite explicit his view that citizens were men, Amar insisted that citizens were entitled to go about their business and their political activities secure in the knowledge that their homes and families were being looked after by their wives. Women's groups continued sporadic activity after this, but by the end of 1793 all agitation by women had ceased.

As women's political participation was brought to an end and their family roles were officially cultivated, citizenship became inextricably connected not only with masculinity, but also with the prerogatives and privileges of being a husband and a father. In the course of these developments, the idea that citizenship was a masculine prerogative was extensively argued and demonstrated. The gendering of citizenship involved the very explicit and extensive reworking of images and ideals of masculinity. As both Lynn Hunt (1984) and Dorinda Outram (1989) have shown, in the early stages of the French Revolution new images of masculinity were developed and officially promoted. The personality of Hercules became more and more prominent in revolutionary iconography. Stoicism and self-control—both accepted as attributes of masculinity—came to be seen as important in new models of political behaviour.

As successive governments became more conservative on questions of social policy in the mid and later 1790s, there was some concern about whether the family legislation of the early 1790s allowing divorce and limiting paternal control was too liberal and might contribute to the breakdown in social order. This legislation remained in force until the early nineteenth century, when the new Civil Code introduced by Napoleon in 1804 eradicated the legislative gains for women. The Napoleonic Civil Code re-established and possibly strengthened patriarchal power within family life. It set up a framework for marriage which echoed the *ancien régime* requirement for parental consent for marriage. Women under the age of 21 and men under 25 could not legally marry without parental consent, and if parents disagreed, it was the father's view that counted. Parental control was also extended in duration. The age of majority was set at 30 and those under this age were deemed to be children subject to the authority of their parents. Under the Napoleonic Code, a father was given the right to have a child imprisoned for up to six months if he deemed it disobedient, another echo of the *ancien régime*. The Code not only reasserted the power of parents but also it re-established the authority of husbands over wives. A husband was charged with the protection of his wife, while she in turn owed him obedience. Women were designated as legally incompetent: unfit to witness certificates of marriage, birth or death; unable to sue in a court of law without their husband's consent and unable even to make or receive a gift or inheritance or succession without their husband's consent. So complete was the disregard of and distrust for women under the Code that a husband was required even to witness the birth of his children and to declare a child his own before it could be recognized as legitimate. Husbands were given unconditional control over family property and over the wages or earnings of their wives. Husbands were also given the power to determine all aspects of marital life: the nature and location of a residence, the schooling of children, etc. Some historians have interpreted the provisions of the Code which prohibited paternity suits as the corollary of Napoleon's military background and his concern for soldiers. By prohibiting paternity suits, the Code prevented women from taking action against men whom they claimed to have seduced them. The Code also introduced the sexual double standard into marital law. Adultery was seen as a criminal offence for women, rendering an erring wife liable to imprisonment for a period of between three months and two years. By contrast, an adulterous husband would at most receive a fine. Moreover, adultery was a different crime for men and women: a wife could be charged with adultery on suspicion of any form of illicit sexual conduct. However, a husband could be charged with adultery only if he brought his mistress into the home.

In the aftermath of the French Revolution, then, women were rendered completely subordinate to husbands. Regarded primarily as homemakers, married women needed their husband's permission to engage in paid work. The Napoleonic Code set the legal framework for women in France, in the German and Italian states and in all the countries conquered by Napoleonic armies or which chose to adopt the Code in the course of the nineteenth century as a symbol of national progress. The introduction of the Napoleonic Code in some of the German-speaking states brought a slight deterioration in the legal position of women there. Independently of Napoleon, and before he came to power, there were moves in Germany to reinforce the centrality of maternity and to regulate women's maternal conduct. In the German-speaking regions governed by Prussia, the Allgemeines Landrecht laid down a framework for marriage in 1794, stressing the importance of procreation, and underlining the nature of women's conjugal duties and their subordination to their husbands. Following Rousseau's advice, mothers were enjoined by the law to breastfeed their children and fathers were given the responsibility of determining how long the breastfeeding should continue. Women were, however, entitled to expect protection from their husbands and were given some legal control over their own property. A decade later, when the Napoleonic Code was accepted by the German states, west of the Rhine married women lost any control of their property and were in effect reduced to the legal status of minors. The Code gave men greater control over common matrimonial property and easier access to divorce than had previously been the case. Similarly in Eastern Europe, including parts of the Hapsburg Empire which borrowed from the Code, women were deprived of some traditional rights of inheritance and of power within family life. Similar conditions entailed in Britain, where a married woman legally owned nothing. Her husband owned all her earnings and anything she might inherit. He was entitled to exact sexual and domestic services, even to imprison her to enforce them. Further, she had almost no legal rights in regard to her children.

All of these developments have led to intense historical discussion about the overall impact of the French Revolution on women. Olwen Hufton argues that only small numbers of women were actively concerned about political citizenship or engaged in the Revolution which resulted in their political annihilation. The majority of women—poor, rural women—had few concerns about citizenship, and the Revolution brought them immense physical, financial and emotional hardship which made them long nostalgically for the re-establishment of the Church and the communal solidarity it had symbolized (Hufton, 1992). Taking a longer perspective, but an equally bleak view, Madelyn Gutwirth has argued that 'the enforcement of a regime of separate sexual spheres institutionalized under Jacobinism, with the women retired from all public participation, was to prove to be perhaps the single most unalterable measure effected by Revolution, surviving all the Nineteenth-century's changes of regime' (Gutwirth, 1992). However, other historians put forward a rather different view, pointing to the importance of the idea of political participation for women that the revolution inspired, and insisting on the importance of the revolution for the emergence of modern feminism. While acknowledging the ultimate defeat of women's political aspirations, Darlene Levy and Harriet Applewhite argue that in the years from 1789 to 1795, the revolution provided women with the opportunity to evolve from subjects, sometimes passive and sometimes protesting, but always leaving decision-making to those in power, into participating citizens demanding a say in government (Levy and Applewhite, 1992:

pp. 97–98). This participation dramatically affected the nature of the Revolution and made it genuinely democratic. For historians interested in intellectual and cultural history and in the history of feminism, the French Revolution brought women few lasting gains, especially in terms of new political and legal rights; nonetheless, the claims women made during the Revolution fundamentally altered traditional ways of seeing and understanding sexual difference and citizenship, and raised women's emancipation as a major political issue throughout Europe for the rest of the nineteenth century. Women's activity during the French Revolution made it possible to articulate the ideal of women as active citizens participating fully in the political and social activities of the nation. In a similar way, though citizenship was explicitly made a masculine right and prerogative at this time, the questions of the gendering of rights and of the rights of women was never laid to rest. Indeed, modern feminism was organized around the recognition that women were now subject to new forms of legal and political discrimination.

WOMEN'S VOICES

Women's demands for political rights and a public role were emphatically rejected in the course of the 1790s. However, this did not mean that women retired submissively to the silent world of the home, as demanded by Rousseau. If anything, the participation of some women in public debate and the audibility of their voices increased. Salons declined in number in France and England, as their functions were taken over by learned societies, professional bodies and political parties. However, in other countries, particularly Germany, Russia and Spain, salon women emerged only in the early nineteenth century and were at the peak of their influence by about 1820. Where salons declined, women became increasingly prominent as writers. The expansion in publishing, particularly the increasing number of journals and magazines, provided an outlet for women writers. Writing offered many middle-class women from a humbler social class than the *salonières* a voice and the chance to earn a living. Despite Rousseau's strictures on the importance of marriage, domesticity and financial dependence for women, there were significant numbers of unmarried women in Western Europe. Moreover, many married women were deserted by their husbands, or found themselves married to men who were unable or unwilling to support them and who made it necessary for the women themselves to work for their support and that of their children. Works of some 400 women writers were published in England in the last two decades of the eighteenth century. For many of them, literature was a profession and a way of supporting not only themselves, but also their families. While no other European country replicated entirely English developments, by the late eighteenth and early nineteenth centuries, there were increasing numbers of prominent women writers in France, the German and Italian states and in Central Europe.

In England in particular, it is clear that the popularity of fiction played an important part in the rise of the woman writer. The novel allowed great scope for women because of its concern with the domestic world of family and private relationships and because it did not require the classical education or the knowledge of classical literature still deemed essential for poetry and drama. Thus the late eighteenth century saw the emergence of best-selling novelists like Fanny Burney or Ann Radcliffe, and the early nineteenth-century writers such as Maria Edgeworth and Jane Austen. Women did not only write novels. In Britain, Catherine Macaulay became a historian who was widely read. Her countrywoman Hannah More published plays, poetry, biblical dialogues and moral and religious tracts as well as her immensely successful *Strictures on the Modern System of Education* (1799). Though the French Revolution ultimately silenced women's political voice, like the wars which followed, it led to an outpouring of historical reflections, personal reminiscences and memoirs from French women, from English women like Mary Wollstonecraft and Helen Maria Williams, and from women in the German states and as far away as Greece. Indeed, women writers became involved in all the literary fields evident in their own countries. Thus Italian women were prominent in the writing of opera librettos, while their English and French counterparts were actively engaged in journalism.

The increasing number of women writers was made possible by economic change and developments within the world of publishing. The decline of patronage from wealthy and titled individuals, and the expansion of a literary market with more commercial publishers, more journals and a growing number of local lending libraries, all helped to provide women writers with ways to publish their work. There were specific magazines and journals written for and by women, like the *Lady's Magazine* in England or the *Journal des Dames* in France. Other women were able to make a living through editorial work or contributions to journals. Thus in England, Mary Wollstonecraft worked as an editorial assistant for a radical monthly journal, the *Analytical Review.* Although women were able to make use of the commercial world of publishing, nonetheless, as Carla Hesse has recently pointed out, they faced considerable problems when it came to legal questions about who actually owned their work and what their rights within it were (Hesse,

1989: pp. 469–487). In France it was not until 1793 that the law recognized an author's claim to property rights in a text. Prior to that, ideas were thought of as a gift of God, revealed in a text, but not created by an author. Both male and female writers had been protesting against this, and finally in 1793 the national convention passed what has been seen as 'the declaration of the rights of genius', giving male authors claims to their work. These rights were not extended to women. Although married women in France were given some new legal rights—the right to inherit and to sign contracts—they were still subject to their husband's authority and could not appear in a court without his support and consent. This in turn meant that in any legal dispute about publication rights, a woman required her husband to fight for what was, after all, his name. Married women were generally unable to publish work without the consent of their husband. In Britain too, married women had no legal standing and both their literary work and any money they might earn from it belonged legally to their husbands. Hence while women's voices could increasingly be heard in this period, women could still not participate in the literary world on the same terms as men.

Within the literary world, moreover, women were still confined in what they could write about and more particularly by prevailing perceptions of their literary abilities. This gendering of art was made very clear in the dominant aesthetic values and critical language of the late eighteenth century, which set the masculine 'sublime' against the feminine 'beautiful'. Mary Wollstonecraft's feminist anger was directed as much against the aesthetic and critical approaches which denied women true literary stature as it was against the legal and political structures which denied them those rights. Just as she had attacked Edmund Burke for his political views, so too in her *Vindication*, Wollstonecraft attacked his influential *Philosophical Inquiry into the Origin of the Sublime and the Beautiful*. For Burke, as for his contemporaries, the highest art dealt with the sublime. He contrasted the sublime with the beautiful, but in ways which made the former masculine, while the latter was feminine. The sublime, for Burke, was exemplified by the awesome grandeur of rugged natural land and rock forms, especially the Alps. However, it was also evident in the spectacle of powerful men gazing on or overcoming nature, in images of the kinship between gifted men and God as the creator of nature, or of men exercising their terrible strength and overcoming any natural obstacles which prevented them from gaining a particular goal. Burke contrasted the sublime with the beautiful, which he regarded as more graceful, but less overwhelming or significant. He applied the term beautiful to that which was small, delicate and graceful either in art or in nature, including women and the works they created.

While the sublime was masculine, the beautiful embodied those qualities that men found desirable, especially in women. Wollstonecraft charged Burke with having convinced women, 'that *littleness* and *weakness* are the very essence of beauty and that the Supreme Being, in giving women beauty in the most super eminent degree, seemed to command them, by the powerful voice of Nature, not to cultivate the moral virtues that chance to excite respect, and interfere with the pleasing sensations they were created to inspire.' Thus eighteenth- and early nineteenth-century women writers or artists had to contend with a set of aesthetic values which immediately diminished the value of what they produced.

The advent of the woman writer coincided also with the rise of Romanticism towards the end of the eighteenth century. While disputes about the nature of Romanticism and the place of gender and of women within it continue, several recent writers have argued that Romanticism served to privilege and empower men, largely because it incorporated a new and very explicitly masculine idea of creative genius. One of the key features of Romanticism was its emphasis on the importance of feelings and emotions as denning human characteristics and as the source of creativity, knowledge and moral insight. Romanticism stressed the importance of feeling in opposition to the Enlightenment idealization of reason. The hero of Goethe's novel *Wilhelm Meister's Apprenticeship* in 1824 (originally published in German in 1795) exemplified a masculinity untethered by the materialist concerns of business, work or domesticity. Wilhelm Meister personified the liberal tenets of autonomy, and brought together feeling and reason, combining 'the brightest and most capricious fancy, the most piercing and inquisitive intellect, the wildest and deepest imagination... his faculties and feelings are not fettered or prostrated under the iron sway of Passion, but led and guided in kindly union under the mild sway of Reason' (Carlyle, 1874: p. 23). This form of 'intellectual manhood' was characteristic of Romanticism, and of the desire for an alternative to the mediocrity of bourgeois norms, of a 'new Poet for the world in our own time, of a new Instructor and Preacher of Truth to all men.' For Romantics, intuition, sensation and feeling, rather than reason, were the key to knowledge and truth. While this stress on feeling linked Romanticism to femininity, it did not lead to the idea that women, who were generally seen as more emotional than men, had any superiority in terms of their imaginative or creative capacities. It was rather the case that exceptional men, and particularly men of genius, combined these feminine characteristics with masculine physical and intellectual strength. Romanticism thus developed a particular ideal of androgyny, in which the highest creative power was associated with a person who combined masculine and feminine characteristics, but always within a male body. For the Romantics, creative power or genius was the quality of greatest worth and, as Christine Battersby has argued, a genius was always a man who combined his masculine attributes (especially his bodily strength and sexuality) with feminine intuition and sensitivity (Battersby, 1990: p. 103). By contrast, a woman with a masculine mind was seen as unnatural or monstrous. The Romantic idea of a genius also involved a sense of a man, battling alone, alienated from the surrounding culture, seeking solace in the natural world where he could find spiritual peace and a sense of the immense power of God, as the creator of nature. However, this image, too, drew on ideas about men as the explorers of unknown continents, or as solitary beings who devoted their time to discovering the wonders of nature. Within the Romantic world view, as was made so clear by Rousseau in *Émile*, women were identified with society, with the world of triviality, everyday life and with corruption. The figure, who stood alone, seeking an authentic life and a close connection with the natural world, was always a man.

Romanticism gave a high place to feminine characteristics, although this did not mean that there was any marked empathy between romantic writers and women. On the contrary, women were depicted as exotic and strange in the writings of most Romantics, and were the supreme and mysterious objects of male desire. In some cases, as Anne Mellor has argued, the Romantic ideal of love did involve a sense of man and woman as spiritual soul mates. In these cases, however, the woman had no separate identity as she came to mirror or to be absorbed into her male lover. Describing his love of Mary Godwin (the daughter of Mary Wollstonecraft), the English poet Percy Shelley explained, 'so intimately are our natures now united, that I feel while I describe her excellencies as if I were an egoist expatiating upon his own perfections' (Mellor, 1993: p. 25). For Mellor, Romanticism is characterized by its extreme tendency to deny, obliterate or efface women, and to absorb feminine qualities into men. This effacement and absorption are seen most clearly in the way Romantic poets and writers attempt to appropriate the reproductive powers of women. Shelley in his *Defence of Poetry*, for example, described the poet as a mother bringing forth a work of art as if it were a child. By usurping the mother's womb, the poet becomes like God, sole ruler of the world. Mary Shelley's novel *Frankenstein* critiques this assumption about women's reproductive powers. The novel depicts a monster which is created—and then rejected and ignored—by the young scientist, Frankenstein. Frankenstein seeks the creative power of women, but feels none of the care or concern for his progeny that women feel for their babies. Shelley's novel has been read as an allegory of the ways in which the creative capacity of women was denied in Romanticism, much as it was in politics during the French Revolution.

The intensity of attempts to silence and erase the voices of women in the late eighteenth- and early nineteenth century in Europe points to anxieties about the place and potential power of women and about the stability of the gender order. For much of the nineteenth century, this gender order was debated and renegotiated as women's participation in home, in the workforce and in the political arena became more and more pronounced.

References and Further Readings

Primary Sources

Burke, Edmund (1965 [1790]), *Reflections on the Revolution in France* (New York).

De Gouges, Olympe (1986 [1791]), 'Declaration of the Rights of Woman and the Citizen', in B. Groult (ed.), (Paris: Oeuvres).

More, Hannah (1799), *Strictures on the Modern System of Female Education* (London).

Rousseau, Jean Jacques (1911 [1762]), *Émile*, trans. (New York: Barbara Foxley).

Wollstonecraft, Mary (1988 [1792]), *A Vindication of the Rights of Woman* (New York).

Wollstonecraft, Mary (1975 [1796]), *Maria or the Wrongs of Woman* (New York).

Sexual Difference and the Enlightenment

Abelove, H. (1989), 'Some Speculations on the History of Sexual Intercourse during the Long Eighteenth Century in England', *Gender*, 6: 125–130.

Goodman, D. (1994), *The Republic of Letters: A Cultural History of the French Enlightenment* (New York: Ithaca).

Hill, B. (1987), *Eighteenth Century Women* (London).

Hull, I. (1996), *Sexuality, State, and Civil Society in Germany 1700–1815* (Ithaca).

Jordanova, L. (1990), *Sexual Visions: Images of Gender in Science and Medicine Between the Eighteenth and Twentieth Centuries* (London).

Laqueur, T. (1990), *Making Sex: Body and Gender from the Greeks to Freud* (Cambridge, Mass).

Lloyd, G. (1984), *The 'Man of Reason': Male and Female in Western Philosophy* (Sydney).

Scheibinger, L. (1989), *The Mind Has No Sex? Women in the Origins of Modern Science* (Cambridge, Mass).

Spencer, S. (ed.) (1984), *French Women and the Age of Enlightenment* (Bloomington).

Steinbrugge, L. (1995), *The Moral Sex: Women's Nature in the French Enlightenment*, (trans. P. Selwyn) (New York).

Wertheim, M. (1995) *Pythagoras' Trousers: God, Physics and the Gender Wars* (New York).

French Revolution and the Origins of Feminism

Caine, B. (1997), *English Feminism, 1780–1980* (Oxford).

Godineau, D. (1990), 'Masculine and Feminine Political Practice during the French Revolution, 1793–Year III', in H. B. Applewhite and D. G. Levy (eds), *Women and Politics in the Age of the Democratic Revolution* (Ann Arbor).

Gutwirth, M. (1992), *The Twilight of the Goddesses: Women and Representation in the French Revolutionary Era* (New Brunswick).

Hufton, O. (1992), *Women and the Limits of Citizenship in the French Revolution* (Toronto).

Hunt, L. (1984), *Politics, Culture and Class in the French Revolution* (Berkeley).

Hunt, L. (1992), *The Family Romance of the French Revolution* (Berkeley).

Landes, J. (1988), *Women and the Public Sphere in the Age of the French Revolution* (Ithaca).

Landes, J. (1992), 'Representing the Body Politic: The Paradox of Gender in the Graphic Politics of the French Revolution', in S. E. Melzer and L. W. Rabine (eds), *Rebel Daughters: Women and the French Revolution* (New York and Oxford).

Levy, D. G. and Applewhite, H. B. (1992), 'Women and Militant Citizenship in Revolutionary Paris', in S. E. Melzer and L. W. Rabine (eds), *Rebel Daughters: Women and the French Revolution* (New York and Oxford).

Melzer, S. E. and Rabine, L. W. (eds) (1992), *Rebel Daughters: Women and the French Revolution* (New York and Oxford).

Outram, D. (1989), *The Body and the French Revolution* (New Haven).

Proctor, C. E. (1990), *Women, Equality, and the French Revolution* (New York).

Scott, J. W. (1996), *Only Paradoxes to Offer: French Feminists and the Rights of Man* (Cambridge, Mass).

Taylor, B. (1992), 'Mary Wollstonecraft and the Wild Wish of Early Feminism', *History Workshop Journal*, 33: 197–219.

Women Writers and the Age of Romanticism

Battersby, C. (1990), *Gender and Genius: Towards a Feminist Aesthetic* (London).

Butler, M. (1981), *Romantics, Rebels, Reactionaries: English Literature and its Background, 1760–1830* (Oxford).

Carlyle, T. (1874), 'Introduction', Goethe, *Wilhelm Meister's Lehrjahre*, trans. T. Carlyle (London).

Hesse, C. (1989), 'Female Authorship and Revolutionary Law', *Eighteenth Century Studies*, 3: 469–87.

Kirkham, M. (1983), *Jane Austen: Feminism and Fiction* (Brighton).

Mellor, A. (ed.) (1988), *Romanticism and Feminism* (Bloomington).

Mellor, A. (1993), *Romanticism and Gender* (New York and London).

Yaeger, P. S. and Kowalski-Wallace, B. (eds) (1990), *Refiguring the Father. New Feminist Readings of Patriarchy* (Illinois: Carbondale).

2 Spaces and Places: Changing Patterns of Domesticity and Work

—*Barbara Caine*

The impact of industrial capitalism on European economies and societies in the period from 1780 to 1920 brought about a transformation of work and the workplace, and of home and the meaning of domesticity. Industrialization also produced new understandings and representations of gender. The advent of new sources of power, new workplaces and new technologies brought major changes in the sexual division of labour, and a new image of men as industrial workers. The complementary development for women centred on the image of the housewife, located in the home or the private sphere, which was designated as a specifically feminine space and location.

Patterns of industrialization differed significantly from one country to another. In Britain, new methods of agriculture, the establishment of textile factories and the application of steam to manufacture brought what continues to be defined as an industrial revolution in the period 1780–1830. By contrast, France industrialized much more slowly, with substantial development in railway construction and factories getting underway only in the mid-nineteenth century. In Germany and Russia, industrial expansion occurred still later in the century: after 1870 in Germany and in the 1890s in Russia. Despite the different pace of industrialization, however, there were some common patterns throughout Europe concerning women's work, wages and general conditions in relation to those of men. For the most part, industrialization served to emphasize and to make more rigid the sexual division of labour. The emergence of the industrial work that was introduced in the nineteenth century was undertaken by men. In factories and mines, on railways, roads and ships, for example, the vast majority of workers were men, and these new kinds of work brought in turn a new idea of the 'worker' as one engaged on a full-time basis in industrial labour. This industrial worker, alongside the traditional male artisan, on the one hand, and the middle-class professional or businessman, on the other, served to underline the idea that work itself was a masculine activity and indeed was central to the idea of masculinity. While the range of occupations available to men expanded with industrialization, finding work became ever more difficult for women. The introduction of factories and larger workshops, which served to separate home from workplace, and the long working days which came with them produced immense problems for women who had to combine paid labour with familial responsibilities. Increasingly, married women sought home-based work or part-time and casual work which allowed them to supervise families. Trade unions, socialist groups and the many professional associations emerged in the mid-nineteenth century that served to constrain the prospects for women workers. These work organizations were all concerned to improve working conditions for men. They were dominated by men in terms of their membership, and often sought the exclusion of women from particular occupations, or indeed from any kind of paid work.

The conception of the masculinity of work and the workplace had as its counterpart the idea of the home as a private and feminine sphere. The notion of 'separate spheres' for men and women developed first through a middle-class pattern in which a male household head engaged in the public sphere of work and political activity, working to support his family while his wife and daughters remained at home. The notion of separate spheres fitted very neatly into prevailing ideas of sexual difference. Work was clearly the necessary activity of strong, energetic, rational and independent man. By contrast, immersion in the home and dedication to husband and children suited the temperament and emotions of women. Throughout Europe, separate spheres were regarded as integral to the social, civic and moral order. In Britain, in the late eighteenth and early nineteenth centuries, the growing influence of evangelical religion brought a new emphasis on home and family as the basic unit in religious observance and moral order. By contrast, in France, from the 1790s onwards, the new Republic demanded close family ties and maternal duty in order that children would learn civic virtue and their duties as citizens at their mother's breast. In the German states and the Habsburg Empire, the new emphasis on family life and on the home emerged in the early decades of the nineteenth century, and was associated closely with the post-Napoleonic Restoration, political conservatism and the reassertion of the importance of hierarchy in the state. Thus for all their political and social differences, evangelicals, republicans and conservatives held common views about the nature of the public sphere, about sexual difference, women's activities and the importance of family life.

The sense of home promulgated by the middle classes at the beginning of the century also became an ideal among skilled artisans and even socialists in the mid and later nineteenth century. As a result, the question of women's work and indeed the very idea of the 'woman worker' became extremely problematic (Scott, 1993). While the vast majority of women had to engage in paid work to support themselves and their families, the range of employment opportunities available to women and their wages were all set in a framework that viewed them as supplementary or casual income earners, whose major commitment and responsibility was to marriage and family life. Moreover, since in this ideological framework women were suited only to domestic life, certain forms of paid employment, for example many kinds of industrial or agricultural work, were almost unthinkable for women, and others, especially any form of domestic service, seemed 'natural' or suitable. It was by no means the case, however, that domestic labour was any less arduous for women than other forms of employment. Many women protested against the confinement they faced in their conventional work and domestic roles. Some demanded greater opportunities to work in order to support families or to develop financial independence. Others sought rather to gain access to a wider public world through an emphasis on the tasks they undertook at home.

In this chapter, we explore the ideal of family and home that developed in the nineteenth century alongside industrialization and urbanization. We begin by looking at the development of the new style of domestic life evident in the middle class, with a male breadwinner and a family and a home concerned with consumption rather than production. We then look at the impact of this model of family life on the working class, focusing on the gendering of work and on the difficulties this entailed for working-class women.

FAMILY LIFE AND HOME

For many historians, the economic, political and social developments of the nineteenth century produced a new class society in which the values and beliefs of the middle class came to dominate all others (see Chapter 3). Hence the nineteenth century is often referred to as the 'bourgeois century' and it was among the bourgeoisie, or the middle class, that the importance of the home was first extolled and that the new model of family life first appeared. From the late eighteenth century onwards, in both Britain and France, the close-knit family was one of the prominent features of bourgeois urban life. The meaning of the term 'family' changed over the second half of the eighteenth century, as it increasingly referred to the unit composed of parents and children, in contrast to earlier meanings which had stressed either lineage groups or households with apprentices. This new meaning of family derived from the middle-class pattern in contrast to an aristocratic one. Family life in turn played a major part in establishing a distinctive middle-class life-style in which domestic affection, intimacy and a sense of domestic duty were extolled and seen to provide the basis for a superior social and moral order. In the late eighteenth and nineteenth centuries, love between husband and wife began to replace financial or social interest as the proper basis of marriage, while parental love, especially that of a mother for her children, was regarded as essential for harmonious family life. Maternal devotion was also seen as an integral part of a woman's nature, and as something which differentiated civilized women from their 'savage' female counterparts.

This distinctive and morally superior middle-class family and its new domestic life style also became the basis of the middle-class demand for a new social and political status. As Catherine Hall and Leonore Davidoff have shown, in Britain during the first half of the nineteenth century, the capacity to provide a comfortable home to maintain a wife and children was regarded as a primary indication of a man's independence, of his status as a gentleman and of his entitlement to political rights and recognition (Davidoff and Hall, 1987). In France too, the middle-class family had a particular role to play, and the middle-class family man was given a special political status. As Isabel Hull has argued, the Napoleonic Civil Code served to protect the married, propertied male citizen and 'his private social status as presumptive family father and producer of wealth became the basis for his greater, state-guaranteed rights' (Hull, 1996). Before 1848 the claims for political rights made by the middle class in the German states were not recognized and, consequently, men retreated to the domestic world and shared with women a deep involvement in family life. Ute Frevert argues that a certain amount of mockery was directed towards middle-class men who devoted themselves to domestic life rather than seeking a wider use for their abilities (Frevert, 1989). Later in the century, however, the unified German nation recognized the political importance of the middle-class male household head (see Chapter 4).

In the eyes of some historians, the emergence of a more affectionate family and the enhancement of women's maternal role lessened the patriarchal nature of family life and improved the status of women. The ideal wife as depicted by Hannah More or Jane Austen in England at the turn of the nineteenth century was a genuine 'helpmeet' to her husband, valued and beloved in accordance with her dutifulness and devotion. In this view marriage was a companionate relationship, husbands and wives were domestic and social companions as well as sexual partners. Yet, as middle-class women became immersed in domestic and family life, they withdrew from some of their economic activities, and became economically dependent on their husbands or fathers. Though many women in the middle ranks participated in family businesses in the eighteenth century, from the 1780s onwards, middle- and upper-middle-class women withdrew from paid labour so that they could devote themselves fully to family life. In both England and Germany, this process was completed by about 1850, after which time, middle-class women were expected to devote themselves to the home. Unpaid philanthropy or charity work was their main activity beyond the domestic hearth. In France, the prevalence of small family firms rather than larger businesses which could employ paid labour meant that some middle-class women continued to be economically active well into and beyond this period. Bonnie Smith has shown that despite the existence of maternal societies and a literature extolling maternity, the bourgeois women of the Nord worked alongside their husbands for long hours each day well into the 1840s, putting children out to wet nurse or sending them to boarding school so that they would not interfere with their labours. By the 1850s and 1860s, however, these women, too, were devoting themselves to domestic activity and religious observance. Where once female virtue had included the capacity to work hard for a family business, it was now defined in terms of managing a family and maternal devotion. Bourgeois men made very clear their sense that business was no place for women. It is worth pointing out that women who had once prided themselves on their robust health were now being described as delicate and in need of special care (Smith, 1981: pp. 53–90).

The middle-class emphasis on the moral basis of family life had its material counterpart in the expansion of the home, which became a focus for new middle-class patterns of consumption. Middle-class homes grew considerably in size and grandeur during this period. Indeed, the home provided a significant market for textiles, furniture and artefacts, the manufacture of which supplied middle-class incomes. From the 1860s and 1870s, electricity was harnessed to the home, bringing light and more efficient heating. In a similar way, the design and building of comfortable homes and villas located in suburbs away from the centre of towns and cities increased the demand for architects, builders, painters and decorators, as well as credit services, banks and lawyers. It also involved the expansion of new industries which supplied furniture and ornaments, garden implements and plants. Thus the middle-class home provided the basis for new professions and for an expansion of commercial services and enterprises.

Care of home and family and a constant concern with maternity were ostensibly regarded as integral to women's 'nature'. However, the immense number of works in every language which set out to instruct women in their natural role and to explain exactly what wifedom, mothering and domestic care involved, seem rather to question the extent to which, even in the nineteenth century, family life and domesticity were seen as 'natural' for women. During the Napoleonic era, dozens of French manuals on home economics and family welfare were published, seeking to instruct the women about their bodies, sexual identities and roles and about all aspects of child-rearing including infant cuisine. The predominant German-language literature for women in the later eighteenth century still depicted women as *Hausmutters* (literally 'house-mothers'), assuming they would preside over agricultural estates with their husbands. By the 1830s, however, the *Hausmutter* had been replaced by the *Hausfrau* ('housewife'), whose concerns centred on domestic life. Some of the qualities expected of the *Hausmutter* were evident also in the *Hausfrau*. Frugality, orderliness and the notion that the household was the prescribed sphere of woman's existence lost their specific economic focus, but they remained as foundations for bourgeois social ideas of womanhood, shoring up the notion that women should be the guardians of the private sphere of life while men gained new roles in the marketplace and the workforce (Gray, 1987). The period 1780–1830 saw an absolute explosion in English-language publications explaining to women their duties and roles as wives, daughters and mothers. All of these works contained a range of discussions, extending from direct information about child care and domestic activities to moral and religious exhortation. Manuals on motherhood and women's duties were not only remarkably similar across Europe, but were also translated from one country to another. Thus, the preface of an extremely popular English book of the 1840s, Sarah Lewis' *Woman's Mission* (London, 1839) made clear that the work was largely derived from a French work by M. Aimé-Martin, *De l'Education des mères de famille, ou de la civilisation du genre humain par les femmes* (Paris, 1834).

Some of the impetus behind this early and mid-nineteenth-century outpouring of works on women's duty may have lain in the belief that women's domestic role was closely connected to the wider social, political and moral world. The 'home' over which women presided was not only simply a physical space, but was constituted also in moral terms. The best known and fullest English exposition of this ideal of home was set out by John Ruskin in his essay 'Of Queen's Gardens', in *Sesame and Lilies* published in 1865. Home for Ruskin had a powerful metaphorical meaning. It was 'a place of Peace; the shelter not only from all injury, but from all terror, doubt and division.' Unless it functioned in this way, Ruskin insisted, a house could not truly be a home. It was the duty of women to shut out the external world of work, toil, strife and moral delinquency and to utilize their moral and emotional qualities to ensure that the house became truly a home. Ironically, in his insistence on the need to separate the home from the outside world, Ruskin demanded that they be connected. A properly constituted home would protect its inmates from external dangers and exercise a benign influence on the external world. If the home was properly run and organized, Ruskin argued, and if women carried out fully their domestic and moral duties, there would be a diminution of social and political disorder, sexual promiscuity and war (Ruskin, 1865: pp. 77–79). Ruskin was clearly following Rousseau from a century before, but only up to a point. While Rousseau argued against any activity of women outside the home, Ruskin believed that modest and chaste wives and mothers had a responsibility to engage in philanthropic and charitable work, and especially to attempt to reform other women who had fallen from virtue. Rousseau, in his great fear of women's sexuality, saw the very presence of women outside the home as an invitation to vice. By the time that Ruskin was writing, the ideal of women's virtue was rather more widely accepted, especially in regard to middle-class married women. It was believed that the virtue of these women could be utilized to assist their weaker sisters.

A number of paradoxes and contradictions were evident in the relations within the domestic sphere. In the first place, while the ideal home was presided over by a woman and seen as her 'natural' sphere, she did not own it. Women, like the children they bore and the house in which they lived, all belonged to their husbands. Indeed, in Ruskin's view, 'a true wife, in her husband's house, is his servant; it is in his heart that she is queen' (Ruskin, 1865: p. 75). As we have already seen, the precise powers of husbands and fathers varied from one country to another, but they were always extensive, throughout the nineteenth century. Maternity was deemed the highest moral, religious and social duty for women. However, women's care of children was under the control of their husbands. Fathers had extensive rights in regard to their children (see Chapter 1). While designated a 'female sphere', the home and the family were legally and conventionally under male control and authority. The ideal of home as a place of leisure and contentment was derived from the viewpoint of the men who returned to it at the end of the day, rather than from the women who lived constantly within it. Home was certainly not a place of leisure for women. Wealthy women may simply have presided over an army of servants, but the majority of middle- and even upper-middle-class women had a range of domestic tasks which could include either supervising or providing lessons for children, making clothes, shopping, cooking, arranging social events, etc. Moreover, whether or not the lady of the house was directly engaged in these activities, the vast majority of servants who carried them out were women. It was no secret that maintaining homes required extensive labour, and indeed many manuals for women stressed the need to make sure that all housework was done while the lord and master was out at work so that he could enjoy not only peace, but also harmony and domestic order on his return.

The paradoxes underlying family life extend also to the idea of it as a 'private sphere'. The idea of 'privacy', of the home as a secluded haven, safe from prying eyes, was basic to the middle-class ideal of home. At the same time, throughout the nineteenth century, the home was increasingly subject to public debate and to intervention and regulation by governments and intellectuals. Much of the intervention in home life was a result of a growing scientific interest in the question of maternity. As we saw in Chapter 1, medical thought throughout the eighteenth century paid particular attention to defining and classifying women's reproductive systems. This was accompanied by an emphasis in medical manuals on the importance of reproduction and of motherhood as the centre of women's lives. In the process, the physiological details of motherhood, of pregnancy, birth and breast-feeding became matters of widespread scientific and general discussion. Ruth Perry argues strongly that the new emphasis on motherhood in the late eighteenth century involved a 'colonization of the female body for domestic life', with a consequent denial to women of their sexuality (Perry, 1991: p. 167). The significance of motherhood and the responsibilities of mothers for the care and education of their children were also widely discussed. Medical treatises, sermons, moral and educational literature of many kinds stressed the importance of breast-feeding as something which was good for women, essential for the health of their children and beneficial for the nation as a whole. The vogue for breast-feeding was accompanied by a new language and a series of images which depicted the maternal breast as the fountain of both physical and moral nourishment. During the French Revolution, public ceremonies and pamphlets insisted that children were to drink in republican values at the breast (Jacobus, 1992). Later in the nineteenth century, British medical manuals showed children drinking in moral virtue and physical health at the breast.

The most significant change in ideas of motherhood across the nineteenth century was the shift from the earlier concern with the moral and religious importance of motherhood, to the later emphasis on questions of physical health and well-being. The rise of the medical profession in the mid-nineteenth century was accompanied by the establishment of new specialist disciplines including gynaecology and obstetrics, which dealt specifically with women's reproductive systems. However, the development of these female branches of medicine was accompanied by a new stress on the extent to which women deviated from the norm set by the healthy male body, and a view of women as fundamentally weak, fragile and in need of constant medical attention. In the eyes of many nineteenth-century doctors, and influential intellectuals like Jules Michelet, every feature of the reproductive development of women, from the onset of menstruation through pregnancy to menopause, was a form of illness and had to be guided and controlled by a medical specialist (Jalland and Hooper, 1986). The medical, educational and political concern about motherhood and child care, about family life and education, about the relationship between domestic order on the one hand, and social and political order on the other, served to make women's private activities a source of public debate and discussion. This is evidence of the practical impossibility of creating any absolute distinctions between the public and the private sphere. The new emphasis on the private world of home served at least as much to make women's activities visible as to restrict their scope.

These paradoxes about gender are evident also in regard to the moral connotations of home and the place of family life in ideas of social and civic order. As both Rousseau and Ruskin make clear, women and their domestic government determined the tenor of social and political life. Many nineteenth-century authors were far more explicit in their demand that women 'regenerate society' and that they ensure that their families have the right religious and moral or political values. However, through all of this, women were expected to be the religious and moral guides and leaders of men to whom they were in every way subordinate. They were expected to raise the moral and religious tone of their family, household and local community—and through that of the wider economic and political world—a world to which they were denied any direct access.

The tensions between this new sense of women's virtuous domesticity with its religious underpinning, and the secular nature of the masculine political world were evident in much of Europe, but they were particularly marked in Catholic France. Women's greater religiosity, their close ties with local priests and their dependence on parish churches and religious charities had made many of them antagonistic to the disestablishment of the Church carried out by the revolution. When the Church was re-established, the support it gained from women reinforced a belief already held by some secular-minded liberals that it was through women that the priests attempted to exert control not only over the domestic life, but also over the social life and the political behaviour of men. The secularism and anti-clericalism of many French radicals and republicans led to a powerful attack on the alliance between women and the Church and their presumed conspiracy to limit the freedom of independent men.

THE WORLD OF WORK

In the nineteenth-century Europe, the corollary of representations of the domestic sphere as feminine was the conception of the new world of work as masculine. The vast majority of the new forms of work which came with industrialization were undertaken by men. Although some women worked in factories, particularly in textile and clothing factories, most factory workers were men. The mining and metallurgical industries, like the chemical and electrical industries, were almost exclusively male. Men monopolized the senior and the skilled positions even in textile factories. Employers who were installing new machinery in nineteenth-century factories automatically assumed that only men would have the strength and the skill to manage this complicated new equipment. In some cases, this reflected the fact that men had worked as mechanics or had overseen domestic machinery before moving into factories. It also reflected the ways in which masculine traits, and manliness itself, were deemed to be essential to the notion of 'skill', making men into superior workers (Rose, 1992: pp. 23–35; Phillips and Taylor, 1980). Moreover, men's work was very visible in the nineteenth-century towns and cities which were being transformed by new methods of transport. While some women were certainly street sellers, most women worked indoors. By contrast, rail and road laying, building and dock work were exclusively masculine. Thus men were closely associated with the work which was bringing into being new industrial cities.

The association of work with masculinity became a central feature of radical politics and of labour organization in the nineteenth century. The new emphasis on work and the separation of home and workplace meant that for very large numbers of working-class men, work served to define their identity. To be employed as a skilled worker, gave a man economic and social status. In Britain, the skilled male worker could aspire to independence: to be free to sell his labour power; to support himself without the aid of charity; to have some freedom in regard to the regulation of his trade. Independence for male workers carried with it also the connotation which was central to the ideal of middle-class male independence: namely the capacity to maintain dependents within the home, to have a wife and possibly daughters who did not have to engage in paid work. The ideal of manly independence led to strong support from many working men for legislation which would exclude women from particular forms of paid labour, or would limit drastically their working hours. In many cases, hostility to women's paid work reflected fears from working men that the lower wages paid to women would reduce their wages too. As Anna Clark and Sally Alexander have recently shown, the need to reassert and to maintain their patriarchal privileges, so strongly felt by male working-class radicals in Britain led to considerable domestic, familial and social tension (Alexander, 1994; Clark, 1995). Few male radicals, socialists or trade unionists were prepared to listen to the claims and demands of women. Rather they insisted that women remain under the protection of their menfolk. Radical political groups, like the British Chartists of the 1830s and 1840s, indicated that they shared this sense that women did not belong in the public sphere by campaigning for manhood rather than universal suffrage, and by ignoring the demands of their womenfolk for political rights.

The insistence that work was a masculine prerogative is evident elsewhere in the nineteenth-century Europe. In Germany, working men's associations established during the revolutions of 1848 were generally open only to men. Moreover, in those industries employing women such as printing and cigar-making, for example, the General German Workers Association set up by the socialist Ferdinand Lasalle in 1863, and other new men's associations, joined male tailors in demanding an end to women's industrial labour. Other socialist and trade union organizations in Germany, and especially the workers educational association, rejected this view and insisted on women's right to work, but little was done to attract women to trade union or socialist organizations or to push demands for better pay and conditions for them (Frevert, 1989).

The close identification of work with men, alongside the ideal of a family wage earned by men, made the 'woman worker' seems an oddity and an anomaly. From about 1820 onwards, the 'woman worker' was the centre of considerable debate among social and political reformers and in literature. This was not, as Scott and Alexander have argued, because there was any significant change in the quantity of women's work in this period compared with the preceding one. Rather, concern about the 'woman worker' arose because contemporary ideas about sexual difference and about the importance of domesticity made the idea of women working, and especially of women working outside the home, a disturbing one. It is undoubtedly the case that new industrialized forms of work outside the home posed serious problems for women because they could not combine paid work outside the home with the supervision of children. Further, the image of factories, mines and workshops as male spaces increased moral concerns about their suitability for women. The novelist Elizabeth Gaskell, writing in the 1840s, was concerned about how women who worked full time in factories would learn the appropriate skills for domestic life (Gaskell, 1848). Other critics feared the impropriety, sexual promiscuity and disorder that women might bring if they worked in inadequately supervised places. In the view of the socialist writer Friedrich Engels, the employment of women in preference to men in some tasks or industries because they were cheaper to employ, threatened an inversion of the family order by making women breadwinners while men were unemployed. For Engels, as for the widely read French novelist Emile Zola, heavy and dirty labour for women raised the issue of sexual difference; in this new industrial order both men and women seemed 'unsexed' (Engels, 1892) as women lose their feminine qualities and men their manliness.

Regardless of these strictures, women continued to work throughout the nineteenth century. Although many trade unions and socialist groups advocated a 'family wage' which would enable men to support their families, only a very small number of skilled workers were able to provide for their families. Throughout the nineteenth century, most urban workers were in the same situation as peasants and other rural workers, requiring that every member of the family contribute labour or earnings if the family was to get by. The traditional rural family economy in which members of a family all worked together in an agricultural or craft-based enterprise changed its form in urban centres. For the most part, families no longer worked as a unit; instead, they were wage earners who pooled their earnings. However, the family economy continued to underlie the survival of both rural and urban workers.

In Europe, work by women followed a traditional pattern. Agricultural change occurred irregularly across Europe and brought with it a range of different situations. The slow pace of industrial development in France and Italy and its late advent in Germany and Russia, meant that for many women agricultural work continued to be the norm. In Germany and in France, about half of the female labour force continued to be employed in agriculture until after the First World War. Women were accustomed to extremely heavy agricultural work. In peasant communities throughout the nineteenth and early twentieth centuries, for example, women were expected to provide food and clothing for the family and to engage in a variety of different forms of agricultural labour: dairy work, feeding and supervising poultry, growing vegetables or working in the fields when planting or harvesting were underway. In France, women augmented their income with lace-making. In western Prussia, small holdings continued as they did in France. However, new and labour intensive crops like potatoes and beets meant that many women were engaged in very heavy field work.

In countries where capitalism had been applied to agriculture, creating enclosures and new large-scale farms, women's work underwent the most dramatic change. Large farms which employed agricultural labourers introduced patterns of work which resembled those in factories, in that they required full-time work on particular tasks and made it impossible for women to combine farm work with family duties (Frader, 1987). This was the case in England where enclosures had removed common land and thereby made it impossible for women to engage in independent agricultural production. Many women were forced off the land. Some became wage labourers, often working in agricultural 'gangs' on other farms. Similarly in eastern Prussia, where the emancipation of serfs brought land enclosures and large capitalist farms, women worked as full-time agricultural wage labourers. While there were very different patterns for the sexual division of labour in different countries and different peasant communities, it is clear that rural women worked for as many hours as men and in jobs that were as heavy. Early twentieth-century studies suggest that in Russia and in Ireland, peasant women were engaged in considerably more hours of arduous labour than were men, and that they were excluded from many of the masculine recreational activities.

The advent of factories certainly brought some new work for women. Textiles factories provided work for quite large numbers of women spinners and weavers in Britain and France in the early and mid-nineteenth century and in Germany, Austria and Russia in the later part of the century. Women were also employed in the clothing, food, tobacco and paper industries. The numbers and percentages of women engaged in factory work varied from one country to another. Britain had the highest percentage of women engaged in factory work. From 1841 to 1911, the percentage of female factory workers rose from 35 to 45 per cent of the female labour force. By contrast, in both France and Germany it remained at about 25 per cent of the female labour force (Frader, 1987: p. 318). National figures tend to be somewhat misleading, however, as industrial work for women, as for men, were heavily concentrated in particular areas. In Germany, for example, women made up about 60 per cent of workers in the Bielefeld linen industry, while in Britain, women were engaged in textile factories largely in the north of England, in Lancashire and Yorkshire.

Factories demonstrated in the starkest way the incompatibility between the demands of paid work and family responsibilities which came with industrialization. Factory conditions were fairly similar across Europe and in all cases involved workers in extremely long hours of work during which it was impossible to leave the factory. In many places, factories were locked and workers could not get out. Factory working days were generally between 12 and 15 hours, and were regulated strictly by the clock. Workers were fined for being late and were given only very short breaks for meals. Hence, the women who undertook factory work were generally young and single. They were expected to leave once they married. Factory work was poorly paid and working conditions were harsh and difficult for men as well as women, but young women were also vulnerable both to sexual exploitation and to harsh discipline from male factory overseers (Frevert, 1989; Glickman, 1984). Many men shared with women the harsh life of the factory worker, but no women were in positions of power within factories. Commissions of inquiry in Britain, and the memoirs of articulate working women like Jeanne Bouvier in France or Adelheid Popp in Germany illustrate the harshness of factory conditions: the fines for late work, the beatings of those whose work was seen as inadequate, the dangers of machinery which was poorly maintained and not protected and the constant sexual harassment (Frader, 1987: p. 320).

The advent of the factory did not bring out-work or home-based work to an end. Grey Osterud has shown how the hosiery industry in Britain provided work for women at home, seaming and finishing off the stockings which were woven in factories. There was also an expansion in unskilled ‘slop work’, centring on the making of basic clothing like shirts, or furniture making, box-making, book-binding, flower-making, which often employed people in workshops (Osterud, 1986). Workshop wages were usually lower than those of factories, and their conditions resembled those of factories in terms of their long hours and strict regulation. Low rates of pay meant that women who worked at home might have even longer hours than those who worked in factories and workshops, but this option was often the only possible one for women who had both to work and to care for children.

Ironically, while middle-class ideals of home and family life made work seem aberrant for women, it was middle-class homes which provided the largest amount of paid work for women. Seeking work as a servant was a traditional part of rural life, where the daughters of tenant farmers had long worked on neighbouring farms or in towns as servants to earn a dowry. In the nineteenth century, however, domestic service expanded its scope and changed its form dramatically. Until the late eighteenth century, employing servants was largely an aristocratic privilege. In the course of the nineteenth century, domestic service, as Joan Scott says, 'became more democratic'. Increasing numbers of middle- and upper-middle-class families came to need servants (Scott, 1993: pp. 399–405). As service was less and less associated with agrarian life and farm work, and more and more concentrated on middle-class urban homes, it also became a feminized occupation. Domestic servants throughout the nineteenth century were overwhelmingly female and, conversely, domestic service was often the largest category of women's employment. In both London and Berlin in the 1860s, approximately one-third of all women aged between 15 and 24 were domestic servants. In St Petersburg, the number of men and women domestic servants was more or less the same, but by 1890, the number of women had almost doubled, and the percentage of women in domestic service was almost one-third, the same as in London (Glickman, 1984: p. 60).

Factory work was frowned upon for women, but domestic service did not attract criticism from those many middle-class commentators concerned about working-class family life and morality. Middle-class observers and authorities regarded factories and mines as undesirable because they were often dirty and dangerous, allowed girls or women to work alongside men without any supervision, and encouraged, it was thought, promiscuous sexual contact. Industrial work also deprived women of any training in domestic life. Domestic service, by contrast, was seen as unexceptionable, and indeed as a desirable way to educate working-class girls in the domestic arts and customs of the middle class. Most nineteenth-century commentators applauded domestic service as beneficial, but later historians have questioned this evaluation, pointing out that domestic servants were vulnerable to excessive workloads, to sexual exploitation and to cruel treatment in unregulated settings. The lives of domestic servants were extremely hard and often unrewarding. Servants were most often employed alone, as 'maids of all work', or at most with one or two fellows. Their conditions, their hours and their rates of pay were completely unregulated. Sometimes servants were paid annually, or even at the end of a number of years. Most servants lived in and thus could be on constant call. Many were not provided with adequate sleeping or living accommodation. Fortunate servants might sleep in an unheated attic. Others might be required to sleep in closets or in a corner of the kitchen. They were under constant scrutiny, could be called on at any time and were vulnerable to the sexual demands of employers.

Because they lived in, servants lacked the control of their non-working hours available to other workers. Their capacity to carry on any form of social or sexual life was minimal. Any suggestion that a servant girl was engaging in a sexual relationship would almost guarantee her dismissal and the women who remained servants throughout their lives were generally unmarried and celibate. In many cases, girls worked as full-time or live-in servants only until they married, but substantial numbers of older domestic servants lived permanently as celibate dependents in the homes of employers.

For those seeking to explore the world of women's work in the nineteenth century, census figures and surveys are always problematic because they seem to underrepresent women's work. Writing about London in the 1830s and 1840s, Sally Alexander points to the discrepancy between statistics which show only some 60 per cent of working-class women as being employed at a time when it is clear from other evidence that among the working class it was assumed that all family members, including married women, should contribute to the family income. This discrepancy can be explained by looking at the very different patterns evident in women's work as compared with that of men (Alexander, 1994: pp. 3–12). While women's work in factories and workshops bore some resemblance to the full-time work sought by men, much work undertaken by women was casual and part-time, and therefore scarcely noticed. In the nineteenth century, as in the twentieth, many women managed to combine their economic needs and their family responsibilities by doing part-time work, which was never included in formal census data or statistics, including cleaning and charring, sewing, washing and laundry work.

The idea that men were the major family income earners and that women worked only in a supplementary character served to define women as unskilled and provided the framework for wage differentials. Inevitably this meant that women always earned considerably less than men. The sexual basis of wages is most evident in the very low rates of pay available to those women engaged in specifically female activities: domestic service, sewing, millinery, cleaning and laundry work. Wages in these areas lagged significantly behind those available to women engaged in factory work. In Berlin by the late nineteenth century, as Ute Frevert has shown, a full-time domestic maid of all work earned only about one-third of the wages of a woman employed in the linen industry and considerably less than half the wages of a female factory worker (Frevert, 1989). Female factory workers earned between half and two-thirds of the wages of male factory workers. Women earned only a fraction of men's wages regardless of the industry: in factories manufacturing textiles and clothing, pottery and china, and processing wood, paper, minerals and metals. Validations of this situation included claims that women were less literate and less efficient than men, or that they worked at lighter and easier tasks. Recent research in Britain, Germany, France and Russia challenges these claims, and shows that women earned lower wages because of normative assumptions about the masculine nature of work. Rose Glickman argues that in Russian factories women did work which was as difficult, as heavy and as dangerous as men's tasks, but accepted lower wages because they saw no alternative and because they tended to share the assumption that their primary duty was to their family (Glickman, 1984). Moreover, Kathleen Canning and Sonia Rose point also to the fact that women earned less than men even when they were engaged in exactly the same tasks (Canning, 1992; Rose, 1992). Wages were set in accordance with sexual assumptions about the needs and entitlements of the wage earners rather than in accordance with any precise measure of output.

Low wages were also a marked feature of the lives of the many women who were engaged in non-industrial labour, mainly as outworkers or in workshops. In cities like London, there was a vast amount of work in clothing, hat making, food preparation, furniture making, box making and in the manufacture of other household necessities. Most of the skilled trades as bespoke tailors, or cabinet-makers or chefs, for example, were undertaken by men. The concern among tailors and other skilled workers that women's competition lowered wages generally was clearly combined with a new sense of the proper location of women within family life and with a demand for a family wage which would enable men to support their families. A few women counted as highly skilled dress-makers or milliners, but the vast majority of women were regarded as semi- or unskilled and worked for very low wages. In many of these areas, especially those connected with fashion or with food, work was seasonal with immensely long hours during the fashion 'season' and periods of little or no work before and after. All of this meant that a very large proportion of women workers received an income which was inadequate to their needs. Seasonal slumps or ill-health could deprive them of any income at all.

In view of the extreme moral concern expressed about women's work throughout the nineteenth century, and most particularly the fear that it would lead to sexual promiscuity, it is ironic that the generally low level of wages, and the intermittent periods of unemployment, often meant that women, especially young women, had no way to earn a living at all unless they resorted to prostitution. While some women clearly chose prostitution, seeing it as offering better pay and conditions than what was available in any of the other avenues open to them, others were driven to it through the sexual inequalities which they confronted at work. In many cases, working women were expected or required to provide sexual services to their employers or overseers. This was so for domestic servants, for shop assistants and for women employed in industry and agriculture. In other areas of employment, casual or intermittent prostitution was taken for granted. The urbanization which accompanied industrialization and the development of leisure as an industry with shopping precincts, dance halls, theatres, promenades, hotels and bars increased the opportunities for prostitution and by the mid-nineteenth century, prostitution was rife in all European cities. Every city in England had at least one area notorious for prostitution and in London, prostitutes were thought to number at least 100,000 by mid-century. Other major cities had similar figures: contemporary estimates suggest that Berlin had about 16,000 prostitutes in 1870, rising to 40,000 by 1909; St Petersburg, which had a population of 1.5 million by the turn of the twentieth century, was estimated to have between 30,000 and 50,000 prostitutes.

In her final work, *Maria or the Wrongs of Woman* (published after her death in 1796), Mary Wollstonecraft pointed in a very graphic way to the immense difficulties women faced in supporting themselves, and to the ways in which this drove them into prostitution, or into relationships based solely on their need for economic support and their agreement to engage in sexual intercourse to provide it. The need of working-class women for paid employment was a matter of discussion among feminists within the utopian socialist movements of the early nineteenth century. In Britain, socialist feminists wrote and spoke at length on the double difficulties they faced as a result of the sexual division of labour and low wages, on the one hand, and from the hostility of their own menfolk to the very idea that they should engage in paid work, on the other (see Chapter 3). This was less of an issue in France, where the participation rates of married women in paid labour were higher than they were in Britain throughout the nineteenth century. Nonetheless, most of the women who became involved in the Saint-Simonian movement identified themselves clearly as workers and insisted on their right and their ability to combine paid with family responsibilities.

The need for paid work for women was a central concern to all the feminist and philanthropic organizations which began to emerge in the mid-nineteenth century. In Britain, the extreme hardships of middle-class women who did not have husbands, fathers or brothers to support them had been of concern to feminists from the 1840s. Harriet Martineau, a very well known writer and journalist, published an influential article in 1859 in which she sought to show 'the full breadth of the area of female labour in Great Britain', and to demand recognition of the varieties of work done by women and of the huge numbers of working-class women forced to be self-supporting. The census results and various major surveys, she argued, now revealed that, contrary to popular beliefs, 'a very large proportion of the women of England earn their own bread.' The census of 1851, she argued, showed the increase in the numbers of women involved in paid employment: 'While the female population has increased (between 1841 and 1851) in the ratio of 7 to 8, the number of women returned as engaged in independent industry has increased in the far greater ratio of 3 to 4' (Martineau, 1859: pp. 277–330). Women were now employed in many forms of agriculture; in mining and extractive industries; in many industries concerned with 'the produce of the waters', including catching, curing and selling fish; in a wide variety of crafts and trades and in domestic service. New occupations for women included manufacturing, especially the textile, lace and ribbon industries, as well as telegraphy and clerical. Increasing numbers of women were also engaged in the keeping of lodging houses.

Martineau's article provided the stimulus for the establishment of a number of British campaigns to expand the range of paid employment available to women, including the creation of the Society for Promoting the Employment of Women in 1859, which established employment bureaus, training schemes and particular forms of work like printing. In a similar way, in the 1860s and 1870s, in Germany, Russia and the Habsburg empire, middle-class feminists and philanthropists began to organize ways to extend paid employment for women, sometimes through the setting up of co-operative workshops or training schemes. The St Petersburg Society for Women's Work was established in the 1860s. The Viennese Women's Employment Association, founded in November 1866, initiated what is referred to as the 'era of the organized woman' in Austria (Good, Gardner and Maynes, 1996). Its immediate impetus was the widespread economic distress which followed the defeat of Austria by Prussia earlier that year, and which had made many women, both married and single, destitute and in need of employment. This organization was followed by a series of other associations dedicated to the improvement of women's education and to the support of lower-middle-class girls by assisting them in obtaining appropriate training. While essentially philanthropic, the Viennese Women's Employment Association recognized the need for financial independence for women.

The capacity of philanthropic groups or of middle-class feminists to address the needs of working-class women was challenged in the 1880s and 1890s and in the early twentieth century by a number of women associated with the labour movement or with socialist organizations. In Britain, women like Barbara Hutchins and Beatrice Webb associated with trade unions and the Fabian Society, in Germany, Klara Zetkin as the leader of the women's organization set up by the German SPD, in Russia, Alexander Kollontai, the leader of the Bolshevik women's group—all insisted that the needs of working women could only be addressed from within the framework of socialism. The specific issues over which there was major disagreement between these women and middle-class feminists and philanthropists were industrial legislation and trade union membership for women. For the most part, middle-class feminists opposed any form of industrial legislation that applied to women and not to men and they also opposed trade unions as interfering with the freedom of individuals.

The whole question of work for women, and the related issues of family responsibilities on the one hand, and special industrial legislation on the other, is a complex one. Many middle-class feminists demanded the right of women to work on the same terms as men. In Britain, this involved a direct conflict of views between the old-style economic liberalism of the women's movement and the much more interventionist ideas of socialists and members of the labour movement. In the 1880s and 1890s members of women's movements continued to oppose any industrial legislation which was applied to women and not to men. Such legislation, in their view, denied that women were rational adults capable of ascertaining or following their own interests. It served also to reduce the employment opportunities and the income-earning capacity of women. Many women associated with the labour movement attacked this approach. They opposed the political and economic framework on which it was based, arguing that feminists lacked any understanding of the problems of industrial labour. Beatrice Webb, for example, insisted that protective legislation, far from restricting the freedom of women, was essential to that freedom since it offered the only way to improve their pay and conditions of work.

While it is clearly the case that working women needed protection, throughout Europe the labour codes and legislation of the late nineteenth century were more concerned to ensure the pre-eminence of men as household heads and primary income earners, and to ensure that women's maternal role was recognized, than to ensure women's rights as workers (Canning, 1996; Stone, 1995). This issue was a dilemma within the rapidly expanding socialist and labour organizations, many of which were committed to the idea that a man should earn a family wage sufficient to support his wife and children. The question whether women should be treated as equal to men as workers, and entitled to equal pay and conditions, or whether they needed special protection, was debated across Europe by socialist and labour organizations, along with the question whether, and on what terms, women could join socialist organizations. The 1893 conference of the Socialist International not only passed a resolution demanding equal pay for men and women, but also spelled out particular conditions which should apply to women's work, including the eight-hour day, a prohibition of night work and of work in jobs which might be detrimental to their health (Sowerwine, 1987). Of all nineteenth-century questions about gender, women's needs as workers and how women's work can best be combined with their family responsibilities have remained the hardest to resolve.

References and Further Readings

Primary Sources

Aimé-Martin, Louis (1834) *De l'Education des mères de famille, on de la civilisation du genre humain par les femmes*, Paris.

Engels, Friedrich (1976 [1892]) *The Condition of the Working Class in England*, New York.

Gaskell, Elizabeth (1985 [1848]) *Mary Barton: A Tale of Manchester Life*, London.

Lewis, Sarah (1839) *Woman's Mission*, London.

Martineau, Harriet (1859) 'Female industry', *Edinburgh Review* 109, 222 (April): 293–336.

Michelet, Jules (1854) *Oeuvres Complètes* (ed. P. Viallaneix), Vol. 16, Paris.

Ruskin, John (1865) 'Sesame and Lilies', republished in *The Complete Works of John Ruskin* (1897), Boston.

Zola, Emile (1956 [1887]) *Germinal*, London.

Family Life and Home

Angerer, M. (1996) 'The discourse on female sexuality in nineteenth-century Austria', in D. F. Good, M. Gardner and M. J. Maynes (eds) *Austrian Women in the Nineteenth and Twentieth Centuries*, Oxford and Providence.

Davidoff, L. and Hall, C. (1987) *Family Fortunes, Men and Women of the English Middle Class 1780–1850*, London.

Delamont, S. and Duffin, L. (1978) *The Nineteenth Century Woman: Her Cultural and Physical World*, London.

Donzelot, J. (1980) *The Policing of Families*, trans. R. Hurley, London.

Frevert, U. (1989) *Women in German History: From Bourgeois Emancipation to Sexual Liberation*, trans. S. McKinnon Evans with T. Bond and B. Norden, Oxford and New York.

Gray, M. (1987) 'Prescriptions for productive female domesticity in a transitional era: Germany's Hausmutterliteratur 1780–1840', *History of European Ideas* 8, 4/5: 413–426.

Hull, I. (1996) *Sexuality, State, and Civil Society in Germany, 1700–1815*, Ithaca. Jacobus, M. I. (1992) 'Incorruptible milk: breast-feeding and the French Revolution', in S. E. Melzer and L. W. Rabine (eds) *Rebel Daughters: Women and the French Revolution*, New York.

Jalland, P. and Hooper, J. (eds) (1986) *Women from Life to Death*, Brighton.

Perry, R. (1991) 'Colonizing the breast: sexuality and maternity in eighteenth-century England', *Journal of the History of Sexuality* 2, 2: 204–234.

Ross, E. (1993) *Love and Toil: Motherhood in Outcast London, 1870–1918*, New York.

Smith, B. G. (1981) *Ladies of the Leisure Class: The Bourgeoises of Northern France in the Nineteenth Century*, Princeton.

The World of Work

Alexander, S. (1994) *Becoming a Woman and Other Essays in the 19th and 20th Century*, London.

Canning, K. (1992) 'Gender and the politics of class formation: rethinking German labor history', *American Historical Review* 97, 3: 736–768.

Clark, A. (1995) *Struggle for the Breeches*, Berkeley and London.

Frader, L. L. (1987) 'Women in the industrial economy', in R. Bridenthal, C. Koonz and S. Stuard (eds) *Becoming Visible: Women in European History*, Boston. Frader, L. L. and Rose, S. O. (eds) (1996) *Gender and Class in Modern Europe*, Ithaca, New York and London.

Glickman, R. (1984) *Russian Factory Women: Workplace and Society, 1880–1914*, Berkeley.

Good, D. F., Gardner, M. and Maynes, M. J. (eds) (1996) *Austrian Women in the Nineteenth and Twentieth Centuries*, Providence.

John, A. V. (1986) *Unequal Opportunities: Women's Employment in England 1800–1918*, Oxford.

Lown, J. (1990) *Women and Industrialization: Gender at Work in Nineteenth-Century England*, Cambridge.

McClelland, K. (1989) 'Some thoughts on masculinity and the "representative artisan" in Britain, 1850–1880', *Gender and History* 1: 164–177.

Osterud, N. G. (1986) 'Gender division and the organization of work in the Leicester hosiery industry', in A. John (ed.) *Unequal Opportunities*, Oxford.

Phillips, A. and Taylor, B. (1980) 'Sex and skill: notes towards feminist economies', *Feminist Review* 6.

Pinchbeck, I. (1981[1930]) *Women Workers and the Industrial Revolution*, London.

Rose, S. (1992) *Limited Livelihoods, Gender and Class in Nineteenth Century England*, Berkeley.

Scott, J. W. (1993) 'The woman worker', in M. Perrot (ed.) *History of Women in the West*, Cambridge, Mass.

Scott, J. and Tilly, L. (1975) 'Women's work and the family in nineteenth-century Europe', *Comparative Studies in Society and History* 17: 36–64.

Sowerwine, C. (1987) 'The socialist women's movement from 1850 to 1940', in R. Briderthal, C. Koonz and S. Stuard (eds) *Becoming Visible: Women in European History*, Boston.

Stone, J. F. (1995) 'The Republican brotherhood: gender and ideology', in E. A. Accampo, R. G. Fuchs and M. L. Stewart (eds) *Gender and the Politics of Social Reform in France*, Baltimore.

Walkowitz, J. R. (1980) *Prostitution and Victorian Society: Women, Class and the State*, Cambridge.

Nationalization of the Female Citizenry: Fascist Italy and Nazi Germany 3

—Vandana Joshi

While the first two chapters have looked at the gender issue from the perspective of the twin revolutions of the long nineteenth century, namely the French Revolution and the Industrial Revolution, we now turn to the most important historic force of the twentieth century, namely Italian Fascism or, in the German case, National Socialism. Scholars today are not so comfortable about clubbing the two together mainly because National Socialism was driven by an extreme form of racism and anti-Semitism. It categorised humans on the basis of their biology and transformed German society through its complete biologisation. Race and gender were two pivotal aspects of this process. We take up the question of race in the next section of the volume and discuss Nazi gender politics in the present one. In this biotic view, men and women were essentially and immutably different biologically and therefore ought to have different destinies. Hitler and Mussolini, in their effort to win over the women of their countries, may have rhetorically stated that this difference did not make any of the two less insignificant and that both were equally important for national regeneration, but in reality this difference was value loaded, judgemental and derogatory towards women.

In spite of this, both Hitler and Mussolini were immensely popular. While they may appear at the first glance to be extreme right wing and conservative in prescribing maternity to women, driving them back to their home and hearth and condemning working women, the two were full of contradictions and initiated a lot of measures that were radical and unconventional. While they prescribed domesticity to women, they simultaneously activated them in the war efforts for multiple tasking in the public sphere. They condemned women's dabbling in politics, yet women were an important support base for their parties as they drew their power from mass support. And at least in the initial stages, they provided enterprising women, even feminists, some autonomy on the women's issue. We also observe that the two regimes, despite differences, deployed jingoism, narcissistic national pride and imperialism to erase fault lines that existed in highly fragmented class societies of interwar Europe. Gender divide was one of them.

Hitler and Mussolini rode the crust of popular mass movements. Their appeal stretched across gender, class, region, confession and generation. Fascism was a playground for stirring masses and rallying them behind the nationalist cause, but interestingly it also demonstrated that women, in spite of being positioned below men, worked with equal enthusiasm for the fatherland and contributed their bit to the national, imperial and war efforts. Historians agree that fascism truly nationalised women and invited them to history in their masses, an experience that men had had a century back as activists, citizens and voters. Women participated in all activities that their fascist leaders assigned to them as mothers and wives. They carried out these functions not just in the private sphere but also in the public arena as social mothers, volunteers, secretaries, teachers, labour, unpaid agricultural or household assistants, nurses, snoops, denouncers, jailors, concentration guards and colonisers.

GENDER AND THE POLITICS OF VOTE; VESTIGES OF LIBERAL-DEMOCRATIC PAST

It did not matter if women had the vote or not. Why? This question puzzled historians in general and feminists in particular given the long and protracted history of the suffragists before the onset of fascism in the continent. Early historians, mainly men, put forth the argument that women were ruled by their hearts more than their heads in their support for Hitler and Mussolini. Herrmann Rauschning, a Nazi ideologue, believed that it was women's vote that brought Hitler to power. In *Hitler Speaks*, he noted the emotional effect Hitler had on women. 'One must have seen from above, from the speaker's rostrum, the rapturously rolling, moist, veiled eyes of the female listeners in order to be in no further doubt as to the character of this enthusiasm (Evans, 1976, 125–6). Fest, who claimed that 'the women discovered, chose and idolised Hitler', echoed the same sexist bias, when he said, 'the overexcited, distinctly hysterical tone of Hitler's meetings sprang in the first place from the excessive emotionalism of a particular kind of elderly woman, who sought to activate the unsatisfied impulses within her in the tumult of mighty political demonstrations before the ecstatic figure of Hitler' (Evans, 1976, 125–6). William Shirer, known for his *Berlin Diary*, similarly commented, 'I was a little shocked at the faces, especially those of women, when Hitler finally appeared on the balcony for a moment... If he had remained in sight for more than a few moments, I think many of the women would have swooned from excitement (Shirer, 1970: 22–3). These male observers reflect not only a sexist bias but also the prevalent dominant patriarchal cliché equating the will to surrender to women or ascribing subordination to women.

The myth that Hitler exercised some special influence in the female psyche is busted by the election results of the Reich's presidency in which Hitler and Hindenburg were the main contenders in 1925 and 1932. The ballot paper given to men and women was of different colours and the results revealed that women on both occasions preferred the venerable conservative Hindenburg to Hitler casting 58 and 56 per cent votes in his favour in the first run off. In fact, Hindenburg got 52 per cent of women's vote and 44 per cent of men's vote, while Hitler received 27 per cent of women vote and 28 per cent of men's vote (Bremme, 1956: 231–5). Had only women's vote mattered Hitler would not have come that far in the first place. Nonetheless, the Nazis made sweeping gains between 1928 and 1932 and women represented a substantial chunk among their supporters. In Bavaria, traditionally a Catholic stronghold, the Nazi vote increased by 199 per cent among men and 231 per cent among women between 1928 and 1930. In the parliamentary elections of 1930, 52 per cent of the Nazi voters in Leipzig were women, in Cologne 42 per cent and in Frankfurt 58 per cent. In fact, the overall percentage of women voters for the Nazis increased from 42 per cent in the 1928 elections to 49 per cent in 1930 (ibid.; Falter 1984: 47–59). Nonetheless, the percentage that supported Hitler was substantial and needs to be explained.

Feminists forwarded their own explanations, which sought to find a rationale behind women's choices. In 1973, Renate Bridenthal and Claudia Koonz blamed the pseudo-emancipation that the Weimar Republic offered to women. Women were granted legal equality and the right to vote but Bridenthal and Koonz believed that it hardly proved emancipatory since the social and economic structures remained patriarchal and became increasingly susceptible to right wing and Nazi forces. In fact, the modern woman as single, self-conscious, job-oriented and emancipated person became a threatening symbol of self-seeking independence in the conservative circles and attracted negative attention and publicity. Contrary to this much publicised emancipated woman, Bridenthal and Koonz argue, the large majority of women actually lost status in the Weimar Republic rather than increased independence. As modern techniques started appearing in agricultural sector, dairy and poultry farms and acquired higher status they were masculinised. Though women constituted nearly half of the work force in the agricultural sector only one-sixth of them occupied management positions in 1925 and only one-twelfth in 1933. In agricultural farms too they lost out to men as head of the farms. While in 1907 women headed 14 per cent of the independent farm households, in 1925, this had slipped to 12 per cent and by 1933 it was down to 10 per cent. Moreover, most of their farms were tiny. During the years of inflation and depression, the smaller farms were absorbed by the middle-sized ones, reducing the number of female owners. This led to increasing family friction and frustration among women. Their daughters had no incentive to stay and most of them migrated to the cities to get absorbed by the urban job market.

In the urban job markets, they got jobs as salesgirls, secretaries and industrial labour. This had two contradictory effects. Firstly, these new jobs were conspicuous and gave an impression to men that women were becoming emancipated and thus invited hostility. Secondly, these jobs were less rewarding and were such that the men would not have taken them up in any case (Bridenthal and Koonz, 1984: 55–6). In spite of the tall claims of the government of equal wage for equal work, the promise remained on paper. The job of secretaries and sales girls demanded only young girls, and with age instead of getting promotion they got phased out. The big managerial positions remained elusive for women. Thus, concluded the authors, without an appealing alternative, women persisted in their loyalty to their familiar '*Kinder, Küche and Kirche*' ethos. Women saw emancipation more as a threat than a blessing (ibid.: 56). Women's apprehension about losing their traditional niche in society was akin to men's fear of proletarianisation. Thus, when Hitler told women that politics was a dirty business and not suited for women, obviously, he struck a responsive chord. This picture indeed captured the reality of young women who migrated to the cities while largely ignoring the lives and politics of the mass of women living in the countryside and the urban housewives who were untouched by back to the hearth call. It is doubtful if women voted on the basis of women's issues alone.

A far broader explanation was offered by Richard Evans who argued that women's choices were determined by the twists and turns of the women's movement. His analysis sees women as makers of their destinies, as members of organisations that represented their interests (Evans, 1977).

The mainstream nineteenth-century women's movement was launched under the auspices of the BDF or the League of German

Women's Associations. Largely middle class and liberal, the BDF consciously kept away from socialist and communist strands, while the socialist women were subsumed under the mainstream left. The BDF from the late nineteenth century onwards increasingly suffered from a liberal and democratic deficit and like the mainstream political scenario fell under the spell of illiberal, racial-nationalist and social Darwinist ideas rather than the earlier liberal individualistic ones. Prevalent Ideas of race hygiene, eugenic reforms and promotion of prolific mothers penetrated in the League's politics. In fact, even ideas such as the disenfranchisement of the mentally abnormal and the illiterate, ban on the racially mixed marriages and sterilisation of the alcoholics were already doing rounds in the League much before the rise of Hitler.

This social Darwinist turn was complemented by an anti-worker or anti-socialist attitude, which could be seen in two of the most numerically preponderant organisations, namely, the National Union of German Housewives Association and Union of Rural Housewives Association. While the former had a membership of 200,000 in 1931 the latter boasted a membership of 90,000. These housewives organised themselves to keep their housemaids and working-class women's wages down. In that sense, they were undercutting the collective bargaining power of socialism. Similarly, salaried lower middle-class women organized themselves to protect their interests and the German Colonial Women's League joined their male counterparts to clamour for colonies and imperialist expansion (Evans, 1977: 240–1). In addition, there were a host of organisations, such as the Woman Postal Workers Union and the Women's Group of the Trade Union League of Salaried Employees, all petty bourgeois in composition, who fought for their own narrow interests. This tore up the fragile fabric of the nascent Weimar Republic, Germany's first attempt at the bourgeois democratic republic. During the economic crisis, as the struggle for economic survival of the nation intensified, the BDF was driven on the defensive unable to give them an amiable solution. Both the housewives' associations deserted the BDF, as they thought that it was an organisation of women workers. It was these numerically rich organisations that provided the ultra-conservative racist parties a mass base in the late twenties and early thirties. With the emergence of the Nazi party in this period, they willingly threw in their lot with the Nazis considering them the most viable solution to the problems of Weimar Republic. By 1929, the BDF itself was forced into a wholesale surrender of the women's rights on account of its inadequacy on both ideological and practical fronts. When the Nazis came to power, the BDF was already claiming its compatibility with National Socialism since it had been in support of the Nazi eugenic policies, and its condemnations of the Revolution of 1918 and the Treaty of Versailles.

Thus, not only was it the failure of emancipationist ideology, but also the pull of mainstream politics, which drove a huge number of women towards the Nazi party. This is what explains their voting pattern, which was not remarkably different from their male counterparts. Obviously, class fears and class solidarity played on women and men of the same class. This means that the fear of proletarianisation affected men as well as women from the middle classes, and working-class men and women in large parts turned to the communists instead of social democrats between 1929 and 1933, while Catholic men and women remained more or less loyal and consistent in their voting pattern even in the crisis years. Women's choices in the larger picture were conditional upon factors like class, region, religion and economic uncertainties. They were not solely based upon women's issues.

In Italy, in the post-war years, the middle-class liberal women's movement split and allowed the infusion of nationalist propaganda, which went counter to the traditional democratic and pacifist leanings of the movement (de Grand, 1976: 950). Much like in Germany or the rest of Europe, it moved closer to national-conservative forces with a strong anti-socialist bias. On the other hand, the socialist wing of women's movement subordinated the women's question to the question of class, which also happened in much of Europe. There were two political strands that were not discriminatory towards women. D'Annuzio's constitution for the city of Fiume gave full civil and political rights to all citizens above the age of 20 without regard to their sex. Futurism, another intellectual strand sharing common grounds with the fascists, confronted traditional positions on women and the family and included women's right to vote in their programme. Mussolini himself tactically supported women's suffrage in the initial phase.

EARLY FASCIST AND NAZI 'FEMINISTS'

Women 'fascists of the First Hour', i.e., early members of *Fasci Femmenili* or women-only fascist group belonged to the traditional conservative elite, who valued fascism mainly as a means of defeating the 'Red Threat'. Though they mobilised a significant section of women from lower middle classes, the leadership remained in the hands of upper-middle-class or aristocratic women. Many of the early female fascist leaders had experienced public life as philanthropists. They had a superior educational background than the rank and file male fascists. They were drawn to the movement because of the events at Fiume and were intellectually influenced by the Futurists and Irredentists. Early feminist leaders also came from a liberal feminist tradition rather than a radical or socialist one. Nonetheless, they were ambitious and enterprising and their dreams and aspirations reflected a curious mixture of feminism, anti-socialism, patriotism, strong nationalism and philanthropic activism. Social motherhood was a strong component of their philanthropy (Williams, 2010: 83).

Early female fascists, whether feminists or not, chose to behave, much like their German counterparts, more as members of their class and social milieu rather than their sex. Coming from overwhelmingly middle- and upper-class backgrounds they thought that Mussolini could save them from the Bolshevik menace and restore the honour of the nation. Angels Maria Guerra, an early activist and sympathiser remembered, 'being a fascist meant loving order, justice, respect. It meant respect for crucifixes in schools, respect for the symbols of the nation, respect for property and the family' (ibid.). Similarly, Elisa Lombardi, who later became director of the fascist women's sports academy, recalled, 'There was nothing to criticise about fascism when it started, when there was the revolution in Italy after the war they spat at soldiers, my brother could not walk around in uniform' (ibid.). In any case, liberalism had not delivered much by way of female suffrage and gender equality. The bill on female suffrage was passed in the lower house in 1919 but was rejected by the senate (de Grand, 1976: 949).

This disappointed Italian suffragists who had hoped, like many of their European counterparts, to be granted the right to vote after successfully responding to the nation's call by carrying out many jobs reserved earlier for men only. Nationisation of women in Italy occurred under authoritarian and illiberal terms. To be sure, the liberal regime anyways had been hostile to the women's vote thinking that women's inherent loyalty to the Catholic Church and Pope would weaken their social base. Mussolini realised the feminist anxiety regarding the issue of female suffrage and made correct strategic moves in the early phase to attract female constituency. He supported the vote for women in his early days. On 14 May 1923, when he presided over the opening of the IX Congress of the International Alliance for Women's Suffrage in Rome, he stated that, so far as this government was concerned, he was authorised to declare that the fascist government had resolved to grant the vote to several categories of women, beginning at the local level. He did not believe that enfranchising women would have catastrophic consequences but in all probability it would have beneficial results because women would bring to the exercise of these new rights their fundamental virtue of balance, equilibrium and prudence (de Grazia, 1992: 36). He also gave the female wing relative autonomy in the initial phase. They were free to organise their conferences and lobby for feminism demands. There was a blend of patriotism and feminism in their agendas. They debated openly and organised political activities independently.

Many of the feminist concerns that women fascists raised in Italy were later condemned by the regime. The more enterprising, self-conscious and vocal women were replaced by more subservient ones in the later years. In 1924, when the fascists were in the process of establishing their iron grip over the system, Mussolini appointed a former Red Cross nurse and 'fascist of the First Hour' Elisa Majer Rizzioli to the new position of Inspector of the Fascist Women's Groups with a seat on the party directorate. His choice of even a moderate feminist was not appreciated by the patriarchs in the party as coming events would demonstrate soon. In November 1925, the suffrage was granted to certain limited categories of women, i.e., over the age of 25 in local elections. These women had to qualify one of the following categories: decoration for war service, civil merit, soldier's widows of good moral conduct, mothers of the war dead, literate head of the family, completion of elementary education and payment of 100 Lire as tax. It potentially enfranchised 17,00,000 women compared to 9 million men. In any event, all of this was rendered irrelevant from 1926 onwards when local councils started receiving nominations of fascist functionaries. The vote, in general, was rendered useless in the dictatorship.

Majer Rizzioli did not last much either. She was replaced by Angiola Moretti, her ex-clerical assistant, too young to have learnt feminism and too docile to air independent women's views. During the late 1920s feminists like Rizzioli and Pia Bartolini of Bologna who spoke explicitly of 'fascist feminism' were ousted or faced complete marginalisation. A new age of female cooperation dawned on Italy.

After 1925, women's organisations failed to make any impact on the general course of fascism. Socialist feminists, a force to reckon with at the turn of the century, were betrayed by their bourgeois sisters and suppressed by the regime. The other two politically active groups that remained in the fray were Catholic women that abided by fascist teachings and fascists women themselves. They remained numerically rich and made great contributions to the national-fascist culture and society, although realising that they would receive neither honours nor economic compensation for their work. The fascists were totally unresponsive to their demands, complaints or proposals. This does not mean, however, that women as a segment of the population were ignored. They were indeed important and were effectively nationalised. They had become exemplary wives and mothers, angels of the hearth and civil militia in the service of the state. Devoid of actual power in the political domain, they served an important function in the fascist rhetoric about the role of women in society and polity, and received honorific titles and welfare benefits as healthy mothers, dutiful wives and citizens. It is in the domain of domesticity and civic virtues as patriotic citizens that they found solace and a sense of purpose.

In Germany, similarly, early Nazi women combined anti-socialism, maternalism and social reform. In addition, the German brand had a heavy dose of anti-Semitism, racial and eugenic ideas and a strong female agency in their political activities. While their concerns and efforts were appreciated in the early years, their enterprise, independence and ambition were not. After the Nazi seizure of power, all feminist organisations were banned like all other political formations. Early Nazi women faced marginalisation within the party and the leadership was given in the trusted hands of Gertrud Scholtz Klink, a docile and pliant widow.

Let us have a quick look at the early Nazi women and their vision. Elisabeth Zander, one of the earliest Nazi organisers launched a double crusade for motherhood and Hitler. In her newspaper, she championed the cause of German motherhood, urged the women to leave politics to men and join in her motherhood crusade to show their patriotism and increase the birth rate. She organised the German Women's Order, created a dense network of cell mothers that would spread Nazi beliefs at the grass root level to the disenchanted and the alienated. Her followers organised charities, donations and cared for the fighting SA units. She was more enthusiastic about anti-Semitism, anti-communism and racial purity than the party high command in the 1920s (Stibbe, 2003: 92 ff).

Ultra conservative Guida Diehl launched a New Land Movement in the 1920s, declaring inner revival as its aim and defined women's movement in terms of a spiritual–moral struggle. Her inner renewal redirected women's desires away from false hopes of emancipation to the true needs of motherhood. Diehl wanted women to be removed from paid labour outside the home and proposed subsidies to enable mothers to remain at home and devote their time to mothering. Her solution to the falling birth rate was a state-sponsored baby boom, something that was actually realised by the Nazis (Koonz, 1991: 83–4 ff).

Lydia Gottschewski organized women under the banner of 'spiritual motherhood'. She called upon women to dedicate themselves to motherhood, by which she meant not just biological motherhood but also all tasks requiring protection and nurture of the weak. She was vociferously anti-Semitic and anti-Marxist who blamed all wrong on Judeo-Bolshevism.

Among the early Nazis, Sophie Rogge Börner was perhaps the only one who challenged the Nazi biological view on gender. An anthropologist by training Börner in her book, *Back to the Mother Right*, warned against the glorification and deification of motherhood. She foresaw the danger of an all-male Nazi elite and saw the danger of women being turned into breeding machines. She also criticised women's stereotyping into mothers (ibid.: 113–14 ff). After 1933, she protested against the masculine framework of the Nazi party, which she saw as disadvantageous to women. She demanded women's entry into public life because she thought male dominated institutions had brought the humanity on the brink of destruction. She was an ardent racist and eugenicist who thought that women of the best race should reproduce more quickly to prevent Germany from turning into a racial swamp.

These early Nazi leaders had their own ambitions and dreams, which they wanted to realise once the party attained power. Even while they propagated housewifery and motherhood for the mass of women, they wanted to exercise their motherly or womanly influence as public women. They had political ambitions for themselves. Intense rivalries existed among them in the early thirties. However, these women leaders were not a part of Hitler's inner coterie. They could not influence Hitler. Besides, men like Strasser, Lay, Hess and Frick were competing among themselves for this constituency. Once the Nazis acquired state power, they wanted to reorder the women's wing and replace these competing female leaders with one woman who could translate Nazi doctrines into practice without questioning and quarrelling with the male party bosses. Gertrud Scholtz Klink was just such a woman, mother of 11 children, 32-year-old widow, much younger than the existing leaders like Paula Siber, who had by then left her other competitors like Gottschwiski, Diehl and Zander behind, and had hoped to lead the German women for the party. Scholtz-Klink had no interest in ideological things, was more comfortable in administrative compliance to orders from above, had left the evangelical Church, was widow of an SA fighter who had devoted herself to the rearing of her 11 children and was now available to serve the party in the most dedicated manner.

Under her command women were told to stay away from politics and take interest in their primary calling, i.e., motherhood. After the Nazis eliminated all liberal individualist women with personal ambitions in politics from their ranks and put faithful and pliant female leaders at the helm, they set out to implement their agendas in gender politics.

FASCIST GENDER POLITICS

Gender politics was an integral part of the fascist social engineering project. Their vision of a new society encompassed more masculine men and more feminine women, more virile men and more productive women. They were modernist utopians who believed they could remodel societies according to their whims, at the root of which was a biological notion of gender and race. Even though they may have relegated public women to a secondary position, women as a gender had a significant place in their social engineering project. Women were understood to be cultural and racial repositories of a fascist nation, whose offspring would inhabit the conquered territories. Their role was crucial to the regeneration of the nation. It was the recognition of this role and the dignity that most mothers found in this destiny which partially explains why a large majority of women rallied behind the fascists at a time of emotional, psychological, economic and social uncertainties, when nations were projected to be fighting a battle of survival in the international arena, but as we shall see later, this was just the beginning. Nonetheless, there was a clear demarcation between men's and women's spheres of activities, at least in the peaceful years, later the gender roles were rearranged to cater to the contingencies of war.

MARRIAGE AND MOTHERHOOD

Josef Goebbels, the propaganda minister of the Reich, expressed the Nazi view on women in no uncertain terms when he made a statement in *Die Frau*, an important women's journal, 'It should not be unknown to you that the National Socialist movement, as the only party keeps women away from direct everyday politics. That is why it is bitterly attacked in many respects, but unjustly so. We are attacked not because we do not care for them but because we care for them a bit too much. We have held them away from parliamentary democratic intrigues that have determined the German politics of the last fourteen years... but it should not remain unsaid that things that belong to men must remain with them like the politics and the valour of the folk. It is no adverse criticism of women. It is only a reference to their capabilities and predispositions in the areas that best correspond to their ways... On the danger of being considered reactionary, I say clearly that the first, the best and the most suitable place for a woman is her family and the most wonderful job that she can accomplish is to bestow children upon her land and her folk' (Schmidt and Dietz, 1983: 74). No wonder

Goebbel's wife Magda was mother of six children. This was also the only family that remained loyal to Hitler and his vision till the bitter end and participated in the collective suicide committed in the Berlin Bunker involving Hitler and Eva. Adolf Hitler wrote in Mein Kampf, 'The German girl belongs to the state but becomes its citizens with her marriage for the first time' (Hitler, 1962: 491). Marriage in the Nazi vision was equated with reproduction. Special provisions were made for an increase in the birth rate such as divorce for unproductive marriages and recognition of unmarried motherhood if the mother was racially pure. Ideally speaking, a women's role lay in guaranteeing the increase and preservation of the Aryan species. Unlike the liberal, democratic or feminist spirit that emphasized on the growth of women as individuals, womanhood was equated with motherhood in the fascist vision.

EULOGISATION OF MOTHERHOOD THROUGH RHETORIC, RITUALS AND SYMBOLS

In terms of rhetoric, motherhood was meant to alleviate women's status above that of woman as a self-seeking and self-centric individual, a trait of liberalism that was vigorously condemned by the fascists. Hitler's ideas on motherhood were orchestrated by the propaganda ministry through posters, exhibitions and advice literature. Pictorial depictions of young and healthy mothers surrounded by children of various ages could be found in textbooks, magazines and newspapers and were meant to inspire and train an entire generation in the virtues of motherhood. Hitler turned his mother's birthday into Mother's Day, which was celebrated with rituals and ceremonies to honour German mothers. Mother's Cross of Honour were conferred on prolific women. An iron Cross for four children, a silver Cross for six and a gold Cross for eight were conferred on Aryan mothers. This added a powerful symbolic value to motherhood for these crosses were put at par with gallantry awards. The Nazis accorded the same value to the battle for birth on the home front as it did to soldiers fighting for the fatherland at the front.

In Italy, the fascist love of rituals and propaganda could be seen in state–managed pageantry speeches during public ceremonies and rallies which were aimed at encouraging women to reproduce. From 1933, a 'Mother and Child Day' was celebrated on 24 December to publicly honour prolific mothers and their children. The choice of Christmas Eve for this celebration was no coincidence but a clever appropriation the Catholic cult of Virgin Mary to the fascist cause. Italian motherhood was associated not just with the mother of God but also with the Virgin's chastity, the joyous birth of Jesus and his sacrifice for humanity. The highlight of the first ceremonial year was the national rally in Rome in which the most prolific mothers from all 90 provinces were passed in review like prize breeding stock. The roll call trumpeted not her name but the number of her live births (de Grazia, 1992: 71). The venues of the prize-giving ceremonies were adorned with visual displays of rocking cradles laden with fruits (Williams, 2010: 65). Once the war started, mothers were exhorted to take up reproduction at war footing for the survival of the race.

This ritualisation and symbolism had a pragmatic concern at the core. It was directly connected to the falling birth rate and rising male unemployment, both of which were Europe-wide phenomena. The fascists adopted a carrot and stick policy to achieve these twin objectives. They sought to make motherhood more attractive and rewarding by introducing various pro-natalist welfare policies favouring mothers of 'pure blood and sound health'. Both regimes introduced a marriage loan, a child allowance, income tax benefits and several other concessions to big families.

Among the pro-natalist measures introduced in Italy was a 'bachelor's tax' which was levied proportionally on unmarried men between 25 and 65 of age using a sliding scale to make the youngest pay the most in addition to deducting a flat rate of 25 per cent from gross income. Priests, infirm and servicemen on active duty were exempted. Fathers of large families got preference in state sector jobs. The age of consent was lowered. The money thus raised was used for mother and child welfare programme. Tax reduction, free medical care, tram tickets and school meals were other such benefits for members of large families. However, the threshold was fixed at a minimum of seven living children for such benefits. Thus, only a minority benefited from such large-heartedness of the state. In the 1930s, marriage loans on the German pattern were introduced in Italy too but they covered only the low income groups under 26. Family allowance was introduced in the state sector from 1928 and was extended to industrial workers in the mid-thirties. These were to be repaid at 1 per cent and the principal was partially cancelled with the birth of each child.

In Germany, marriage loans were introduced right in the beginning. The loans were sanctioned to the fathers even though the prerequisite was that the mothers would leave the job market to make room for men. This condition was later waived as Germany geared itself for the war, achieved full employment rates for men and required assembly line workers. One-fourth amount of the 1,000 Marks loan could be paid off with the birth of each child, which meant that bearing four children could free the family from the burden of the loan completely. However, only eugenically and racially, healthy couples could avail themselves of the loan. The loan was to be redeemed as vouchers meant for buying furniture and other necessary durables for children and the family. This was also a way of promoting small-scale business as against supermarkets as the vouchers could be redeemed only in small outlets. It was believed that big stores were monopolised by the Jews. Thus, even a measure, which looked like a welfare provision for mothers had a gender and racial spin to it. Recipients of such benefits also received concessions on water and electricity bills, railway and tram ticket, free theatre tickets, reduced rent and so on. The money for this was raised by taxing eligible singles at the rate of 2 to 5 per cent of their income.

Alongside the carrot for the worthy couples, the fascist stick outlawed birth preventive measures banning contraceptives, abortion and sex education. Abortion had a long history in Europe. It was condemned by the Pope, liberal states and fascists alike yet it continued to be practiced in poor city quarters, backstreets and in hinterlands because of economic and moral reasons. In Italy, the fascist Public Security Laws of November 1926 and Rocco Code of 1930 made abortions more risky than ever, even though medical termination on health grounds was permitted contrary to Church belief. State anti-abortion campaigns started targeting untrained midwives who attended child birth in majority of the cases. These were the women who helped villagers get rid of unwanted pregnancies as well. Fascists launched a rigorous campaign to train and professionalise midwives and to keep an eye on them, especially for the role they played in backstreet abortions. If they were caught performing abortions, they were sent to political confinement, a punishment also meted out to homosexuals as violators of demographic policies (Williams, 2010: 67). Punishments for homosexuality and abortions were more serious in Nazi Germany. Long spells in the concentration camps were usual for the homosexuals. Abortions were strictly prohibited for the racially worthy women. Undergoing, aiding and abetting abortions called for two years of imprisonment in peacetime and invited death penalties in wartime.

Italian fascists adopted a two-pronged strategy to increase the birth rate among women: ruralisation—a call to return to villages—and demographic campaign. The demographic campaign was linked to the ruralisation campaign as the peasant stock was understood to be more prolific and less polluted by the easy virtues and feminism of urban areas. The peasant stock was praised in propaganda campaigns as a symbol of social and racial cohesion, large households and a nurturer of family values. The fascist propaganda projected two contrasting female images. One was the *donna-crisi*: cosmopolitan, urbane, skinny, hysterical, decadent and sterile. The other was the *donna-madre*: national, rural, floridly robust, tranquil and prolific. Middle-class city women who preferred to have lesser children with sounder health and better upbringing belonged to the first type, while the prolific rural peasant stock belonged to the latter. The ruralisation campaign also meant to revive the romantic and mythological era of primordial and pristine ways of nature where men and women carried out their 'natural' duties rather than competing with each other in the urban labour market for jobs. This meant leaving industrial and urban jobs to men and sending women back to reproduction and farm work. This was applauded by some women as Latin feminism, which, unlike the 'sterile foreign feminism of individual's rights', valued women's maternal duty to the family and nation.

In Germany, Walter Darré, the protagonist of 'Blood and Soil' model, projected village women as the prototype of Aryan womanhood: simple, innocent and uncorrupted by the polluting and artificial city culture. These women were most suited to give the desired boost to the flagging birth rate. It was the supposed continuity of their genealogy, which assured him of the purity of the race and also the cultural ways of rearing children in the national socialist way. Darré considered the 'unpolluted' German countryside, insulated from the relatively easy virtues of city dwellers, as the best location for rearing the 'Aryan stock' (Münkel, 1996: 427).

Most of these reproductive strategies, however, primarily addressed mothers who produced children within the nuclear family mould, and many of the western democracies too were resorting to such measures to raise their birth rates. As Ann Taylor Allen points out, not just male politicians, even feminists in the first half of the twentieth century were worried about the falling birth rate and considered it a threat to the military and political survival of their respective nations, a worry that was heightened in the inter-war period. This era saw a marked rise in maternal politics, which resulted in granting the mothers generous welfare benefits and social protection in all of Europe (Allen, 1993: 101).

MOTHERHOOD AND ILLEGITIMACY

The Nazis and fascists went far beyond the prevalent ways to increase reproduction. Unlike conservative regimes and wartime democracies, they introduced many unconventional policies, which legitimised, encouraged or accepted out of wedlock children, inaugurating a new sexual morality. During the war soldiers could not come home on leave so frequently. In case their relations with women of pure blood resulted in pregnancies but the relationship was not legalised for some reason, several provisions were made by the Nazis to provide them sanctity, security, full legal status and welfare benefits. Such alliances were known as emergency marriages, post-mortem marriages (in cases where soldiers died leaving behind pregnant single women), long distance marriages, subsidiary marriages and so on, depending upon the context. They encouraged divorces where the extra-marital alliance had better potential to bring children and the chances of reproduction in existing marriage were bleak due to frigidity, abortion, refusal to conceive or irretrievable breakdown, which was judged by three years of separation. The Nazis went so far as to bestow the title of 'Frau' to all unmarried German women, a title that eluded them even in the progressive Weimar era because it was seen as undermining the sanctity of marriage. In spite of vociferous demands by feminists and socialists to grant unmarried women the title of Frau, the Weimar Republicans had found it outrageous and shelved the matter aside when it came up in the parliament for discussions. The Nazis, on the other hand, granted unmarried women this privilege as right. They broke Christian, bourgeois and republican conventions of sexual morality in this regard.

The Nazis craving for racially pure children made them adopt an ingenious way outside the traditional institution of marriage. Heinrich Himmler, head of the elite SS forces set up *Lebensborn* homes which were located away from the cities in the picturesque surroundings of the countryside where children stemming from extramarital alliance of the SS officials and racially desirable women in all of occupied territories could be delivered. Of course, the SS wives could also take advantage of these homes, which they did in wartime when cities came under bombing attacks, but the number of illegitimate children far outnumbered the marital ones. These children were conceived and delivered in absolute secrecy and mother and child both enjoyed all social welfare benefits. The regime made painstaking efforts to keep their respect and dignity intact in order to save them from stigmatisation. The money for this enterprise was raised from a tax levied on the SS and bachelors had to pay more than the married ones.

Italian fascists also condemned traditional, bourgeois and Catholic morality with regard to illegitimacy and unmarried motherhood. The traditional and Christian way of dealing with illegitimate children was *Ruota*, a system of anonymous abandoning of infants in orphanages in order to salvage the honour of the girl and her future chances of marriage. Infant mortality rates were high in these orphanages as children routinely suffered from diseases and neglect. If they managed to survive, they were offered to foster families from where they landed as cheap labour in the market. The Great War increased the number of illegitimate children manifold. The fascists saw in this their urgent calling. They set up the OMNI, the national mother and child welfare agency, which took over the care of mothers and children who fell outside the normal family structure. This meant typically unwed mothers, widows, abandoned mothers and other single mothers staying on the margins of society. The OMNI was charged with finding solutions to their moral, economic and social problems and with their complete integration in society. The first step taken in this direction was to prevent mothers from abandoning their infants by giving prenatal medical and financial support three months prior to delivery. The next step was to make it possible for the expectant mother to be with the child after delivery, and the third was to have the child recognised by the father. Every year after 1927, ONMI claimed to have prevented thousands of cases of infant abandonment, filed paternity suits on behalf of mothers, found jobs for the needy and pressed the parents to legalise such unions (de Grazia, 1992: 68–9). ONMI's undertaking was the fruition of many earlier reformers' and feminists' dreams for the rights of such mothers and children. Illegitimate births were now treated as natural births and the parenthood as natural motherhood/fatherhood. Feminists for years had been complaining that these children forever suffered the stigma of 'child of the unknown', which was stamped on their birth certificates. This birth certificate had to be produced in school, job market, youth group registration and so on, forever creating embarrassment for such children. Giving care and rights to the illegitimate children and abandoned mothers had been a long-standing feminist demand which fascists were the first to fulfil in terms of providing mother and child all social welfare benefits that were granted to legitimate children and married mothers. Equally important was the showering of care and concern and the removal of the stigma of illegitimacy. Majority of women and most of the feminists may have found these measures satisfying and pro-women.

However, this model of radical maternalism had a flip side too with rather alarming implications for feminist, egalitarian and democratic practices. These measures were exclusivist in letter and spirit, which made it a hallmark of Nazism and which was later implemented in Italy as well. The Nazis took stringent anti-natal measures to wipe out the undesirable races and ethnicities. They devised equally ingenious exclusivist, anti-natal measures to prevent the reproduction of 'undesirable races'. As Gisela Bock argued in her path-breaking work, forced sterilisations were conducted upon eugenically and racially 'unfit' persons, which demonstrated Nazis' commitment more to anti-natalism rather than pro-natalism (Bock, 1986). From January 1934 until the outbreak of the war, about 320,000 people were sterilised on grounds of feeblemindedness, schizophrenia and alcoholism, mental or physical abnormalities on arbitrary and subjective grounds. Gabriele Czarnowski argued how even for the 'racially acceptable' couples the institution of marriage came to be regulated through genealogical and racial approval, if couples wanted to take full advantage of maternal benefits. Banning abortions and promoting births among the 'racially healthy' went hand in hand with forced sterilisations and abortions on eugenically unfit Germans, Gypsies and foreign labour in wartime. The Gypsies were branded as asocial and work shy. Similarly, undesirable German men, women and children became targets of clinical negligence and wilful murder under Action T4 scheme, which was the precursor to the mass murder in death factories like Auschwitz. Murder of the 'undesirable' children went hand in hand with child friendly policies for the racially desirable offspring.

This racial and exclusivist aspect of motherhood and childhood makes us keenly aware of the opportunities and perils of fascist 'welfare maternalism'. On the one hand, the Nazis went out of their way to provide benefits and remove stigma for the racially pure; on the other, they went after those who did not pass their race and eugenic criteria and punished them equally vociferously. For the racially pure they fulfilled long-standing feminist demands in the reproductive sphere but simultaneously snatched the basic civil and human rights of birth, life and freedom from those who did not fit into their racial views. This is a site where we can observe an inter-play between race and gender as also feminism and fascism. While women were subordinated to men in fascism and could thus consider themselves to be at the receiving end, when we compare them to racial and social outsiders, there is no doubt who was the bigger sufferer and victim of Nazi politics. In other words, race trumped gender or sexism. Women from the desirable race were beneficiaries of many fascist policies even though they may have faced discrimination in political aspect. Aryan women were victims at times, beneficiaries many a time and perpetrators in certain contexts, but racial and social outsiders, whether men or women, were almost always victims of the Nazi regime.

The more serious aspect of this maternalism was, therefore, the racial aspect of Nazism, which was also transported to Italy in 1939 when the latter implemented racial and anti-Jewish laws as a collaborator of Nazi Germany. This kind of maternalism denied women of the unwanted race the 'natural' right to and choice of motherhood, the same natural right, which fascist asserted in case of illegitimate children of desirable mothers. The Nazi racial laws of September 1935 banned marriages between non-Jews and Jews and created difficulties for mixed couples and their children, even though they were granted some immunity. In the war years forced workers from the conquered territories were regulated purely on the basis of their 'racial worth'. Birth and motherhood were strictly discouraged among forced workers by various means. Among the seven million forced foreign labour, on whose shoulders the demanding agricultural work and dangerous munitions work rested, were millions of women too. It was largely owing to the labour of these workers that German women could be spared of the demanding and risky war work. These foreigners were graded according to a racial hierarchy in which the north-western workers were better off than the eastern and southern ones and the Soviet workers were the worst sufferers. All worked under humiliating circumstances, were underpaid, lived in labour camps and were deprived of family life.

Initially the pregnant or ailing women were dispatched to collection camps and sent back to their native countries to avoid the costs of having to care for them. From 1943, abortions were encouraged in these cases. If it was too late for that, then their children were sent to child collection centres where they were either starved to death or murdered with lethal injections. Children who were found to be 'racially fit' on the basis of their appearances were snatched from their parents to be given to German foster parents for Germanisation by the welfare service. This points to how welfare workers, nurses and the so-called 'care givers' were deeply racialised. We should also remember that the majority of these 'care givers' were women. How such 'feminine sectors' of professional work traditionally associated with care and concern were brutalised by the Nazi and how they functioned unproblematically in this era is an indicator of the perils of majoritarian welfare policies. While such exclusivist welfare policies might have appeased women of the majority community, they simultaneously punished innocent minorities without eliciting any outrage and protest from German feminists and human rights activists. This also shows us that women of the same creed, in spite of being the second sex, enjoyed a privileged status when compared with ethnic and racial minorities, who were persecuted due to their race more than their gender, even though gender agonies and humiliations might have been more intense in some cases.

GENDER AND THE PUBLIC SPHERE

This section explores those aspects of fascism, which connected motherhood and 'womanly activities' to the larger public sphere such as imperial quest, war and industrial work, all considered traditional male spheres.

The fascist cult of motherhood was directly connected to the imperial quest. Both Italy and Germany saw population growth as an index of national virility and the essential condition for inhabiting the conquered territories. It is another matter that most of the male population was used as cannon fodder in the Second World War resulting in large-scale loss of population once again. France and England were seen as sterile in comparison with rejuvenated fascist states ready to conquer and inhabit new territories. Demographic theories and imperialism reinforced each other in this vision. Imperialism complemented ruralisation and demographic campaign. It was an integral component of their gender politics.

From the late nineteenth century onwards, anti-Enlightenment, illiberal and irrational forces started colouring the idea of nationalism. The Late nineteenth-century European nationalism was wedded to imperial ambitions. Germany and Italy as young nations and late beginners in the race for colonies wanted to compete with Britain and their European counterparts. This age of new imperialism, which resulted in a rush for dividing Africa amongst powerful European nations also triggered a new domestic politics. In order to divert the attention of the masses from prevailing inequalities at home, the ruling elite tried to lure the lower classes towards newly acquired colonies. These colonies in Africa offered fresh opportunities to make a fortune or build new carriers at the cost of the subject populations and in doing so ease the tension arising from increasing inequalities in the mother country. This reflected in the emergence of a new kind of language in the public sphere. This language biologised politics by presenting nations as organic communities that must multiply faster and spread out. Nations had to have a healthy population of young people who would go and occupy colonies and add to the glory of the nation. Numbers became important for imperial ventures, and imperial ventures became important for the masses as imperial expansion gave new opportunities to the masses that were increasingly turning towards socialism and communism for a more egalitarian distribution of resources at home. The conservative ruling elite of these young nations thought that diverting public attention to the colonies and showing their people the dreams of occupying distant land would ease tensions at home. At the turn of the century, imperialist leagues prospered in both these countries.

What did this have to do with gender politics? Certainly, a lot! Women were thought to be the ones who could rejuvenate the nation by giving it bounties of children who would inhabit the conquered territories. The question of gender was as important as race. Colonial encounters in the age of new imperialism when Europe's self-esteem and confidence were at their apex led to an arrogant understanding of what was earlier understood to be difference. Differences between Europeans and others such as Asians and Africans were earlier seen as differences of culture and religion. Now race increasingly replaced those earlier ideas and came with a set of biases that created essentialist hierarchies. Traits and characteristics according to racial biology came to be understood as fixed and immutable. Similar notions pervaded gender politics of the era. Men were thought to be virile, aggressive, ambitious and outgoing and woman were understood as submissive, sacrificing and complacent. The latter were important for the nation primarily as producers and nurturers of coming generations. These ideas were to blossom and grow under fascist and Nazi regimes.

Post First World War political scenario gave a further push to these ideas in central and eastern Europe, which divided nations between victors and vanquished. In the aftermath of the First World War, Europe witnessed the birth of many new nations in the eastern and southern part of Europe on the basis of American president Wilson's principle of national self-determination. However, rather than vindicating national self-determination, the Treaty of Versailles and the inconsistencies in the implementation of the Wilsonian principle, fuelled more discontent among these nations. Aggressive nationalist ideology of fascism and Nazism provided people of these disgruntled countries just the right discourses at home to bolster their self-esteem. Interwar fascism has to be placed in this international context to make sense of national politics, which blunted the edge of existing ideologies such as socialism, pacifism, feminism—all of them internationalist in appeal and perspective—which were ultimately sacrificed at the altar of nationalism. Women's ambitions, dreams and roles cannot thus be seen in isolation and, therefore, this larger context has to be kept in mind while assessing women's position and roles in these regimes.

Not just as mothers and life-givers, women also became willing supporters as colonisers and social workers in the imperialist drive. German women became active agents of Germanisation in the occupied territories of the Reich. Elizabeth Harvey studied this aspect of women's empowerment as imperial and racial agents (Harvey, 2003). German women had a more direct and active role in occupied Poland as missionaries in bringing German culture, manners, hygiene and efficiency to these supposedly uncultured and chaotic people. German female colonisers furthered the racial imperial goals of the regime. This job involved not only evacuating Polish inhabitants for the conquerors but also settling ethnic Germans from farther east in the evacuated Polish territory. These eastern Germans were culturally very different from the Germans living in Germany and thus had to be Germanised. This task fell upon German women colonisers who worked as educationists, welfare workers and civilisers of a people they considered inferior. While subordinated to the commands of men at home and in public in their fatherland, these missionary women were filled with a sense of superiority. For example, one Frau Bauer, a 27-year-old sales assistant-turned volunteer in Poland thought that it was a call from the stars and that she must accept this and help the German East European settlers who had come to Germany to find a homeland in occupied Poland (ibid.: 104 –5). They also took pride in the leadership positions they occupied while dealing with the colonised, in a sense making up for the power deficit suffered at home.

Women could also be found as direct perpetrators in concentration camps and jails as guards, a particular one among them, Irma Grese, was nicknamed the bitch of Belsen and the beast of Auschwitz because of her regular whipping and beating of inmates. She was as sadistic and cruel as any of her male colleagues. Countless women acted as nurses who selected euthanasia patients—many among them children—for wilful murder by administering lethal injections and as callous staff in orphanages that housed foreign children.

Italian women's enthusiastic support for Mussolini's imperial mission is documented in the weeks after 18 December 1935, when thousands of women followed the lead of Queen Elena who offered her wedding ring—her dearest possession—to the Ethiopian war cause. Among these women were war widows and mothers of fallen soldiers, wet nurses, the Church's 'brides of Christ' and the unwed. They all offered what they could: gold rings, brooches, gifts, intimate family mementos and other ornaments. In all 2,262 kilos of gold was collected and a new union was created between women and the imperial nation (de Grazia: 77–8). The ring ceremony triggered a scrap metal drive and gave a huge impetus to enlisting women's support to fascist institutions. Coupled with this imperialist cause was economic frugality in household management, austere habits and autarchy in buying national products to contribute to war efforts.

THE FAMILY, COMMUNITY AND PRIVATE SPACES

The family was the germ cell of the nation in the fascist project. Intense political activity differentiated it from traditional conservative regimes. In fact, the totalitarian claims of the regime started with the family, which became the nursery for learning fascist values and behaviours.

The family became the focus of population, eugenic, racial and educational policies and thus a target of fascist propaganda and a source of human resource mobilisation for various imperial political requirements. The family lost its previous liberal status as a sacrosanct unit and was exposed to state intervention like never before. Its members, men, women and children, were called upon to serve the state in many other capacities. Not just that, members of the family were often found assuming intimidating postures at times. Scores of denunciations filed with the Gestapo against husbands and fathers bear testimony to a contestation of power, which went on among family members within the four walls of private homes (Joshi, 2003: 43–86). In the neighbourhoods, women denouncers acted as watchdogs of the community and reported Jews, communists, socialists, foreigners and all those who were suspect in the eyes of the Nazis. The provision of denunciations opened the channels of communications with the prerogative arbitrary powers like the Gestapo, criminal police and the judiciary, which women appropriated to threaten and punish vulnerable sections of society. Interestingly, the nature of these denunciations was not always political but had morality, sexuality, jealously, inferiority, envy and a whole lot of psychological and emotional reasons, which were presented as political. Through these 'political denunciations', the dictatorship opened a consensual space which ordinary women filled up by voluntarily approaching a dreaded police organ such as the Gestapo and thus participating in the persecution of others. The fact that false accusations went totally unpunished, speaks volumes of the power that ordinary Aryans, men and women, acquired over those condemned by the Nazis on racial and political ground.

GENDER AND HIGH POLITICS

Women did not acquire leadership positions in either fascist Italy or Nazi Germany. In political terms, Gertrud Scholtz Klink or Angiol Moretti—leaders of women's mass organisations in Germany and Italy respectively—did not wield as much power as a district party head. Their job was to essentially prepare womenfolk to follow orders rather than take political initiative and decisions. Under their leadership, women were called upon to serve the nation in war and peace by organising themselves in various fascist organisations. After banning all pre-existing women's organisations, the Nazis organised the rank and file of women under the auspices of German Women's Enterprise (DFW), while the elite were organised under the National Socialist Womanhood or NSF, whose membership touched 2.3 million in 1938 (Burleigh and Wippermann, 1991: 249).

The Nazis charted the entire course of life for their citizens irrespective of gender from childhood onwards. From the age of 10, young boys would be recruited to *Jungvolk* (young boys) and girls to *Jungmädel* (young girls). Then they graduated to *Hitler Jugend* (Hitler Youth) and BDM (German Girls' League) respectively between 14 and 18 years of age. Boys could then either be part of the SA, SS or Labour Front and women could go on to join NSF or DFW. In between, for one year, they also had to do a compulsory labour year on the farm, army or household to shed their class inhibitions and inculcate love of hard physical work. All of this was compulsory and any defiance to this was not taken lightly, more so if accompanied by any other form of non-compliance. Further, 7.5 million young people were thus organised collectively in 1933, which was to increase manifold thereafter (ibid.: 202). Young boys and girls participated in political, social and leisure activities, creating a new youth culture outside the influence of the family. This culture also suppressed an existing alternate youth culture by intimidating those who were associated with jazz, swing or communist groups.

Similarly, in Italy women's fascist organisation, *Fasci Femmenili*, was founded in 1919 for middle-class women who were active in the public sphere looking after social welfare and poor relief. While women's involvement in the public sphere may have been empowering in some sense, their power vis-à-vis their male leaders was clearly circumscribed. Augusto Turati, Party Secretary of the ruling fascists from March 1926, sent a circular rebuffing a demand from women activists to be allowed to wear black shirts, which stated bluntly, 'The black shirt is the virile symbol of our revolution and has nothing to do with the welfare task that fascism has given women' (Williams, 2010: 85).

This notwithstanding, fascists organised women in different sections to carry out assigned tasks efficiently and smoothly. In 1933, the Section for Rural Housewives was established as an umbrella organisation to organise rural women, which provided services to peasant women and also alerted them to practice autarky in consumption and rational farming practices under Taylorism in agriculture. The Rural Housewives Section also conducted courses on domestic science, hygiene and child care. In 1937, female labour was organised in the Section for Women Workers and Outworkers (SOLD), which offered some training in work skills and support in applying for state benefits. It also worked with maids and working-class housewives and organised outings, short holidays, leisure and sports activities for them. Girls and boys were organised in separate groups. Girls aged between 8 and 12 joined the *Piccole Italiane* (Little Female Italians) and were promoted to *Giovani Italiane*

(Young Female Italians) between 13 and 18. In 1937, both girls and boys became part of the *Gioventu Italiana del Littorio* or Italian Youth of the Lictors graded according to age groups. For girls these were essentially nurseries for future motherhood, where they learnt 'doll drills', domestic science, gardening, first-aid, alongside some sports and leisure activities. By 1939, about 31,80,000 women and girls were active in party sponsored groups (Allen, 2008: 52).

GENDER AND EDUCATION

The entire educational system was revamped to suit the state's requirement, inculcate fascist values and fight prevalent morality. Nazi educational system was to give practical shape to Hitler's stated aim in the *Mein Kampf*, 'future motherhood is to be the main aim of the female education (Hitler, 1962: 491). The Reich's education minister, Rust, was given charge of revamping the educational system to rear more masculine men and more feminine women. This clear polarisation between sexes led to the opening of *Frauenschule* or women-only schools, which gave priority to home economics and spiritual training over natural sciences. Concepts such as the law of heredity, racial hygiene and noble race lay at the heart of biology classes to prepare the girls to choose racially worthy husbands and rear their offspring in the 'real Aryan manner'. The home economy classes taught women to be simple and thrifty, shun luxury and love of foreign cosmetics and develop a sense of autarky. The geography course was designed to awaken the consciousness that Germans were the true representatives of the pure Nordic race and history classes were aimed to develop a heroic view of the Aryan past besides advancing imperialist and aggressive ideas. On the other hand, boys learnt Latin (a prerequisite for higher education) for four hours while the girls had to do compulsory needle work. School-leaving girls had to undergo one year of obligatory labour service as agricultural or household assistant, to avoid which most parents married off their daughters after schooling. Besides, a national Mother's Service set-up mother schools that trained young women in household jobs, maternal health and child care. Another agency called People's Economy offered courses in home economics, sanitation, cooking and so on.

GENDER AND THE JOB MARKET

The fascists understood unemployment mainly as men's problem even though female population was higher than male population and the Great War left many single mothers and widows in its wake. They attacked women as double earners and used various means to expel women from the job market. Job positions were reserved for war veterans in Italy. In November 1933, the government imposed severe limitations on the rights of women to compete in state civil service examinations. In 1938, a law restricted female employment in private and state enterprises to 10 per cent. While retaining women in areas requiring female workers, the government aimed to remove women completely within three years. The Nazis exhorted double earners to leave the job market to men, settle at home as housewives and procreate. Marriage loans, as shown earlier, were supposed to drive working women gently out of the job market, while a restrictive quota of 10 per cent was imposed on higher education for women. They were kept out of higher position in the bureaucracy, barred from the judicial and armed services. It assumed that women could neither be trusted with rational decision-making, nor deployed in risky jobs such as direct combat.

Psychological pressure was applied on women through propaganda, which derided women's liberal individualistic ambitions and competition with men. Too much of education was condemned as a bad impact, which distracted them from their motherly and housewifely duties. Universities were seen as centres of middle-class snobbery.

Fascist policies of discrimination in the job market ran into pragmatic difficulties once the war started. With able-bodied men marching to the front, the home front faced an acute labour crisis. In Italy, in spite of discouragement, women dominated in traditional areas of teaching and nursing. In nursing, there was a steady increase from 28,490 in 1911 to 44,598 in 1921 and 73,668 in 1931 (de Grand, 1976: 959). It was precisely in the years after 1935 that women's number in universities and teaching institutes increased dramatically. While the teachers' training institutes had 26,769 female as against 2,225 males, the number increased to 71,439 for females and 42,753 for males (ibid.: 966). In the universities, their enrolment increased from 3.9 per cent in 1911–12 to 17.4 per cent in 1942–43. The number of female doctors also increased. There was a rise in white collar and professional jobs. The largest drop was registered in the agricultural sector, precisely where the fascist wanted women to retreat.

Traditional civilian jobs performed by men were to be filled by women as able-bodied men marched to the front. The regime sought to train and acquire women for jobs ranging from civil services, assembly line labour forces to managers of private and agricultural enterprises. To justify their use of women, especially in the assembly line production where they were urgently required by the state in view of the labour shortage in the armament industry, the Nazi regime adopted a new public posture, which reflected in their wartime propaganda and changed policies.

The blood and soil model of Walter Daree, which lost its urgency in the war years, was replaced by the social engineering model to justify women's presence in the labour market. This model was prepared by the technocratic elite who developed pseudo-scientific theories using conventional wisdom about the nature of women, and concepts from Social Darwinism, industrial psychology, anthropology and medical sciences to suit their purpose. The Nazis now emphasised women's psychological makeup which was more suitable for repetitive, mechanised and monotonous assembly line work.

One major mouthpiece of this model was the Institute of Labour Research, which worked closely with industrialists in dismantling ideological and emotional barriers in blending rationalisation with German National Socialism or indigenous rationalisation. Employers were repeatedly urged to feminise the work force, which meant splitting up the tasks before taking women into war production. Under no circumstances were women to be allowed to look into the inside of the machine. They had to be kept unskilled for it was believed that they lacked scientific temper, abstract thinking and observation. But this 'biological inferiority', according to the institute, was not general, for example, in case of the women, their sense of touch, temperament and manual precision was developed to a much higher degree than that of men. The institute argued that these skills could be utilised in the conveyor belts (Schmidt and Dietz, 1983: 195). While the regime tried to justify women's engagement in the job market, especially at the bottom rungs of the industry, they were apprehensive about deploying them in harmful munitions industry. Unlike the Americans and Britons who were successful in employing women in the auxiliary services, the Nazis refrained from it for fear of discontent in the soldiers. The separation allowances for soldier's wives were most liberal in Nazi Germany; so, these wives did not have to slog it out in the job market or respond to the call of the state to fill vacancies left by soldiers in the industries and danger zones. The Nazis deployed slave labour from occupied territories to do the most demanding and dangerous jobs and thus spare their women.

HISTORIOGRAPHY

Historiographical Trends

Historiography related to Nazi Germany has been much richer and far more diverse in comparison with the fascist Italy. This can be explained by the extreme brutalities and human rights violations both in and outside the Nazi-occupied Europe during war years. Ever since the collapse of Nazi regime, historians have had to deal with this era of unprecedented horror. German historians have had to modify their conservative and defensive stance repeatedly when faced with a volley of questions from their Anglo-American colleagues. These questions have generated waves of historiographical debates regarding the peculiar nature of German past and its process of modernisation, necessitating a reflection on its destructive imperial ambitions and aggressive anti-Semitism in dealing with war and the Holocaust. For this reason, the Nazi past is one period that does not seem to pass for German historians and public alike. It is a period that not only presents standard methodological and ideological issues, but also problems related to ethics, morality and conscience. We deal with some of these issues in Chapter 5. As a result, this period is perhaps one of the most well-researched areas in human history, and gender history is no exception to this trend.

This section, therefore, focuses on historiographical trends related to Nazi Germany rather than fascist Italy where this field is still developing. Contemporary feminists, who witnessed the rise and growth of fascism in Italy and Germany, responded in various ways. Some, as we have seen in the course of the chapter, aligned themselves willingly with the latter hoping that their long cherished desired would be fulfilled, and some of these especially in the realm of motherhood were indeed fulfilled, even if circumscribed by race and ethnicity. Some got free rein to organise their own activities at least in the initial years. Several others whose feminism was aligned with pacifism, socialism, internationalism, democratic and human rights were indeed alarmed by the rise of this phenomenon. Feminist movement, in that sense, was not cohesive and was already in fragments when fascist forces started gaining ground in the interwar era. Many of these internationalist and leftist feminists left their own countries and took refuge in democratic and neutral countries. Anita Augspurg and Lyda Gustava Heymann were two such feminist-pacifists who left Germany in the wake of the Nazi takeover in 1933. Besides their rejection of Nazi politics, Augspurg also feared personal vendetta from Hitler because in 1923 she had applied for Hitler's expulsion due to his Austrian origins and sedition. Many others opted for inner exile and silence in public pursuits.

After the collapse of fascist powers in Europe, the biggest concern of all was to restore normalcy and democratic order. For gender politics, it meant giving the vote to those women who were deprived of it not just in erstwhile dictatorships, for example, Italy and Germany (where it was restored), but also France, which had kept the vote away from women until then. The Second World War had been by far the most destructive war not just in terms of material losses but human lives. For nation states, the war meant a loss of young male populations as many lost their lives on the front. Many were still missing or were taken as POWs and many returned home as half men with an amputated arm or leg. Demographically, the war created a major imbalance between genders. Europe had many more women than men, but all could not get married or find partners. Of all available men several were physically damaged and psychologically shattered. Many others were missing or taken as POWs. They found it difficult to adjust to the everyday life after the war, especially in the vanquished countries. Physical separation of spouses in the war years also led to increasing rate of divorce, remarriage or simply break up of marriage. Post-war women's magazines, advice manuals and entertainment magazines started regular columns on how to re-establish the sanctity of marriage and restore normalcy in family relations. Psychologists, moralists and Christian reformers were preoccupied with this theme and for more than a decade, 'normalisation' of gender relation in private, i.e., re-establishment of the authority of the husband and restoration of the family as an institution was akin to the democratisation of the polity or the public sphere.

This order of things changed with the students' revolt of 1968, which questioned the authority of the patriarchs in the private sphere and a strong authoritarian and anti-left attitude of the political elite in the public sphere. The second wave of feminism was an offshoot of this anti-authority movement. The feminist movement of the 1970s spilled out on the streets of Paris, Berlin, London and many other big cities of Europe. The feminist legacy lived on in the intellectual world, which was shaken in very fundamental epistemological ways. This second wave feminism produced a wide range of literature on subjects related to women's oppression and suppression in society. A critical engagement with women's role in fascism also started with this.

Feminists of this generation faced a peculiar dilemma while studying fascism and Nazism. How did they manage to rally so much female support behind them in Italy and Germany when they were pursuing such anti-feminist policies? Fascism and Nazism were indeed seen as movements with a backward march for women in the early 1970s. Additionally, in the post-Auschwitz scenario, Nazi regime became synonymous with industrialised mass murder of innocent civilian populations. Were just Hitler and his clique responsible for this heinous crime, or was the social base much wider (women being part of it)? Issues such as these have engaged historians and social scientists ever since then. This also posed questions to feminist history writers who were at that time engaged in finding a positive identity for women by recovering their past, a general trend that can be witnessed in the contemporary Western world. Feminist theory and writing, as young burgeoning disciplines, did not want to get soiled with the murky past of inhuman crimes and atrocities. German feminists, thus, maintained an uneasy silence on these matters for long.

Earlier paradigms that developed in the 1970s and 1980s to confront this problem saw women either as pure victims of or, at the most, passive accomplices to Nazi crimes. It was comfortable to see women as victims of the National Socialist regime, as mere objects, who were discriminated against by the *Männerstaat*. Margret Lück, for example, characterised the National Socialist state as a dictatorship of men. Only men occupied leading positions in the government and elsewhere. Because of their position as leaders, it was, in her view, men who defined the status of women in the system and ascribed a feminine role to women, casting them out of the spheres of public life and active politics (Lück, 1979: 122). Some feminist historians declared women to be particularly resistant to fascism and by implication considered them to be totally uninvolved in the crimes of National Socialism (Stephenson, 1981). Most saw the National Socialist regime as an extreme form of patriarchy, which snatched away all the rights hitherto won by women through concerted efforts of the women's movement. It was a period described in terms of degradation with disastrous consequences, or regression into an existence marked by humiliation and deprivation of rights. Feminist historians usually started with the description of the women's emancipation movement before 1933, outlined its gains, and then portrayed a backward march with the seizure of power by the Nazis. The list of discriminatory measures was endless: ban on double earners, removal of women from the job market, marriage loans for those who left work to get married and indulged in procreation, compulsory labour service, restriction on female students to 10 per cent in the universities, recognition of women primarily as mothers and so on. Even the gender-neutral measures of the Nazis in the realm of the house and family were put forward as evidence for the terrorist basis of gender politics by some (Kuhn and Rothe, 1982 (1): 138). Ute Frevert cautioned that political ideology and policies should not be confused with social reality. It should not be forgotten that the actual outcome of the policy was sometimes different, and often diametrically opposed, to its intended effects. Moreover, an approach which holds that Nazism exercised absolute tutelage and deprived citizens of their rights, tempts us to regard women as nothing but victims of an omnipotent, totalitarian polity which excluded them, and the helpless prey of a chauvinist, elitist band of male rulers. The logical conclusion from this argument is that if women allowed themselves to be 'mastered' by an instrument of repression for a whole 12 years, they must have been pitifully stupid, naïve and cowardly (Frevert, 1988: 251). Besides, characterising house and family as women's domain is itself problematic. Did men, as heads of the household, have no role to play there? Did they not exercise their powers in this realm to subordinate women? Was it really women's uncontested domain?

Such a scheme could barely find women as active agents in the Nazi regime. However, this could hardly be inspiring for constructing a positive identity among women. So, where did they find positive impulses? In the resistance movement, the same powerless, innocent victims were turned into active agents in the form of resistance fighters (Kuhn and Rothe, 1982 (1): 18). Not just that, women in the post-fascist context, suddenly becomes the procreators, nurturers and protectors of positive social values and sensibility. They were visualised as bearers of anti-fascist culture and builders of post-Nazi society in view of their role in the reconstruction. Why, however, should these productive qualities be restricted to anti-fascist culture; why, asked Gudrun Brockhaus, should they not to be applied also to the fascist disregard of culture? (Brockhaus, 1991: 113). Besides, the argument about women's activity as being vital for sustaining the war-torn and post-war societies could well be turned into a counter-argument against it for sustaining a criminal regime like National Socialism. Thus, the same qualities became weaknesses when the question of involvement in the National Socialist past came up and strengths when the question of resistance was raised.

This feminist self-projection faced criticism on other counts as well. Frigga Haug, for example, pointed out that women could also be in a position to be active agents. Unless external pressure could be proved, every subordination, even patriarchy, could only function with the consent of the subordinate. Similarly, Ute Frevert suspected that the immense ability of the regime to mobilise the population, and the relative rarity of deliberate acts of political resistance, suggest that women who satisfied the political, racial and social requirements—and the vast majority did—did not perceive the Third Reich as a women's hell (Fervert, 1988: 252).

To escape this mutually contradictory stance and still save women from active involvement, a second position was developed with two representative variants. The first one was Margarete Mitscherlich's psychoanalytical model. She diagnosed anti-Semitism as a disease prevalent among men, which resulted from their unresolved oedipal crisis. The unconscious psychological motives for the development of anti-Semitism, such as the projection of hate for fathers, the shifting of incestuous desires onto a different group of people (i.e., Jews), aggression and rivalry, were of relevance primarily to the male psyche (Mitscherlich, 1985: 151–2). Mitscherlich gendered anti-Semitism by arguing further that there was a male and a female anti-Semitism that derived from the difference between the two sexes in the development of their superegos. Adopting the controversial Freudian position of ascribing a strong superego to men and a weak one to women, she argued that women were less vulnerable to the narcissistic and aggressive anti-Semitism of the masculine kind. Women's anti-Semitism rather stemmed from their identification with male prejudices. So went her argument, 'Women like all other oppressed ones of the society tend to identify themselves with their aggressors. This tendency to conform is tied to the great fear of losing love' (ibid.: 160).

Strongly critical of this explanation, Karin Windaus-Walser in turn feminised the oedipal crisis. She asked: How about the resolution of Oedipus complex in women? How about the female projection of incestuous desires and hatred of mothers on to Jewesses? Were there no women living in the anti-Semitic, narcissist paradise where everything evil was shifted on the Jews and everything good to the 'Aryans'? Did women not integrate themselves into this narcissism of men by projecting everything evil on to the Jews? Mitscherlich's escape into psychoanalysis served her to establish that it was only the longing for love that compelled women to become anti-Semitic, that they were only secondarily anti-Semitic, that their inner psychic world had remained pure, unpolluted by hatred, sadism, murderous and persecutory instincts (Windaus-Walser, 1988: 111). One has to really ask oneself if women only followed men or if they had their own agendas, their own motives in being anti-Semitic. Mitscherlich's explanation saw women as lacking in initiative, denying them both positive and negative agency, and attributed perpetration to them only indirectly in the context of Nazi crimes. The second model of female complicity was forwarded by Christine Thürmer-Rohr. It was different from that of Mitscherlich's in that it attributed an active role to women in complicity by ascribing an active interest to women in perpetuating patriarchy. Women had an active interest, so went the argument, in playing the role assigned to them by men for it promised them *free spaces*, the guarantee of a definite sphere of life and a piece of their own world as premiums for their good conduct (Thürmer-Rohr, 1987: 42). However, she adhered to the idea that the 'murderous normality' in which women lived was man made and to the idea that men have been the prime perpetrators in the past and present. What Christine Thürmer-Rohr simply meant by complicity was that women prepared themselves for a world conceived and determined by men and that they followed the ideas of men about themselves, that they supported the man and his world. Complicity reduced itself to corruptibility through the patriarchal system and its ideology. Instead of passive victims, we have active victims, commented Walser (ibid.: 112). What was new about this explanation was that conformity did not come from compulsion but from self-interest in the reward. Thus, the feminist dilemma of not being able to overcome the status of the 'second sex' remained unresolved and was reproduced further. The message was that women shared the guilt of Nazi crimes but only secondarily and insofar as they supported and reaffirmed the doings of men. They did so by denying their own feminine self.

The real polemic, which took the shape of a *Historikerrinnenstreit* of sorts, however started with the publication of American feminist historian Claudia Koonz's book, *Mothers in the Fatherland* in 1987. While Koonz was looking for gender participation at the societal level among the perpetrators, her critic Gisela Bock was preoccupied with gendering victims and ascribing victimhood even to 'Aryan' women in the same vein as Jewish and Gypsy women. This was a problematic proposition as the two kinds of victims, if both could be considered victims at all, did not share the same destinies, which varied from survival to extinction in quality and monstrously in quantity. This difference in perspective between the two became visible in Bock's criticism of Koonz's book, which started with a juxtaposition of a large number of sterilised female victims to a handful of policy makers and desk perpetrators. This approach treated victims as a gendered mass and found hardly any women among the perpetrators (Bock, 1989: 563). Koonz brought lower-level women functionaries like nurses, teachers and social workers to book for making sterilisation policies a reality with their active collaboration (Koonz, 1987: 7). Her contribution lay in dragging female professional murderers, activists of various women's organisations, who were cogs in the wheel, average wives and mothers alike into the arena of active perpetration. Though she talked most of the time about Nazi women, SS wives and women of Nazi organisations, she also implicated ordinary women who maintained an atmosphere of normality inside the homes in an environment of hatred.

In Hitler's Germany, women provided in a separate sphere of their own creation the image of humane values that lent the healthy gloss of motherhood to the 'Aryan' world of the chosen. In addition, wives gave the individual men who confronted daily murder a safe place where they could be respected for what they were, not what they did (ibid.: 419).

Koonz's anchoring of female guilt to sacrificing mothers and dutiful homemakers proved to be hazardous and invited criticism from German feminists. The private sphere, a 'place' apart from the brutal world, offered a respite to people at both extremes of the moral spectrum. Guards and commandants, victims and resisters—at the outer flanks of the Nazi world—all needed the psychological 'space' offered by a home (or at least the myth of one), to gather strength with which to face the deformed world outside. In the Nazi world, man and woman operated in radically separated spheres (ibid.: 419–20).

On the other hand, Bock in her work highlighted the gender agony of those women who became victims of the sterilisation policy of the regime (Bock, 1987). Others like Koonz, Walser and von Saldern found the sterilisation policy more racist than sexist and rejected the same parameter to judge the victimhood of sterilised 'Aryans' and gassed non-Aryans. Further, Bock exonerated all housewives and mothers of any responsibility for Nazi crimes. For her the real contribution of women to Nazi crimes was in their non-traditional function external to the home. Adelheid von Saldern found this position hardly productive, for denying any notion of a specifically female guilt in the traditional female sphere neglected the structural interconnection of the private sphere and the public sphere. While women were certainly less powerful than men were, they were by no means powerless. The question that we should ask is not whether women enjoyed power or not, but rather what kind of spaces and possibilities were available to women as housewives and mothers where they could and did exercise power. Housewives and mothers should not be seen and judged as merely bearers and nurturers of children. There performed many other functions at home and for the *Volksgemeinschaft* at large. In Nazi Germany, they were seen as repositories of the Nordic race and as guardians of the purity of 'Aryan' blood. The regime entrusted to them the responsibility of keeping the *Volksgemeinschaft* racially pure and of guarding it against 'political enemies'. Women internalised these teachings very well when they denounced Jews, racially foreign workers and political opponents of the regime including sometimes their own husbands. They ostracised and boycotted Jews, and 'averted their gaze' when Jews were being deported. They enriched themselves with the belonging of deported Jews. As mothers and housewives they reared their children in the Nazi spirit and sent them to Hitler Youth or BDM. They even organised themselves in women's groups, where they drew psychological and emotional strength from each other, felt like a strong female collectivity, even against their own men at home. They psychologically and emotionally supported their warring sons and husbands (von Saldern, 1994: 155). They separated their children from the children of the *Volksfeinde* at home, in schools and in neighbourhoods. Windaus-Walser rightly asked, 'Should we not think about the power of the mother or matriarch, which showed its ugly side in National Socialism, when we are talking about the power of the father or patriarch?' (Windaus-Walser, 1988: 113–14). Around the same time when Koonz was pointing a finger at German women for collaborating with the regime, a critical self-reflective effort began on the part of German feminists towards problematising women's role in the perpetration of crime. Angelika Ebbinghaus and her team wrote biographical accounts of women perpetrators like social workers and concentration camp supervisors in a victim/perpetrator paradigm (Ebbinghaus, 1987). In a sharply polemical way, Windaus-Walser attacked all previous feminists who had offered apologetic explanations of victimhood, of an allegedly abused, functionalised or corruptible second sex in the National Socialist regime. The blessing of female birth could, henceforth, no longer be used as an excuse. The high point of the polemic reached with the publication of *Töchter Fragen NS Frauengeschichte*, the leading voice of which claimed Auschwitz and Nazi crimes as negative feminist property and placed women's role therein at the centre stage of feminist discourse (Gravenhorst, 1990: 17–37).

From the identity building project in the 1970s and the 'unclaimed baggage approach towards Nazi Germany's crimes, women historians moved to heated debates centred on the roles and responsibilities of women in the Nazism in the 1980s and 1990s to now generate a far more diversified field of knowledge that does not carry the ideological burden and engages with hitherto ignored areas of research that have broken the mould of victim-perpetrator and explored the finer nuances of power play at various levels. This recent trend paints the picture on a larger canvas and in shades of grey. In this picture German women are also depicted as victims of aerial bombing, as rape victims of the marching Soviet and Allied forces towards the war's end and as victims of Nazi state when they were found to be romantically involved with the POWs. The behavioural patterns are seamlessly merged in what is called the history of everyday life in National Socialism. Historians of women, gender and sexuality have opened up an entire range of behaviour and situations peculiar to war and genocide, which are difficult to fit inside the watertight frames of victims and perpetrators. Birthe Kundrus and Vandana Joshi have made us aware of the agonies of German women who were incarcerated for being romantically involved with the POWs, during the Nazi regime because these relations were criminalised and later because their behaviour was found embarrassing in the post-war era of the normalisation of gender relations

(Kundrus, 2002; Joshi, 2011). Women historians have discovered 500 bordello barracks near military camps on the eastern front and the special comfort barracks running in the death camps. Birgit Beck, in her study of institutionalised mass rape tells us that far from being sex workers these women were arrested for petty crimes, black marketing or had offered themselves to secure safety and security for their family members (Beck, 2004). Atina Grossmann and Regina Mühlhäuser have investigated Soviet soldiers' mass rape of German women at the end of the war and mass rapes of Eastern women by the Germany army a distinct form of crime against female civilian populations in the war zone (Grossmann, 1997; Mühlhäuser, 1999). The edited volume by Dagmar Herzog, Brutality and Desire, has rewritten history of war and sexuality in many ways. While it challenges conventional military history by bringing gender dynamics into the history of soldiering and combat, it simultaneously explores a whole range of sexual behaviours ranging between sexual violence and sexual desire in the war zone. Here again, women are not treated just as victims and men as perpetrators, but as agents, who negotiate their survival and coexistence, fears and pleasures, desires and compulsions as victors and vanquished in the altered power relations.

Essential Readings

Bridenthal, R. and C. Koonz (1984), 'Beyond Kinder, Kirche, Küche' in R. Bridenthal, M. Kaplan, and A. Grossman (eds), *When Biology Became Destiny,* New York.This essay offers a feminist explanation for the rise of Nazism in Germany.

de Grand, Alexander (1976), 'Women under Italian Fascism', *The Historical Journal 19*, 4: 947–68 is one of the early conceptualisation of the women's question in Italian fascism.

de Grazia, Victoria (1992), *How Fascism Ruled Women,* California University Press. Grazia's work gives a critical and comprehensive survey of the era from a feminist viewpoint.

Evans, Richard (1977), *The Feminist Movement in Germany*, London: Sage Publications. It is a pioneering work of a British historian to write on the feminist movement in Germany with a ground-breaking explanation for the rise of Hitler.

Frevert, Ute (1988), *Women in German History,* Oxford: Berg. It is a general survey by a German feminist historian, which addresses some critical issues regarding women's participation in Nazi regime.

Koonz, Claudia (1977), 'Mothers in the Fatherland' in Renate Bridenthal and C. Koonz (eds), *Becoming Visible. Women in European History,* Boston.

Koonz, Claudia (1987), *Mothers in the Fatherland: Women, the Family and Nazi Politics,* New York.

Mason, Tim (1976), 'Women in Nazi Germany', *History Workshop Journal*: 74–113.
Pine, Lisa (1997), *Nazi Family Policy, 1933–45*, Oxford: Berg.
Stephenson, Jill (1981), *The Nazi Organisation of Women*, London.
Stibbe, Matthew (2003), *Women in the Third Reich*, London: Arnold, is a synthetic account on the subject.
Williams, Parry (2010), *Women in Twentieth Century Italy*, Hampshire: Palgrave. This broad and synthetic survey gives us the most updated and insightful account of women in Italian fascism.

Further Readings

Works dealing with specific aspects of women in Nazi Germany:

Allen, Ann Taylor (2008), *Women in Twentieth Century Europe*, Basingstoke: Palgrave.

Burleigh, Michael and Wolfgang, Wippermann (1991), *The Racial State*, Cambridge: Cambridge University Press, places race at the centre stage in understanding the real nature of Nazi state and has a special chapter on women.

Evans, Richard J (1976), 'German Women and the Triumph of Hitler', *Journal of Modern History 48*, 1: 123–75.

Fest, Joachim (1963), *The Face of the Third Reich*, Munich.

Harvey, Elizabeth (2003), *Women and the Nazi East. Agents and Witnesses of Germanisation*, London, highlights the role of German women engaged in the civilising mission in occupied territories.

Hitler, Adolf (1962), *Mein Kampf*, Boston, Hitler's autobiography.

Joshi, Vandana (2003), *Gender and Power in the Third Reich: Female Denouncers and the Gestapo 1933–45*, Basingstoke: Palgrave. This work dwells on a unique aspect of popular collaboration, namely, denunciatory practices in everyday life, and the role ordinary women played in private and semi-public spaces in the persecution of fellow citizens by the Gestapo.

Rauschning, H. (1939), *Hitler Speaks*, London.

Shirer, William (1970), *Berlin Diary*, London, an American journalist's account of Berlin during Nazi Germany.

The following works deal with intertwined aspects of maternalism, welfare politics, illegitimacy, and race:

Allen, Ann Taylor (1993), 'Maternalism in German Feminist Movements', *Journal of Women's History* 5, 2: 101.

Herzog, Dagmar (1998), '"Pleasure, Sex, and Politics Belong Together": Post-Holocaust Memory and the Sexual Revolution in West Germany', *Critical Inquiry 24*, Winter: 393–444.

Joshi, Vandana, 'Maternalism, Race, Class and Citizenship: Aspects of Illegitimate Motherhood in Nazi Germany', *Journal of Contemporary History,* 46, 4: 832–53.

Kundrus, Birthe (2002), 'Forbidden Company: Romantic Relationships between Germans and Foreigners', *Journal of the History of Sexuality*, 2(1–2): 201–12.

Müller, Robert (1994), 'The State of Women's Welfare in European Welfare States', *Social History* 19, 3: 385–93.

Historiographical debate:

Beck, Birgit (2004), *Wehrmacht und sexuelle Gewalt. Sexualverbrechen vor deutschen Militärgerichten 1939–1945*, Paderborn: Schöningh.

Grossmann, Atina (1997), 'A Question of Silence?', in Robert Müller (ed.), *West Germany under Construction*, Ann Arbor: University of Michigan Press.

Herzog, Dagmar (2009), Brutality and Desire: *War and Sexuality in Europe's Twentieth Century*, Hampshire: Palgrave.

Herzog, Dagmar (2003), 'Desperately Seeking Normality: Sex and Marriage in the Wake of the War', in Richard Bessel and Dirk Schumann (eds), *Life after Death: Approaches to a Social and Cultural History of Europe during the 1940s and 1950s,* Cambridge: 161–92, for an excellent survey and evaluation of post-war literature.

von Saldern, Adelheid (1994), 'Victims or Perperators? Controversies about the Role of Women in the Nazi State', David F. Crew (ed.), *Nazism and German Society 1933–45,* London: 141–65, for the English-speaking readers to have a glimpse of the issues at stake.

Books and essays related to the women historians' dispute:

There is a host of literature on this subject, including a debate between Koonz, Claudia and Gisela Bock (1989) which was launched in the pages of *Geshichte und Gesellschaft 15:* 563–79; (1992) *18*: 392–99, 400–04. The debate resurfaced in Gravenhorst, Lerke and Carmen Tatschmurat (eds), *Töchter Fragen NS Frauengeschichte* (1990), Freiburg: Kore.

Brockhaus, Gudrun (1991), 'Opfer, Täterinnen, Mitbeteiligte', in Lerke Gravenhorst und Karmen Tatschmurat (eds), *Töchter Fragen NS Frauengeschichte,* Freiburg.

Ebbinghaus, Angelika (ed.), (1987), *Opfer und Täterinnen. Frauenbiographien des Nationalsozialismus,* Noerdlingen: Franz Greno.

Gravenhorst, Lerke (1990), 'Nehmen wir Nationalsozialismus und Auschwitz ausreichend als unser negatives Eigentum in Anspruch?' in Lerke Gravenhorst and Carmen Tatschmurat (eds), *Töchter Fragen NS Frauengeschichte*: 17–37.

Haug, Frigga (1982), 'Opfer oder Täter? Über das Verhalten von Frauen', in Frigga Haug (ed.), *Opfer oder Täter?* Discussion, Argument SH 46: 4–12, Berlin.

Lück, Margret (1979), *Die Frau im Männerstadt: Die gesellschaftliche Stellung der Frau im nationalsozialismus*, Frankfurt a. Main: Peter Lang.

Mitscherlich, Margarete (1985), *Die Friedfertige Frau,* Frankfurt: Fischer.

Schmidt, Dorothea (1987), 'Die Peinliche Verwandtschaften - Frauenforschung zum Nationalsozialismus', Heide Gerstenberger and Dorothea Schmidt (hrsg.), *Normalität und Normalisierung,* Münster: 50–65.

Similar ideas are expressed by Rommelspacher, Birgit (1994), 'Das Selbstverständnis des weißen Feminismus und Antisemitismus bei Frauen' in Margrit Brückner and Birgit Meyer (eds) *Die Sichtbare Frau—Die Aneignung der Gesellschaftlichen Räume,* Freiburg.

Thürmer-Rohr, Christina (1987), *Vagabundinnen, Feministische Essays,* Berlin.

Windaus-Walser, Karin (1988), 'Gnade der Weiblichen Geburt', in *Feministische Studien*, Jg. 6.

Books in German that have been used in the chapter:

Bock, Gisela (1986), *ZwangsSterilisation im Nationalsozialismus. Studien zur Rassenpolitik und Frauenpolitik,* Opladen: Westdeutscher Verlag.

Bremme, Gabrielle (1956), *Die Politische Rolle der Frau in Deutschland*, Goettingen.

Czarnowski, Gabriele (1991), *Das Kontrollierte Paar. Ehe und Sexualpolitik im Nationalsozialismus*, Weinheim: Deutscher Studien Verlag, is instructive on how eugenics and racial health 'permeated the institution of marriage'.

Falter, Jurgen (1984), 'Die Wähler der NSDAP, 1928–1933', in Wolfgang Michalka ed. *Die Nationalsozialistische Machtergreifung*, Paderson.

Mühlhäuser, Regina (1999), 'Massenvergewaltigung', in Veronika Aegeter et.al. (ed.), *Geschlect hat Methode*, Zürich: Chronos.

Representative works describing these discriminatory measures are: Kuhn, Annette and Valentina Rothe (1982), *Frauen im Deutschen Faschismus*, 1 and 2.

Schmidt, Maruta and Gabi Dietz (1983), *Frauen unterm hacken Kreutz*. Berlin.

Thalmann, Rita (1984), *Frausein im Dritten Reich,* München, 94–104.

Wiggerhaus, Renate (1984), *Frauen unterm Nationalsozialismus,* Wuppertal, 5.

4 Race and Nation: An Intellectual History

—*Eric D. Weitz*

On December 10, 1948, the United Nations General Assembly approved the Universal Declaration of Human Rights. It was a great achievement that extended and deepened the venerable democratic principles espoused by the American and French Revolutions. The approval had come after months of difficult negotiations spearheaded by Eleanor Roosevelt. However, the delegates apparently had very few disputes when it came to defining the categories that constitute the human population. After stating in the lead article that '[a]ll human beings are born free and equal in dignity and rights', Article 2 of the document went on to declare, 'Everyone is entitled to all the rights and freedoms set forth in this Declaration, without distinction of any kind, such as race, colour, sex, language, religion, political or other opinion, national or social origin, property, birth or other status.' Article 16 declared that everyone has a right to a nationality. Article 26 mandated that everyone has the right to education, which should 'promote understanding, tolerance and friendship among all nations, racial or religious groups.'[1]

How is it that the categories of 'race' and 'nation' appeared so self-evident, so natural to the delegates, that they required no further definition and hardly any negotiations about their meanings?[2]

Just a few years later, in 1955, and just a short walk from the UN building, the Museum of Modern Art (MoMA) displayed in its galleries *The Family of Man.* It would become the most famous photographic exhibition of the twentieth century. After its initial five-month run in New York City, *The Family of Man* toured the world for eight years. It appeared in 37 countries on six continents and was seen by over nine million people. The exhibition catalogue has been published in scores of languages and remains a popular item to this day. The brainchild of Edward Steichen, the famed photographer and onetime director of the Department of Photography at MoMA, the exhibition contained 503 photographs, which he had culled from over 10,000 images that had been submitted by amateurs and professionals from around the world. In Steichen's words, the exhibit 'was conceived as a mirror of the universal elements and emotions in the everydayness of life—as a mirror of the essential oneness of mankind throughout the world.'[3] Yet the power of the still image is such that the stunning photographs seem also to capture a certain timeless, unchanging quality of the people on display, as if they were the very embodiment of the distinct nations and races that make up the 'essential oneness' of the human family. A small caption identifies the country of each photograph, fixing the notion of distinct nations in the mind of the viewer.

The Family of Man is a testament to the ideas of peace and human rights espoused by the UN in its Universal Declaration of Human Rights. Yet how is it that *The Family of Man* also assumed the division of humanity into races and nations with a certain fixed and timeless quality to them? And how is it that the categories that could be celebrated as representing the wonderful diversity of humanity were the very same categories through which states organized the most extreme violations of human rights, namely, genocides?

The categories race and nation are not, in fact, self-evident; they are not natural, timeless ways of understanding human difference and of organizing political and social systems. The word 'race' dates only from the late fourteenth century and is of either Latin or Arabic derivation; its usage first became prevalent in the sixteenth century.[4] 'Nation', rooted in the Latin *natio*, is a word with a much longer but also very diverse lineage. Like the Greek *ethnos* and *genos*, it simply meant a group of people, and writers from the ancient to the early modern world used it to describe all sorts of collectives: a kinship group, people with similar customs, the subjects of a particular state, or those with a common social function like students or even bonded labourers. Well into the Middle Ages, 'nation' was often used pejoratively to refer to foreigners.[5] However, in the modern period, the term has undergone such a profound transformation by becoming tightly bound to politics—to the form of the nation-state—that it has only a limited and restricted association with its earlier meanings.

Race and nation, far from timeless concerns, represent modern ways of understanding and organizing human difference. Ancient chroniclers' were, of course, well aware of the great diversity of human life. Through the encounter with others, they sought to define better the particularity—and the higher moral and cultural standing—of their own people.[6] They often wrote and acted with enormous condescension and venom toward those outside their own group. In his *Histories*, written in the fifth century B.C.E., the historian Herodotus marked out the chasm that lay between the civilized Greeks and their barbarian neighbours by depicting, for example, the brutal customs of the Scythians, who lived as nomads and decorated their horses with the scalps of their victims.[7] In the Hebrew Bible, the Israelites' status as a chosen people gives them license utterly to destroy their opponents. After the walls of Jericho collapsed, the Israelites under Joshua's command 'devoted to destruction by the edge of the sword all in the city, both men and women, young and old, oxen, sheep, and donkeys… They burned down the city, and everything in it.'[8] And so it goes with the other cities Joshua conquered—the Israelites 'destroy' or 'slaughter' everyone and everything in their path.[9] They humiliated rival kings by hanging their dead bodies for a day before unceremoniously dumping them into caves or covering them with rocks.[10]

But for all their intense hostilities toward outsiders, the Greeks and the Israelites did not think in terms of race, of fixed and immutable characteristics of a people, or of nation in its modern political sense. Neither Herodotus nor the anonymous authors of the Hebrew Bible ever imagined that in the lived world, all people of a particular group had to be politically unified with their own state. In the Bible's recounting, it took centuries of Jewish existence before the Israelites got a king and a state, and God himself was disappointed at their desire for political organization.[11] For a chosen people, the only true covenant was with God. The unified Kingdom of Israel lasted less than 100 years, and the prophets who followed its division called not so much for the restoration of the political unity of the people as for their adherence to God's law. As for the Greeks, their political world was one of many city-states, with no sense that Greeks could or should live all together within a single political system. They warred against one another as much as they came together in alliances against external enemies like the Persians. When Alexander created a Hellenistic Empire in the fourth century B.C.E., it was, like all premodern empires, a vast multi-ethnic creation, and its rulers never imagined that all the subjects had to be of the same ethnicity or religion.

Nor was membership in a particular group completely closed and defined only by lineage, as the proponents of modern race thinking argued. To be sure, in the Bible the Lord's covenant is granted to a specific group, the children of Israel. But membership in the chosen people lay open to whoever accepted the covenant and Yahweh's commandments;

it was not restricted to those who could claim, however fancifully, 'blood' descent from the patriarchs. The Hebrew Bible recounts many instances of conversion and many allies, including those of quite different physical appearance from the Israelites. Kush (Ethiopia), a powerful nation, is counted among the friends of the Lord, Nubians among those who will eventually join in the covenant. In Psalms, Ethiopians are included 'among those who know me', and God 'records' and 'registers' them—that is, he enters them in the book of life as faithful worshipers.[12] Individual Kushites play honoured roles as a wife of Moses, a messenger to David, and an intercessor for Jeremiah.[13]

Christianity and Islam were even more open to those beyond the original community of believers, since both asserted the universal stature of their religions without identifying any particular people as chosen. Christians defined themselves from the outset as a community of salvation in Christ's body, not an ethnic, national, or racial group. As Saint Paul wrote to the Colossians: 'in that renewal there is no longer Greek and Jew, circumcised and uncircumcised, barbarian, Scythian, slave and free; but Christ is all and in all!'[14] The great expansion of Islam resulted at least in part from its openness to all those who accepted Allah as the sole and indivisible God and Muhammad as his messenger.

Greeks considered themselves the most elevated people of all because they emphasized reason without excluding the passions, holding the two in appropriate balance. They generally used an environmental—not a 'blood' or, in modern terms, racial—theory to explain the differences among people. Climate and terrain made some people fierce, others gentle, some wise, others savage, gave some a penchant for reason, others for the senses.[15] When people migrated from their area of origin, they, or at least their descendants, would adapt to the temperaments that prevailed in their adopted homeland. Herodotus related that when the Scythian traveller Anacharsis returned home after travels in Greece, he was killed because he had adopted Greek ways, and a similar fate awaited the Scythian king Syclas when his followers found him celebrating the rites of Dionysus.[16] Herodotus also described 240,000 Egyptian troops, left at guard posts unrelieved for three years, who decided to go over to the Ethiopians. 'The result of their living, there was that the Ethiopians learned Egyptian manners and became more civilized.'[17] Culture and customs could be adopted or abandoned, they were not 'natural' to the physical body, and nothing prevented the intermixing of groups. 'Barbarian' was not a racial but a political and cultural concept, a term of contempt for those who had not mastered reason and rhetoric.[18]

Medieval Europeans often depicted outsiders in the vilest terms, as shown by even a cursory reading of the Church's condemnations of heretics and its tracts against Muslims and Jews. In the twelfth century, for example, Christian theologians condemned the heretic Henry of Le Mans by describing him as an animal, a 'ravening wolf in sheep's clothing' and a 'malicious fox' who moved about stealthily and deceptively. They also charged Henry with an assortment of sexual transgressions, from patronizing prostitutes to adultery to homosexuality. The 'potent poison' of his speech supposedly 'penetrated... the inner organs' of his listeners.[19] From the medieval *Song of Roland* to Luther's sermon about the Turks, Europeans depicted Muslims in similar fashion and associated dark skin with sin and apostasy.[20] The fervent language, which made beasts out of humans and awakened the deepest sexual anxieties, was not terribly different from the way North American slave-holders depicted Africans and Nazis described Jews.

Some scholars profess to see these medieval European expressions as evidence for the emergence of a 'persecuting society' that then developed in a linear fashion to the modern world.[21] But overall the evidence for the medieval world is too mixed, the ruptures of the modern world too great, to permit any claim of continual development from medieval attitudes to modern race thinking and nationalism. Despite all its grotesque characterizations of 'the other', the medieval Church held to its theological view that all people could be saved; it even welcomed Ethiopian Christians who made their way to Italy in the early fifteenth century. And only the barest glimmers of the modern nation-state are evident in the medieval period.[22]

To locate die birth of modern conceptions of race and nation, we need to turn to the eighteenth century, when Europeans developed new ways of understanding difference and invented new forms of politics. The intellectual and political leaps of this century did not emerge suddenly. They were rooted in nearly three centuries of overseas travel and conquest, which revealed a world far more diverse than anything Europeans had previously imagined. In association with New World discoveries, they also established more cohesive and assertive states and, perhaps most fatefully, colonial societies in which the benighted status of slavery became associated, for the first time in human history, with people of one and only one skin colour. But before we explore the historical emergence of race and nation, some definitions are in order.

RACE, NATION AND ETHNICITY

Race and nation represent ways of classifying difference. The two categories have never been hermetically sealed off from one another; rather, the lines between them are fluid and permeable. Nonetheless, for the sake of analytical clarity, it is important to dissent angle them and to define the characteristics of each form of identity.[23] And they have to be defined in relation to a still more general term, 'ethnicity'.

The members of an ethnic group typically share a sense of commonality based on a myth of common origins (descent from Abraham in the case of the Israelites, from Hellen in later Greek accounts), a common language, and common customs. Ethnicity is the most open and permeable form of identity. Whatever the myth of common origins, outsiders are usually able to assimilate into the ethnic group by marriage and acculturation. Ethnic groups develop into nations when they become politicized and strive to create, or have created for them, a political order—the nation-state—whose institutions are seen to conform in some way to their ethnic identity, and whose boundaries are, ideally, contiguous with the group's territoriality.[24] In terms of acceptance of outsiders, nationality oscillates from fairly open to tightly closed forms. In the modern world, the states in which citizenship definitions are based upon political rights tend to be the most open (the United States, France); those that define citizenship by ethnicity tend to be the most closed (Germany, Romania).

Race is the hardest and most exclusive form of identity.[25] Race is present when a defined population group is seen to have particular characteristics that are indelible, immutable and transgenerational.[26] Race is fate; there is no escape from the characteristics that are said to be carried by every single member of the group, bar none. Races can 'degenerate' if they become 'defiled'; they can go on to still greater accomplishments if they become 'pure'. But the essential characteristics of each race are seen as immutable, and they are borne *in the blood* by every individual member of that race. While racial distinctions have most often been based on phenotype, race is not essentially about skin colour but about the assignment of indelible traits to particular groups. Hence ethnic groups, nationalities, and even social classes can be 'racialized' in particular historical moments and places.[27]

Unlike ethnicity, race always entails a hierarchical construction of difference. Racial movements and states understand their creation and defence of a racial order as the great historical task of making the political and social world conform to the reality of nature, with its fixed system of domination and subordination. While ethnicity is often self-defined—and this was Max Weber's classic, subjectivist definition of an ethnic group—racial categorizations are most often assigned to a group by an outside power, usually a state, though over time, the group may then develop its own racial consciousness.[28] Ethnicity or nationality by no means always or necessarily takes on racialized forms, but the possibilities are certainly present, all too easily present when modern states seek to limit the pool of citizens and strive actively to shape the very composition of society. Moreover, while biology provided the pseudo-scientific underpinnings for race thinking in its heyday, roughly from 1850 to 1945, race can also have a cultural basis. As the French theorist Etienne Balibar writes: '[B]iological or genetic naturalism is not the only means of naturalizing human behaviour and social affinities... *[C]ulture can also function like a nature*, and it can in particular function as a way of locking individuals and groups a priori into a genealogy, into a determination that is immutable and intangible in origin... [This perspective] *naturalizes not racial belonging but racial conduct*.'[29]

While ethnicity has existed since time immemorial, race and nation emerged together historically in the Western world from around 1700 onward.

NEW WORLDS AND NEW IDEAS

Slavery was a standard and accepted institution of human societies until the nineteenth century. But slavery in the Americas expanded so forcefully and became such a central element of New World societies because it was intrinsically bound up with the rise of a global system of commercial capitalism.[30] By the eighteenth century, the colonial powers had made slavery a condition only of Africans and their descendants, a historically unprecedented development in which the debased condition of slavery became linked to people of only one skin colour. The origins of 'racial slavery' are much debated by scholars, some of whom see its emergence as the result of long-standing and deep-seated European prejudices against blacks and the concomitant cultural prohibitions on enslaving whites and Native-Americans; others assert that traders and plantation owners simply found it more economical to enslave Africans.[31] Even if one accepts the former explanation, in the eighteenth century 'mere' prejudice gave way to a far more comprehensive way of articulating and legislating human difference, a perspective that would also underpin many of the genocides of the twentieth century. Race thinking, formulated in the complex interactions among Europeans, Native-Americans, and Africans, established a fixed hierarchy of difference rooted in the body. Race locked Africans into a position of eternal inferiority and also explained the middle ranking of Native-Americans and the superior position of Europeans on the racial scale.

Race was made as European thinkers pondered the meaning of slavery and the world of great diversity. It was also made in colonial societies, in the interactions 'on the ground' of Europeans, Native-Americans and Africans. The many sexual relations and even marriages across these lines and the 'mulatto' progeny that resulted confounded-dear lines of difference and became the flashpoints for establishing far more rigid boundaries designed carefully to demarcate groups from one another.[32] By attempting to place people in fixed categories, colonial legislation and social practices contributed decisively to the making of race. In the British colonies the matrilineal organization of Native-American societies and the relative power—economic, social and sexual—that Indian women possessed seemed a direct threat to the more fervently patriarchal organization of English social life.[33] Many settlers feared that their European-derived religion and culture would dissipate in the unstable conditions of the colonies. In the early years of colonization, many of the settlers had expected Indian women to become assimilated into British colonial society by adopting British mores. They even expected Indian women to change physically; over time, through their relations with white men, their skin tones would 'blanch', which would also signify transformed inner beings.

But in the course of the eighteenth century, ideas of fixed differences rooted in die body took hold as British settlers expanded their hold on the land. European men who engaged in long-term relationships with Indians or Africans were increasingly seen as endangering the entire colony.[34] A series of laws in the British colonies, starting with Virginia in 1691, banned marriages between white colonists and blacks or Indians and, in many cases, mulattoes as well. Additional law as in North Carolina slapped supplemental taxes on those who had intermarried prior to the legal ban on such unions. The virulent language of the laws reflected a new level of racialization, and the tones would reverberate into the twentieth century (as we shall see in subsequent chapters). The intent of the new legislation was to prevent the 'abominable Mixture and spurious Issue' that resulted from mixed unions.[35] As Kirsten Fischer writes:

> Laws against intermarriage helped define racial boundaries and contributed to the meaning of "race" itself. The 'expanding scope of the prohibition, which went from banning an "Indyan" spouse to outlawing marriage to someone with even one nonwhite grandparent, made race seem like a physically real and transferable substance, as if some essential "Indianness" coursed through blood lines in diminishing strength with every generation of added "whiteness." Only after three generations would such a mixture be so diluted as not to pose a significant threat of pollution to "white" blood. Marriage laws naturalized the idea that race inhered in the body as something substantive that was passed on to others.[36]

Older environmental and cultural understandings of difference—the kind of understanding that ancient Greeks and Hebrews had articulated—were overthrown with this newer conception that difference was rooted in the body itself and constituted a definable essence, for good or bad. This fatal move had to do with the colonists' perceived need to articulate their differences from—and superiority to—the Native-Americans they conquered and the Africans they enslaved. The higher moral and cultural status of Europeans was now seen to inhere in their very bodies, the lowly status of Indians and, especially, Africans in their darker-skinned bodies. In response, Native-Americans also began to transform their traditional understandings of difference into racialized ones, as did, ultimately, Africans and their descendants.[37] Racialization attempted to establish clear lines of difference among the three groups but also entailed a homogenizing process within each population.[38]

In this setting, 'virtue' and 'honour', especially of white women, became synonymous with monoracial sex and marriage. A whole set of limitations on slaves—their inability to control the status of their own children, restrictions on their movements, prohibitions on their carrying firearms and engaging in trade—further demarcated them from Europeans and Indians and solidified a racial caste system in the British colonies.[39] But perhaps more than anything else, the violence exercised against Africans defined the new reality of race and demonstrated, despite the continued existence of free black communities, the association of slavery and blackness. Over the course of the eighteenth century, the colonies regulated and limited the violence that could be exerted against white servants. In contrast, whites could enact virtually boundless violence against slaves. Since the atrocities were often visible on the bodies of slaves in the form of amputations or brandings, they served further to codify racial conceptions that rooted difference in the collective body of each group. Sexual violence—the liberties slave owners took with their female slaves, the legal right slave owners had to castrate male slaves who ventured to challenge their subordinate status—only intensified this trend. Rape and castration signified the ultimate physical and psychological power of the master, the utter dehumanization of his victims, but also his underlying, quaking fear.[40] As Fischer writes, 'the divergence in legally acceptable forms of violence reinforced the idea that the bodies of African Americans were innately different and inherently "black." Violence was a social practice, another performance of race that transformed official categories of race into a physical relationship.'[41]

In the modern world, then, the 'social death' of slavery, the complete dehumanization of slaves, became, for the first time, congruent with a population seen to possess a particular skin colour. Slaves in previous societies had been subject to all sorts of bodily exactions and tortures, had been disparaged and denigrated. But few slaves in complex civilizations had been so completely demeaned as those in the New World. As David Brion Davis writes, 'In no ancient society was the distinction between slave and freeman so sharply drawn as in America.'[42] If slavery, by the eighteenth century, had made an essentially homogenous 'black' race out of Africans of highly diverse ethnicities, it had also turned Europeans and Indians into races, since any individual categorization has to be part of a relational system.

In close connection with the creation of racial slavery, Europeans after 1500 strove to make sense of a world they now knew was much larger and much more variegated than they had ever imagined, and of a Christendom shattered by the Reformation into many competing groups. The effort to understand this new, exciting and troubling world unfolded in both political and scientific realms, fields of endeavour that were, in any case, not so sharply distinguished as in our own day.

According to Hannah Arendt in her classic work, *The Origins of Totalitarianism*, Thomas Hobbes was the theorist who first broke radically with the received understandings of politics that had dominated ancient and Western society for nearly two millennia.[43] By positing that humankind existed naturally in a state of war and all individuals sought to pursue their egotistical interests, Hobbes destroyed the classical political check on race thinking and nationalism, the non-racial, non-national distinction between virtue (or faith) and barbarism (or sin). Moreover, Hobbes contributed to the general secularization of European thought, a development that breached two powerful tenets of Christian thinking that, previously, had also served as a defence against race thinking. In Christian dogma, all human beings are imperfect; every individual embodies both sinful and divine characteristics. As Christian teachings weakened, an opening was created for a Manichaean perspective, one that 'externalized evil'.[44] Bangerous, sinful traits could be cast in toto onto other population groups, leaving—depending on the proclivities of the writer—Aryans or Nordics, English, French, or Germans, pristine and divine, the embodiment of strength, goodness and achievement. As the body of Christ waned as the symbol of community, the racialized body, radically segregated by skin colour, arose to take its place. This new symbol was rooted in the Christian spiritualization of the body but eliminated 'the Cliristological element'.[45] To the extent that the human body is, in Christian theology, ephemeral, it can never be seen as the ultimate determinant or symbol of moral or political value. But when secularization broke through that limit, the body was set free to become a symbol of a different sort: the racialized body now became the outer marker of inner worth, or of inner damnation.

The French philosopher Jean Bodin expressed such a perspective by arguing that human characteristics derive from nature, and the inner being is evident in outer, bodily forms. Men are formed not in politics but in nature.[46] Such an interpretation commingled easily with John Locke's emphasis on observation and Montesquieu's division of the human species into immutable groupings based on geography and climate. Unsurprisingly, Montesquieu praised the inhabitants of the north, the well-governed English and Scandinavians who had created liberty from its origins in the Germanic tribes. But Africans, he wrote, were beyond the pale: 'It is hardly to be believed that God, who is a wise Being, should place a soul, especially a good soul, in such a black ugly body. It is so natural to look upon colour as the criterion of human nature.' In these two brief sentences, Montesquieu made four significant moves in the direction of race thinking. He gave eternal characteristics to human groups based on skin colour; argued that physiognomy, outward appearance, expresses inner being; made one group, Africans, incapable of ever joining the circle of the elect; and 'naturalized' skin colour as a marker—'it is so *natural*', he wrote. Hence, the correct political order had to reflect particular racial properties.[47]

But a fully developed theory or race required a new science of humankind. This is what anthropology, an Enlightenment invention, provided. Enlightenment thinkers fervently sought to redefine the place of humankind in nature. Their critique of Christianity had undermined the primacy of religious dogma, setting human beings adrift in a sea of uncertainty. They had to be reanchored, and a desanctified, presumably scientific 'nature' provided the weight.[48] Moreover, travel accounts from Persia, India, the South Sea Islands and the west coast of Africa came to constitute a veritable genre in the eighteenth century, the stories of strange and exotic places and peoples very popular with an increasingly literate public. The great variety of cultures, languages and appearances had to be explained. Religion, philosophy, and science, anthropology preeminently, all joined the fray.

Through their penchant for careful observation, scientists had already begun to categorize the natural elements of the universe. The Swedish botanist Carolus Linnaeus in the eighteenth century rigorously, even maniacally, classified all sorts of plants, establishing a methodology and a general scientific attitude about the virtues of classification that prevail to the present day. Soon after Linnaeus, geologists began to classify rocks and started to understand how to read prehistory through sedimentary layers. From the determination to categorize all flora and fauna in the world it was but a short step to categorizing human beings in a similarly rigorous, supposedly scientific manner.

Linnaeus himself had made some rough categorizations of the human species. He identified the European as 'ingenious', the Asian as 'melancholy', and the African as 'crafty, lazy and careless'.[49] Other writers, less scientifically minded than Linnaeus, popularized the concept of race in historical and class terms. The Comte de Boulainvilliers defended the French nobility as a unified caste descended by blood from one of the Germanic tribes, the 'Francs'. They had conquered the 'Gaules', whose descendants now were the commoners of the realm, the myriad elements of the Third Estate. The two classes of France were not united under the banner of king or nation; they were distinct entities, divided by blood descent, and their only contact entailed the conquest and rule of the one over the other.[50]

But the key figure in the emergence of the new disciple of anthropology was Johann Friedrich Blumenbach (1752–1840), whose *On the Natural Variety of Mankind* insisted on both the unity of the human species and the diversity within it, a diversity that could be accounted for only through rigorous scientific observation.[51] His 'epoch-making catalogue of human races', in Peter Gay's words, included just five, each assigned to its own region of the globe—Caucasian, Mongolian, Ethiopian, American and Malay.[52] For the next 200 years, just about down to the present day, scientists would dispute the number and types, but not the effort to define and categorize races, Blumenbach's own collection of skeletons, the raw material of his scientific researches, would be rivalled only by the anthropologists of the nineteenth century who began to collect skulls and measure the cranium as a way of determining race-linked intelligence.[53]

At the same time, Enlightenment thinkers pondered the diverse origins of humankind and located difference in the body, another strain of Enlightenment thought radically postulated equality among men. This is, of course, the Enlightenment that figured so prominently in the language of the American Declaration of Independence and the French Declaration of the Rights of Man and Citizen.

By creating republics, the American and French revolutionaries made the nation the critical locus of political rights. In so doing, they dramatically altered the received understanding of 'nation'. No longer was the term reserved for the aristocracy or other legally defined groups. Instead, the American and French revolutionaries fused the concepts of nation and people, as reflected in the stirring words that begin both the Declaration of Independence and the Declaration of the Rights of Man and Citizen. Both the Americans and the French understood their movements as world-historical in significance, as expressed in the many metaphors of illumination that accompanied their efforts—the beacon, the shining light, the city on the hill bathed in sunlight. More practically, the French, by conquering the continent, carried the idea of the nation all across Europe. As Eric Hobsbawm writes about the impact of the French Revolution on the meaning of the nation: 'whatever else a nation was, the element of citizenship and mass participation or choice was never absent from it... The equation, nation = state = people... also implied a multiplicity of nation-states so constituted.'[54]

Yet from the outset the meaning of the nation was laden with tension. As numerous feminist scholars have argued, the concept of equality was in fact highly gendered. The French Revolution opened up possibilities for imagining gender equality, as in Olympia de Gouges's Declaration of the Rights of Woman, penned just a few years after the Declaration of the Rights of Man and Citizen. Yet none of the revolutionaries was willing to go so far as to institute the equality of the sexes in law. In fact, as Joan Landes has argued, the French Revolution invested the concept of citizenship with qualities deemed to inhere only in men, like rationality and eloquence, and thereby inscribed a much more rigid division of the sexes that presumed the subordination of women.[55] Furthermore, citizenship was also limited to men of property, in important ways, the unpropertied were placed in a category with women, both considered dependents and therefore incapable of acquiring the independence and rationality upon which a republic had to rest.

Most important for the topic of this book, both revolutions articulated the nation not only in terms of gendered citizenship, but also as an ethnic and racial community. To be sure, the linkage of political rights with the sovereignty of the nation marked an enormous advance in democratic practices. The principles of both revolutions continue to resonate around the globe. Yet both revolutions oscillated between understandings of the nation 'as a political community bound by citizenship and as an ethnic or racial community bound by language and descent.'[56] Slaves were denied any rights by the framers of the American Constitution. The reason for this blatant violation of the Enlightenment universalism that underlay the hallowed principles of democracy and the self-creation of a political community had to be located in the body, in the supposedly deficient racial constitution of African-descended populations. Thomas Jefferson, slave owner and Enlightenment thinker, wrestled with this problem his entire life, giving it various turns. Ultimately, his understanding of the irreducible and incommensurable difference between black and white led the author of the Declaration of Independence to articulate a racial definition of the nation in conjunction with his radical republicanism.[57] In *The Federalist Papers*, John Jay articulated well the veil of deception composed of race when he wrote that 'Providence has been pleased to give this one connected country to one united people—a people descended from the same ancestors, speaking the same language, professing the same religion, attached to the same principles of government, very similar in their manners and customs.'[58] For Jay as for so many others, the nation was constituted not just in the political terms of republican citizenship but in terms of race as well, a tendency that burgeoned in the succeeding decades.[59]

'The French revolutionaries, under pressure from slave revolts in the Caribbean, ultimately granted equality to free people of colour and then abolished slavery. But in the long, tortuous discussions on these issues, many revolutionaries advocated an identity for France that was explicitly white and European.[60] Caribbean mulattoes and their supporters in the National Assembly and Convention defended the claim for equality precisely on the ground that the mulattoes were of partly white ancestry. On a less severe note, the attempt to impose linguistic uniformity on a heterogeneous population was also articulated in ethnic and racial terms, since those who resisted standard French came to be seen as 'foreign'. For the French revolutionaries, the nation was never only a political community, the realization of the Rousseauian myth of the social contract.

Indeed, William H. Sewell, Jr., has shown how the abbé Sieyes, the paragon of republicanism, the author of *What Is the Third Estate?* adopted a virulent racialized language that mitigated the political constitution of the nation that his pamphlet so fervently promoted.[61] Sieyes inverted the racial ideology that had developed over the course of the eighteenth century in defence of aristocratic privilege. He endowed commoners with all the noble (and inheritable) traits, the aristocracy with all the nefarious (and inheritable) traits. In defining who precisely could be a member of the nation, Sieyes deployed two key ideas—social utility and biological health—that we shall see deployed in each of the subsequent cases of genocide. Social utility became, perhaps, the most ubiquitous language of modernity, one used by liberals, socialists, communists, fascists and nationalists generally, often with a racial tenor. To Sieyes, the members of the aristocracy could never be members of the nation because they performed no socially useful acts. They did not *produce* but lived a life of leisure off the labours of others. The nobility, he claimed, 'is not part of our society at all; it may be a burden for the nation, but it cannot be a part of it.'[62] The nobility was even dangerous to the health of the nation. 'The nobility constitutes a "horrible parasite eating the living flesh of an unfortunate man"; nobles are "vegetable parasites which can only live on the sap of the plants that they impoverish and blight."'[63] Were nobles to be included, the social body of the nation would be completely sapped of its vitality. Sieyes writes:

> Do not ask what is the appropriate place for a privileged class in the social order, it is like deciding on the appropriate place in the body of a sick man for a malignant tumor that torments him and drains his strength. It must be *neutralized*. The health and the order of the organs must be restored, so as to prevent the formation of noxious combinations that vitiate the essential principles of life itself.[64]

This was a language that would reverberate through the decades as race thinking became ever more prevalent in the West, ever more firmly grounded through the proliferation of the nation-state and the rise of the biological sciences.

This 'slippage' from, the nation as a political community to the nation as a racial community became more prevalent when culture, not political rights, was made the defining element in the formation of the nation—an intellectual move accomplished largely by German theorists. Certainly, it is easy to understand why intellectuals in central Europe, devoid of a nation-state, claimed to find the nation in language, culture, and race, while the French, who had something akin to a single state going back centuries, could formulate a political concept of the nation. Johann Gottlieb Fichte and Johann Gottfried von Herder, two of the key figures in the formulation of a cultural concept of the nation, pursued problems set out by Immanuel Kant but focused more clearly on the relation of the individual to the collective. As an individual 'grew into' freedom (in a Kantian sense), moved from the childhood of ignorance and bondage to the adulthood of self-knowledge and freedom, so the political form of the nation-state grew from—and remained organically linked to—the original manifestations of being in language and culture. And if, as Kant argued, there were preexisting mental categories like time and space that made possible the individual's journey of self-discovery, similarly the pre-existing categories of human society were nations or races, timeless, eternal entities that underpinned the journey to collective self-consciousness and self-rule. Freedom is the self-determining nation, and, as Fichte also argued, consists of the individual's recognizing his indivisible connection to the totality. To reach the stage of autonomy and freedom that was its grand destiny, the nation, like the individual, had to struggle; it needed a severe countenance, an aesthetic temperament designed to conquer freedom as one climbs a mountain.[65]

Neither Kant nor Herder nor Fichte ever denied the essential unity of the human species, and Herder specifically rejected the terminology of race.[66] But the problem that preoccupied them, the more telling reality, was the diversity of human beings, a diversity rooted in nature, in God's creation, expressed first in language, then culture, then in political guise through the state. Herder and Fichte wrote about people and nations. But by defining a people as a closed community whose ties to one another were primordial—based in language and culture—the concepts they developed and the language they deployed slid easily into racial categories. Ernst Moritz Arndt, for example, claimed in 1815: 'The Germans have not been bastardized by foreign peoples. They have not become mulatto… The fortunate Germans are a genuine *[ursprüng-liches]* people.'[67] With these kinds of comments, Arndt and others of his contemporaries virtually dissolved the distinction between nation and race, a process we shall see at work in the genocides of the twentieth century.

FROM ROMANTICISM TO RACE SCIENCE

By the turn into the nineteenth century in the West, race and nation had become established, though not necessarily predominant, ways of understanding human difference. New World slavery and more cohesive states; the writings of Hobbes, Linnaeus and Blumenbach; the eruptions of the great revolutions of the late eighteenth century—all these trends contributed to the creation of new systems of classification that placed people in the categories of race and nation. Yet religion, village and empire still framed the lives of so many people and, in various places, they coexisted—sometimes easily, sometimes not—with the more modern forms of race and nation. But over the course of the nineteenth century, new political and intellectual developments would make race and nation, along with gender, the most prevalent and powerful forms of articulating the differences among people and of organizing political and social systems.

In the early nineteenth century, those who provided a cultural definition of the nation also helped create the aesthetic style of romanticism. The romantic hero, noble or demonic, imposed his will on the canvas, the battlefield, or the state. But the romantic hero of the early nineteenth century, triumphing over all adversity, was not an isolated individual. He drew his powers and his creativity from the nation as people. Without that wellspring, he was nothing, a weak being adrift in a void.

Like Kant's self-articulating individual becoming the self-articulating nation, so race thinking and nationalism absorbed the romantic notion of heroic creativity, of intense struggle, of a life of heightened feelings and grand achievements, a life that disparages the mundane. And the romantic hero as symbol of the race or nation was evident in physicality, the powerful presence of a muscular masculinity engaged in battle, politics, or the arts, or, occasionally, the fertile mother of the nation. He was Goethe's creative genius, Byron's Napoleon, Géricault's hussar, and Delacroix's defeated but still heroic Greek fighters at Chios. Romantics venerated the outer, male body as the sign of inner worth and, often, as the symbol for an entire people increasingly understood in a racialized fashion.[68]

The romantic hero, transferred from the individual to the collective, was also given a history in the first half of the nineteenth century.[69] These were histories of conquest and of freedom, of liberties enshrined in Germanic judicial practices and land tenure of old, of freeborn Englishmen, of valiant peasants. The lead actors in the script varied with the location of the scriptwriter: they were Saxons or Franks, Celts or Lombards. Invariably, they represented freedom and greatness; they were 'organic', attached to the soil rather than to the mechanistic, degenerate city. Giving flesh and bones to Herder's theories, the authors identified original languages as the true expression of the *Volk*—literally a 'people', but often written or spoken with mystical connotations. Out of histories of language, landholding, and governance emerged such constructions as 'Anglo-Saxons' or 'Semites' as distinctive racial types. In an often mystical fashion, race, transmitted through blood descent, remained organically entwined with land and language, which gave to each group its particular characteristics. In these accounts, the state was the ultimate expression of the racial characteristics of the *Volk*, almost an epiphenomenon built atop language, culture, and soil.

The search in the eighteenth and nineteenth centuries for the histories of peoples ran parallel with the search for the origins of the species. In fact, the term 'ethnology' was coined in 1839 to describe this combined enterprise of the natural and human sciences.[70] While philologists studied languages and philosophers and historians pored over legal codes, naturalists examined skeletons, animal and human, anatomists exhumed corpses, and geologists explored sedimentary layers. The Aryan myth emerged in the context of this search for biological and historical origins, the positing of human races, and the romantic inclination toward the heroic and the exotic. Like many myths, it carried grains of truth, in this case, in the philological investigations that identified Indo-European languages as having common roots in

Sanskrit. Friedrich Schlegel in 1808 drew many of the diverse elements together in his *Concerning the Language and Wisdom of the Indians*. The roots of classical Mediterranean culture, and its northern European successor, were located in the Indian subcontinent, from where the noble Aryans with their 'organic' language, one uniquely suited to higher thoughts and aesthetic beauty, had migrated. In this mythology, the northern forests debased, darker skinned people. Language thus expressed inner being; in a sense, language was not learned but transmitted by blood descent. From its beginnings in linguistic studies, the Aryan myth would prove long-lasting, inspiring even Nazi quests to Tibet in search of Aryan origins.

Amid this fervent search for the origins and histories of humankind, two key figures loom at mid-century, one a towering, presence even today, the other long forgotten except by scholars. Charles Darwin published in 1859 *The Origin of Species*, and the theory of evolution he postulated, with shattering effects, remains the most profound and forceful explanation for the development of humankind. The Arthur Comte de Gobineau published from 1853 to 1855 his *Essay on the Inequality of the Human Races*. Not much read by contemporaries, it was rediscovered toward the end of the century. Gobineau's *Essay*, the first fully developed theory of race, was a brazen pronouncement that, like Marx and Engels's *Communist Manifesto*, published just a few years before, provided anthropology and a history of the human species.

Gobineau was born on Bastille Day, the anniversary of the revolution he so despised, in 1816. His family background was bourgeois and noble, his career as journalist and government official mediocre, His horror at the perceived decline of France, its ruin by revolution, its supposed domination by hordes of middling and low-level bankers, tradesmen and bureaucrats, was the common stuff of conservative thinking at the time. Gobineau's powerful intellectual invention was to explain this decline, indeed, to explain all of history, by the category of race. Gobineau brought together the strands of thinking of the preceding centuries that had hesitantly, incompletely, begun to explain human society in terms of race.

For Gobineau, the human species was divided into discrete races, each with defined intellectual and moral traits. After pages of verbose ramblings, he finally delivered to his readers his grand theory: '[T]he racial question overshadows all other problems of history,... it holds the key to them all, and... the inequality of the races from whose fusion a people is formed is enough to explain the whole course of its destiny.'[71] In Gobineau's view, races were by definition unequal, and the qualities of each, physiological and moral, were permanent, immutable and inescapable. Moreover, all civilizations decline, and the source of the decline is race mixing.[72]

For all the historical knowledge it revealed, Gobineau's *Essay* descended to a compendium of the most common prejudices. He identified just three races, black, yellow and white, in ascending order. Like all race theorists, Gobineau considered fine outer appearance a symbol of inner nobility. Charlemagne's 'tall and nobly proportioned figure', the 'intelligent regularity of Napoleon's features', and, strangest of all, 'the imposing majesty that exhales from the royal countenance of Louis XIV'—these rather startling examples of beauty were the signs of the glory of the French race.[74] People not of white (or perhaps French) blood may come close to, but will most certainly never attain, true beauty. 'As these races recede from the white type', he wrote, 'their features and limbs become incorrect in form; they acquire defects of proportion which, in the races that are completely foreign to us, end by producing an extreme ugliness.'[75] This inequality in beauty is 'rational, logical, permanent and indestructible'—that is, it is based on racial inequality.[76] The same is true for strength, courage, intellect and morality.

The *Essay on the Inequality of the Human Races* demonstrates just how easy, was the slippage between race and nation, it is often unclear whether Gobineau is writing about Europeans, white people, or, quite simply, the French. In this regard, his book was firmly in keeping with the common tendency of his day to use interchangeably the terms 'English race' and 'English nation' or with the ambiguities that were always present at the invocation of the German *Volk*, a term that simply means people but could connote the citizenry of a democratic polity, the members of the German cultural nation, or a group bound by kindred descent that stamped indelible characteristics upon its members.

Gobineau saw society threatened by race mixing and looked for a 'race of princes', the Aryans, to defend society, history itself, from the mob. But his work conveyed predominantly a tone of profound despair. Gobineau could see only race mixing and degeneration on the horizon, a world full of mediocrity, in which nations will constitute 'human herds', mournfully somnolent, 'benumbed in their nullity',[77]

And that is the extent of Gobineau's profundity, a thinker on the scale of his contemporaries Marx and Darwin he was not. A stylist worthy of his sometime mentor, Alexis de Tocqueville, he was not. But a synthesizer with one inventive thought, he was and he would be dutifully recognized by his successors as the first to perceive the profound 'truth' of race as the dominant, indeed exclusive, factor in the shaping of humankind.[78]

Darwin's contribution to our ways of understanding is so monumental that it almost defies description, in the initial version of *The Origin of Species* he did not use two of the most memorable locutions with which he is associated, 'evolution' and 'survival of the fittest'. His supporters often took his ideas down paths he was loath to follow. In particular, his entire system of thought demonstrated the mutability of species, a position often at variance with the advocates of race. Yet many of his formulations, especially in his later work *The Descent of Man* (1871), proved very congenial to race theorists, some of whom would claim—with at least some legitimacy—to be his intellectual descendants.[79]

Darwin, first of all, provided an explanation for the development of the species. All the varied attempts since the eighteenth century to give to humankind a natural rather than a sacred past had faltered or been incomplete. Now, at long last, humanity had found its compelling historian. But the story had not necessarily reached its culmination. Upon reading Darwin, people found it possible to envisage a further progression of human development. The French Revolution envisaged perfectibility through politics; Darwin posited advance through adaptation, and Darwinians would come to imagine purification through purges, an engineered process of weeding out unwanted traits and peoples to achieve a healthier, more accomplished race.

Moreover, 'Darwin's depiction of the process of human development as a struggle among various species in a harsh environment provided a scientific explanation for what many people considered a natural, eternal condition of human life. From a struggle among species it was but a simple step to argue that human society was characterized by struggle among races, who operated in a harsh world of scarce resources. The analogical argument between the natural and social worlds had a firm, scientific grounding: just as the species progressed through competition, so did human society. One's own group had to be ever vigilant, ever ready to engage the fight, whether for territory, markets, or sea-lanes.

Finally, the great popularization of Darwin's theory rested to a considerable degree on its law-like character. He had uncovered the hidden workings of nature, which, to many of his supporters, meant that he could also explain the social world. Every subsequent race theorist would base his claims, whether 'scientific' or 'mystical', on the nature that Darwin had depicted in *The Origin of Species*—whether or not they had read the work. Profound thinkers like Herbert Spencer and street-corner ideologues alike were drawn to the theory of natural selection because Darwin had articulated it as a simple but very powerful law. From that original law all sorts of subsidiary laws followed. For Spencer, the author of *Survival of the Fittest* and, arguably, Social Darwinism, these were, very importantly, laws of competition by which a 'purifying process [eliminated]... the sickly, the malformed, and the least fleet or powerful.'[80] State policies to protect the weak interfered with the laws of nature, an interference that would wreak social and political havoc and destroy the possibilities of continued progress. Those who occupied the lower rungs were there because they deserved to be. They were deficient intellectually, often morally as well. Such categorizations applied to the working classes and the poor, as well as to the 'lesser' races, who required the direction and tutelage of white Europeans.

Darwin and Gobineau were brilliant synthesizers, both of whom gathered together various strands of thought from the previous centuries and, with intellectual leaps, recast them into radically new systems. Darwin, clearly the more brilliant of the two, drew from Linnaeus's system of categorization, Blumenbach's anthropology, Charles Lyell's geological discoveries, and, of course, his own incisive observations, especially on his famed journey to the Galapagos Islands. For the first time science offered a compelling explanation for the diversity and movement of the natural world. Darwin provided the 'science' that many race thinkers adopted to make their case in a century enamoured of progress and technology.

Gobineau's pessimism might alone have consigned his book to obscurity, so out of tone was it with the mid-nineteenth-century belief in progress. Gobineau's tract is one long lament about race mixing as the source of the decline of civilization. He projected his own aristocratic frustrations onto the world. But by the turn into the twentieth century, his concern with decadence had many adherents. Gobineau needed, however, a more optimistic reading, one that turned his fundamental invention, race, not only into an epitaph, but also into a clarion call for action.

This Houston Stewart Chamberlain provided. English by birth, German by choice, he became an intimate of Richard Wagner's circle and then the composer's son-in-law. Like Gobineau's *Essay*, Chamberlain's *Foundations of the Nineteenth Century*, published in 1899, is a fundamental text of racist thought.[81] Chamberlain, less concerned with the science of race, postulated a mystical 'race-soul' possessed only by Germans, a constituent component of their blood. This race-soul made Germans moral, spiritual and creative, the signs of a special 'German Christianity'. 'In Chamberlain's hands, even Jesus became an Aryan hero. History was made, though by the inhabitants of northern

Europe.[82] Teutons were the ones who developed great ideas, produced magnificent art, created civilization. The Italians of the Renaissance were either Teutons or were saturated with Teutonic blood, whether Lombard, Gothic, or Frankish.[83] '[B]ut for the Teuton', Chamberlain wrote, 'everlasting night would have settled upon the world.' Only the birth of the Teuton has made possible the revival of Hellenistic and Roman culture.[84] With all the bombast and megalomania typical of race theorists, Chamberlain claimed that 'true history, the history which still controls the rhythm of our hearts and circulates in our veins, inspiring us to new hope and new creation, begins at the moment when the Teuton with his masterful hand lays his grip upon the legacy of antiquity.'[85]

The consciousness of being a member of a pure race endows a man, the Teuton in particular, with extraordinary powers. A man of 'pure origins' who is also gifted will tower above those who muddle around in the swamp of race chaos. From the purity of race he absorbs the life force that gives him the ability to achieve greatness in every field of endeavor—war, art, politics, science.[86] Chamberlain disparaged the tendency to make Jews scapegoats for all problems and claimed that Jewish influence was much exaggerated. Yet he also described Jews as materialistic, immoral and conniving, the very antitheses of Greco-Roman greatness embodied in the modern Teuton.[87] "The Indo-European, moved by ideal motives, opened the gates in friendship; the Jew rushed in like an enemy, stormed all positions and planted the flag of his, to us, alien nature.' [88] Yet the Jews were also a model, because they alone had maintained the purity of their blood and therefore possess 'physiognomy, and character'.[89] The Jews, in short, had proven the race principle.[90]

Chamberlain's mystical Aryan hero aroused the suspicions of those who were determined to found race thinking as a science. Chamberlain's verbose writing, grand historical claims and absurd assertions were the very antithesis of the scientific spirit. Scientific race thinkers looked to Darwin, Chamberlain to Wagner and his medieval Teutonic heroes. Indeed, Chamberlain's writing had something of the epic quality of a Wagnerian composition, though without any of the opera's grace and melody. Yet the science and the mysticism of race could also coexist quite easily.

In an era replete with memorable phrases and fluent coinages—survival of the fittest, blood and iron, cross of gold—the British statistician Francis Galton invented, in 1881, 'eugenics'. The word is not much used today—the Nazis made it a term of opprobrium. Yet in the last two decades of the nineteenth century and on into the twentieth, it was bandied about with ease in lecture halls and parliaments, newspaper columns and scientific journals. Learned societies were founded to promote eugenics, mass organizations to popularize it. The term denotes selective breeding for favoured characteristics, and the breeding out of those traits deemed dangerous. Scientists discussed the possibilities with the cool tones appropriate to their disciplines in the austere pages of journals like the *Archiv für Rassen- und Gesellschafts-Biologie'* (Journal for racial and social biology), in seminars and laboratories at the Francis Galton Laboratory for National Eugenics, in lectures to the British Eugenics Education Society and the German Racial Hygiene Society, all of them founded between 1904 and 1907. Just beneath their cool veneer lay a rough-hewn hysteria, the fear that the poor and ignorant were breeding at fantastic rates, while the 'better' classes practiced family limitation. The gene pool (admittedly, a term invented later) would be swamped by deleterious traits, leading to the decline of the race. In yet another memorable phrase, Theodore Roosevelt mused aloud about the dangers of 'race suicide'. With eugenics, race thinking reached an apex of sorts, a merger of anthropology, Darwinism and medicine—a fateful collusion termed by the Germans 'racial and social biology'.

Eugenicist thinking developed out of the great advance of biological and medical knowledge from the 1850s down to World War I.[91] Scientists made enormous strides in identifying the basic mechanisms of the human body. They discovered cell division, leading to the recognition of the cell as the basic organic unit of life, and isolated bacteria that caused virulent diseases, resulting in the triumph of the germ theory of disease.[92] The first real therapies for such scourges as typhoid and diphtheria quickly followed (though tuberculosis proved more difficult), as did extensive public health measures to clean up water supplies, remove waste and reduce overcrowding. Such advances contributed to a growing belief that science reigned supreme, and that society, a sick patient if there ever was one, needed the careful attention of the physician or scientist, who had it in his powers to cure the ills. From government ministers to socialist reformers, people increasingly thought of society as analogous to the body and the race: as a biological organism, whose health needed constant attention, whose vitality was continually in danger of being sapped by killer bacteria borne by the weaker members and by those of completely alien races.[93]

Karl Pearson, the leading British eugenicist after Galton, was a tireless campaigner for the cause. He was convinced that science alone provided the prescriptions that would forestall rampant degeneration and prepare the path for still greater progress of the race. The world that Pearson depicted was a fearful place. The unhealthy, the indigent, the lesser races bred at will, while the 'better' elements, the strong, industrious, and intelligent, limited family size or dissipated their 'stock' in endless luxuries and unhealthy liaisons. The weak, sickly and degenerate threatened to swamp the healthy. Pearson's world was also a combative place, its history defined by virile, masculine contests among the races for domination. The contest could be military; it was also scientific, cultural and economic. Only by expunging the 'lesser races' could the better races thrive: it was their right, indeed, their destiny, to dominate those beneath them, and if, in some fit of feminine sentimentality, the better races chose to renounce the struggle, to pursue a path of peace, they would inevitably degenerate. 'The biological factors', Pearson wrote, 'are dominant in the evolution of mankind; these, and these alone, can throw light on the rise and fall of nations, on racial progress and national degeneracy.'[94]

Yet modern sentiments kept alive the weak and degenerate. Science, the discoverer of nature, would now replace nature's own working, repair the damage that society had done by interfering with nature. 'Race-culture', Pearson wrote, 'will cope with the ills which arise when we suspend the full purifying force of natural selection.'[95] As for the 'lesser races', nothing at all could be done about them.

How many centuries, how many thousands of years, have the Kaffir or the Negro held large districts in Africa undisturbed by the, white man? Yet their intertribal struggles have not yet produced a civilization in the least comparable with the Aryan. Educate and nurture them as you will, I do not believe that you will succeed in modifying the stock. History shows me one way, and one way only, in which a high state of civilization has been produced, namely the struggle of race with race, and the survival of the physically and mentally fitter race.

And if one were to try to mix the races, the result would be utter disaster, the deterioration of the strong without the uplifting of the weak. Presciently and frightfully, Pearson maintained that 'every remedy which tends to separate them [the "unfit"] from the community, every segregation which reduces their chances of parentage, is worthy of consideration.'[97] He warned his countrymen that they were facing 'race suicide' as they watched 'the loss of our former racial stability and national stamina.'[98] But if eugenics became the foundation of state policy and private behaviour, then the future would be glorious indeed. A purified, powerful race would thrive and build an ever more prosperous, ever more creative, society. The Enlightenment belief in the perfectibility of humankind had a new foundation—in race science.

Pearson's German counterpart, Alfred Ploetz, was no less forthright in his calls for the placement of race at the centre of national policy.[99]

In the *Archiv für Rassen- und Gesellschaft-Biologie*, the journal that he founded in 1904, Ploetz argued that science had now proven the inextricable intertwining of body and spirit, physical and mental characteristics. 'All spiritual and intellectual *[geistige]* developments are tightly bound up with our physical development. This was an "iron law" from which no human powers can diverge.'[100] These developments are themselves inseparable from 'race', a grouping with similar life patterns, similar descent and similar reproduction. A biological race is nothing less than the 'maintenance of life in its entirety *[Erhaltungseinheit des Lebens]*' and the 'development of life in its entirety *[Entwicklungseinheit des Lebens]*'.[101] Morality, art and literature—these are the products of particular racial constitutions that are transmitted through the generations by heredity.

Ploetz, too, was keenly alive to the lurking dangers that threatened to dissipate the purity and quality of the inheritance matter that Aryans had passed on for generations. Race mixing, the protection of the feebleminded and the criminal, the limitation on family size practiced by the 'better' elements—these were the dangers that Ploetz and his collaborators repeatedly identified in their research, writings and lectures. Contributors to Ploetz's journal described a menagerie of well-endowed individuals, the finest elements of the race—lawyers, physicians, artists and scientists—who limited the number of their children or failed to reproduce altogether. Not rarely, they succumbed to a life of dissipation, their fine hereditary material destroyed by syphilis and gonorrhea.[102]

Like Pearson, many of the authors in the *Archiv für Rassen- und Gesellschafts-Biologie* advocated state policies to promote births among the better elements, to restrict births among those poorly endowed by inheritance. Should these measures not suffice, then more drastic ones, like compulsory sterilization of the unfit by castrations and ovariectomies, were required.[103] Progressive public health measures would round out the programme. Underlying these state policies was a general science of social biology ploetz proved positively inflationary in his advocacy of new, subsidiary disciplines. Along with 'race biology', there would be race anatomy, race physiology, race pathology, race hygiene.'[104] Race psychology and race sociology could not be far behind. Yet the presumed science of all this often degenerated into a collection of crass prejudices—the musical genius of Mozart and Beethoven rooted in their Aryan racial constitution, the formation of archery clubs as a means of reviving the vitality of the race.[105]

Ploetz also advocated an ethics of race that was derived from science.[106] The code mandated, especially for superior individuals, careful selection of one's partner and the couple's obligation to propagate. Racial ethics meant the promotion of state intervention in the very intimate realms of sexuality and reproduction to foster '*the widest possible dissemination of social virtues and the weeding out* [Ausjäte] *of persistent, debilitating characteristics* [dauernd Schwachen].'[107] Ominously, he wrote:

> The elimination of existing incurable diseases could occur only by extermination or expulsion *[Vernichtung oder Ausstoßung]*... The deficient and defective individuals *[fehlerhaften und defekten Individuen]* that still emerge could only be removed by extermination or expulsion.[108]

Ploetz had imagined the fateful move: extermination of those with unwanted traits.[109]

NATION, STATE AND EMPIRE

Far removed from the laboratories of London and Berlin, and a few decades earlier, the prince-bishop Petar Petrović. Njegoš of Montenegro had written *The Mountain Wreath* (1847). It is an epic poem set in the early eighteenth century, which memorializes a possibly apocryphal event, the slaying of Christian converts to Islam under Bishop Danilo, the Serbian Orthodox ruler of Montenegro. Njegoš writes glowingly of his own land and of the timeless, violent struggle of heroic Serbs against vicious Muslims. In that way, *The Mountain Wreath* connects with another myth, the defeat of Serbia by the Ottoman Turks in 1389 at Kosovo Polje, the Field of Blackbirds, located in contemporary Kosovo. In that story, the Serbian prince Lazar refuses to betray his people and dies a hero's death. In *The Mountain Wreath*, Njegoš depicts the... faithless Turk, with Koran! Behind him hordes of that accursed breed, that they might devastate the whole wide earth, as locusts pestilent lay waste the fields!... From out of Asia where they have their nest, this devil's brood doth gulp the nation's up.[110]

Just a few years later, the Italian conspirator and publicist Giuseppe Mazzini wrote 'Duties towards Your Country' (1854). It was a classic statement of liberalism that called on men to serve, first and foremost, the human family whose oneness derives from God. But God has also divided humanity into nations. Only the greed of governments and conquerors has prevented the realization of God's design—that each nation shall have its own state that extends to its natural geographic borders. When people act together, they will repair what kings and nobles have so unnaturally created. 'Natural divisions, and the spontaneous innate tendencies of the peoples, will take the place of the arbitrary divisions sanctioned by evil governments. The map of Europe will be re-drawn. The countries of the Peoples, defined by the vote of free men, will arise upon the ruins of the countries of kings and privileged castes, and between these countries harmony and fraternity will exist.'[111]

Njegoš and Mazzini represent the poles of nationalist thought in the nineteenth century, the one militant and exclusive, the other more humane and democratic. But both assumed it completely natural that a given state should be built upon an exclusive national group. Their sense of geography was necessarily expansionist, designed to include all Serbian or Italian speakers within the borders of the state. Njegoš provided a powerful story that bound—and continues to bind—the Serbian national idea to the Christian promise of redemption, but a redemption that can be achieved only through struggle and martyrdom against a foe that has been so vilified that he has lost any semblance of humanity. The epic poem also binds the national idea to a defined place, most immediately the prince-bishopric of Montenegro and, generally, all Serb-settled lands. An eighteenth-century event related in written form in the mid-nineteenth century, *The Mountain Wreath* became virtually the official poem of Serbian nationalism in the nineteenth and twentieth centuries. Mazzini was a secular nationalist yet believed that a world composed of nation-states would fulfil the divine plan; he offered a political version of Newton's clockmaker universe. Mazzini also wrote glowingly of mountains and river valleys, linking the national idea to die warm emotions aroused by natural beauty and a sense of place. He made the nation-state the aim of democratic politics and the vehicle of eternal peace and fraternity among peoples. Yet he could never figure out how a state defined by a particular nationality could also encompass people of different linguistic and ethnic backgrounds. If Njegoš had no qualms whatsoever about eliminating foreigners from lands claimed for Serbia, Mazzini simply ignored the problem. Both articulations of the nation were, necessarily, exclusive, even if Mazzini's was far more humane and democratic.

From west to east in Europe, not only in Serbia and Italy, the idea of the nation took hold in the course of the nineteenth century. All across the continent, nationalist movements propagated the idea that a distinctive people (or nation) should have its own state. The advocates of the nation researched the historical origins of their people, wrote or discovered epic poems, developed dictionaries and modernized languages. While they fostered the idea of the nation among many people, nation-states were made in the practical world of politics, and many different political ideologies intersected quite easily with nationalism. The coloration of the nation and nationalism was socialist, liberal or conservative, depending on time and place. The nation found concrete manifestation in the establishment of an independent Greece in the

1820s; in the carving out, later in the century, of other autonomous states in the Balkans, like Bulgaria and Serbia, that were formerly under Ottoman control; and in the creation of Italy and Germany in the 1860s and 1870s. In opposition to Mazzini's profound faith in popular action, many of these states were founded by modernizing elites whose political and social views were profoundly conservative, on by some combination of popular participation and elite direction. Conservatives recognized the power that could come from a population mobilized on behalf of the nation, and feared the consequences if liberals or socialists succeeded in becoming the spokesmen for the national cause. By establishing nation-states, the elites would be able to create, so they hoped, their own nationals, people whose understanding of the nation ran in suitably conservative paths. The nation aroused hopes of liberty and fraternity, but the nation-state was also a disciplining force, one that made nationals in the schools, the army, and the early welfare state pioneered by Germany and Britain. While much of the continent remained dominated by empires, by the turn into the twentieth century the nation had become a critical locus of identity for a great many people. And in the blendings and confusions so typical of the national form, its members were sometimes considered a political community, sometimes an ethnicity, and sometimes a race—or some combination of all three.

'I would conquer the stars if I could', said the British explorer and businessman, the imperialist par excellence, Cecil Rhodes.[112] He never quite realized his dream of a British Africa straight from the Cape to Egypt. Then again, the British Empire celebrated at Queen Victoria's Jubilee in 1897 was quite an accomplishment, the most vibrant expression of the Western drive to dominate the globe. Very quickly, in the last two decades of the nineteenth century, Europeans and North Americans divided most of the vast, remaining areas that had lain beyond their formal control. As with the discovery and conquest of the Americas, the motives were varied, from sheer economic greed to lofty impulses to uplift and Christianize other peoples. Certainly, the flurry to establish direct, formal control—in a word, to establish colonies—reflected a new, higher level of capitalist development and greater economic and strategic competition among the great powers. Once Belgium had staked out a claim in the Congo, and England had declared its predominant interests in Egypt, the 'structural logic' of the Western state system came into play: every other major European state, and soon the United States as well, felt compelled to aggrandize its own territory with colonies abroad. Not accidentally, imperialism and eugenics blossomed together. Eugenics provided an explanation for the domination of the 'lesser' races—they were 'by nature' inferior, hence could only exist to serve the well-being of those better endowed. At the same time, imperialism provided the intellectual material for eugenicism, the race-infused travel accounts, ethnographies, naturalist investigations, and poetry that demonstrated both fascination with and disparagement of other cultures and peoples.

Imperialism was a large, complex development, and the various imperial powers pursued different strategies of domination. But for all of its 'civilizing' missions, imperial domination was often carried out with unspeakable cruelties.[113] Like new world slaves, Africans especially bore the signs of race on their bodies. The Belgian depredations in the Congo constituted one of the worst cases and appalled many Europeans when the news travelled back home. In their headlong exploitation of the Congo's immense resources, the Belgians did not shy away from amputating limbs, flogging backs, executing villagers en masse and setting homes ablaze, all in the attempt to maintain their domination. The death toll ran into the millions. The situation was little better elsewhere on the continent. The Germans savagely repressed rebellions in Southwest and East Africa, carrying out one of the first genocides of the twentieth century against the Herero. All of these forms of repression were public acts—domination required public humiliation as well as direct violence. British conquerors forced indigenous leaders to crawl before them on all fours as they sat regally above them. They executed elders in front of their children and barred the 'colored' from the public spaces reserved for white Europeans and Americans.[114]

But for so many of its European practitioners, imperialism was also a sporting game. Winston Churchill reported from the Sudan in the 1890s for the *Morning Post.* He later described the Rattle of Omdurman, at which the British routed the Sudanese, as '[one] of those spectacular conflicts whose vivid and majestic splendour has done so much to invest war with glamour.' Britain's 'little wars', the colonial conquests, were 'only a sporting element in a splendid game'; those were 'light-hearted days' and 'everyone' (on the British side) who was about to participate in the battle 'was in the highest spirits and the best of tempers.'[115]

As Hannah Arendt understood, the actions of Europeans abroad could not be separated from politics at home. It is then, in the context of Gobineau's claim that history is defined by race, of Darwinism and Social Darwinism, of imperialism and eugenics, that anti-Semitism, that particularly deadly form of race thinking, first emerged. The term itself was coined in 1879 by Wilhelm Marr, a German whose life amounted to a catalogue of failures in journalism, business, politics and marriage. Marr drew upon the philological studies of the preceding 100 years that had first distinguished between Indo-European and Semitic languages.

However tainted the source, it is useful to follow Marr's invention and distinguish between anti-Semitism, with its clear racialist meanings, and the centuries-long Judeophobia of Christian society. One can scour the literature and find traces of a racialist conception of Jews in medieval Europe. The Spanish Inquisition, in its hunt for *conversos*, certainly came to define Jews as a racial group, whose Jewishness was constituted 'in the blood', not by a freely chosen lack of faith in Jesus. Bishops and priests used a language of vilification barely surpassed by the Nazis, and Jewish communities often endured the most brutal persecutions. Yet the overwhelming reality remains that the Universalist teaching of the Church prevented a racialist understanding of Jews. Race thinking in general and anti-Semitism in particular became possible only with the advance of secular society and Enlightenment thoughts, which proclaimed the formal equality of men and enabled Jews to move out of the confined spaces of the ghetto.[116] Except in Iberia, the path of conversion always remained open to Jews. Few took the path until the Enlightenment and the French Revolution fostered Jewish emancipation and created the dilemma of assimilation.

Initially, in the late eighteenth and early nineteenth centuries, assimilation was a problem only for Jews—the agony of deciding whether to convert to Christianity to remove the stigma of Jewishness and to enhance one' possibilities in a more mobile, but still largely Judeophobic, society. The advance of race thinking over the course of the nineteenth century made assimilation a problem for the general society, because now race thinkers cast Jewishness 'in the blood'. Jews became a constant, pulsing threat to the purity of the racial group, the 'hidden Jews' particularly dangerous because they steadily and secretively worked their degenerative impulses into the noble, upstanding, Aryan racial body.

The specific charges against Jews were hardly new. They drew upon long-standing Christian Judeophobic myths. Jews were accused of rituals in which they murdered Christian babies on Passover and used their blood in the making of matzos (the 'blood libel'). The 'wandering Jew', condemned to a rootless existence because he had helped in the crucifixion of Jesus, haunted the imagination of a world that placed great value on 'rootedness'—literally, to the soil and property; metaphorically, to a fixed and secure place in a world in which so much was in flux. Jews were accused of an unrelenting drive toward economic domination, of concern merely with material matters, of sexual licentiousness, particularly with Aryan girls and women. The language was virulent, as bad as, or worse than, that used about African slaves. But the bodily metaphors used in medieval society about Jews became even more dangerous when articulated in conjunction with the germ theory of disease and eugenics, now it was possible to imagine the 'therapies' that could deal with the 'diseased microbes' and the 'parasites' that sucked the life out of the healthy host. As ever, these virulent epithets are far more revealing about the accusers than about the accused. They betray the most deep-seated psychological anxieties—about sex; bodily pollution, whether through blood or semen; gender, with Jews often depicted as weak and grotesque, at times in a feminine manner, the diametric opposite of the noble and virile romantic-racial hero. To extirpate the Jews, and to remove or exterminate then would purify the Aryan race and open up unlimited vistas of happiness. In the anti-Semitic vision, racial warfare against the Jews would resolve not only all political and social problems, but also—though this went unspoken—the most profound psychological and sexual anxieties.

Yet from the outset a curious contradiction marked anti-Semitic thought. How could anyone truly fear the decrepit, bent-over creature that was invariably depicted as the Jew? A lurking, if grotesque, admiration is evident in the writings of Gobineau, Chamberlain and even Hitler, who saw in the decrepit Jew evidence that Jews had maintained their racial purity. The imagination of anti-Semites was boundless; the political will and techniques had to await the twentieth century.

CONCLUSION

Historians like to be attentive to the openness of the past. They strive to consider the variety of possibilities present at any given moment, the 'paths not taken' as well as those that were travelled. But the categories of race and nation became such powerful currents of the modern world, principles so fundamental to the organization of state and society and to the self-conception of so many people, that it is almost impossible to imagine our contemporary world without them. So many diverse strands—political, social, intellectual—went into their making, and they came to fulfilment in the twentieth century with the extension of the nationalities principle around the globe and the organization of 'overtly racist regimes' like those of the United States in the Jim Crow era, apartheid South Africa and Nazi Germany.[7]

The New World discoveries, the utter strangeness of the Americas and the revelations of the immense diversity of the world's population, resulted in vastly altered ways of understanding difference and of exercising domination. New World plantation owners did not invent slavery, which had existed in biblical times and in virtually all societies. But the scale of New World slavery and its association with one, phenotypically distinct group, black Africans, meant that New World slavery became an institution of a radically different order, to explain their degradation of this land with slavery, a land first thought to be a Garden of Eden, the fertile, life-giving 'nipple" of the earth, as Columhus called it, slaveholders and their apologists formulated an understanding of black skin as the mark of sin and submission, both seen as innate, inheritable characteristics.[118]

These views commingled with the great intellectual advances of the Scientific Revolution and the Enlightenment of the seventeenth and eighteenth centuries, which forged new ways of categorizing human beings. A culmination of sorts came with the emergence of anthropology: the definition of humankind's place in nature was the very raison d'être of this new discipline. To understand man-in-nature required developing a paradigm of order out of the diversity of humankind, a diversity ever more evident and expansive as Europeans continued their explorations of the globe. Theorists in the eighteenth and nineteenth centuries made that order hierarchical on a racial scale marked by gradations of inferiority and superiority. Nationalism, also postulated upon difference—often of a 'natural' kind based in language and an unchanging culture—lent added credence to anthropology.

In the course of the nineteenth century, national and racial thinkers further replaced the notion of community based on politics or religion with the idea of the unbreakable national or racial bonds among distinct peoples. Upon that basis physicians and scientists layered a new understanding of the human body and human evolution that seemed to confirm racial categorizations. Although Darwin's ideas were in eclipse among scientists by the turn into the twentieth century, his revolutionary theories had become immensely popular.[119] Race theorists argued by analogy, substituting races for species and turning all of human history into a struggle among races for the survival of the fittest. Through biology and medicine, race thinking infiltrated the professions and state bureaucracies. Race thinking rose from street politics and penny pamphlets to the highest echelons of society and was as much, perhaps even more, the province of the 'better' classes as it was of the popular classes.[120] In the racial-scientific agglomeration postulated by race theorists, inheritance determined all the essential characteristics of human beings. And the quality of inheritance rested not only on individuals and families, but also on the entire racial group to which they belonged.

Darwinism and then eugenics joined science and medicine to the Enlightenment sense of the perfectibility of humankind—even if Darwin himself posited only a non-teleological progression, not perfectibility.[121] From the mid-eighteenth century, the prescriptions for perfectibility were many and varied, ranging from the virtue of the French Revolution to Hegel's unfolding spirit to Marx's masses of proletarians mounting the barricades for socialism. Ploetz and Pearson gave a new dimension to such sentiments, one rooted in the popularization of Darwinism and medicine. As ever, the path to perfection was not easy; there were enemies along the way, and they had to be vanquished. To flee the contest was to free from history as nurture and the consequences could only be, at best, a kind of purgatory, a long stagnation in the languid world of racial imperfection. Imperialism, overtly organized around the domination of non-European peoples, lent credence to the popularized views of Darwinism and eugenics. Race thinking, around 1870 a history, mythology and anthropology of the human species, had become, by 1900, a science as well. More dangerously, science and medicine had begun to provide the ideas and techniques by which the population could be manipulated, purged of its ailing elements and refined to the lofty stage of pristine purity. Biology had developed techniques of immunization against harmful bacteria; it was now possible to imagine biological-political techniques for dealing with the harmful scourges of human society.

Certainly, not all adherents of the theory of natural selection were racists, and the pioneers of the bacteriological revolution were generally liberal minded. Thomas Huxley, so ardent a defender of Darwin's theory of evolution, was no less ardent an opponent of Social Darwinism. He argued vociferously for the autonomy of the ethical realm.[122] Franz Boas, for decades the dean of American anthropologists, challenged the notion of immutable racial traits, emphasizing, in opposition, the role of environment in the shaping of human cultures.

Nonetheless, by 1914 race thinking and nationalism had become pre-dominant and pervasive in the West. At all levels of society, many people believed that racial characteristics were hierarchical, inheritable and immutable, and that they entailed not only physical but moral and intellectual qualities as well. Many also took it for granted that at least among Europeans, nations should have their own states, and the regnant multinational empires—Ottoman, Habsburg and Russian—were considered relics, of the past that could not long last in the twentieth century.

The cataclysm of World War I only intensified the tendency to think in racial and national terms. The first total war in history required the full mobilization of all of society's resources, human and material, for the practice of violence. Total war required total victory; amid the massive death toll, a war of empires nation-states became a war of nation as race versus the racial enemies. According to George L. Mosse, propaganda attacks on the enemy in previous wars had only exceptionally involved complete, all-encompassing condemnations of a people.[123] But total war meant also the total dehumanization of the enemy in official propaganda, which lent a fateful tenor of racialization and brutalization to the conflict.[124]

Moreover, the post-war settlements enshrined the nationalities principle of the political map of Europe. In the American view so forcefully advocated by President Woodrow Wilson, only within a nation-state could democracy flourish. The Great Powers, then, produced a settlement that affirmed the rights of some self-proclaimed nations to establish their own states. Despite the platitudes of protection in the treaties, the very notion that states should be the exclusive representatives of particular nationalities presented grave problems for specific populations throughout central and eastern Europe. It is perhaps no surprise, then, that the situation of Jews deteriorated markedly all over the region—not just in Germany—in the 1920s and 1930s, because they were the consummate outsiders wherever the nationalities principle was affirmed.[125] Nor is it a surprise that the 1923 Treaty of Lausanne legitimated both the forced removal of some 800,000 ethnic Turks from an enlarged Greece and 1.2 million Greeks from their historic homelands in Anatolia, and, in effect, the genocide of Armenians by abandoning the Armenian state that had been recognized in the prior Treaty of Sèvres.[126] In light of these developments, it might not have appeared so strange to Soviet officials in the 1930s and 1940s that they should brutally remove from border areas entire populations whom they considered security threats, or to the Nazis that there was anything so amiss about organizing massive migrations of ethnic Germans into the Reich from all over central and eastern Europe as a corollary to the forced expulsions of Jews.

World War I had other effects that were decisively related to the subsequent escalation of genocides in the twentieth century. The war established a new model of a powerful interventionist state that tried to manage everything in sight, because only the state had the capacity to mobilize resources on the scale required by total war. Afterward, both Soviets and Nazis would look back with admiration upon the powerful World War I states, Imperial Germany in particular, which they then sought to replicate.

World War I also created aesthetics of violence that reverberated through the post-war period.[127] The massive death toll of the war made violence on such a large scale, almost normal and, to some, a necessary, even desirable way of shaping the future society and the character of the new man and new woman who would inhabit it. For every Erich Maria Remarque, the soldier-turned-pacifist author of *All Quiet on the Western Front*, for every

Wilfred Owen, the English poet who so powerfully depicted the brutality of warfare and the tragic waste of death, there were at least as many like Ernst Jünger and Gabriele D'Annunzio, the men who in their post-war writings continually returned to the theme of heroic combat, ennobling death, in his books *In Stahlgewittem* (Storm of steel), *Das Wäldchen 125* (Copse, p. 125), and many, many others, Jünger wrote glowingly of the machines of death, the tanks, cannons, guns and railroads that he naturalizes and aestheticizes, imparting an almost erotic sensibility to the practice of killing.[128] Large segments of the Left, long considered antiwar in its predominant sentiments, came to idealize political violence as the path to the future. Even the political and social centre, especially in Germany, but also elsewhere, become radicalized by the unprecedented scale of wartime killings and deprivations, a process that found expression in dreams of ever greater victory over a racialized enemy.

And out of the war came a series of revolutions, the most profound societal transformations that penetrate to the very core of individual and collective existence. The crises of World War I provided both Bolsheviks and Nazis with the opportunities to seize power. The Bolsheviks acceded to power in 1917, aided by the enormous popular discontent with the deprivations of war, which ultimately deprived the czarist system of all legitimacy. The Nazis came to power amid the immediate crisis of the Great Depression, but also because the Weimar Republic could never quite master the immense social, economic and political issues that the war had left in its wake. Without World War I, it is hard to imagine either movement's coming to power. From the legacy of World War I, both Soviet and Nazi leaders adopted a casual attitude toward human life, a willingness to countenance death on a massive scale; a model of a powerful, interventionist state; a commitment to political violence as the means of societal progress and each after its own fashion, the ideologies of race and nation.

End Notes

1. "Universal Declaration of Human Rights," General Assembly res. 217A (III), U.N. Doc A/810 at 71 (1948). Text available at *http://www1.umn.edu/humanrts/instree/b1udhr.htm* [27 August 2002].
2. The major discussions were over whether the word "color" should be added to the document in addition to "race," and whether "national," "nationality," or "national origin" was the appropriate term. See Johannes Morsink, *The Universal Declaration of Human Rights: Origins, Drafting, and Intent* (Philadelphia: University of Pennsylvania Press, 1999), 102–5.

3. Edward Steichen, *The Family of Man* (1955; New York: Museum of Modern Art, 1997). Information on the exhibition from *http://www.moma.org/ research/archives/highlights/1955.html* [29 August 2002] and *http://www. clervaux-city.lu/index1.htm* [29 August 2002]. *The Family of Man* is now on permanent exhibit at the Château de Clervaux, Luxemburg.
4. See Werner Conze, "Rasse," in *Geschichtliche Grundbegriffe: Historisches Lexikon zur politisch-sozialen Sprache in Deutschland,* ed. Otto Brunner, Werner Conze, and Reinhard Koselleck (Stuttgart: Ernst Klett, 1984), 5:135–78, and Léon Poliakov, *The Aryan Myth: A History of Racist and Nationalist Ideas in Europe,* trans. Edmund Howard (New York: Basic Books, 1971), 136–37. Poliakov claims that the term "race" derives from the Arabic *ras,* but the etymology seems much disputed. In any case, it is clear that aside from some scattered and isolated uses in the medieval period, the word "race" became prevalent in the Romance and Germanic languages beginning in the sixteenth century.
5. See the very interesting, older article by Guido Zernatto, "Nation: The History of a Word," *Review of Politics* 6:3 (1944): 351–66.
6. See François Hartog, *The Mirror of Herodotus: The Representation of the Other in the Writing of History,* trans. Janet Lloyd (Berkeley and Los Angeles: University of California Press, 1988).
7. Herodotus, *The Histories,* trans. Aubrey de Sélincourt, rev. ed. John Marincola (1954; London: Penguin, 1996), 4.16–29 (pp. 222–26), 4.64 (p. 235).
8. Josh. 6:21–24.
9. For example, ibid., 8:24, 10:38, 11:20.
10. Ibid., 8:29, 10:26–27.
11. "And the Lord said to Samuel: 'Listen to the voice of the people in all that they say to you; for they have not rejected you but they have rejected me from being king over them.'" 1 Sam. 8:7.
12. Ps. 87:4–6.
13. Frank M. Snowden, Jr., *Before Color Prejudice: The Ancient View of Blacks* (Cambridge: Harvard University Press, 1983), 44–46.
14. Col. 3:11.
15. See Snowden, *Before Color Prejudice,* 82–87; Herodotus, *Histories* 9.122 (p. 543).
16. Herodotus, *Histories* 4.76–80 (pp. 239–41).
17. Ibid. 2.30 (pp. 96–97).
18. The Greeks, writes the classicist Frank Snowden, "developed no special theory concerning the inferiority of blacks" (*Before Color Prejudice,* 87, generally 85–87). And if that was the case, then there could be no special theory of "whiteness," the one being logically dependent upon the other.

19. See the section on Henry of Le Mans in Walter L. Wakefield and Austin P. Evans, eds. and trans., *Heresies of the High Middle Ages: Selected Sources* (New York: Columbia University Press, 1969), 108–9, 112–13, 122, 124. Some of these comments are by anonymous sources, others by the famed Bernard of Clairvaux.
20. On the latter point, see, for example, James H. Sweet, "The Iberian Roots of American Racist Thought," *William and Mary Quarterly* 54:1 (1997): 143–66.
21. For a review of the literature and critique of this thesis, see David Nirenberg, *Communities of Violence: Persecution of Minorities in the Middle Ages* (Princeton: Princeton University Press, 1996).
22. For a recent important and learned discussion along these lines, which emphasizes the instability and fluidity of premodern ethnic categorizations and depictions of blackness, see Benjamin Braude, "The Sons of Noah and the Construction of Ethnic and Geographical Identities in the Medieval and Early Modern Periods," *William and Mary Quarterly* 54:1 (1997): 103–41. See also Nicholas Hudson, "From 'Nation' to 'Race': The Origin of Racial Classification in Eighteenth-Century Thought," *Eighteenth-Century Studies* 29:3 (1996): 247–64. I find Braude's contribution more convincing than Sweet, "Iberian Roots," both published in the same thematic issue of the *William and Mary Quarterly* devoted to the construction of race.
23. Rogers Brubaker and David D. Laitin, "Ethnic and Nationalist Violence," *American Review of Sociology* 24 (1998): 428 n. 1, contend that the term "ethnic" encompasses "nationalist," but this position seems misplaced to me.
24. On the definitions of ethnicity and nationality, see some of the excellent collections that have appeared in recent years, such as Montserrat Guibernau and John Rex, eds., *The Ethnicity Reader: Nationalism, Multiculturalism, and-Migration* (Cambridge: Polity, 1997); Geoff Eley and Ronald Grigor Suny, eds., *Becoming National: A Reader* (New York: Oxford University Press, 1996); Omar Dahbour and Micheline R. Ishay, *The Nationalism Reader* (Atlantic Highlands, NJ: Humanities Press International, 1995); and John Hutchinson and Anthony D. Smith, eds., *Nationalism* (Oxford: Oxford University Press, 1994).
25. I am drawing here on the recent theoretical and historical literature on race, e.g., George M. Fredrickson, *Racism: A Short History* (Princeton: Princeton University Press, 2002); idem, *The Comparative Imagination: On the History of Racism, Nationalism, and Social Movements* (Berkeley and Los Angeles, University of California Press, 1997); Ronald Aminzade, "The Politics of Race in and Nation: Citizenship and Africanization in Tanganyika," *Political Power and Social Theory* 12 (2000): 51–88; Stephen Cornell and Douglas Hartmann, *Ethnicity and Race: Making Identities in a Changing "World* (Thousand Oaks, CA, Pine Forge Press, 1998); Eduardo

Bonilla-Silva, "Rethinking Racism: Toward a Structural Interpretation," *American Sociological Review* 62:3 (1997): 465–80; Michael Omi and Howard Winant, *Racial Formation in the United States: From the 1960s to the 1990s,* 2d ed. (New York: Routledge, 1994); Étienne Balibar and Immanuel Wallerstein, *Race, Nation, Class: Ambiguous Identities* (London: Verso, 1991); and David R. Roediger, *The Wages of Whiteness: Race and the Making of the American Working Class* (London: Verso, 1991). I leave aside some differences on particular issues among these authors and stress the common features of their interpretations.

26. See Fredrickson, *Racism,* who writes that it is "when differences that might otherwise be considered ethnocultural are regarded as innate, indelible, and unchangeable that a racist attitude or ideology can be said to exist" (5).

27. Notably, one strand in the development of racial ideology originated as a defense of aristocratic class privilege in eighteenth-century France. See the discussion of the comte de Boulainvillier's writing in Hannah Arendt, "Race-Thinking before Racism," *Review of Politics* 6:1 (1944): 36–73, here 42–47, and in Ivan Hannaford, *Race: The History of an Idea in the West* (Washington, DC: The Woodrow Wilson Center Press, 1996), 188, 195–96.

28. See especially Cornell and Hartmann, *Ethnicity and Race,* 15–38, and Omi and Winant, *Racial Formation.*

29. Balibar, "Is There a 'Neo-Racism?'" in idem and Wallerstein, *Race, Nation, Class,* 22, emphases in original. See also the similar formulation in George M. Fredrickson, "Understanding Racism: Reflections of a Comparative Historian," in idem, *Comparative Imagination,* 84–85.

30. For a very forceful argument about the modernity of New World slavery, see Robin Blackburn, *The Making of New World Slavery: From, the Baroque to the Modern, 1492–1800* (London: Verso, 1997).

31. There is, of course, an immense literature on the connection of race and slavery, which goes back at least to Eric Williams: "Slavery was not born of racism: rather, racism was the consequence of slavery," which is the general approach I follow. See Williams, *Capitalism and Slavery* (Chapel Hill: University of North Carolina Press, 1944), 7. For the recent economic argument, see William D. Phillips, Jr., *Slavery from Roman Times to the Early Transatlantic Trade* (Minneapolis: University of Minnesota Press, 1985), 173–84. For a counterposition, see David Eltis, "Europeans and the Rise and Fall of African Slavery in the Americas: An Interpretation," *American Historical Review* 98:5 (1993): 1399–1423. For the differences in European attitudes toward Native Americans and Africans, on which there is also an immense literature, the classic works of Winthrop D. Jordan, *White over Black: American Attitudes Toward the Negro, 1550–1812* (Chapel Hill: University of North Carolina Press, 1968), and David Brion Davis, *The Problem of Slavery in Western Culture* (Ithaca: Cornell University Press, 1966), are still a good entry point into the discussion. For recent considerations, see David Brion Davis, "Looking at Slavery

from Broader Perspectives," *American Historical Review* 105:2 (2000): 452–66, and idem, "Constructing Race: A Reflection," *William and Mary Quarterly* 54:1 (1997): 7–18. Ira Berlin, *Many Thousands Gone: The First Two Centuries of Slavery in North America* (Cambridge: Harvard University Press, Belknap Press, 1998), emphasizes the changing forms of race and sees its full-blown character emerging first in the nineteenth century.

32. For this issue in a later colonial context, see Ann Laura Stoler, *Race and the Education of Desire: Foucault's "History of Sexuality" and the Colonial Order of Things* (Durham: Duke University Press, 1995).

33. See Kirsten Fischer, *Suspect Relations: Sex, Race, and Resistance in Colonial North Carolina* (Ithaca: Cornell University Press, 2002).

34. Ibid., 55–97.

35. Ibid., 86.

36. Ibid.

37. See Nancy Shoemaker, "How Indians Got to Be Red," *American Historical Review* 102:3 (1997): 625–44.

38. See Hudson, "From 'Nation' to 'Race.'"

39. Fischer, *Suspect Relations,* 129–30.

40. See Jordan, *White over Black,* 136–78.

41. Fischer, *Suspect Relations,* 160–61.

42. Davis, *Problem of Slavery,* 47. See also M. I. Finley, "Slavery," in the *International Encyclopedia of the Social Sciences,* ed. David L. Sills, Vol. 14 (New York: Crowell, Collier and Macmillan, 1968), 307–13, here 308, 309, and the excerpts from Emperor Constantine's regulations in Phillips, *Slavery,* 27. Despite the quotation, generally Davis, *Problem of Slavery,* and Orlando Patterson, *Slavery and Social Death: A Comparative Study* (Cambridge: Harvard University Press, 1982), emphasize, at times implicitly, the continuities between premodern and New World slavery. Two factors seem different to me: the congruence of slavery and blackness, as argued above, and the integration of slavery into the dynamic, commercial, and capitalist world economy of the early modern era.

43. See Hannah Arendt, *The Origins of Totalitarianism* (1951; Cleveland: Meridian Books, 1958), 139–43, and Hannaford, *Race,* 191–94.

44. See the classic article by Eric Voegelin, "The Growth of the Race Idea," *Review of Politics* 2:3 (1940): 283–317.

45. Ibid., 293–294.

46. See Hannaford, *Race,* 155–58.

47. See ibid., 197–202, quotation 199.

48. As Davis writes: "Insofar as the Enlightenment divorced anthropology and comparative anatomy from theological assumptions, it opened the way for theories of racial inferiority." *Problem of Slavery,* 446.

49. See Hannaford, *Race,* 204.
50. Arendt, "Race-Thinking before Racism," 42–47'.
51. See Voegelin, "Growth of the Race Idea," 295–302.
52. Peter Gay, *The Cultivation of Hatred,* vol. 3 of *The Bourgeois Experience: Victoria to Freud* (New York: Norton, 1993), 72.
53. See Stephen Jay Gould, *The Mismeasure of Man,* rev. ed. (New York: Norton, 1996).
54. Eric Hobsbawm, *Nations and Nationalism since 1780: Programme, Myth, Reality,* 2nd ed. (Cambridge: Cambridge University Press, 1990), 18–19, Among the major writers, only Elie Kedourie, *Nationalism,* 4th ed. (Oxford: Blackwell, 1993), seems resistant to the almost universally positive view of the nationalism of the French Revolution.
55. Joan Landes, *Women and the Public Sphere in the Age of'the French Revolution* (Ithaca: Cornell University Press, 1988).
56. Hannah Arendt argued quite differently, that race thinking undermined the principle of nationality. See "Race-Thinking before Racism," the ideas of which were reworked into her classic *Origins of Totalitarianism.*
57. See Peter S. Onuf, *Jefferson's Empire: The Language of American Nationhood* (Charlottesville: University Press of Virginia, 2000), esp. 147–88.
58. Quoted in Walker Connor, "Man Is a National Animal," in idem, *Ethnonationalism: The Quest for Understanding* (Princeton: Princeton University Press, 1994), 201.
59. Amid a huge literature on the interplay of race and nation in U.S. history, see, for example, Gary Gerstle, *American Crucible: Race and Nation in the Twentieth Century* (Princeton: Princeton University Press, 2001); Roediger, *Wages of Whiteness,* and Reginald Horsman, *Race and Manifest Destiny: The Origins of American Racial Anglo-Saxonism* (Cambridge: Harvard University Press, 1986). Gerstle shows the swings back and forth in the twentieth century between racial and political definitions of the nation.
60. On the issue of race in the French Revolution, see Carolyn E. Fick, "The French Revolution in Saint Domingue: A Triumph or Failure?" in *A Turbulent Time: The French Revolution and the Greater Caribbean,* ed. David Barry Gaspar and David Patrick Geggus (Bloomington: Indiana University Press, 1997), 51–75; Lynn Hunt, ed., *The French Revolution and Human Rights* (Boston: Bedford Books, 1996), 51–59,101–18; Shanti Marie Singham, "'Betwixt Cattle and Men': Jews, Blacks, and Women and the Declaration of the Rights of Man," in *The French Idea of Freedom: The Old Regime and the Declaration of Rights of 1789,* ed. Dale Van Kley (Stanford: Stanford University Press, 1994), 114–53; David Geggus, "Racial Equality, Slavery, and Colonial Secession during the Constituent Assembly," *American Historical Review* 94:5 (1989): 1290–1308; and

Jacques Thibau, ed., *Le Temps de Saint-Domingue: L'esclavage et la révolution française* (Paris: Éditions Jean-Claude Lattès, 1989). On the earlier debates in eighteenth-century France, see Sue Peabody, *"There Are No Slaves in France": The Political Culture of Race and Slavery in the Ancien Régime* (New York: Oxford University Press, 1996).

61. William H. Sewell, Jr., *A Rhetoric of Bourgeois Revolution: The Abbé Sieyes and "What Is the Third Estate?"* (Durham: Duke University Press, 1994).
62. Sieyes quoted in ibid., 58.
63. Sieyes quoted in ibid., 59.
64. Sieyes quoted in ibid., 62. Emphasis in original.
65. On Kant as a philosopher of nationalism, see Kedourie's forceful, though controversial, argument in *Nationalism.*
66. Though Kant did argue in *The Different Races of Humankind* (1775) that within the unity of the species, there are distinct races, which are based on geography but then acquire a certain immutability.
67. Quoted in Arendt (in German), in "Race-Thinking before Racism," 49 n. 26.
68. The cult of the body as the marker for inner being had already been formulated by Enlightenment scientists and *philosophes* like the Dutch anatomist Peter Camper and his German counterpart Johann Kaspar Lavater. See George L. Mosse, *Toward the Final Solution: A History of European Racism* (Madison: University of Wisconsin Press, 1985), 17–34. See also Suzanne L. Marchand, *Down from Olympus: Archaeology and Philhellenism in Germany, 1750–1970* (Princeton: Princeton University Press, 1996).
69. See Hannaford, *Race,* 235–76.
70. Ibid., 258.
71. Arthur comte de Gobineau, "Essay on the Inequality of the Human Races," in *Gobineau: Selected Political Writings,* ed. Michael D. Biddiss (New York: Harper and Row, 1970), 41.
72. Ibid., 164.
73. Ibid., 135–37.
74. Ibid., 113.
75. Ibid.
76. Ibid.
77. Ibid., 173.
78. Gobineau was not alone, only particularly effective as a propagandizer. The Scottish anatomist Robert Knox, in a much quoted line, said: "Race is everything in human history." And: "Race, or hereditary descent, is everything;

it stamps the man." Quoted in Gay, *Cultivation,* 73, from Robert Knox, *The Races of Man* (1850; 1862 ed.), 8, 6.

79. This is an immense area of controversy within scholarship on Darwin and the theory of evolution. For one recent study that firmly links Darwin's intellectual system and personal beliefs to Şocial Darwinism, see Mike Hawkins, *Social Darwinism in European and American Thought, 1860–1945* (Cambridge: Cambridge University Press, 1997). For the contrary view, even more forcefully stated, see Ernst Mayr, *The Growth of Biological Thought; Diversity Evolution, and Inheritance* (Cambridge: Harvard University Press, Belknap Press, 1982), 385–86, 493–94.

80. Quoted in Gay, *Cultivation,* 41. As he does throughout the multivolume *Bourgeois Experience,* Gay qualifies the received views, in this case, of Spencer as a heartless misanthrope. Gay shows his more humane side as well. For a more extended analysis that firmly places Spencer in the Social Darwinist camp, see Hawkins, *Social Darwinism,* 82–103.

81. For a succinct discussion, see Mosse, *Toward the Final Solution,* 105–???.

82. Houston Stewart Chamberlain, *Foundations of the Nineteenth Century* (New York: John Lane, 1910), l:lxv.

83. Ibid., lxvi.

84. Ibid., lxvii-lxviii.

85. Ibid., 257.

86. Ibid., 269.

87. Ibid., lxxvii-lxxix, 329–493.

88. Ibid., 330–31.

89. Ibid., 334.

90. Ibid., 253–55.

91. These paragraphs draw on Paul Weindling, *Health, Race and German Politics between National Unification and Nazism, 1870–1945* (Cambridge: Cambridge University Press, 1989). See also Daniel J. Kevles, *In the Name of Eugenics: Genetics and the Uses of Human Heredity* (Berkeley and Los Angeles: University of California Press, 1985).

92. Robert Koch isolated the anthrax bacillus in 1876 and the tubercular bacillus in 1882, and other scientists soon identified the bacterial causes of diphtheria and typhoid.

93. See Paul Weindling, "Theories of the Cell State in Imperial Germany," in *Biology, Medicine and Society, 1840–1940,* ed. Charles Webster (Cambridge: Cambridge University Press, 1981), 99–155, and idem, *Health, Race and German Politics,* 19, 39.

94. Karl Pearson, *The Scope and Importance to the State of the Science of National Eugenics,* University of London, Galton Laboratory for National

Eugenics, Eugenics Laboratory Section no. 1 (London: Dulau and Co., 1909), 38.

95. Pearson, *Scope and Importance to the State,* 12. See also idem, *National Life from the Standpoint of Science,* University of London, Galton Laboratory for National Eugenics, Eugenics Lecture Series no. 11 (Cambridge: Cambridge University Press, n.d.).

96. Pearson, *National Life,* 21. See also idem, "The Bearing of Our Present Knowledge of Heredity upon Conduct" (1904), in *National Life,* 102–3; and idem, *The Problem of Practical Eugenics,* University of London, Galton Laboratory for National Eugenics, Eugenics Laboratory Lecture Series no. 5 (London: Dulau and Co., 1912), 31–34.

97. Pearson, *Scope and Importance to the State,* 40.

98. Pearson, *Practical Eugenics,* 36. Also 38 for the term "race suicide".

99. See Weindling, *Health, Race and German Politics,* 120–33.

100. Alfred Ploetz, "Die Begriffe Rasse und Gesellschaft und die davon abgeleiteten Disziplinen," *Archiv für Rassen- und Gesellschafts-Biologie* (hereafter *AfRGB)* 1 (1904): 1–26, quotation 3.

101. Ibid., 7–8.

102. See, for example, Karl Munn, "Tatsachen zur Frage der ungenügenden Fortpflanzung der Intellektuellen und ihrer Ursachen," *AfRGB* 13 (1918–21): 171–75.

103. Weindling, *Health, Race and German Politics,* 100–101, 185–86. German eugenicists followed with great interest American legislation that allowed the compulsory sterilization of the mentally and physically handicapped. See, for example, G. von Hoffmann, "Das Sterilisierungsprogramm in den Vereinigten Staaten von Nordamerika," *AfRGB* 11 (1914–16): 184–92.

104. Ploetz, "Begriffe," 11.

105. Alfred Ploetz, "Neomalthusianismus und Rassenhygiene," *AfRGB* 10 (1913): 166–72; Albert Reibmayr, "Zur Entwicklungsgeschichte der wichtigsten Charaktere und Anlagen der indogermanischen Rasse," *AfRGB* 7 (1910): 328–53; and Weindling, *Health, Race and German Politics,* 153.

106. See Alfred Ploetz, "Ableitung einer Gesellschafts-Hygiene und ihrer Beziehungen zur Ethik," *AfRGB* 3 (1906): 253–59, and Gustav Ratzenhofer, "Die Rassenfrage vom ethischen Standpunkte," *AfRGB* 1 (1904): 737–48.

107. Ploetz, "Ableitung einer Gesellschafts-Hygiene," 256. Emphases in original.

108. Ibid., 255.

109. Weindling, *Health, Race and German Politics,* 131, provides a somewhat more cautious interpretation of Ploetz's position before World War I. "Yet the most altruistic and humane method was to control reproduction. Ploetz concluded that if no more weaklings were bred, then they need not

be exterminated" (131). In one of the passages to which Weindling refers, Ploetz writes, "If no more defective traits *[Schwachen]* are reproduced, then they do not need again to be expurgated *[ausgemerzt zu werden]*" ("Begriffe," 26). But what if the traits are not expurgated? And some of Ploetz's other writings were not even this tentative.

110. *The Mountain Wreath of P. P. Nyegosh,* trans. James W. Wiles (London: George Allen and Unwin, 1930), lines 3–6, 18–19.

111. Giuseppe Mazzini, "Duties towards Your Country," in *Introduction to Contemporary Civilization in the West,* 3d ed., vol. 2 (New York: Columbia University Press, 1961), 540–43, quotation 541.

112. Quoted in Raymond F. Betts, *The False Dawn: European Imperialism in the Nineteenth Century* (Minneapolis: University of Minnesota Press, 1975), 33.

113. For one recent, extraordinary discussion, see Sven Lindqvist, "*Exterminate All the Brutes": One Man's Odyssey into the Heart of Darkness and the Origins of European Genocide,* trans. Joan Tate (New York: New Press, 1996).

114. Depiction of the Ashanti king and his mother crawling to the British in ibid., 54–57.

115. Quoted in ibid., 53–54.

116. I follow here Arendt's argument in *Origins of Totalitarianism* rather than some newer studies that claim to see an unbroken line of antisemitic sentiment in Germany. The more recent arguments revive the approach of some of the studies of the 1940s and 1950s that were far less sophisticated than Arendt's. For the older argument redux, see Daniel Jonah Goldhagen, *Hitler's Willing Executioners: Ordinary Germans and the Holocaust* (New York: Knopf, 1996), who seems unaware of the lineage of his own views.

117. The phrase "overtly racist regimes" is from Fredrickson, *Racism.*

118. Quotation from Davis, *Problem of Slavery,* 4.

119. Not until the late 1930s and the "new synthesis" of population ecology and genetics did Darwin again become the central figure for scientists. See Mayr, *Growth of Biological Thought.*

120. Some of the classic studies of race thinking in general and antisemitism in particular picture them more as the ideologies of the "mob" or the "rabble," as in Arendt, *Origins of Totalitarianism.* Older intellectual surveys, like George L. Mosse, *The Crisis of German Ideology: Intellectual Origins of the Third Reich* (New York: Grosset and Dunlap, 1964), also implied that race thinking became operative when it descended from intellectuals like Fichte and Jahn to the popular classes. I follow more recent studies that stress the biomedical di mensions of race thinking and its deadly application by highly trained professionals and bureaucrats.

121. Darwin and his followers had great difficulties with the issue of "evolutionary progress." For a careful consideration of the problem, see Mayr, *Growth of Biological Thought,* 631–34. Mayr's conclusion is that Darwin resisted the notion of any finality to evolution but of course recognized that species progressed by becoming more diverse and more complex (though complexity is not always a mark of greater adaptability to the environment). This would mark a difference between his views and those of race theorists, who did believe in perfectability.
122. Thomas Huxley, *Evolution and Ethics* (London: Macmillan, 1893).
123. George L. Mosse, *Fallen Soldiers: Reshaping the Memory of the World Wars* (New York: Oxford University Press, 1990), 173–74.
124. See, for example, many of the propaganda posters reproduced in Peter Paret, Beth Irwin Lewis, and Paul Paret, *Persuasive Images: Posters of War and Revolution from the Hoover Institution Archives* (Princeton: Princeton University Press, 1992).
125. See William W. Hagen, "Before the 'Final Solution': Toward a Comparative Analysis of Political Anti-Semitism in Interwar Germany and Poland," *Journal of Modern History* 68:2 (1996): 351–81.
126. See the still valuable work by Stephen Ladas, *The Exchange of Minorities* (New York: Macmillan, 1932). Most thoroughly on Armenia, see Richard G. Hovannisian, *The Republic of Armenia,* 4 vols. (Berkeley and Los Angeles: University of California Press, 1971–96).
127. There is a huge literature on the cultural impact of the war. Among the most important works are Omer Bartov, *Murder in Our Midst: The Holocaust, Industrial Killings, and Representation* (New York: Oxford University Press, 1996); Modris Eksteins, *Rites of Spring: The Great War and the Birth of the Combat and Identity in World War I* (Cambridge: Cambridge University Press, 1979); and Paul Fussell, *The Great War and Modern Memory* (London: Oxford University Press, 1975).
128. Ernst Jünger, *Copse 125: A Chronicle from the Trench Warfare of 1918,* trans. Basil Creighton (London: Chatto and Windus, 1930).

The Apogee of Racism: Nazi Germany 1933–1945

5

—Vandana Joshi

Nina was in her early fifties in the Fall of 1998 and had already spent nine years in therapy. She had a horrendous story to tell, which she desperately wanted to share with a sympathetic listener. She eventually found one in Dan Bar-On, a Jewish psychologist and Holocaust researcher. She faxed a message telling him that while she could not find out what her father had done during the War, she was certain what she knew was only the cover story. She suspected that her father had somehow been involved in criminal activity. Nina's father had ordered her mother to shoot their two children, who were seven and nine years old respectively, at the end of the Second World War. Her mother had followed this 'order'. Nina recently found the death certificates of her two siblings. She learnt that her siblings had been brought to a hospital in Berlin on 7 May 1945, with bullet holes in their heads.

However, once her father saw that the reality after the war, under Allied occupation, was less threatening than he had previously anticipated, he convinced her mother to give birth to a new child, Nina, who was named after one of her dead siblings. Her mother died a couple of years later and her father remarried and wiped out any trace of his previous family, including family pictures or letters. It was only through therapy that Nina could face this terrible hidden past of her family and try tracing its origin.

Dan Bar-On has many such stories to share about troubled parent–child relationships in the post-Holocaust era when many children discovered their parents' criminal pasts. In most cases, the father-perpetrators maintained a loving and caring environment at home in the shadow of inhuman crimes and atrocities. However, when defeat became imminent, many parents behaved in the most unpredictable manner and went to unimaginable lengths to steer clear of the crimes they had committed. Not many of us know such private stories laden with guilt, horror, and suspense, of troubled relations among family members, between fathers and sons, grandfathers and grandsons, and even children and parents. What we all know of, however, are the Nuremberg Trials, a series of judicial dramas much publicized by the western press, which also attracted popular attention in Germany.

The first and the best known of these was the trial of the major war criminals before the International Military Tribunal (IMT), which tried 22 of the most important captured leaders of Nazi Germany. Eleven of them received death sentences, some committed suicide in custody, while others were either acquitted or received sentences between 10 and 20 years. Twelve subsequent trials under the auspices of the American military government at Nuremberg, against leading medical, judicial, military, administrative, SS, and Gestapo officials, led to 144 convictions and 35 acquittals. Numerous other trials of individual war criminals were also held in the Soviet, British, and French occupation zones, and in the occupied territories. This, however, was the tip of the iceberg.

The social base of Nazi crimes was much wider. Besides the dreaded institutions like the Gestapo, SS, SA, SD, and criminal police, civil institutions like the judiciary, finance, railways, housing, medical, industrial, and administrative state organs were all deeply involved in the evacuations, deportations, and murders of the innocents. Over 15 million Germans were party members.

Even after the Allied powers resolved to cleanse these institutions and professions through a de-Nazification drive, the retribution was slow and half-hearted. A major reason for this was the growing tension between the Soviet Union and the western democracies, which culminated in the Cold War. The West found a new enemy in the Stalinist Soviet Union. It was perceived as an immediate threat compared to a vanquished enemy and a bygone era.

At a more popular level, the Allied powers asserted that a de-Nazification drive had to be undertaken to establish a democratic order in Germany. This resulted in a rush among the rank and file of the Germans to find erstwhile victims, who could issue a statement of sympathy, clearing them of the burden of inhuman crimes, besides turning to churches or civic authorities. In popular parlance, these statements were called *Persilscheine*, Persil is a popular brand of detergent and *Scheine* means certificates. The sooner one could obtain a character certificate washed in Persil, the quicker was one's incorporation in the job market and civil society.

Nonetheless, feelings, thoughts, and deeds related to Nazi crimes kept surfacing in the public sphere through the media and debates conducted by historians. They went through phases of suppressions and eruptions in different times and places. Mastering the past had been a tough challenge for Germans and their national psyche. While the western public ranted with news of Nazi crimes, Germans, directly involved in the perpetration of crimes, deeply suppressed these realities in their private lives. Burying the unpleasant immediate past for a palatable present, was their recipe for life after the Second World War and the holocaust. It is for this reason that historian Dan Bar-On's stories are so significant. They show us a way of dealing with a troubled past; a way beyond the media glare, publicity, political drama; a way to cleanse the conscience through self-reflection; a way far more meaningful than the victors' justice. Voices, such as those of Nina and many others who exhumed corpses of their criminal forefathers and ancestors, were expressed from within a society, which had to carry the burden of guilt and remorse long after the Nazis were dead.

The question of guilt and responsibility in perpetrating crimes against humanity is not confined to Nazi Germany alone. Such atrocities have been committed by many societies in the world. The Nazi atrocities have raised numerous ethical questions about the entanglement of professionals like judges, who claim to have followed the law of the land in persecuting tens of thousands on racial and ethnic grounds, therein ignoring the call for truth. The same holds true for doctors and nurses who violated their basic oath of protecting human life when they chose their patients for euthanasia killings and fatal laboratory experiments. Nazi Germany's history is a past that never seems to pass, not just for Germans but for all those who love peace, democracy, human dignity, freedom, and rights, most of all the right to life, which was under attack within and outside the Third Reich.

The danger is all the more serious because it was not a traditional coup d'état, a military dictatorship, but a potent combination of tricks, political intrigue, ingenious propaganda techniques, mass support, Hitler's rabble-rousing speeches, and economic instability of a defeated nation, which brought the Nazis to power. In spite of the popularity that the Nazis enjoyed, the party never got more than 37 per cent of the vote. Other factors which accentuated this impact were the splintering of the leftist opposition, the disappearance of the liberal-democratic middle ground, and the volatile political situation of Germany in the interwar period. Nonetheless, it is important to remember that Hitler came to power through democratic means and destroyed democracy once he seized power. But equally significant is the fact that that Hitler's dictatorship remained popular almost until Germany's final collapse and his suicide in a bunker in Berlin. There was very little, or almost no organized protest or opposition to his regime. Even today, there are numerous ex-soldiers who take pride in Hitler's regime. Except for the defeat in war, it was not a bad deal for them.

The history of Nazi Germany tells us how human virtues were violated and unprecedented violence was unleashed on the declared enemies of the nation, inside and outside the Reich in the 12 years of its rule. Its central feature was the extreme hatred of peoples it considered different and inferior on racial grounds. It identified, stigmatized, marginalized, and ultimately, annihilated all of them as lives unworthy of living. The scale and method of this annihilation were unimaginable and unforeseen in a land which was once known to be the land of poets and philosophers. In fact, after the emancipation of the Jews in 1869, it was perhaps the most comfortable place for the Jews to live in, offering them chances of upward mobility like nowhere else in the continent.

How could it all have happened in Germany? The narrative of events avoids an intentionalist route. The author believes that there was no law of inevitability that governed German history; that things could have been different at several turning points in the twentieth century; that just one man could not possibly have decided the fate of an entire nation or a continent. In other words, historical circumstances turned certain fringe ideas into mainstream reality at a specific juncture, and that these developments have to be understood in their historical context. Some historians might like to trace the eliminationist strand of Nazi Germany as far back as Luther and the militarist/authoritarian strand to Bismarck, while others emphasize the strong socialist, Catholic, and democratic currents from below that made parliamentary politics truly democratic, socialist, and radical in its agendas. The German Social Democratic Party inspired its continental counterparts and boasted of the largest number of deputies in the parliament in 1914. We will discuss some of these paradoxes later, and turn now to the rise and fall of Nazi Germany in the context of interwar Europe.

FIRST WORLD WAR AND THE POLITICAL UPHEAVAL

The First World War was welcomed by all in Germany as the dawn of a new era. There was a certain euphoria about the War in Europe and all involved nations hoped to benefit from 'the Great War', as it came to be known. Millenarian sentiments and apocalyptic visions ran high. But this was just the beginning. What was hoped to be a quick victory turned out to be a protracted struggle. Soldiers had to fight for every inch of land, living in trenches for days. They watched dead bodies of their comrades being nibbled at by rats, smelt the stench of decaying corpses and explosives, heard sounds of bombshells and faced blindness due to poisonous gas attacks every day. Food supplies became a problem as early as 1915. In April 1917, the first major strike occurred due to cutting of bread rations. The civilian government broke down and the reins of the government were practically taken over by the Chief-of-Staff Hindenburg and General Ludendorff. Towards the end, fresh pass outs from school became the cannon fodder of nations at war, so sensitively portrayed by Eric Maria Remarque in his novel, *All Quiet in the Western Front*. The Great War was as psychologically devastating as it was tedious and impersonal. It exhausted material and human resources of the entire continent. From a prosperous and industrialized creditor continent, Europe became an abode of misery, indebtedness, and anxieties. More than anything else, the Great War initiated and bred a culture of violence. As the war was over and the demobilized soldiers returned home, they brought this culture of violence home. The instability of the Republic and economic problems left the generation of front soldiers craving for more violence.

Until the beginning of 1918, Germany was doing quite well at the front. She also drove a hard bargain with the newly triumphant Bolsheviks in Russia. The Germans extracted huge swathes of land from Russia in the Treaty of Brest-Litovsk and transferred 5,000,000 soldiers from the Eastern to the Western Front. Lenin was eager to end the war and offer his people land, bread, and peace (Evans 2004: 58). With the new spring offensive plan, the Germans hoped and propagated that victory did not seem far. In August 1918, the Kaiser proclaimed that the worst was over. But soon after, things took a dramatic turn. The heavy losses inflicted by General Ludendorff in the spring offensive propelled the American entry into the Western Front with unprecedented supplies of troops and provisions. The German troops and their morale started to crumble under American pressure. Further blows came when Bulgaria, their partner, sued for peace and the Italians started a southern offensive against the Habsburg armies. Military leaders Field Marshall Hindenburg and General Ludendorff informed the Kaiser that the war was almost lost. However, due to a tight censorship, the government was able to maintain the myth of a final victory, while the soldiers continued to perish in the trenches.

THE SPARTACUS UPRISING

Meanwhile, domestic unrest was rising in January 1918. There were more strikes; the mood of war-weariness and a desire for peace could be sensed among sailors and soldiers, even though official propaganda and policies goaded the rank and file to put everything at stake for the eventual glorious victory. It was from this split between the policies of the army elite and the experiences of rank and file that the first sparks of the Spartacus uprising erupted. At the end of October 1918, naval officers, in a bid to salvage their honour decided to fight the British fleet, but the sailors mutinied in Wilhelmshaven and Kiel. Within a few days the uprising spread to many parts of Germany. Workers', soldiers' and sailors' councils on the Bolshevik pattern sprang up in many palaces, which wrested control of the administration from local governments. On 8 November, a Republic was declared by Kurt Eisner in Bavaria, a south German state. Threats of strikes and civil unrest loomed large.

The generals sensed imminent defeat and strict peace terms from the allied powers. Saddled with the uprising at home and the vindictive attitude of the victors, the military elite quietly handed over the reins of government to the weak civilian government of Max von Baden. He tried to establish contacts with the Emperor, but the Emperor had already escaped from Berlin, which was in the grip of revolutionaries, to Holland. In a fit, von Baden announced the abdication of the Emperor and decided to put Friedrich Ebert, the SPD leader, at the helm of affairs. Ebert's colleague Philipp Scheidemann went to the balcony of the Reichstag to declare a republic in an attempt to prevent the proclamation of a more radical 'Soviet Style' Republic, preparations for which were in full swing in Berlin. The latter republic was being designed by the USPD, a faction of the SPD and the Spartacus League, which was to become the communist party (KPD). Their republic was taking shape in many locations where sailors, soldiers, and workers came together to organize their councils. Berlin was under the control of these revolutionaries, the reason why Weimar, a small town in East Germany and the birth place of Goethe, was chosen as the site for the proclamation of a democratic parliamentary republic with the SPD, Catholics, and democrats as coalition partners.

The leaders of the rival Spartacus League, Rosa Luxemburg and Karl Liebknecht, wanted a truly republican army consisting of workers, sailors, and ordinary soldiers, a socialisation of the means of production, a transfer of all powers to the workers' and sailors' councils, and many more fundamental changes in the existing system. Afraid of alienating the old elite, the army and civil servants, the leader of the SPD and Weimar Republic, Friedrich Ebert, quickly entered into an agreement with the army to quell the Spartacus uprising in January 1919. The Free Corps (privately financed paramilitary groups of demobilized soldiers) were roped in. Hundreds of revolutionaries were butchered mercilessly in the streets of Berlin and elsewhere. The bodies of Rosa Luxemburg and Karl Liebknecht were hacked into pieces and thrown into the *Landwehr* canal, which flows through the heart of Berlin. Kurt Eisner's Republic in Bavaria was also suppressed by the Free Corps by May 1919. Eventually, a successful right-wing regime under Kahr was installed in Bavaria, which offered a heaven to the anti-republican, right-wing radicals. Hitler was nurtured in this climate. The foundation stone of the democratic Weimar Republic was laid on the corpses of leftist revolutionaries. This type of violence repeatedly occurred against the communists in the republic's brief life. This legacy of violence split the German left into two bitter enemies: the Communist Party or the KPD and the SPD. The former converted many SPD members to its cause in the late 1920s. The two leftist factions kept fighting among themselves, the KPD branded the SPD as social fascists, while the SPD called them stooges of the Soviet Union. Meanwhile, the Nazis took full advantage of this split and rapidly made inroads into a cross section of society during the Great Depression.

To come back to the post First World War scenario, after the suppression of the Spartacus Uprising, the democratic parties campaigned for the general elections of 19 January 1919. The SPD gained 385 seats, the largest, but still short of absolute majority. It had to enter into an alliance with the Catholic Centre Party (Zentrum) and the German Democratic Party (DDP) to form a government. The National Constituent Assembly was convened in Weimar on 6 February and Ebert was elected the Republic's first president.

THE MYTH OF STAB-IN-THE-BACK IN THE INTERWAR PERIOD

To many soldiers at the front, Hitler being one of them, the news of the defeat and armistice was earth shattering. This was not, however, the case with the commanding top officials who knew that they were fighting a losing battle. Generals like Ludendorff believed that the Jews were behind many of the evils like communism, socialism, defeat, democracy, and so on. In fact, senior officers in the army ordered the so-called Jewish Census in October 1916 with the hope of accumulating statistics that would show that Jews' proportion among the soldiers was less than their share in the population, but the Census revealed just the opposite and its findings were suppressed. After the war, Ludendorff, Hindenburg, the

Kaiser, and the conservative right-wing spread a myth that the war was lost due to a stab-in-the-back by the revolutionaries of 1917, and that the army had been a victim of a secret, planned, demagogic campaign, which had doomed all its efforts to failure. This myth served two functions: firstly, it covered German military failures by blaming the defeat on the revolutionaries; secondly, the Emperor abdicated ignominiously and the military leadership quickly facilitated the entry of democratic force in the political front to set up a new government and negotiate with the Allied powers, what they knew would be a harsh treaty. In this way, they were able to create hatred towards the revolution and democratic forces while hiding their incompetence. The revolutionaries were dubbed as Jews, communists, and all other 'subversive elements' of Germany, including the socialists and democrats. They accused the latter of first stabbing the army in the back, and then committing the double crime of overthrowing the Emperor and signing the Armistice. Free Corps members formed secret assassination squads to kill those whom they regarded as traitors to the nation, including the democratic politician Walther Rathenau; the radical socialist and founder of the break-away Independent Social Democratic Party (USPD) leader, Hugo Haase; Centre Party Deputy, Mattias Erzberger; and Spartacist revolutionaries such as Rosa Luxemburg and Karl Liebknecht. Tens of thousands of ex-soldiers with right-wing, nationalist leanings joined the ranks of the Free Corps. They broke strikes, attacked communists, socialists, and Jews and enjoyed killing. Klaus Theweleit wrote an account of these and the Nazis in his *Male Fantasies*, which has acquired the status of a cult classic. He used Freudian and Foucaultian methods to study around 200 autobiographical and literary accounts of the Free Corps and Nazis. *Male Fantasies*, through these accounts, enters into the psychic world of these early fascists and comes up with disturbing and startling insights on their brutal desires, craving for power and violence, hatred of women (esp. revolutionary), psychic fears and anxieties. These ex-soldiers and right-wing early fascists brought the cult of violence from the battlefield to the streets and public spaces in the interwar years, admired the rifles and machine guns, were deeply anti-Semitic and anti-women, and took pleasure in destruction. Hitler, in his demagoguery, used the myth of November criminals to drum up nationalist frenzy and hatred towards the leftist elements in society.

THE VERSAILLES TREATY

Germany emerged from the debris of the First World War beaten, humiliated, and destroyed. She had lost her Emperor, her fleet, her air force, and the size of her army had been severely limited. On the western frontiers, the Rhineland was demilitarized, the Saar was put under the temporary administration of the League of Nations, and her mines and minerals was given to France. France also acquired Alsace and Lorraine, which were wrested from her by Bismarck, while Eupen and Malmedy were given to Belgium. On the western side, Austria was enlarged at Germany's expense owing to the prohibition on the unification of the two. Posen and part of Prussia were given to Poland in the north-east to give her access to the sea. Danzig was declared a free city. Memel and her hinterland were given over to Lithuania. In all, the territorial clauses of Versailles cost Germany 25,000 square miles or 13 per cent of her territory, three-quarters of her iron ore deposits, 26 per cent of her coal, 38 per cent of her steel capacity, and almost seven million inhabitants. Most damning for Germans, however, was the war-guilt clause, which squarely put the responsibility of starting the First World War on Germany, and to atone for her crime, she was saddled with years of reparations, in total of 132 billion gold Marks, as established in 1921 (Holtfrerich, 1986: 146–49). The Weimar Republic also inherited Imperial Germany's debt of some 150 Billion marks for financing the war.

The war-guilt clause was immensely unpopular with the Germans and so was the payment of reparations, a point to which we shall return later. On hindsight, one could say that the Allied powers went wrong strategically. Either they should have imposed the Versailles Treaty on the monarchy and the conservative military elite, forces who were actually responsible for waging the war, or they should have been a bit lenient on the republicans. This did not happen for the Allied powers insisted that the monarch should abdicate before the peace process could begin. Anti-German feelings ran so high at the end of the War that Eric Campbell Gedde's slogan during a rally before the Versailles Peace Conference, 'We shall squeeze the German lemon until the pips squeak!' became a universal cry overnight, and more than the Britons, it was the French and Belgians who later followed it in letter and spirit.

THE WEIMAR REPUBLIC

The Versailles Treaty was signed by the leaders of the Weimar Republic, which was established by a coalition of progressive and truly democratic forces. It was these forces that had to bear the burden of guilt and reparations of the Allied powers and also face rebuke from society for having accepted these humiliating terms. Whenever a flash point emerged, the Republic and its creators took the beating for anything and everything that went wrong with the Weimer Republic. The right-wing cashed on each failure of the Weimar Republic. It castigated them as November criminals and accused them of stab-in-the-back. Hitler regularly drummed up hatred of the democratic forces and institutions with the same allegations.

Ironically, the Weimar Republic was one of the most advanced welfare democracies that one could have had at that juncture of history. All adult men and women had the right to vote. The system of proportional representation in volatile times made it almost impossible for any single party to acquire absolute majority. In this system, however, no vote was ever wasted. The number of seats that a party occupied corresponded to the percentage of votes it won in the general elections. Five per cent votes translated into 5 per cent seats in the parliament and 40 per cent votes meant 40 per cent seats. This means that small parties did not have much of a chance, except for playing junior partners in a coalition, but it was very challenging for any single party to get two-thirds majority to emerge victorious. At the height of their popularity, the SPD won 38 per cent votes in 1919 and the Nazis 37.8 per cent in 1932. The entire period of 14 years of democracy saw about 20 different cabinets, each lasting on an average for 239 days or 8 months. Coalition governments were unstable and weak by nature, as different parties squabbled over personalities and policies. At the same time, some long-term continuities were seen in certain ministries such as the ministry of justice, which was used as a bargaining chip for forming coalitions leading to a succession of ministers, but some others like the foreign ministry with Gustav Stresemann, as the German People's Party deputy, survived nine successive cabinets and six years in office. Otto Gessler remained army minister in 13 successive governments spanning over 8 years. The same was true of Heinrich Braun, a Catholic deputy who remained labour minister (Evans, 2003: 87). Such ministries followed consistent policies and provided stability to the otherwise volatile system.

Among the worst pitfalls was the emergency power of the elected president to rule by decree under Article 48. The president was elected through a separate universal vote and chosen for seven years. Friedrich Ebert in the initial years and Brüning during the Great Depression made sweeping use of this prerogative to legitimize many of their high-handed actions that undermined the democratic spirit of the constitution. Many of the extreme left-wing executions were legitimized post facto by Ebert.

The welfare arm of the Republic was quite strong. About the same time as Ebert reached an understanding with the army to suppress the radical elements, it also struck a deal with employers to protect workers interests to some extent. This negotiation called the Stinnes-Legiens agreement, named after the employers' and trade union's leaders respectively, negotiated some crucial concessions to labour. These included: the legitimation of trade unions as representatives of workers, a smooth reincorporation of returning soldiers to their previous jobs, the establishment of 'worker's committees' in enterprises exceeding 50 employees, settlements between employers and employees, an eight-hour working day and the institution of a 'Central Committee' made up of representatives of workers and employers to resolve both short and long-term labour-related issues (Fulbrook, 1991: 23).

The Weimar Republic built on the already existing welfare system by making it more comprehensive and elaborate. It was a confluence of social Catholicism, Protestant philanthropy and social democratic egalitarianism (Evans, 2003: 139 ff.). Its welfare provisions incorporated war widows and their children, irrespective of their legal status or unemployment and health benefits to the juveniles, youth, war disabled and other vulnerable sections of society, backed by a massive housing scheme, expansion in the medical profession, hospital beds, and infrastructure. The Republic faced a lot of difficulties in fulfilling these promises, especially during the crisis years. The economic elite, being naturally inclined towards the right wing, hated the rights that workers had won for themselves. They eagerly waited in the wings to attack the Republic at the opportune moment.

In spite of these provisions, institutionally, Weimar's supporting pillars maintained much of their pre-war character after the November revolution. The army, civil service, police, and judiciary remained very conservative. They remained sympathetic to the monarchist, authoritarian, and right-wing extremists, and averse to left-wing revolutionaries. The Social Democrats had their fair share in this from the early days of the Republic, when Friedrich Ebert rode on the shoulders of the army and free corps to suppress the Spartacus uprising. The Republic had no political will for a thorough radical reform. It merely made adjustments with the established elites in many important quarters of administration. The army, restricted to 100,000 after the Treaty of Versailles, remained elitist under the leadership of War Minister General Groener, who worked in tandem with Ebert to quell the November Spartacus rising. Thus, founded by the militarist elite and the rank and file of the Free Corps, the Weimer Republic suffered from a serious democratic deficit since its inception.

Not only did Ebert seek a helping hand from the army to shatter the dreams of a more radical and egalitarian republic, but the army elite also exercised enormous moral and political influence in the Republic. In spite of the drastic reduction in their size and stature officially, it harboured hopes of resurfacing like a giant, and gobbling up the Republic to restore an authoritarian state. In spite of its hatred of Bolshevik ideology, its pragmatism guided it to cultivate the Soviet Union, the natural foe of western democracy, and silently and secretly train its soldiers in Soviet Russia. The Rapallo Treaty with the USSR in 1922 re-established diplomatic relations between the two countries renouncing claims of reparations or compensation. This also included a secret agreement allowing Germany to remilitarise and train inside the USSR. The Berlin Treaty of 1926 furthered their resolve to remain neutral in the event of war between the two forces in the continent.

We already discussed how Hindenburg and Ludendorff allowed the state power to slip out of their hands on seeing the coming defeat and put the burden of a humiliating treaty on the Republicans' shoulders in the crucial months of late 1918. The command of the army, for about half of the Weimar Republic's life was in the hands of Hans von Seeckt. A reluctant republican, he was an admirer of right-wing putschists like Kapp and Hitler, and maintained the army's neutrality in the face of such attacks on the Republic. He even allowed the abdicated Kaiser's son, Prince William, to take part in military exercise. The rest of the Republic breathed in the shadow of Field Marshall and later President Hindenburg, a highly decorated general, a symbol of Prussian militarism and a staunch supporter of some kind of authoritarian rule. Hindenburg allowed German diplomatic representations and flagships to carry both the republican black-red-gold flag alongside the imperial black-white red flag. At the dedication ceremony for the Tannenberg monument in Hohenstein (East Prussia), the site for German counter-attack against the Russians in late August 1914, the presence of a range of right-wing columns spoke volumes for the politics of the Weimar army. In his speech Hindenberg denied Germany's role in the outbreak of the First World War and resolved to defend the fatherland (Weitz, 2007: 120).

While the army remained generally authoritarian, disdainful of the Republic, openly hostile to left-wing radicals, receptive to right-wing manoeuvres, and operated behind the scenes, the judiciary did not fare much better either. In the mid-1920s, a left-wing statistician, Emil Julius Gumbel, published figures showing that the 22 political murders committed by the left wing led to 38 convictions, including 10 executions and average prison sentences of 15 years. In contrast, 354 political murders committed by right-wing offenders led to 24 convictions, no executions, and prison sentences averaging four months. Right-wing attempts at coups or destruction of the Republic, carried out in the name of saving the fatherland, certainly elicited sympathy from the ruling circle, who had no respect for the Republic. The conservative Kapp Putsch of 1920 brought a brief period of confinement for Kapp. Similarly, Hilter's violent and extra-constitutional Beer Hall Putsch in 1923 earned him a five-years sentence, but he was released in one year.

In fact, his public trial provided him the opportunity to turn the witness box into a rostrum from where he propagated his cause for hours, and the jail confinement of just 13 months gave him enough leisure and comfort to dictate his *Mein Kampf* to a fellow prisoner and follower. He emerged as a far more mature propagandist and strategist thereafter. While the Putschist attempts might have proved to be good training grounds for right-wing nationalists, such efforts sealed the fates of left-wing activists altogether. As noted earlier, the attacks made on the system by the Novemberists and the Spartacists led to violent clashes between free corps and the revolutionaries on the streets of Berlin and Munich and resulted in much bloodletting. Even sympathizers and leftist intellectuals and journalists were dealt with an iron hand by the judiciary. Carl von Ossietzky was sentenced to 18 months' imprisonment for publishing an article in his magazine, *The World Stage*. The article revealed that the German army was training with combat aircrafts in the Soviet Union, an act banned by the Versailles Treaty. Another journalist, Felix Fechenbach, was sentenced to 11 years' imprisonment for publishing the Bavarian files from 1914, related to the outbreak of the First World War. Coming as it did in 1919, his offence was judged as no less than high treason because this lent support to the Allied idea of the German guilt in starting the war, and thereby weakening Germany's position in peace agreement (Evans, 2003: 136). He was judged alongside rogues and murderers by a summary special court, which was set up to deal with the November Revolutionaries of 1919. This court anticipated the Nazi Special Court, which carried out similar functions.

These negative and positive features of the Weimar constitution have to be placed within the peculiar socio-economic context, which put the constitutional features to harsh testing on numerous occasions before the Republic finally collapsed. The Weimar Republic's economy and society remained extremely volatile, deeply fragmented and anxiety-ridden leading to a sharp polarisation of the population at the end. The boiling points was reached on many occasions in quick succession and deepened the fundamental cracks within the system. For these reasons, we now turn first to the economy, then to the political developments in the last phase of crisis, and then to the Great Depression to be able to understand the rise of Hitler and the collapse of democracy.

WEIMAR REPUBLIC'S ECONOMY

Like many other eastern and central European economies, Germany too was facing an unprecedented crisis. The Great War left Germany much poorer than its pre-War levels. The industrial production was reduced to 42 per cent and grain production to 48 per cent as compared to 1913. Post-war material shortages, huge debts resulting from waging a war, the burden of reparations, and the costs of demobilization by providing work for millions of returning soldiers in concrete financial terms meant deficit spending (Feldman, 1975: 47; Overy, 2001: 34–73). To deal with the shortfall between revenue and expenditure, governments resorted to populist inflationary policies of printing paper money, increasing employment and economic activity, rather than burdening people with heavy taxes. The German economy, which was already reeling under debt from the Great War days, had hoped that the benefits of a victory would make up for the losses of war. On the contrary, it was burdened by reparations in the post-war scenario. Germany was exporting its products to a competitive international market with devalued German currency. This meant an unfavourable balance of trade because exports were cheaper while imports were expensive. This fed into the existing inflationary situation.

The amount of taxation required to meet the cost of reparations, social welfare programmes, and the normal running of the government without inflationary consequences would have involved trebling the pre-War tax levels relative to national income at a time when living standards had already taken a dip. To accomplish this challenging task, a strong government with a solid popular backing was required because this demanded great sacrifices (Heinz Haller, 1976: 140–1). This kind of realistic politics, accepting harsh political and economic post-War circumstances, could have made the democracy sustainable and credible, even though cumbersome for a few years. Instead, the Weimar democracy obstinately refused to burden its citizens financially with increased taxation. Politically, it gave way to myths, lies, and propaganda. The one who was best at it, Hitler, ultimately won the game, a point to which we shall return later.

It is within this context that the hyperinflation of 1923 should be understood. When Germany was unable to pay the reparation any longer, the French and Belgian troops entered the industrial Rhineland province in January 1923 and occupied it. The German government resorted to the policy of non-cooperation and promised to bear the cost of passive resistance. It printed paper currency recklessly without backing it with economic resources. Hyperinflation, in sum, meant: too much of printed money in circulation of too little worth. A US dollar was equal to 24,000 Marks in April, 353,000 Marks in July, 4,621,000 Marks in August, and 98,860,000 in September, and by December 1923, the figure ran into trillions (Evans, 2003: 105). The image of Germans carrying a cartload of currency notes to buy a loaf of bread was widely publicised. Prices doubled and trebled several times in a day making shopping with paper money almost impossible. People's savings, incomes, hopes, and aspirations dashed to the ground, prices skyrocketed, and the economy came to a standstill. It was the salaried class, of course, who suffered the most. The poor and the unskilled, living on meagre incomes and welfare doles, suffered terribly, but the middle and upper middle class, the backbone of German society until then, did not fare better either. According to Gerald Feldman, an upper-level civil servant, in 1922 took home only 1.35 per cent more income than an unskilled worker (Feldman, 1993: 546). Pensioners, savings accounts holders, and others, who had saved each penny for the future, saw their savings evaporate as the currency increasingly lost its value. This created an unforeseen 'levelling' in society, which had a very damaging impact on the middle-class psyche and status. This phenomenon has been referred to by historians as the 'fear of proletarianisation'. The respectable middle class, which prided itself on standing above the proletariat, thought that its prestige and social standing had gone down drastically creating an existential crisis in their ranks. On the other hand, a minority such as speculators, mortgage holders, those earning in foreign currency, and industrialists, especially those who had built their assets on loans, benefited hugely for they could return their loans in paper money which was increasingly losing its real value.

Social resentment became acute. Industrialists blamed workers of earning high wages and burdening the economy with welfare costs, while workers blamed industrialists of speculation and profits seeking. People in the city blamed those living on the countryside of feasting while they were carrying cartloads and standing in long queues for bread. Jews especially came under attack as speculators and profiteers who enriched themselves at the cost of others. Almost everybody blamed the Republic and the Allied powers. Politically, the economic chaos reflected in putsch attempts and uprisings both from the right and the left. A communist-inspired uprising rocked Saxony, Thuringia, and Hamburg, while in Bavaria, Hitler, then the leader of young NSDAP or National Socialist German Worker's Party, made his first attempt at capturing power through an insurrection. This failed attempt, known as the 'Beer Hall Putsch' of 8 and 9 November 1923, earned him a brief jail sentence and gave him a lot of publicity and opportunity to display his demagogic skill in the public trial following his arrest.

On balance, this crisis gave a rightist turn to politics. Nationalist sentiments ran high, hatred of the Allied powers intensified and the Allied reparations were blamed for all of Germany's ills. The Republic shared the brunt too. One must not forget, however, that it was perceptions and aspirations which were at play rather than the grim realities. Had the Germans emerged victorious, their terms would have been harsher for the vanquished, as was evident from the Brest-Litovsk Treaty with the Bolsheviks in Russia. In any event, economic collapse in the face of massive burdens of war seemed to put the world upside down for Germans who considered normality by the yardstick of pre-War Germany: which had been a glorious empire, rivalled Britain for colonial and naval supremacy, and had a robust industrial economy and general prosperity. Even though post-War Germany was impoverished as much due to post-War reparations as for fighting the War on the basis of bonds and credits, the perception of normal Germans was that the end of the War would bring peace and normality, which they mythically associated with Imperial Germany of 1913. Everything appeared to be abnormal to them in the Weimar Republic. It had become a beaten nation, a burdened economy, and a 'sold out democracy' a stark contrast to the former glorious empire, not-with-standing that the Emperor had vanished from the scene without owning up his failures.

In concrete terms, politically the government lost total credibility, so did Chancellor Wilhelm Cuno, an incompetent centre-right representative. In mid-August, the SPD withdrew support from the government and Cuno resigned. The new coalition government, now including Gustav Stresemann as Chancellor, was appointed by the SPD. On 26 September, he ended passive resistance and resorted to rule by decree to handle multiple crises. The government beat back both right-wing and left-wing revolutionary attempts, as mentioned above, established a new currency called *Rentenmark*, which was backed by industrial and agricultural assets, and in Fall 1924 by gold standards, to stop inflation. By spring 1924, the pre-war 12-hour shift, instead of eight hours, returned and employers were given rights to hire and fire workers. This showed the reversal of workers' gain and a conservative shift of the polity and economy. Many other social welfare gains won in 1918–19 beat a retreat. The scene was set, however, for a meaningful dialogue with the Allied powers. Germany adopted the Dawes Plan, named after the American banker Charles G. Dawes, to bail herself out of the economic crisis and also facilitate America's entry into her market (Weitz, 2007: 141–3). Dawes provided Germany some breathing space before the reparations could be restarted in full swing. Short-term loans from abroad, particularly from America, were introduced to bring the German economy back on rails. To sort out political problems, in October 1925, the Locarno Pact was signed by Germany, Belgium, Britain, France, and Italy with separate agreements between Germany and Poland, and Germany and Czechoslovakia. While it pushed the French and Belgians back to their boarders and made all agree to renounce the use of force, it revalidated the Treaty of Versailles and accepted Germany into the community of nations working towards the peace and security of Europe with the League of Nations. This phase is known as the golden years of the Republic and lasted till 1928.

In these golden years, a liberal democratic culture and economy blossomed. It is controversial how far the golden years were capable of repairing the structurally flawed economy and society, but let us run through some features of change in this era. This was the stable phase of the Republic, but it was largely based on American loans. The economy expanded. Industrial giants went in for rationalisation taking their lead from the American Ford and Taylor enterprises. This is also known as Fordism or Taylorisation. Some of the features of rationalisation were assembly line work, high-speed capital-intensive precision instruments, and a high level of specialisation, monotonous and impersonal work culture, and higher wages and drastic cuts in the number of workers. People of all classes went on a buying spree on credit or otherwise, as long years of crisis and deprivation, war and inflation had taught them how ephemeral life and assets were. So why not enjoy life here and now? Consumerism, entertainment, and living for the moment became the mantra of the poor and rich alike. Fashion, life style, sexual liberation, entertainment, cinema, huge department stores with eye-catching display windows, more nourishing food, growth of a new middle class with much of the workforce engaged in the service sector, shop floors, offices, aspirations of upward mobility in the workers, increased female presence in offices and streets were some of the features of this era of popular consumption.

In August 1929, the Young Plan revised the reparation schedule, setting a new total figure and a reduced annual average of reparations. This was met with intense opposition and provided winds to the sails of the NSDAP. For the moderates, the positive achievements of the Young Plan were considerable: the removal of foreign control and the evacuation of the Rhineland in June 1930, the renegotiation of the reparations, the reduction in international hostilities, and so on. But all of this ran into the sands once the Great Depression set in. The radical right was ever more determined to demolish everything that undermined Germany's position, internationally and nationally.

This brings us to the third and the most decisive phase of the economic roller coaster ride of the Weimar Republic: the Great Depression. It catapulted Hitler's position from being the drummer of a fringe nationalist party to the Chancellor and then President, and indeed, the *Führer* until he breathed his last in the Berlin bunker.

The edifice built during the golden years collapsed like a house of cards with the onset of the Great Depression. Germany's economic prosperity was dependent upon short-term loans, primarily from America. The first signs of trouble appeared on 24 October or 'Black Thursday' when a business crisis led to panic selling on the New York stock exchange, known as the Wall Street Crash. Share prices began to sink dramatically and on 29 October 1929, also known as the 'Black Tuesday', the stock market crashed. Frantic speculators and shareholders overcrowded the Wall Street to sell their shares before the prices dipped further. This sudden bursting of the balloon created a major crisis of liquidity in the market for construction, development, and investment. Firm after firm went bankrupt. This set off the world's biggest banking crisis of the twentieth century. Personal incomes, tax revenues, profits, investments, development activities, and prices dropped, while international trade reduced drastically because of the fall in demand. Unemployment within the US rose to 25 per cent. To deal with the liquidity crunch, firstly the US banks started imposing monitory restrictions and cutting down foreign lending. Such measures were necessary to preserve the gold reserves on which the currency was based. Secondly, the US started calling in their short-term loans from abroad. Like migratory birds, American capital took a flight back to its place of origin. This spelled doom the German economy, which was making a slow but steady recovery in the 'Golden years', largely based on American short-term loans. A major financial crisis erupted in Germany with the flight of the American funds. The economy came to a grinding halt. The financial crisis rapidly snowballed into a production crisis which sucked in both the industrial and agricultural sectors. With heavy retrenchment in the industrial sector, unemployment figures reached a staggering high of six million, far outstripping the rates of the US, from where the crisis had spread to the world economy. By 1932, every third worker in Germany became unemployed, as in comparison to 1929, the industrial production had dropped by 40 per cent. Those who could manage to save their jobs had their scales, working hours, and salaries reduced. It was commonplace to see men with placards around their necks saying, 'willing to do any work', the youth playing cards or roaming aimlessly in neighbourhoods. Men sat listlessly in street corners, initially well dressed waiting to find some work, queuing before their local employment exchange, and later, indulging in criminal activities in total frustration and despair. Children talked about their unemployed fathers from whom they had no hope. Although the working class was the worst sufferer of unemployment, economic difficulties wore down larger sections of the population. Already before the Depression, between 1 October 1923 and 31 March 1924, 135,000 out of 826,000 civil servants working for the railways, post, telegraph, and printing services had been sacked along with 30,000 out of 61,000 white-collar workers and 232,000 out of 706,000 state-employed manual workers. A further wave of cuts came after 1929 with reductions in salaries of civil servants. Further reductions came in 1930 and 1932. Tourist agents, retailing firms, restaurant owners, and others in the service sector suffered as peoples' purchasing power declined. White-collar workers lost jobs and the banking and financial sectors got into major difficulties (Evans, 2003: 242–3). Peasant economies swung in rapid succession between inflation, stabilisation and depression, thereby producing contradictory effects, which made them lose their bearings and produce a general crisis by the late 1920s. While big landlords bought machinery on hire purchase in the initial years of the Republic and modernized their agricultural practices while paying in inflated currency during hyperinflation, the story of small farmers was quite the contrary. They tended to hoard money for a rainy day. The hyperinflation spelled doom for them as their savings evaporated. After the inflation, the government made provisions to ease credit restrictions on agriculture. The small peasants now borrowed heavily, expecting another round of inflation. To their utter dismay, the deflationary policies of Brüning during the Great Depression led to a drastic decrease in the prices of agricultural goods, and peasants were unable to repay the loans. Bankruptcies and foreclosures ruined many small-scale agricultural enterprises, while big landlords, faced with a downturn in agricultural prices, considered the taxes levied by the Weimar welfare state excessive. They did not want to pay high taxes to ameliorate the condition of the marginalized at a time when they were themselves going through a tough time. All of this pushed the countryside into the lap of the Nazi party. The big landlords, who already had conservative authoritarian leanings, also resolved to dump traditional nationalist parties in search of a more radical alternative.

The initial spark was caused by a 'distributional crisis' of unemployment funds. Workers in the Republic relied heavily on state arbitration for wage claims that were contested by employers. The employers claimed that Taylorisation caused wages to become too high and a distributional struggle, according to Harold James, ensued with the onset of the Depression and led to the collapse of the last truly democratic government, led by Hermann Müller of the SPD. The Müller government witnessed large-scale bankruptcies and unemployment and fell over the issue of unemployment cover. With rising rates of unemployment and a recession in the economy, class conflict became imminent and the first shots were heard in the distributional crisis. The coalition partners split on the issue of unemployment insurance. The SPD, a workers' party, did not want any compromise in the unemployment funds, whereas their partners DVP, the representatives of nationalist, right-wing, middle-class interests, argued that the earlier welfare measures could not be sustained in the crisis years. Müller could neither reach a consensus nor acquire emergency powers given Hindenburg's conservative attitude and had to resign. Müller's collapse became synonymous with the collapse of parliament-led cabinets, a surrender of worker's interests, a sharp right-wing turn in politics, and the beginning of the era of presidential cabinets and rule by decree.

This entire crisis had the most disastrous political fallout as many started raising the fundamental question whether the Republic was capable at all of handling the crisis. The right saw in the Republic's failure their golden chance to destroy it for ever. On the other hand, the KPD would have been equally pleased to see the capitalist system crumble, which had neared its 'providential nemesis' due to the internal crisis of finance capital (Evans, 2003: 237–42). Time would prove that out of these two anti-republican trends, the radical right was able to substantiate its claims to power in and out of the parliament.

These two phases of economic crisis, that is, hyperinflation and the Great Depression, created deep anxieties and fears in popular psyche. The lower middle class and middle classes were beset with the fear of proletarianisation, an anxiety of being reduced to the ranks of working classes, or worse still, the unemployed. They were gripped by a sense of being caught between the organised workers below and the organised industrialists above, who had managed to hold their necks above water due to their organised strength. Soldiers, who had returned from the front after a humiliating defeat, now faced unemployment; the youth saw its future bleak; and women, unable to fill their children's stomachs, were filled with a sense of deep despair.

In high politics, this was a time of coalition governments as none could prove absolute majority in the parliament. They fell in rapid succession as they proved totally incapable of mastering the crisis. Müller's successor, Brüning, waded through the Depression era, equipped with presidential decrees rather than support from the parliament. He followed many unpopular policies in a high-handed manner. These included austere deflationary policies which had a serious impact on the well-being of millions living on the edge. Public expenditure of all sorts was cut down. Unemployment benefits were reduced in several ways, means testing became more rigorous and thus humiliating for many, and the period for which benefits could be claimed was restricted. Those unemployed for long periods saw a downward spiral of hope and despair sliding from unemployment insurance onto the state-financed crisis benefit, then local welfare support, and finally, no support at all. By the late 1932, there were only

618,000 people left on the unemployment insurance pay, 1,230,000 on crisis benefit, 2,500,000 on welfare support, and over a million whose period of joblessness overshot all welfare provisions and possibilities of a regular income (Evans, 2003: 253–4). The unemployed sat disoriented in parks and stairwells. Children, reconciled to seeing jobless parents and women had to work for many more hours, spending more time on recycling resources, altering, and mending whatever they possessed rather than procuring afresh. Places associated with healthy leisure activities, street corners, and pubs became centres of violent clashes between the Nazis and communists. The level of violence rose dramatically. We turn to that in the section dealing with the rise of Hitler.

To continue with Brüning's story, deflationary policies forced businesses to cut down labour costs, leading to a fall in the prices of agricultural and industrial goods. Brüning hoped to cut German domestic prices by reducing demand and making exports more competitive at the international market. But this did not prove to be a sensible decision at a time when the entire world was facing recession and the demand was sinking everywhere. The banking crisis of 1931, further led to the collapse of the Darmstadt and the National Bank, making Germany heavily dependent on foreign loans. It was estimated that the budgetary deficit of Germany would require more than the entire gold reserves of the US, making international trade impossible. Brüning saw no alternative but to put a stop on the convertibility of the Reichsmark. This rendered the gold standards meaningless. Theoretically, Germany, in her internal market, could adopt reflationary policies to boost industry and jobs. But Brüning refused to take such measures and continued with the deflationary measures causing popular unrest. All these policies earned him the title of 'the Hunger Chancellor'. But he remained unaffected by popular misery. He intentionally followed these policies to show to the world that Germany had no money to pay the reparations. Germany received a moratorium in 1931 and then, ultimately, had all reparations cancelled at the Lousanne Conference of 1932. However, he had to politically pay a heavy price for these anti-people policies. Even on the political front, Brüning pursued anti-democratic policies. A former army officer, a staunch Catholic, and an avowed monarchist, he had little respect for republican values. He curbed civil liberties and the freedom of expression and publication. Hundreds of newspaper editions, critical of his policies, were banned. Liberals, socialists, and communists alike faced his ire.

Brüning's policies have been a matter of considerable debate ever since. There are those like Knut Borchardt who argue that Brüning found himself in a tight spot. He had almost no room to manoeuvre, given the set of political and financial problems he was facing. Others, such as Holtfrerich, argue that a range of other options were available to him, and were being suggested, but he did not want to explore them due to his authoritarian inclination. However, what remains beyond doubt is that the Great Depression and Brüning's anti-people policies paved the way for Hitler.

The question of whether the Weimar Republic was doomed from the beginning or was an experiment that had gone sour has been a matter of debate among historians. While more hopeful historians like Hagen Schultze mourned, if only people had not 'allowed the Weimar experiment to fail' by thinking about mistaken thoughts and engaging in mistaken action (Schultze, 1982: 425) or if only the Left had not been divided and had been truly committed to the transform economic structure (Ruge, 1974: 473), Gerald Feldman thought that the Weimar Republic was more of a gamble rather than an experiment, which stood no chance of success because of the domestic and external economic burdens (Feldman, 1985: 385). Bessel and many others rightly suggested that the Weimar Republic shared many of the economic hardships along with other eastern democracies which suffered similar political fates. What was special about the Weimar Republic was a unique combination of extreme circumstances, which brought about the most extreme political solution, Nazism. Weimar Germany had the *most* democratic constitution. It developed the *most advanced* social welfare system, but it suffered the *worst* inflation. It had lost and had to pay for the *most* destructive war, and lastly, was *most* savagely affected by the Great Depression (Bessel, 1990: 148–9). It may have survived these problems individually, but collapsed under their collective weight in the hothouse atmosphere of Weimar Germany.

We now shift our focus from the Depression to the rise and growth of Hitler and the Nazi party (NSDAP). Hitler started his career as a failed artist, who survived by selling his paintings, and became a dispatch rider in the First World War. He was blinded briefly due to a poisonous gas attack and like many other soldiers was infuriated by the defeat of Germany and the Treaty of Versailles. He was a typical product of the crisis years whose anger and resentment for the Republic in 1923 was brought to a boil in the notorious Beer Hall Putsch. He was a relative nonentity in the national scene before the onset of the Depression. Nothing fits his success story better than Karl Marx's dictum, 'men make their history but not in circumstances of their choosing'.

The first time Hitler tried to make history was in 1923, but the circumstances were not conducive then. He made history once again in 1933, and this time, he sent ripples across the world. In the following pages, we sketch the interplay of circumstances and the making of a charismatic leader of the twentieth century. A below average pupil in school, Hitler wanted to become an architect and applied to the School of Art in Vienna and failed the entrance tests twice. He led a bohemian life in Linz, Germany, until the First World War broke out in which he volunteered as a dispatch runner. He was nominated for an Iron Cross, ironically by a Jewish officer Hugo Gutmann, for delivering a message from command headquarters to the front through heavy fire. He was temporarily blinded by a mustard gas attack when he heard about the defeat and wept bitterly. He often referred to this 'prophetic moment' in his life, of Germany's defeat and the November Revolution that made him enter politics and change Germany's fate. In fact, at that moment, demobilization and the prospect of unemployment were staring at him in the face and he was not willing to leave the army, unlike many of his comrades, until 31 March 1920. Kershaw, who has written Hitler's most authoritative biography in recent years, makes us aware of how this prophetic moment was just plain myth-making, which helped in creating a *Führer* cult. It was sheer luck and opportunism in real terms that moved Hitler rather than his strength of will in the post-war years (Kershaw, 1998: 105).

What his army career in the post-war period did for him, however, was that it turned him into a drummer, a propagandist. His talent for speaking was discovered by captain Karl Mayr, an associate of Kapp, who recruited him for anti-Bolshevik instruction courses conducted at the Munich University in June 1919. Munich had just gone through a phase of soldiers' and sailors' republic under the leadership of Kurt Eisner and the army was now making concerted efforts to pull Munich out of that spell. From there, he went to conduct a five-day course at the army camp at Lechfeld near Augsburg to inculcate nationalism and drive out the vestiges of Bolshevism among soldiers. It is during these speaking tours that he targeted the Jews and Bolsheviks as twin enemies of Germany and was soon considered as the expert on the Jewish question by the likeminded. In September 1919, he joined a non-descript German Worker's Party on invitation by its head Drexler. From here started his career of a full-time political drummer and propagandist, a hypernationalist radical, who wanted to tear down the entire system founded upon the Versailles Treaty and republican values. He soon acquired a reputation among the right-wing circles of being a fiery speaker who enthralled his audiences in the beerhalls of Munich. By mid-1921, he was able to mobilize even larger crowds to his meetings, displace other leaders, and establish himself as the unquestioned leader. He went on addressing ever-growing crowds in beerhalls and with his rabble-rousing speeches provoking his enemies, mainly the socialists and communists, who often booed him, while the right-wing racist audiences fell under the spell of his guttural, over-excited tone, which seemed to many to be a sincere and passionate obsessive love of the fatherland. His repetitive and simple assertions, aggressive and sarcastic manner of talking impressed many, who believed that he was a man of action and not just an orator. He began slowly, spoke with plenty of bitterness and sarcasm, attacked political figures personally, built a gradual climax and created a cathartic impact on the audience, but left them with a hope that more would come. All listeners, irrespective of their class background, were swept off their feet by his rhetorical skill. The typical issues that he raised were: Germany's great past contrasted with the present pitiable state and the need to turn it into a great power again; betrayal and revolution as twin enemies of the German nation; demand for a greater Germany, land and colony; the reversal of the Versailles Treaty, which to him was the peace of shame, the exploitation of innocent Germans by Jewish racketeers and speculators; freedom from interest slavery; land reform; protection of the middle class; persecution of profiteers; and so on. Hitler chose to make his meetings provocative in order to attract large crowds but also controversial to get the attention of his opponents and the media. To combat the opponents, the NSDAP prepared Strom Troopers (SA), or hall protecting squads by August 1921. The SAs were recruited from demobilised soldiers who had a passion for brawls and were right-wing in political orientation. Ernst Röhm, a junior officer, whose face was disfigured by a shell injury and whose psyche was affected by defeat and revolution, was the architect of the SA. He wanted to create a new warrior class capable of rising above corrupt and incapable politicians and of strengthening right-wing politics along with paramilitary forces.

As mentioned earlier, Hitler's first phase of politics ended with his unsuccessful Beer Hall Putsch in 1923. This was followed by a jail sentence and a ban on the NSDAP. Once he returned, he realized that he had to concentrate his energies on reviving the NSDAP. In any case, from 1924 to 1929, Germany's economy was recovering from the debacle of hyperinflation and there was no such crisis that he could capitalize upon. He just quietly worked on consolidating his position within the right-wing and emerged as its unquestioned leader. He had also realised that he could not attain power through a putsch and thought of strategies to destroy democracy by democratic means. In the 1928 election, the NSDAP won just 2.6 per cent of the vote.

As rightly pointed out by Kershaw, propaganda for Hitler was the key to the nationalisation of the masses, without which there could be no national salvation. Being a drummer for the national cause was the highest calling for Hitler (Kershaw, 1998: 156–7). He had done so in the early 1920s, but the dividends were not as dramatic as in the early 1930s. Why? This was because Nazism was the product of all-pervasive crises. The first crisis of hyperinflation led Hitler to armed insurgency against the Republic, which failed miserably and brought him to jail. When he came out on probation in 1924, Germany was experiencing its golden years of stabilisation, drumming up nationalist sentiments when most of the money on which German fortunes were based would not provide fertile ground, so he worked quietly. He returned to mass mobilisation once again in 1930 and was successful beyond his own expectations. With the Great Depression in the background, we could not agree less with Aldous Huxley, 'The propagandist is a man who canalises an existing stream. In a land where there is no water he digs in vain.' The Nazi movement was just this groundswell of anxiety, which drove the masses to despair during the Great Depression. Their frustration and anger at the system was canalised by Hitler for his cause. The Great Depression and Brünings' anti-people policies, which exacerbated the impact of the Depression, created a crisis in which lay Hitler's golden chance to seize power. Hitler sought to project himself as the saviour of a nation in distress, which he exhorted to rise above factional politics of class and stand united behind one movement and one leader.

How was he able to achieve that? The success formula lay in a combination of strategies and tactics which Hitler adopted: non-stop propaganda; a synthetic ideology; making mutually contradictory promises to different sets of people; borrowing styles and strategies from enemies and friends alike; and practicing politics which had a mixture of mass politics of votes combined with street activism, support from below, as well as cultivating the backing of an elite group comprising the army, industrialists; and landlords; and finally, intrigues in the corridors of power. We examine all these elements one by one.

There were three political figures that influenced Hitler from his early days in Austria. He was inspired by Georg Ritter von Schönerer for his national socialism, a brand of radical German nationalism, anti-liberalism, anti-Catholicism, and anti-Semitism and an espousal of the concerns of small proprietors (Kershaw, 1998: 33–4). He owed his 'Heil' greeting and the *Führer's* tag to this man. Next came Karl Lueger, a leader of the Christian Social Party, whose command over the masses and use of propaganda to influence the psychological instinct of the masses left a deep impression on Hitler. Viktor Adler, a Jewish social democrat, who had immense organisational ability to rally workers in street marches and demonstrations in an organised manner, was the third (ibid.: 35–6).

Hitler's first recruits were the Depression-hit farmers. Two years before the onset of the Depression, the countryside was suffering from sinking food prices, bankruptcies, and indebtedness. In the 1928 elections, the peasants were Hitler's only ray of hope in the east and north. He acquired another constituency in students, an indicator of which was his address in November 1928 at the Munich University where a 25,000 strong crowd thronged to listen to him. It was here that he found Baldur von Schirach, a promising leader for the youth. Others like Otto Strasser and Joseph Goebbels adopted a socialist rhetoric to attract workers to the party. This sector had the advantage of Goebbel's propaganda skills and Otto Strasser's organisational skills. Once the Nazis gained popularity, the lower rungs in the party, led by Otto Strasser, advanced their agenda of socialism in the movement. He churned out pro-socialist propaganda through his own press, the *Kampfverlag*, and continued providing support for the striking metal workers in Saxony, despite Hitler's ban, under pressure from industrialists, on any support to strikers. Goebbels, who was editing the *Angriff*, saw in Strasser a rival and wanted him out of his way. This opportunity came due to Strasser's vocal and relentless support for the socialist cause, while Hitler was trying to cultivate the upper classes to expand his social base. In April 1930, he held a party meeting with some of the important leaders in which he harshly criticised Otto Strasser and the left-wing policies of the strikers. Goebbels, another favourite of his, had been working in the Ruhr industrial area to increase his party's base with socialist rhetoric, but Hitler's messages to all people harbouring a socialist dream was to either stop dreaming and nurturing such agendas or to leave the party. Otto Strasser, who was castigated by Hitler and who later published his version of the verbal altercation between the two in *Kampfverlag*, sensed that his days were numbered in the NSDAP. Before he could be purged, he himself resigned and chose a life of anonymity and exile thereafter. Goebbels also chose to quit socialist rhetoric and swore personal loyalty to Hitler. He went on to propagate Hitler's agendas as they changed with time. After quashing the socialist agenda within the party, Hitler's next move was to ameliorate fear from the ranks of industrialists. One important step in this direction was his address to some 650 industrialists at the Industry Club in Düsseldorf in January 1932. In this address, he emphasized on his commitment to protect private property, value hard work and proper rewards for the able and enterprising. Knowing the ways of the big bourgeoisie, he avoided ranting against the Jews in his hysterical style and assumed a respectable garb ensuring them that he was not that violent low-class unruly street fighter. Though this address did not immediately lead to a fund-raising campaign, it paid dividends in the coming years.

Having dissociated the movement from the socialist wing and having cultivated the support of the industrialists, Hitler simultaneously escalated violence on the streets and intrigues in the upper echelons of power. Apart from sophisticated use of propaganda, Hitler's personal charisma and unique mobilisation strategies were other factors, which made him appear as a unique force on the political horizon in the most trying times. It was his ability to mould the circumstances at the right time, which made him the Chancellor, the man of Germany's destiny.

In the elections of September 1930, the NSDAP achieved its first breakthrough with 6.4 million votes, which translated into 18.3 per cent and 107 seats, making it the second largest party with the SPD as the leading party at 24.3 per cent votes. It was a big leap from the 1928 elections when the NSDAP's count was just 2.2 per cent vote, 12 seats and 0.8 million votes. Its niche areas were the protestant, agricultural, and small industrial towns in the north and north east of Germany, but from 1930 onwards, it widened its network. The Nazis were able to make the best out of the economic distress. According to Richard Hamilton, its appeal spread beyond white collar workers, shop keepers, small businessmen, and farmers to civil servants, professionals, mercantile, and industrial bourgeoisie (Hamilton, 1981). In the general elections of July 1932, with 37.8 per cent votes and 230 out of 608 seats, the Nazis became the largest party, even though it was far short of obtaining absolute majority. Others opine that the Nazi party became a catch-all party of social protest and its appeal cut across generations, gender, regions, professions, and conventional class divisions. Its deft use of rhetoric, skilful use of the media for propaganda, cover-all promises, street politics, clever strategy, and above all, Hitler's charismatic personality and rabble rousing abilities swung the masses towards the Nazis. He was able to pose himself as a saviour of the masses, trapped in gloom, hopelessness, and depression. He promised to rise above petty squabbles of existing parties, create unity of all Germans, and march towards an eternally glorious future. In the anxiety-ridden years, the NSDAP was successful in making inroads into fallow lands and converting many camp followers of other parties. It activated many first-time voters: those who did not turn up to vote before, the young generation, and many among women. The party had a strong appeal among the old generation who thought that conventional nationalist parties no longer had the vigour and determination to destroy the republic and take radical action. A huge right-wing nationalist vote bank shifted to the Nazis. They were particularly liked by the civil servants due to the cutbacks that put hundreds of thousands out of work during the Depression years. They also appealed to the self-employed, particularly in protestant areas (Childers, 1981: 262–9). While the Catholics remained more or less loyal to the Catholic Centre and the unemployed from the working class increasingly turned to communists, some 27 per cent of the Nazi voters still had a working class background (Evans, 2003: 263).

Hitler had the advantage of being a political newcomer, not so far tested (and failed as had all others by 1932), and promised a radical break from the stale and ineffective Republican politics. The Nazis also had the advantage of not having a fixed ideology such as Marxism or socialism, which threatened propertied sections of society. In popular understanding, there was no typical way or a set pattern in which a Nazi politician would behave since they had never ruled before. Their violent acts and bloody solutions were seen by the middle class as a part of the exuberance and overexcitement, which they assumed would sober down once they gained power. Hitler's rhetoric appeal lay in repeating in a simple and affective manner, some of the things that touched the sensitive cord of the masses such as the severe condemnation of the Versailles dictate, November criminals, conceited bourgeois parties and the restoration of national pride and glory, and the protection of Germany from the 'menace of Bolshevism'. Given a choice, the middle class would be happy to tolerate right-wing violence to destroy the Bolsheviks. This made their demagogy far more effective and politics far more manoeuvrable. Hitler could swing his arguments and the tenor of his speeches to suit his audience. He could be virulently anti-Semitic in a typical lower-middle-class milieu, but sophisticated and respectable when facing the big business, for example, in Düsseldorf. He did not make any reference to his anti-Semitism and violent ruffian street behaviour because of the aversion of this class to crude street politics of the radicals.

Hitler made a special effort to win over the army, which was elitist to the core and did not trust a rabble-rousing plebeian. The army also feared the NSDAP's hold over its younger creed, which became clear in 1930, when three young national socialist army officers were put on trial for high treason. This infuriated many others who thought that these officers were being tried for their unselfish love of the fatherland. The trial, like Hitler's own in 1923, offered a big occasion for Nazi propaganda when a defendant's lawyer, Hans Frank, summoned Hitler to the witness box. In his characteristic monologue, he declared that the Nazi party had no intension of indulging in high treason, that it intended to come to power through fully legal means and that he had expelled those who were pushing the party to stage a revolution. He used Otto Strasser's ouster as an example to argue that revolution had no place in his worldview. But he also assured his judges, 'if our movement is victorious in its legal struggle, then there will be a German State Court, November 1918 will find its atonement, and heads will roll (Kershaw, 1998: 338). This public proclamation of faith in the legal route to power was widely publicised in the press. Along with the army, this galvanised a considerable section of upper middle class to Nazi aims and ambitions (Evans, 2003: 149). Already before the failed putsch, in the early 1920s, Hitler was able to cultivate some well-heeled members of Munich. Some of them were: Kurt Lüdecke, a gambler and commercial adventurer, who connected Hitler to Luddendorff and used up his entire income during hyperinflation to support Hitler; Putzi Hanfstaengl, a part American from highbrow Munich culture, who was captivated by this 'virtuoso on the keyboard of mass psyche' (Kershaw, 1998: 187), and whose wife treated Hitler with great warmth and sumptuous meals. Hanfstaengle further introduced Hitler to others from the Munich salon society. For all the high-society connections, NSDAP largely depended on funds raised from membership and entry fees. Propaganda financed propaganda in the 1920s, even though Fritz Thyssen may have made a generous gift of 100,000 gold Marks and Hanfstaengel gave 1,000 dollars to purchase two rotary presses to give American style format to *Völkische Beobachter*, the Nazi mouthpiece (ibid.: 189). The big business did not take interest in Hitler in the 1920s, when he was a fringe phenomenon, but when his party made rapid advances in early 1930, they had to take notice of him. Two distinct contrary views emerged regarding the support of big business to Hitler, one from the Comintern that Hitler was a mere agent of big business and another propagated by the party itself, according to which, Hitler won the hearts and minds of all sections of the populations, including the big business. The reality lay somewhere in-between. The big business did not notice the Nazi party in the 1920s and had to recognise its presence in the early 1930s when it grew by leaps and bounds. Even at that time it spread its funding and most of it still went to the conservative right (Turner, 1969: 56–7), as Hitler remained an unreliable factor with the conservatives. Even in 1932, when the Nazis emerged as the strongest party, the big business stayed firmly behind Field Marshall Hindenberg for the presidential election and behind Franz von Papen for the parliamentary elections. Some individual industrialists funded lavish lifestyles of higher ups like Goering, George Strasser and perhaps, also Hitler, but Hitler earned royalties from his *Mein Kampf* which went through many editions and sold thousands of copies as his popularity increased. He also charged heavy fees to give interviews and contribute to foreign press. A majority of the funding still came from membership dues, entrance fees to party meetings, and donations from small businessmen and trades people rather than big business. The big business truly shed all inhibitions once the Nazis came to power.

No matter how much Hitler tried to convince the court and the big business that his party was interested in following only the legal and sober route to power, the social Darwinist idea of struggle for survival was intrinsic to the party and the entire persona of Hitler. The Nazi obsession with uniforms, boots, order, discipline, and compliance to authority set the Nazis apart from the regular right-wing groups that mushroomed in the interwar period. The Nazi party was not a traditional party; rather it was projected as a movement, full of youth, vigour, energy, and the will to bring about radical change in society. It did not go by manifestos, detailed programmes, and policies, but emotion and energy. Street violence was the other side of the parliamentary politics that Hitler played. This is what held promise for the youth, this is what attracted the anxiety-ridden, nervous youth of interwar generation.

'It was exciting,' said Wolfgang Teubert, who joined the Strom troopers in the 1920s. There was the comradeship, the being-there-for-each-other feeling, which for a young man was something outstanding, at least at that time (Rees, 1997: 31). The SA uniforms, the marches in disciplined columns, the display of physical strength to the enemy, invariably a communist, socialist or Jew, filled the disorientated generation of youth with a sense of purpose. The Strom troopers were raised to guard beerhall meetings addressed by Hitler and other Nazis, which tended to become violent but they were equally violent on the streets while marching, demonstrating, or attacking demonstrators and marchers of other parties. They disrupted meetings held by communists and socialists. Otto Buchwitz, a Social Democratic Reichstag deputy, was regularly harangued by SA men; when he rose to address a meeting, they hurled insults at him. On one occasion, an SA man fired a shot at him causing a panic among the gathered crowd. After that they chased him from home to office. His requests for police protection went unheeded. Further, after the dissolution of the Reichstag in 1932, he was sentenced for three months' jail for possessing a weapon illegally, while not a single SA member was prosecuted. Eventually, his safety was assured by the rank and file of communists who promised him protection from the SA (Evans, 2003: 271).

HIGH POLITICS AND INTRIGUES

Riding high on his electoral success in July 1932, even though far short of the absolute majority, Hitler expected to be offered Chancellorship by President Hindenburg. Hindenburg was far from ready to do that, disdainful as he was of this upstart Bohemian corporal. He thought, all that Hitler could hope for was a Vice Chancellorship, but for Hitler, chancellorship was non-negotiable; so he turned down the offer. This bred frustration in party circles, who sensed trouble in the lower rungs, which were being bred on constant movement and the hope that one day their leader would be at the helm. They feared mass discontentment and upheaval in the rank and file.

When the Reichstag reopened on 12 September 1932, it passed a vote of no confidence on Chancellor von Papen by 512 votes to 42. Franz von Papen was a Catholic with an aristocratic upbringing, who never had a popular base and now he lost his parliamentary base as well leaving no justification for his hold over Chancellorship. With this his intentions of establishing a conservative authoritarian rule with complete disregard of parliamentary politics were also dashed, when the parliament was dissolved and fresh elections announced for 6 December. By now the worst of Depression was over. The Nazi movement lost much of its heat when the vote count could not be translated into power politics and the party lost 2 million votes and its deputy's count was reduced to 196. As vote bank politics hung in doldrums, the politics of parliamentary intrigues took the driving seat, which resulted in a brief chancellorship tenure for Schleicher and the ultimate installation of Hitler to chancellorship. Schleicher was able to rule for a couple of weeks until 28 January. January saw the high tide of intrigues and political machinations. Franz von Papen, together with the agrarian elite, which felt threatened by Schleicher's rapprochement with the unions, believed that any coalition without the Nazis would not work because of their sheer mass base, necessitating an acceptable bargain to Hitler. The idea of the broader elite including the army, the industrial, agricultural, and conservative ruling elite was to offer the Nazis some seats in a mixed cabinet and tame Hitler in due course. In the last week of January, it took several rounds of meetings and the effort of Hindenburg's son Oskar to successfully persuade a reluctant Hindenburg to offer chancellorship to Hitler, who was given two more cabinet seats to accommodate his colleagues, Hermann Goering and Wilhelm Frick.

Once in power, with three cabinet ministers only, what Hitler achieved within a matter of months took everyone by surprise;—the conservatives, who were unable to control the tide of *Führerprinzip*; the leftists, and last, but not the least, the Jews and other minorities for whom the countdown for a deadly downward spiral had begun.

He systematically set out to destroy democracy by perusing a policy of *Gleichschaltung* or coordination. All indicators of a multi-party democracy were replaced by compliance and collaboration in politics, society, and culture. All, except the Nazi party, were banned including their newspapers, journals, leisure associations, and other intellectual and cultural wings. The system of elections was done away with. The German

Parliament building, which caught fire under mysterious circumstances, provided Hitler the golden opportunity to invoke the emergency clause of the constitution. The Enabling Act of 23 March 1933 gave Hitler dictatorial powers. Human rights like freedom of speech, press, and assembly were indefinitely suspended. Communists were incarcerated in what came to be known as wild concentration camps. These were simply unoccupied buildings that were used to detain political prisoners without any judicial proceedings. Special surveillance and security forces were created like the Gestapo or the secret state police, notorious for using third-degree measures to torture political opponents; the SS, an elite force which overshadowed the SA over time and built an empire in the East, which was largely responsible for the mass murder of Jews; criminal police (KRIPO); and Security Service (SD), apart from the already existing regular green police and the SA.

The Nazi propaganda and popular longing for an authoritarian personality at the helm created what some historians call the myth of an all-powerful Führer, who had everything under his able and unquestioned command. However, historians now increasingly subscribed to the view associated with Martin Broszat, who argued that the Third Reich was more of a 'polycracy' with competing command structures, internal rivalries, overlapping jurisdiction, and a multiplication of offices and administrative confusion. This was not a static system of rule but a far more dynamic and volatile system. Nonetheless, the *Führerprinzip* or leadership principal remained a binding factor. Hitler managed to play one ambitious rival against the other and, in general, it was in the context of Kershaw's thesis, discussed elsewhere, of 'working towards the *Führer*' or anticipatory obedience, that made a monumental disaster like the holocaust possible. Old systems of policing and administration were not totally revamped but simply altered to suit the new requirements as no great resistance came their way in any case. Thus, much of what was there in the administrative structure was retained for administering ordinary 'law abiding citizens' and a more powerful prerogative state equipped with arbitrary powers became mightier than the normative state. Ernst Fraenkel's notion of the 'Dual state' remains very useful to understand how power operated. The state in this understanding comprised a normative state (for normal functioning), which was increasingly overshadowed by the prerogative state. The prerogative state was run by the arbitrary powers of the Gestapo, Kripo, SD, Special Courts, People's Court, and the SS. It was this that made the Nazi state so intimidating and terrorising for those who were not wanted by the regime. To complement this, the dichotomy between party and state was never clearly defined and party functionaries rivalled state functionaries in the working of the state. This functioned smoothly in the initial years largely due to economic recovery and early diplomatic victories, which we cover briefly now.

The Nazi economy was to serve the interests of the state. German capitalists appreciated the lucrative contracts and freedom from trade union pressures for higher wages. They obtained a free hand over workers and firms and found nothing objectionable about Nazi economic policies. Much of the welfare mechanisms remained in place, but it was now open only to pure-blooded Germans, which meant that Jews, Gypsies, and other community aliens were robbed of protection and support of all kinds. The economic policy can be divided in three phases, the first phase of which lasted till 1936. Their economic policies remained pragmatic to avoid major structural changes and achieve maximum production. In fact, Kurt von Schleicher had already initiated steps to tame the Depression. Under the command of Hjalmar Schacht, the former president of the Imeperial Bank, Hitler introduced deficit financing and greatly increased public spending on employment, generating mammoth projects such as the construction of the *Autobahn* or highways. Tax incentives and subsidies were introduced to encourage economic expansion and stimulate public demand. To combat unemployment, the already existing six-month work service was made obligatory for all young men in 1935. This assured menial labour supply for monumental infrastructural construction and, in the later years, for military service. While existing property relations were not disturbed, the German economy was increasingly subjected to stringent regulations designed to achieve military objectives later on. Prices, salaries, wages, rents, imports, and exports were subjected to varying degrees of state control. The government also set production goals and determined the percentage of net receipts that businesses were obliged to reinvest in expanded production, mainly in the armament industry. With all this, Germany was able to achieve full employment rates. However, Schacht, as a mature economist, was not in favour of deficit financing over a long period due to its attendant problems. He advocated a traditional export-oriented policy designed to attract foreign exchange, which could be used to restore normalcy. Schacht successfully concluded bilateral trade agreements with a number of countries to secure markets for German manufactured goods and raw material for its industries, but his cautious monetary policies, opposition to deficit financing, and shift to the armament industry was not liked by Hitler. Schacht was soon shown the door as Nazi economy entered its second phase characterised by autarchy and the four year plan in 1936, which was geared towards war.

The reins of Nazi economy, henceforth, came into the hand of Hermann Goering in the second phase, and then Frick, who simply followed Hitler's wishes. Many historians today agree that war became a necessity if Nazi economy had to expand, and thus, there was a deep connection between Hitler's aggressive foreign policy and economy. The two fed on each other.

Besides putting the economy on the rails of deficit financing to create jobs, Hitler achieved quick diplomatic victories, which won him wide acclaim at home and abroad. His early diplomatic manoeuvres resulted in nullifying many of the ill effects of the Versailles Treaty without any bloodshed. Hitler walked out of the disarmament conference, conducted by the League of Nations in Geneva, 1932–3. This was followed by his resignation from the League. In March 1935, Germany won back the control of coal-rich Saar in an internationally supervised plebiscite and announced the reintroduction of military conscription and the expansion of the army beyond the sanctioned limits of the Versailles. At the same time, he revealed the existence of a German air force which had been secretly training in the USSR. Britain further concluded a naval agreement that allowed Germany to exceed the limits imposed by the Treaty of Versailles. In February 1936, the French parliament ratified a defensive Franco-Soviet Pact. Using this as a pretext, Hitler sent a token army into the Rheinland, a demilitarised buffer zone between France and Germany, further violating the Versailles agreement. He was testing the French response but France did not react embroiled as she was in an internal conflict between the right and left that would lead to the election of a Popular Front socialist government.

These quick victories became possible because of what came to be known as the British Appeasement Policy under the British premier Neville Chamberlain. Britain followed this policy in order to avoid another war, which it thought would result in the further weakening of Europe as a continent. There was a realisation, both in the power elite as well as wider British public, that the Versailles Treaty had been driven by the French and Dutch vendetta. The adverse impact of hyperinflation and the Great Depression, Germans carrying cartloads of currency to buy a loaf of bread during the former and the unemployed sitting listlessly in parks and stairwells during the latter, so well publicised in the German press, were etched on the memory of British public, which empathised with the German public. The feeling that the Versailles Treaty had gone too far in the direction of seeking vendetta was indeed widespread in the the British public sphere and British would have liked to avoid another bloody conflict this time led by Hitler. Little did they know at that time that the policy of appeasement would only embolden Hitler to crave for more.

The left-wing alternative to the Appeasement Policy was the Popular Front adopted by the Comintern. Its engineers led by the USSR were indeed the harshest critics of Hitler's policies and were acutely aware of the dangers of promoting his aggressive foreign policies, but almost all of the western powers, including the socialists, were more afraid of a Bolshevik threat than a fascist one and would have chosen to trade with the latter rather than the former. The western powers confirmed their fears of the Soviets by refusing aid to the democratically elected Popular Front government in the Spanish Civil War against the right-wing general, Francisco Franco in July 1936. Both Germany and Italy sent weaponry and personnel to crush the glorious uprising of the Popular Front in Spain. Soviet efforts to commit western powers to an anti-fascist front by promoting a collective security policy in the League of Nations, after the USSR's entry in 1934, similarly fell on deaf ears.

Continuing their appeasement policy, Chamberlain sent his minister of war Halifax to Hitler's mountain retreat Berchtesgaden in November 1937 to assure Hitler that Britain would not oppose a modification of Germany's eastern frontiers if achieved by peaceful means. Taking full advantage of the appeasement policy, Hitler moved swiftly to annex Austria. Hitler was afraid that he might face defeat in a plebiscite on Austrian independence and stationed troops on the border of Austria on 13 March 1938. Austrian Nazis invited Hitler the following day. Hitler marched triumphantly into Vienna, a city where he survived as a street artist after being rejected twice by its elite academy of Fine Arts. The policy of appeasement saw its highpoint in the Czechoslovakian crisis when Nazi-inspired Konrad Henlein demanded freedom from the Prague government for Sudetenland, a German-speaking province. The democratically elected Czech government refused to be intimidated. Sensing the brewing tension, Chamerlain flew to meet Hitler thrice and, once again, bowed to Hitler's demands in the infamous Munich Agreement acquiescing German military occupation of Sudetenland. The agreement was brokered on 1 October 1938, in the presence of Dadalier from France and Mussolini from Italy, while Czechoslovakia and USSR were kept out. Hitler's true aims were soon revealed when he marched into Prague on 15 March 1939, thereby flouting the pledge made in the Munich Agreement not to make any further territorial claims. Hitler overran Czechoslovakia, created the protectorate of Bohemia and Moravia, and installed a pro-Nazi dictator Josef Tiso in Slovakia. Ironically, while Britain watched the destruction of democratic Czechoslovakia, it advanced unconditioned support to the conservative government of Poland in case of a German invasion. It is important to remind ourselves that Poland was one of the biggest beneficiaries of the Versailles Treaty and had gained huge territorial benefits from imperial Germany and the Austrian Empire. The suspicion of Soviet designs refrained western allies to secure Poland on its eastern side in spite of repeated Soviet overtures for an anti-fascist front. Hitler took advantage of the situation and signed the Nazi Soviet Non-Aggression Pact on 22 August 1939, invaded Poland on 1 September, and 1939, which was quickly overrun. Poland was the gateway to the long-term eastward expansion for Germany and also the theatre for the large-scale murder of Jews, Gypsies, and other undesirables in death camps. The occupation of Poland, the fall of France, Holland, and Belgium, and advances in the East, as a result of Hitler's successful *Blitzkrieg*, gave Hitler large territories in the continent to realise his plans of a continental conquest of the *Lebensraum*. However, as time would prove, the structural disjunction between his short-term *Blitzkeig* and long-term involvement with the USSR, rendered him at the mercy of Stalin. His overestimation of Germany's armed strength and underestimation of the collective power, resolve, and resources of the USSR, Britain, and the USA made him eventually a captive in his own bunker, where he committed suicide when Stalin's red army came knocking on his door. As Winston Churchill acidly remarked, Hitler had been free to start a war at a time of his choosing, but he was not free to choose the time of its end, except by surrender. These foreign policy blunders were not a result of his failed tactics but of his long-term policy of the conquest of the *Lebensraum* in the East, to which we shall turn now.

NAZI WORLD VIEW

Nazi ideology became synonymous with Hitler's worldview. According to this, there was no equality between the peoples, but only a racial hierarchy. In this worldview, the German people stood at the top. They were white, blond, blue eyed, and belonged to the Nordic Aryan race. Hitler regarded history essentially as a struggle for survival among races. He relentlessly championed the cause of the Aryan race, which was said to be under threat because of intermarriage and blood mixing, especially from the Jewish people. From Darwin and Herbert Spencer he borrowed concepts like natural selection and survival of the fittest. Charles Darwin himself was not a racist. He was a natural scientist who explained the creation of plants, animals, and humans through the concept of evolution and natural selection. Herbert Spencer later added the famous concept of survival of the fittest to Darwin's ideas, which basically meant that only those species survived on earth in the process of evolution that could adapt themselves to changing climatic conditions. These concepts were meant to be applied to understand the world of nature. However, from the late nineteenth century, such ideas were used by racist white thinkers to justify imperial rule over other peoples categorised as Mongoloid, Negro, Jew, and so on. This was largely done on the basis of external appearance combined with value judgements and stereotyping to which, the concept of heredity was attached. All of this made racial differences appear immutable and natural. These ideas gained currency in Europe as well as America. What was different in Nazi Germany, however, was that these utopian racial ideas transformed themselves into state ideology. Race came to be considered a science and racial-biological institutes were established all over the Nazi empire. Here inhuman experiments were conducted on the so-called racially undesirable people for scientific research and for assessing their racial worth. The Nazi state ultimately annihilated the entire Jewish and Gypsy populations apart from large segments of Slavs and Poles on this basis.

The other aspect of Hitler's ideology related to the geopolitical concept of *Lebensraum*, or living space. This largely shaped his foreign policy consideration. Some of it could be seen already outlined in his *Mein Kampf* in statements such as these, 'Germany must find the courage to gather our people and their strength for an advance along the road that will lead this people from its present restricted living space to new land and soil, and hence, also free it from the danger of vanishing from the earth or of serving others as a slave nation (Hitler, 1971: 646). What it meant in real terms was enslaving other peoples and nations, mainly in the east to serve the Germans.

For it is not in the colonial question that we must see the solution of this problem, but exclusively in the acquisition of a territory for settlement, which will enhance the area of the mother country, and hence, not keep the new settlers in the most intimate community with the land of their origin, but secure for the total area, those advantages, which lie in its unified magnitude (ibid.: 653). A curious contradiction in this policy is the need felt for expanding the geographical living space at a time when Germany was facing a crisis of low birth rate. We have already noted in Chapter 3 on nationalisation of the female citizenry how women were being exhorted by the state to produce more healthy Aryan children. Emboldened by his foreign political successes and the economic logic of his aggressive expansionism, Hitler took, what historians call, 'the flight forwards' towards imperialism and war. The first and primary phase of this imperialism was aimed at the European continent itself, its vast agricultural lands, and its people whom he wanted to enslave. Russia and its neighbouring countries were to be the first targets in this vision. The great pre-Bolshevik Russian Empire, according to Hitler, did not owe its glory to the Slav elements but to the racial nucleus of Germanic organisers, which had been replaced by the Jews in the Bolshevik era. He thought it was the historic task of the Third Reich to restore the Germanic elite to its previous position of dominance. Thus, his anti-Semitism not only guided his domestic, but also foreign political considerations. His ever-expansive ambitious foreign policy is aired in his Secret Book which opined, 'For this earth is not allotted to anyone nor is it presented to anyone as gift. It is awarded by providence to people who in their hearts have the courage to conquer it, the strength to preserve it, and the industry to put it through the plough ... The present distribution of possessions has not been designed by a higher power but by man himself (Hitler, 1962: 15–16.)

If we consider his foreign policy in the light of his worldview, with the *Lebensraum* at its core, we can understand that his responses to the British and allied appeasement policy were just a launching pad and he would have gone ahead with his plans. Of course, his determination and urgency were fanned by the early foreign policy successes. His war aims were inextricably interlinked with his anti-Semitic policy to which we shall turn now.

HITLER'S WAR OF ANNIHILATION ON THE JEWS AND OTHER MINORITIES

We observe that these were not entirely a result of Hitler's intentions, as outlined in the *Mein Kampf,* but a mixture of the original intent along with contingencies. The complete extermination came as the 'final solution', not the first choice. The noose tightened gradually and, in the course of its economic and image-related factors, impeded and slackened the pace of persecution, while pure racism was diluted by religious and pragmatic consideration in determining exactly who a 'Jew' was. In brief, the road from religious hatred to racial anti-Semitism was a long and twisted one. Christians had traditionally accused Jews as killers of Christ, ritual murderers, and usurpers. In pre-modern Europe, the Jews were barred from owning land and lived in separately marked areas called ghettoes, mainly practicing trade, commerce, and money lending to earn a living. Christians had three ways of persecuting them: pogroms, that is, periodic violence, expulsion from the land, and conversion. Modern anti-Semitism based on pseudo-scientific theories of race asserted that race was something immutable and unchangeable. 'Once a Jew, always a Jew' is what the racists propagated and believed. They came to be seen as a problem of hereditary nature, and therefore phrases such as rooting out, extermination and so on were used for them.

However, there was no direct route from Christian hatred to the holocaust. Jews experienced a marked period of growth, prosperity, and stability in the Imperial and Republican eras spanning a period of about six decades. The Christian ways of persecuting the Jews were discarded under the influence of the Enlightenment in several parts of Germany, and the unification made the emancipation universal. Henceforth, they enjoyed full citizenship rights and participated in the public sphere actively. In the following decades, they enthusiastically received a liberal education, entered into civil professions, and participated in the civil, cultural, and intellectual life of Germany. Even their women's literacy and education rates were higher than both Protestant and Catholic Germans. In order to assimilate into the mainstream society, a significant number of Jews converted to Christianity and intermarried with gentiles. In modern Germany, Jews had largely middle-class profiles as compared with the East, where they still remained overwhelmingly poor, ghettoized, and persecuted. The Weimar Republic brought more prominence and visibility to the Jews who could be seen in the forefront of change and progress in all walks of life: commerce, finance, education, legal and civil services, medicine, the arts, and sciences. The presence of Jews in progressive and revolutionary movements, in experimental arts and other creative pursuits, was quite noticeable. It is common knowledge that many of the noble laureates of Germany were of Jewish decent. That this bred social jealously in many ordinary Germans is borne out by several cases of denunciations registered by the Gestapo during the Nazi period.

ESTABLISHMENT OF A RACIAL STATE

Once in power, the Nazis realised their dream of creating an exclusive racial community of people (*Volksgemeinschaft*). This meant a radical reorganisation of society along vertical lines as opposed to horizontal divisions, like class, caste, gender, for example. Nazis created a society, which was divided into people worthy and unworthy of life, a division between life and death, inclusion and exclusion, on the basis of the accident of birth in a particular racial group. Who were these undesirables? This included peoples like Jews, Gypsies, Poles, Russians, and Blacks, especially half Blacks living in Europe. The chief target of attack in number and visibility were Jews, and therefore, it is in order to quickly touch upon major milestones of the anti-Semitic or anti-Jewish policies, which eventually led to mass murder.

The statistics of the German Jewry reflect that at no point did they exceed 1.09 per cent of the total population. By 1933, roughly 500,000 Jews lived in Germany. Most German Jews were concentrated in large cities. During the Nazi regime, Jews were gradually de-classed as a result of their step-by-step pauperisation, starting with the April 1933 boycott of Jewish businesses. Various laws and decrees dispossessed them of their government jobs, private practices, properties, businesses, and in the end, even their personal belongings. This legal discrimination was combined with terror attacks on them through the SA men, which culminated in the *Reichskristallnacht* (night of broken glass) on the nights of 10 and 11 November 1938. There were some 400 pieces of anti-Jewish legislation promulgated by the Nazis. The first two laws came in April 1933 namely, the Law for the Restoration of the Professional Civil Service and the Law Concerning Admission to the Legal Profession. These resulted in large-scale dismissal of Jews from these professions. Nuremburg Laws, which came into effect from 15 September 1935, declared that only persons of German or related blood would henceforth be German citizens enjoying the protection of the German empire. This meant that Jews, Gypsies and other minorities were no longer to be citizens. Marriages between Jews and German were forbidden. Extramarital relations between Jews and Germans became a crime. Further discriminating laws came in 1938, which were promulgated to expel them root and branch from businesses, legal, medical, and teaching professions. The pauperisation drive was intensified after the *Reichskristallnacht*. By the Decree of 12 November 1938, all Jewish property and businesses, retail or wholesale, were to be Aryanised. Jews were forced to sell their properties to the Aryans at a throwaway price.

The widespread rejection of the violence and hooliganism unleashed by the party on the *Reichskristallnacht* made the Nazis take another route leading to Auschwitz and the organised mass killings. Henceforth, wild actions and legal persecution gave way to deportations and destruction.

Not all Jews, however, went through the same process at the hands of Nazis. Even in the Third Reich, Jews were not a mass of undifferentiated people. Not all had escape routes, just as not all were physically eliminated. Certain categories of Jews got a differential treatment. Those who had fought for the 'Fatherland' in the First World War comprised the first category. They were given some 'concessions', and 'milder punishments' in the initial years. The differential legal treatment could not shield them for long. Finally, their destiny led them to the death factories via Theresienstadt ghetto. Persons of 'mixed Jewish blood' were another category. The Jews living in mixed marriages also enjoyed certain immunities. Mixed marriages were divided into two categories, privileged and not privileged. The 'privileged Jews' consisted of Jewish husbands, who had German wives, provided the couple had one or more children classified as mixed children of the first degree, and Jewish wives who had German husbands, provided that the children were classified as mixed children of the first degree, or that the couple was childless. At the time of the deportations, privileged status was enjoyed by the Jewish parent of a mixed child. If the only mixed child had been killed in action, and the now childless Jewish wife lived in a mixed marriage, she enjoyed immunity from deportation for the duration of the marriage. The Jews living in a privileged marriage also escaped unscathed from the Holocaust to a great extent. A 'non-privileged Jew' was the Jewish parent whose half-Jewish children were classified as Jews or a childless Jewish husband in a mixed marriage (unless his only mixed child had been killed in action). In the above categories of mixed marriages and mixed children, it was not so much blood and race that decided the fate of the victims as their religion. Jews who survived also included those who emigrated, if they were not captured and killed from the neighbouring countries and were able to leave the frontiers of the Reich before it was too late. In the initial years, the regime forced the Jews to leave the country. For the Jews, it was never emigration, always only escape. The highpoint of this tendency was witnessed during the aftermath of the *Reichskristallnacht*, the night of the broken glass (9–10 November 1938). The Jews were rounded up en masse and thrown in concentration camps. The Gestapo files show that a large number of them were set free on the assurance that they would leave the country for good.

From the night of the broken glass onwards Jews kept moving from one place to the other, their belongings became lesser and lesser, were appropriated by the state, neighbours, colleagues, and others in a superior position than them, depending upon the context. Once the War started, Jews were separated from ordinary Germans by introducing a yellow Star of David, which all Jews were forced to wear on their breast. This identity mark was stamped on their passport, all legal documents and houses. They were kept in Jewish houses and deported to Poland from 1941 onwards.

And death came of them in many forms but most notoriously in killing centres where gas machines killed them in their masses within minutes with industrial, scientific precision. As Germany occupied Austria, Poland, France, Belgium, Holland, Russia, and established puppet regimes in Southern Europe, they combed entire occupied territories to collect Jews and deported them to killing centres where they were all gassed. A large number of their worldly goods landed on the Auschwitz ramp and were appropriated by the SS. One can see samples of the left-over artefacts: shoes, spectacles, brushes, toothpaste, soap, clothes, hair, prayer mats, suitcases, utensils, and even textiles using their hair as raw material in the Auschwitz memorial museum today.

THE ART OF DECEPTION IN NAZI GERMANY

Language is generally viewed as a means of communicating thoughts and feelings through words. We assume responsibility for the words we utter because freedom of speech is not freedom from responsibility. The Nazi regime invented a language to deceive people and deny responsibility. Euphemisms abounded in their official communications. Detaining political and racial victims without judicial proceeding, indefinitely, in the Gestapo torture chambers was called 'protective custody', which implied that if they were set free they will be lynched by people. 'Public outrage' was the term used for organised lynching, pillorying, blackening of faces and shaving off heads, mostly for humiliating racial offenders. Such acts were undertaken by party enthusiasts in the name of the people. The most dreaded court, which routinely announced summary executions, was called *Volksgerichtshof* or the 'People's Court' and all justice was dispensed here in the name of the people. The ramp at Auschwitz on which selections were done was called *Himmelfahrt* or singular journey to heavens. It was on this ramp that Jewish doctors were engaged to choose who would go straight to the gas chamber (mostly women, children, and infirm men) and who would survive until their last drop of blood and sweat is spent on heavy manual work. Auschwitz Birkenau, where they were consigned to hard labour, had an inscription at the entrance gate saying 'work liberates' (of course, from life). Some of the words used for mass killings were special treatment, final solution (used for Jews), euthanasia (mercy killing), selection, disinfection, evacuation, deportation. The communities selected for murder were compared to vermin, rats, pests, carriers of diseases in Nazi propaganda, thereby justifying their murder as necessary for freeing the Aryans from epidemics, plagues and infections. The gas chamber was called the disinfection area, and these looked like a bathroom equipped with fake showerheads, which released poisonous gas killing them within minutes.

These lies and deceptions went beyond words, and an entire propaganda machinery, called the Ministry of Cultural Enlightenment, was set up under Goebbels, to indoctrinate people to develop Nazi sensibilities. It essentially meant approval for their various racial programmes and active support for inhuman, murderous policies, the nazi regime employed a language to deceive in communicate its racial messages, and recruit people to its cause. A large range of propaganda films, both fiction and documentaries, were made to spread hatred of Jews, the most infamous being 'The Eternal Jew'. It was full of stereotypical images of the orthodox Jews with flowing beards wearing kaftans, even though German Jews were difficult to tell from their outward appearance because of their highly assimilated nature. On the map of the earth, the movement of rodents was compared to that of the Jews. The voiceover constantly referred to the Jews as vermin, rats, and pests in order to create a parasitic, inhuman image of the entire people.

Another film called 'I accuse' justified the murder of the physically and mentally challenged by creating a melodramatic situation where a professor was shown deeply in love with his terminally ill wife whose sufferings he could not endure and decided to free her by giving her an overdose of morphine. The actual killing operation of the disabled, euphemistically called euthanasia, however, did not bear any resemblance to the emotionally charged scenario of the film. It was the result of a cold, calculated, and clinical procedure and a precursor to the gas chambers in death factories.

The Triumph of Will, which went on to become a cult propaganda documentary, showed the indomitable spirit of the Nazi party, its disciplined marching column, it mass following, and the hysteria of the crowd upon seeing their *Führer*. The film was a majestic show of Nazi power at its height, leaving even the worst sceptic spellbound by the magic created by its director Leni Riefenstahl. The radio was called the people's receiver. It became available at affordable price to keep people in close touch with the *Führer*. At the same time, listening to foreign broadcasts was declared a criminal offence.

The entire system of education was designed to communicate Nazi ideology, which was outlined in *Mein Kampf*: 'No boy or girl must leave school without having a clear insight into the meaning of racial purity and the importance of maintaining the racial blood unadulterated.' History and geography lessons were distorted to suit Nazi worldview and new subjects like racial biology and racial hygiene were introduced in the school curriculum, as well as in the teachers' training programmes. Classrooms became unbearable for Jewish children as they were targeted and ridiculed by teachers and the taught alike before they were finally expelled from there.

ORDINARY PEOPLE AND THE HOLOCAUST

In Hitler's biography, Kershaw propounded the famous thesis 'working towards the *Führer*'. Hitler in this work is projected as a chaotic, insensitive, non-stop talker, who neither wanted nor was capable of engaging in long-term careful planning. He was passionate but hardly meticulous and hated getting trapped in bureaucratic red tape. His underlings made their own sense from the long monologues they received from him and 'worked towards him'. They wanted to please him and knew for certain that inviting his ire could cost them their jobs so the successful ones were those who fulfilled his wishes and did not question him. This applied just as much to lower functionaries, bureaucrats, party zealots, and so on. The net result was that Nazism in power acquired a huge mass base and a mammoth force of willing workers in whatever capacity. As Alf Lüdtke and many others opine, the active participation of sectional heads, administrators, and even the clerical personnel, in fulfilling the job of 'their agency' or 'their company', was more than mere passive obedience or 'just following orders', as many would argue before the trial courts in the post-War era. Active participation and involvement was also a part of the picture where organisational routines and bureaucratic forms created or reinforced a semblance of order and regularity (Lüdtke, 2000: 82). This is as far as the bureaucracy is concerned. In fact, the number of ordinary people with no special obligation to fulfil the expectation also willingly collaborated in the brutalisation and criminalisation of everyday life under the Nazis. This has been shown in the work of Christopher Browning's *Ordinary Germans: Reserve Police battalion 101 and Final Solution*, and in a far more controversial and popular work of Danial Goldhagen, *Hitler's Willing Executioners*. Both of them primarily analysed this battalion to draw their own conclusions about the behaviour and impulse of this battalion, which consisted of conscripts, about 500 of them from working class backgrounds and many war veterans. The most conspicuous thing about them was that they were very normal, very ordinary. They were neither party members nor members of the SS and were assigned the job of killing the Jews for they were the only ones available. Yet they did this job with great efficiency, were deeply involved in anti-Semitic and racist propaganda and killing. In his graphic portrayal, Browning talks about peer pressure, brutal socialisation, prevailing anti-Semitism, and a sense of superiority that drove them to kill Jews in their hundreds, without any remorse and guilt. None expressed the wish to get transferred even though the option was open. The same men fared far worse in Goldhagen book, *Hitler's Willing Executioners*, who argued that Germans contained a specific brand of eliminationist anti-Semitism in them. Driven by this hate ideology, the 101 Police battalion killed the Jews with great relish. One major contribution of these two works was that Nazism was pulled out of the sphere of psychoanalysts who gave

Freudian explanations of murderous behaviours, trying to establish that there was something abnormal about the Nazi killers, that they were somehow pathological, abnormal cases. Studies such as those of Browning and Goldhagen awaken our sense to the mundane and everyday aspect of killings and mass brutalities and thereby make us keenly aware of the presence of murderers amidst ordinary people. They convey the important message that one did not have to be a psychopath to go on a killing spree. We can get closer to the normality of Nazi crimes and brutalisation of society when we study the dossiers of Gestapo functionaries. Recent studies have shown that the conventional image of the Gestapo as the omniscient, omnipotent, and omnipresent agent of the Nazi power apparatus has been largely a 'myth', first propagated by the Nazi state itself and then believed by resistance fighters, scholars of totalitarianism, and ordinary people. This myth played a very important political and social function not only in instilling fear and eliciting compliance among ordinary people, but also allowed leftists and other radicals to justify the absence of organised mass protest, the decimation in their own ranks and their own growing isolation. Ordinary people, after the collapse of the Third Reich, could then conveniently say that protest or even the thought of it was 'too dangerous' as the Gestapo had their spies and informers posted in every nook and corner, had an unfailing surveillance system, and was super-efficient in cracking down on the opponents. This myth has been busted in the last two decades or so by historians who have adopted an Foucaultian approach to study everyday life in Nazi Germany. Notions of state power, surveillance, discipline and punishment in this approach are not studied as mechanisms operating from above only. Rather, the whole system operated on a cellular basis, which involved not just the top political, police and the SS Empire but also ordinary people who policed each other. Nazi Society in other worlds was a self-policing society and denunciations were instrumentalized to this end very effectively. A large number of infractions were not the Gestapo's own discovery but a result of voluntary reporting by ordinary citizens: neighbours, colleagues, relations, spouses and passers-by. These denouncers were not motivated by anti-Semitic, racist, and Nazi ideology, but by a host of interpersonal malicious motives. (Gellately, 1990; Johnson, 1999; Joshi, 2003; Klaus Michael Mallmann and Gerhard Paul, 1991). In the Gestapo dossiers of persecuted individuals, the Gestapo functionaries do not appear as omnipresent and omniscient agents but ordinary desk workers, who simply wrote down denunciations filed by ordinary citizens and then followed up the matter. There is no denying that once an infraction or wrongdoing was reported, they investigated the matter quite thoroughly, although the crack down on the communists, Jehovah's witnesses, socialists, and other 'political enemies' largely became possible because of paid informers and the regime-utilised lists already available from the previous era. But the consensual space for their actions and the participation of willing collaborators increased dramatically due to the provision of denunciation. This act of popular collaboration was successful in creating terror and complicity in society. Many, of course, derived also material advantage through such acts but it was a constellation of many factors, which Alf Lüdtke calls a patchwork of practices, calculated and experienced motives that created the willingness and complicity among the masses (Lüdtke, 2000: 90). A three-volume collection of oral history compiled by Niethammer clearly demonstrates that people, by and large, had positive memories and recollections of the Nazi past. Even the recollections of industrial workers, a traditional vote bank of the leftists, had positive memories of the reconstruction and economic upswings of 1936–37 and the peaceful years until the outbreak and the first three years of the War (Niethammer [ed.], 1983, 1983, 1985).

Organised workers indeed remained resistant to Nazi propaganda in the days of the Great Depression. Undoubtedly, the popularity and vote bank of the KPD increased remarkably during the Depression due to the support of the unemployed working class. Nonetheless, once the Nazi regime consolidated itself, its rule was almost hegemonic and even the SOPADE reports of the illegal correspondences of the SPD in exile observed great passivity among working masses even though they may have noted general dissatisfaction and tried to maintain an illusion of workers uprising. Alf Lüdtke has attempted to resolve this puzzle for us in his analysis of everyday behaviour patterns of workers in their mundane life beyond organisations and workplaces to working class neighbourhoods and families. For him, the key to the workers' complacency lay in their *Eigensinn* (stubborn self-reliance) and the myth of German quality work. Worker's efficiency, dexterity, and pride in the work remained enthused with a sense of Germanness. It was this *Eigensinn*, argues Lüdtke, that created a unique bonding which cut across regions, genders, generations, and other variations and created a sense of oneness in German workers, who increasingly saw themselves as national labour (Lüdtke, 2006: 129–51). He extends this understanding to soldiers in war who were, in fact, largely workers drafted as soldiers. They 'accomplished' the job of soldiering in the spirit of factory work with 'German virtues' of quality work, dexterity, precision, dedication, cool determination, and industry. Never mind if it was factory work or killing; both had to be accomplished with efficiency. Lüdtke arrives at this understanding on the basis of letters from the front, autobiographical accounts, and so on. He cites a one-off case of Janka, a worker/soldier with an anti-fascist background, who had fought in the Spanish Civil War against Franco. In his autobiographical text, he noted that his machine gun company had successfully ambushed and completely destroyed a full load of Franco's soldiers. It was for him a 'good job' that the company had done. At the same time, on hindsight, he began to reflect: "Killing people is not work." But may be a soldier sees it that way and most of the soldiers are workers. What they do is just work (ibid.: 144). He was an exception. For the large majority of worker-soldiers, killing and destruction was just a job done well.

HISTORIOGRAPHICAL DEBATES AND CONTROVERSIES

Nazi Germany has been one of the most researched areas of historical enquiry and, therefore, has been subjected to innumerable approaches, debates, and controversies. In the previous section, we have already discussed some of them and would now turn to certain other trends. Many would argue that this epoch can never be historicised, never be considered a period of history. It is a past that never seems to pass, asserted a right-wing German historian, Michael Stürmer, who wanted to make it a usable past. He is pitted against those who believe that the Nazi past is unmasterable, for example, Charles Meier, because of the singularity of its crimes. At one level, it evokes strong emotions and problems of morality and philosophy at another, making it quite challenging for historians to be 'neutral', 'objective', or indifferent. The *Historikerstreit* or the historians' dispute of the 1980s is the prime example of that. However, after bitter and acrimonious debates that it launched in Europe and America, most of the sober historians agreed that the debate created more heat than light. For this reason, I would not go into the details of the issues involved. I choose instead to talk about some of the more substantial controversies and approaches, which have revised our understanding of the origins, nature, and course of Nazi Germany.

Just as there has been a tendency among western historians to trace the Nazi drives all the way back to Prussian militaristic traditions, Bismarck and even Luther, the post-war German historians on their part tried to detach the Nazi past from its historical moorings, passing it off as a bolt from the blue, or indeed, very un-German in essence. In the post-War years, German historians tried to explain the rise of Nazis as a *Betriebsunfall* (industrial catastrophe) or a bolt from the blue, denying any connection between Germany's preceding eras and the Nazi Germany. This trend was challenged by Fritz Fischer in 1961 with his German publication later translated in English as *Germany's Aims in the First World War 1914–1918*. He argued on the basis of intensive archival research that Germany had prepared extensive plans for a world war much before the outbreak in 1914 implying that it had imperial ambitions of world domination. Germany merely used the pretext of Archduke Franz Ferdinand's assassination as an opportunity to instigate Austria to declare war. Even though he was talking about the First World War, his thesis had a strong bearing for the Second World War, highlighting the continuities of foreign political ambitions and imperial desires not only of the heads of the state (Emperor or Hitler) but also domestic pressure groups who pursued aggressive imperial goals, particularly in the East and Africa. This idea was expanded in his subsequent works such as the war of illusion, primacy of domestic politics, and so on. He also produced archival evidence for ideas related to ethnic cleansing in Russia and the *Lebensraum*, implying that Hitler was not ingenious and singular in pursuing genocidal politics and that these ideas were widely popular in the ruling elite much before Hitler's domination of Germany. Fritz Fischer inspired an entire generation of new left students and scholars in and beyond the borders of Germany to legitimately attack the German right, which had swept the Nazi crimes under the carpet.

In the 1980s, Hans Ulrich Wehler further advanced the argument by suggesting social imperialism as the core of Germany's domestic policy, which in turn determined foreign policy of war, militarism, and imperialism. Wehler's much talked about Germany's special path to modernisation was first illustrated in his work, *The German Empire* (Berg, 1985). Wehler took the aid of both Marx and Weber in propounding his theory, which took a long-term view of the ultimate disaster of 1945. The special path that Germany took was a distorted path to modernisation where pre-existing feudal modes of behaviour continued to prevail upon the bourgeoisie and society. According to this argument, the German bourgeoisie failed to wrest power from the ruling aristocracy in 1848, unlike its Anglo-French neighbours. In the following two decades, the Prussian aristocracy staged a revolution by unifying Germany and also completed the process of industrialisation. While Germany did industrialise, the top positions in the army, civil services, and politics remained in the hands of landlords or *Junkers*. It was their value system that was aped by the aspiring bourgeoisie, which Wehler called the feudalisation of the bourgeoisie. Thus, cultural modes of behaviour remained feudal in orientation and practices, such as the persistence of duelling, inherited status, decorations and titles, paternalism, and so on, in spite of the economic triumph of industrialisation and capitalism. While in other western European countries, capitalism marched alongside social mobility, carriers open to talent, political parliamentarianism, and democratisation, Germany's industrialisation could not keep pace with social and cultural modernisation. As the popular demand for democratisation rose, the pre-modern elite tried to divert the issue by arousing nationalist imperialism and anti-Semitism. With the collapse of the monarchy in 1918, the old elite grew even more desperate and reinvented themselves as the Nazi party. They successfully rallied the feudalised bourgeoisie, manipulated disgruntled petty bourgeoisie, industrialists, top civil servants, army, and politicians. This explanation was criticised most notably by Eley and Blackbourn, who suggested that the realities of the process of modernisation and industrialisation were so complex that making models would serve no purpose. They argued that the German bourgeoisie was not feudalised and, in fact, talked about the embourgeoisment of German nobility and society.

Among the recent trends, one witnesses the virtual disappearance of the generic concept of fascism, and the replacement of class by race as an explanatory tool, which is considered far more central to understanding the working of National Socialism. Proponents of this would agree with Eley and Blackbourn that the German society, before the onset of Nazism, was very much a modern society with a modern bourgeois culture and would stubbornly fight any claims that Nazism was a throwback to the barbaric past of an otherwise civilised society or an accident. They place this modernity in the realm of culture, governmentality, welfare, and other means of controlling and engineering society. These historians take their lead from the works of Detlev Peukert, Foucault, and the Frankfurt School to explore the dark sides of modernity or the so-called pathologies of modernity. They take the challenges presented by modernity seriously rather than consigning bad aspects of modernity to an imagined medieval island of convenience where barbaric utopias exist even today.

In this approach, rationalisation and science, especially the discursive field of 'biopolitics', play a key role as markers of modernisation. Biopolitics is concerned with issues of health, reproduction, and welfare, and understands society as a body, which can be improved, controlled, monitored, and regulated according to the wishes of the rulers and elite. From the 1990s, modernisation has been debated in Germany in connection with National Socialism, which was seen as a culmination point of a certain kind of biopolitics of modernity.

Modernity, in this view, is characterised by a distinctive *Machbarkeitswahn* or man's obsession with making things possible. This belief translates into man's omnipotence and an ambition that society can be comprehensively transformed through social engineering projects, such as urban planning, public health, educational reforms, and social welfare. The moderns in Germany were, in that sense, profoundly optimistic. On the other hand, they were also haunted by a sense of a permanent crisis: the undermining of Christian values, the collapse of the old structure, the emergence of new social formations and mass culture, the proletarian milieu and its attendant problems such as pollution, public health disasters, criminality, industrial conflict and so on. They, thus, oscillated between optimism and despair. The belief in progress existed alongside the fear of degeneration, collapse, and chaos.

In addition, science played a key role in defining both the optimism and pessimism of modernity. On the one hand, it was constantly discovering, naming, defining, measuring, quantifying, and investigating new problems and threats. On the other, it was constantly discovering solutions to these problems. Science was the language both of crisis and crisis management. In this process, science itself became a legitimating agency, a total system of knowledge. Many historians refer to this belief as scientism or instrumental rationality (Dickinson, 2004).

The bio-medical sciences played a crucial role in what might be called 'biologisation of the social', and the history of Nazi Germany, in this perspective, can be understood as one of continuity from 1860s onwards in which the Darwinian evolutionary theory played a crucial role. Darwinism naturalised the faith in progress or inevitability but also a sense of existential threat, of the inevitable necessity of change if extinction was to be avoided. Eugenic in particular, that is, the study of the (alleged) inheritance of physical, intellectual, and social characteristics in human populations, occupied a key place. In this account, the history of modern Germany is a history of a peculiar national variant of biopolitics. Biopolitics is understood as an extensive complex of ideas, practices, and institutions focused on the care, regulation, disciplining, improvement, and finally, the shaping of individual bodies as collective body: the national body. Biopolitics, thus, involves medical practices from individual therapy, personal hygiene, public health campaigns, social welfare programmes, tax policies, race sciences, demographic policies, psychiatry, psychology, beauty and fitness regimes, and so on. The overarching aim of this was to create a more powerful and wholesome society to maximise efficiency and health. Expert knowledge was created to cater to the project of 'normalisation' and the corresponding 'pathologisation' of difference or what is not considered normal, fit, and useful. This dual process of creating binary opposites, with positive and negative values, served as the critical legitimating discourse for policy decisions and targets. The concept of biopolitics was introduced by Michael Foucault in his analysis of power. Through this concept, he intended to designate a new configuration of relations of domination and subordination. From the end of the eighteenth century onwards, some would say mid-nineteenth century, political power progressively took over responsibility for the population as a living mass. Biopower therefore started to distinguish itself from the traditional sovereign power not just because of its all-inclusive nature but also owing to its direct involvement with 'the productivity' of life. It no longer concentrated on the individual and his property, but life itself: birth, reproduction, illness, disease, and death. According to Foucault and his followers, the theory of race, in its evolutionist version, has functioned as an effective vector for the naturalisation and biologisation of the object of power. In the name of preservation and healing of life, power becomes capable of carrying out an immediate political valorisation and functionisation of biology. When racism turns into a state ideology, it also becomes the theoretical point of reference for a practice that, to make life productive, is able to organise in a hierarchical manner and differentiate, to include and exclude beings from the human field, and make the death of one a necessity for the life of all. It represents, for Foucault, the extreme and exemplary way in which power manages to carry out a colossal enterprise of regimentation and killing, while talking of the 'law of life' and of the 'humanity reborn'. The idea of race further activates a mechanism of power in generating a device for producing collective identification and an identity construction provided by the body and by biological life, which is extremely powerful and dangerous compared to any other kind of community rhetoric. The focus on the centrality of biopolitics to modernity allows us to locate and make sense of this new picture of the Nazi racial state in two critically important ways. It not only establishes continuities between Imperial, Weimar and Nazi periods but also between Germany and the rest of the modern world. Through this lens, Nazism appears not as a bolt from the blue but an integral part of modernity and as a modern project of universal renovation. While the *Sonderweg* model explained Nazi horrors in Germany's inability to modernise, the biopolitical model puts the genocidal politics at the centre of modernity. Germany appears here not as a nation having trouble modernising, but as a nation of troubling modernity (Dickinson, 2004: 5).

The Nazi totalitarianism is often considered the extreme and emblematic example of a biopolitics that legitimised itself on the basis of racial assumptions, intimately connected to the new sciences of life. Thus, Deltev Peukert opined that 'national socialism pushed the utopian belief in all embracing scientific final solutions of social problems to the ultimate logical extreme' (Peukert, 1987: 248). Peukert was an early exponent of the problematic and troubled modernity of which Germany was the classic example. Against Eley and Blackbourn's assertion that Germany experienced a silent bourgeois revolution in economy and society, which transformed Germany by the end of the nineteenth century into one of the most modern industrial nations of the world, Peukert asked why she then plunged into genocidal barbarism after 1933? His answer was that Germany was an example of the pathologies of modernity and that it showed the dark side of modernity. Peukert called for a sceptical de-coupling of modernity and progress, arguing that historians must raise questions about the pathologies and seismic fractures within modernity itself, and about the implicit destructive tendencies of the industrial class society, which National Socialism made explicit and which it elevated into mass destruction (ibid.: 15).

Rather than the persistence of pre-industrial class relations, as argued by Wehler and his followers, Peukert believed that Nazi Germany presented a case of classical modernity, which was introduced in the imperial period in the late nineteenth century and experienced its crisis years in the Weimar period. This unresolved crisis gave birth to the Third Reich. The NSDAP was at once a symptom and a solution of the crisis (ibid.: 42), at the core of which stood a utopian view of social welfare policies aimed at achieving the final solution to social problems. Race here was the formula that defined and resolved the 'problem'. Nazi Germany was a society in which advanced capitalism, bureaucratisation, and rationalisation existed alongside social disciplining and normalisation whereby instrumental reason and the spirit of science assumed a hegemonic role in ordering the society. Geoff Eley argued for a re-periodisation of the late nineteenth and early twentieth centuries to stress the coherence of the years between 1890s and 1930s as a unitary context in which definite themes of social hygiene, national efficiency, and racialised nationalism coalesced, and remarked that the ground for the final solution was being discursively laid even in the period before the Great War through the diffusion of 'eugenicist and related ideologies of social engineering' (Eley, 1996: 31). Thomas Rohrkämer argued that National Socialism 'shows modernity's most fatal potential' (Rohrkämer, 1999: 50). Omer Bartov suggests that modern war and totalitarianism necessitate and devise final solutions in which humanity is perceived as a mass of matter to be moulded, controlled, moved, purged, and annihilated. Others such as Foucault conceptualized this troubled modernity as aspirations of modern regimes to indulge in social disciplining. Elias saw it as the pathological consequence of the civilizing process and Habermas as the colonisation of living worlds.

This conceptualisation of the world biologises society and socialises biology; humanity becomes an organism in need of radical surgery or a social construct in need of sociological reordering. Hence, the vast population transfers, brutal operations of ethnic cleansing, eradication of whole social classes, and ultimately, outright genocide, become the 'final solution'.

Alltagsgeschichte or the history of everyday life is another approach, which has produced a barrage of literature in the recent past. We have already observed this in the section relating to workers responses to Nazi Germany or the prevalence of denunciatory practices in the works of Alf Lüdtke, Robert Gellately, Lutz Nietheimerm and Vandana Joshi among others. These studies show how patterns of prejudice, complicity, and collaboration can be discerned in everyday life of ordinary Germans. The *Alltagsgeschichte* approach has been far more useful than the Wehler-led Bielefeld School in suggesting that below the barbarity and the horrors of the regime, lay patterns of social normality that were, of course, affected by Nazism in various ways, but predated and survived it. The role of Nazi ideology, hence, becómes 'relativised' in the context of a 'normality' of everyday life shaped for much of the time by non-ideological factors. It is the normalisation of brutality in everyday life, normality in the face of Auschwitz, war, persecution, and murder of the 'physically or mentally unfit' that is the most disturbing aspect of Nazi Germany, and not only the commands from above. It is the everydayness, the banality of the crimes, which should alert us to the danger, that is forever present and has arisen many times over since then, and should concern us as a democratic and freedom-loving people.

Essential Readings

Bessel, Richard (1990), 'Why Did the Weimar Republic Collapse?', in Ian Kershaw (ed.) *Why Did German Democracy Fail*, New York: St. Martin's Press. (This edited volume by Kershaw has some of the leading experts on Weimar economy engaging in a lively debate about whether Weimar Republic offered initial promise but failed to deliver due to insurmountable problems or whether it was doomed to failure from the beginning.)

Browning, Christopher (1992), *Ordinary Germans: Reserve Police Battalion 101 and Final Solution*, and in a far more controversial and talked about work of Danial Goldhagen (1996) Hitler's *Willing Executioners*. Both offer some reading for the economic difficulties facing the Weimar Republic that set the stage for the Nazis.

Burleigh, Michal and Wolfgang Wipppermannn (1991), *The Racial State: Germany 1933–1945*, Cambridge: Cambridge University Press, puts racism at the centre of the Nazi rule.

Evans, Richard (2003), *The Coming of the Third Reich*, London, New Delhi; (2005), *The Third Reich in Power*, London; and (2008), *The Third Reich at War*, London. (This trilogy offers the latest and most comprehensive coverage of the Third Reich.)

Feldman, Gerald (1975), 'Economic and Social Problems of German Demobilization, 1918–19, *Journal of Modern History* 47.

Feldman, Gerald D. (1985), 'Weimar from Inflation to Depression: Experiment or Gamble', in G. Feldman (ed.), *Die Nachwirkung der Inflation auf die deutsche Geschichte 1924–1933*, R. Oldenbourg Verlag: Munich.

Feldman, Gerald D. (1993), *The Great Disorder: Politics, Economics and Society in the German Inflation, 1914–1924,* New York, offers a good survey of the first phase of the crisis years and hyperinflation in Weimar Republic.

Fulbrook, Mary (1991), *History of Germany, 1918–2000: The Divided Nation*, Oxford: Blackwell Publishing, gives a long-term brief coverage of contemporary German history.

Hamilton, Richard F. (1981), Who Voted for Hitler, Princeton University Press, and Childers, Thomas (1981), The Nazi Voter: The Social Foundations of Nazism in Germany, 1919–1933, NC: Chapel Hill. (These books offer fact and analysis of the voting patterns in Weimar Germany and social base of the Nazis.)

Holtfrerich, C. L. (1986),*The German Inflation 1914–1943,* Berlin: New York.

James, Herold (1986), *The German Slump, Politics and Economics 1924–1936*, Clarendon Press: Oxford.

Overy, Richard (2001), 'The German Economy, 1919–1945', in Panikos Panayi (ed.), Weimar and Nazi Germany: Continuities and Discontinuities, Pearson, London/New York.

Peukert, Detlev, (1987), *Inside Nazi Germany*, New Haven and London: Yale University Pres. It offers a critical modernist perspective on the Third Reich.

Turner, Henry Ashby (1969), 'Big Business and the Rise of Hitler', *American Historical Review*, 75.

Further Readings

Bartov, Omer (2001), 'Social Outcasts in War and Genocide: A Comparative Perspective', in Robert Gellately and Nathan Stolzfus (eds), *Social Outsiders in Nazi Germany,* Princeton: Princeton University Press.

Blackbourn, David and Geoff Eley (1984), *The Peculiarities of German History*, Oxford: Oxford University Press.

Broszat, Martin (1981), *The Hitler State: the Foundation and Development of the Internal Structure of the Third Reich*, London: Longman.

Browning, Christopher R. (2004), *The Origins of the Final Solution: the Evolution of Nazi Jewish Policy, September 1939–March 1942*, Lincoln: University of Nebraska Press.

Crew, David F. (ed.) (1994), *Nazism and German Society 1933–45*, Routledge: London, brings together experts on various historiographical issues.

Dickinson, Edward Ross (2004), 'Biopolitics, Fascism, Democracy: Some Reflections on Our Discourse about "Modernity"', in *Central European History*, 37, 1: 1–48.

Eley, Geoff (1996), 'Introduction 1: Is there a History of the Kaiserreich?', in Idem (ed.), *Society, Culture, and the State in Germany', 1870–1930*, Ann Arbor: University of Michigan Press.

Gellately (1990), *The Gestapo and German Society: Enforcing Racial Policy, 1933–45*, Oxford

Hitler, Adolf (1971), *Mein Kampf*, Houghton Mifflin: Boston.

Kersaw, Ian (1998), *Hitler: Huberis 1889–1936*, London: Penguin Books; and (2000), *Hitler, Nemsis 1936–45*, London. (A two volume biographical account of Hitler from a celebrated social historian's perspective.)

Kershaw, Sir Ian (2000), *The Nazi Dictatorship: Problems and Perspectives of Interpretation*, Bloomsbury: London.

Lüdtke, Alf (2000), 'Everyday Life and German Fascism', *History Workshop Journal,* 50, Autumn: 74–92.

Lüdtke, Alf (2006), 'War as Work', in Alf Lüdtke and Bern Weisbrod (eds), *No Man's Land of Violence: Extreme War in the 20th Century*, Goettingen: Wallstein Verlag.

Mallmann, Klaus Michael and Gerhard Paul (1991), *Herrschaft und Alltag: Ein Industrierevier im Dritten Reich*, Bonn: Dietz; Johnson, Eric (1999), *Nazi Terror*, Basic Books; Vandana Joshi (2003), *Gender and Power in the Third Reich: Female denouncers and the Gestapo 1933–45*, Palgrave; These three works highlight ordinary people's compliance and complicity in Nazi crimes through their acts of denunciation

Niethammer, Lutz (ed.) (1983), *Die Jahre weiss man nicht wo man die heute hinsetzen soll*, Berlin/Bonn: Dietz; (1983), *Hinterher merkt man, dass es richtig war, dass es schiefgegangen ist*, Berlin; Niethammer and Alexander von Plato (eds), (1985), *Wir kriegen jetzt andere Zeiten*, These three accounts based on oral history that trace patterns of compliance in everyday life.

Peukert, Detlev (1987), *Inside Nazi Germany,* New Haven, 248.

Raul, Hilberg (2003, c1961), *The Destruction of the European Jews,* Yale: University Press.

Rees, Laurence (1997), *The Nazis: A warning from History*, BBC Books: London. (A popular account based on his BBC film with the same title.)

Rohrkämer, Thomas (1999), 'Antimodernism, Reactionary Modernity and National Socialism: Technocratic Tendencies in Germany, 1890–1945', *Contemporary European History*, 8, 50.

Ruge, Wolfgang (1974), *Deutschland 1917–1933*, Deutscher Verlag d. Wiss., VEB :Berlin, 473.

Schleunes, Karl (1970), *The Twisted Road to Auschwitz; Nazi Policy toward German Jews, 1933–1939*, Urbana: University of Illinois Press. (It follows a functionalist approach to argue that the Holocaust did not result from a blue print that Hitler made in his writings, but was the last station after passing through a series of measure to 'solve' the Jewish question.)

Schulze, Hagen (1982), *Weimar Deutschland 1917–1933*, Severin und Siedler: Berlin, 425.

Taylor, Telford (ed.) (1962), *Hitler's Secret Book*, New York.

Theweleit, Klaus (1987/9), *Male Fantasies: Volume 1: Women Floods Bodies History Volume 2: Male Bodies: Psychoanalyzing the White Terror*, Minneapolis : University of Minnesota Press. (This is a pioneering study of the mind and psyche of the demobilised soldiers of the Great War many of whom made up the rank and file of the SA.)

Wehler, H. W. (1985), *The German Empire, Dover, N.H.:* Berg Publisher.

Weitz, Eric (2007), *Weimar Germany: Promise and Tragedy*, Princeton: Princeton University Press.

In Pursuit of Social Justice: Modern European Socialism, 1850–1940

6

—*Sharon A Kowalsky*

As an ideological movement, socialism has taken on many forms. Its origins can be found in utopian yearnings for a better society that stretch back as far as recorded history. Early philosophers beginning with Plato's *Republic* tried to imagine a more perfect world based on social harmony, communal values and egalitarianism. Some implemented these ideas in small agricultural communities. Often, utopian thinkers, particularly those situated within the Christian context, found their perfect society in their vision of the next world or the afterlife. Modern socialism, in contrast, argued that a utopian society based on communal values could be realized in the present world and on a large scale. It evolved out of the specific historical context of rapid industrialization and urbanization in nineteenth-century Europe and was a product of that environment. Modern socialism emphasized a secular vision of society that focused on improving current conditions by achieving economic equality, particularly for the underprivileged. It sought to promote communal property ownership and equal access to resources. It based its ideas on rationality, natural law and notions of working-class solidarity. It stressed community, social justice and the welfare of one's fellow human beings at a time when it seemed that traditional ways of organizing society were being destroyed and the pursuit of individualism prevailed. Finally, it responded to the failure of other ideological movements to address adequately these issues and concerns. Most supporters of modern socialism came from the lower orders of society, those most directly affected by and least likely to benefit from the transformations brought about by industrialization. Moreover, these groups were underrepresented in the political systems of industrializing Europe. Modern socialism thus became a workers' movement and sought to appeal to this stratum of society.

As it evolved, modern socialism developed two distinct strands. One branch focused on working within established systems to promote and implement socialist-oriented reforms that would improve the conditions of the labouring classes and eventually establish a true socialist system. The approach became possible in Western Europe during the second half of the nineteenth century as more and more regimes, under pressure from their populations, established representative political bodies. Socialists could and did use these institutions to promote their agendas, and often succeeded in gaining considerable political influence. The other avenue taken by socialists focused on the necessity of revolutionary change to establish a socialist society. Adherents of this approach refused to work within existing political institutions, opting instead to destroy the establishment to create a new socialist society. While revolutionary socialists proliferated throughout Europe alongside democratic socialists, they tended to gain a stronger foothold in countries that lacked representative institutions and legal avenues to pursue reform, particularly Russia. The two strands of socialism coexisted uneasily throughout the period in question.

Modern socialism also had an international orientation, stressing that only with world revolution could socialism be fully realized. As the only major political movement to establish international organizations, it sought to break down national, religious and ethnic boundaries, asserting universal human values. Yet, modern socialism evolved in different ways based on particular national circumstances. Socialists found it necessary to work within their national frameworks to pursue their agendas, but at the same time they also advanced their international goals. The interactions of socialists beyond their national contexts helped not only to broaden the scope of the movement, but it also revealed fundamental differences in approach that the various national organizations developed. Despite its international outlook, modern socialism had difficulty overcoming the particularities of the modern nation-state.

This chapter explores the origins of modern socialism, its major theoreticians and practitioners, its establishment as a political force within various national contexts and its international aspects. Because a clear, unified approach for achieving socialist goals never emerged within modern socialism, it is not possible to provide a comprehensive account of the movement. Rather, this chapter seeks to highlight the most significant moments and issues in its evolution. In doing so, it illustrates the central role that socialism played in the development of modern European society and politics.

THE ORIGINS OF SOCIALIST THOUGHT IN EUROPE DURING THE AGE OF REVOLUTION

In May 1796, François Noël (Gracchus) Babeuf (1760–1797) was arrested by the French government for attempting to overthrow the Directory and re-establish the Constitution of 1793. Babeuf was hardly what one might consider a socialist. Under the Old Regime in France, Babeuf had worked to support the legal foundations of aristocratic privilege as a land surveyor and feudal tax collector. After the 1789 revolution, however, he threw himself into political activity and became a journalist and activist for peasant land rights. In 1790, Babeuf was imprisoned for inciting tax riots, providing him with solid revolutionary credentials. Jailed again during the terror for criticizing the government's economic policies, he was released in July 1794 and was shocked by the shifts in policies of the new leaders, the Directory, as they stifled the freedom of expression and democracy that had flourished after 1789. Babeuf began to organize a conspiracy, the 'Conspiracy of the Equals', to overthrow the Directory and establish, eventually, a collectivist society. He based his beliefs and efforts on Enlightenment notions of natural rights but argued that happiness was not possible without social equality and the elimination of private property. His vision of society looked backward to a premodern communal tradition concerned with the fair and equal distribution of property and wealth. He saw the Directory as corrupt and parasitical and sought to end its abuse of the people. Babeuf came to believe that only violent revolution led by a revolutionary elite would be able to bring about economic equality. Indeed, Babeuf differentiated between notions of freedom, which he equated with misery and exploitation, and equality (Kolakowski, Vol. 1, p. 185). For his revolutionary ideas and his attempts to implement them, Babeuf received the death penalty and was executed in May 1797, providing socialist revolutionaries their first martyr.

Babeuf's ideas and goals provide a good starting point to begin our exploration of modern European socialism. His vision was rooted in Enlightenment thought that emphasized natural rights and he valued the idea of the premodern community as the way to achieve equality. At the same time, many of Babeuf's ideas pointed toward the development of modern socialism. He stressed equality and simplicity not out of religious conviction but because he believed they provided the most efficient ways to guarantee equality and social welfare. He understood social struggle in moral terms as one of equality, justice and sacrifice versus duplicity and ambition. In this way, Babeuf sought to deal with the corruption and abuse he saw in his own society. Indeed, early socialist thought emerged in the first half of the nineteenth century as one response to the massive changes occurring in European society with the advent of industrialization. Socialist thinkers sought solutions for the dislocation and upheaval they saw around them. They were often concerned with contemporary problems of poverty and unemployment, believed in the value of education, sought to improve the status of women, and wanted to address social welfare issues. These intellectuals drew upon the foundation of Enlightenment thinking, seeking to figure out how to achieve ideas of individual and natural rights in the changing context of industrialization.

Socialist thought in the early nineteenth century emerged out of a combination of the Enlightenment, the French Revolution and the Industrial Revolution. Enlightenment discussions about natural rights and natural law helped plant the seeds of socialist ideas. Jean-Jacques Rousseau (1712–1778), in particular, envisioned a society where people could return to the simplicity of rural life and their natural state. He stressed the importance for individuals to place the needs of the community, or the 'general will', above their own interests and argued that individuals entered into a 'social contract' with each other, not with any state or government. He understood privilege as deriving from the unequal distribution of property and his 'social contract' prohibited its personal accumulation. In this way, Rousseau undermined the traditional sources of power and authority, prioritizing human nature and republican democracy over monarchies and aristocratic privilege. His ideas and those of the Enlightenment in general helped to challenge the divine right of kings to rule and facilitated the development of revolutionary ideas and parliamentary democracies. The French revolutionaries of 1789 sought to do away with aristocratic privilege and feudal authority, creating a society based on merit where all male citizens had equal opportunities for political representation and political engagement. In its ideal, the French Revolution attempted to reconfigure the basic structure and shape of French society, and provided a model for both the ways that freedom and equality could be expressed in politics and the excesses that could befall revolutionary movements. Finally, the Industrial Revolution helped to shape early socialist ideas as new technologies both exposed social inequities and suggested possibilities for social and technological advancement. Many early socialists were also influenced by the plight of the peasantry, made worse by policies such as the enclosure system in England that prevented peasants from accessing land. Indeed, early socialists often condemned urban and industrialized society, with its widespread poverty and disease, and looked longingly to an ideal future rooted in the romanticized image of the preindustrial countryside. For many, socialism became an 'alternative framework that negated, exposed, and superseded all previous ideologies' (Wuthnow, p. 365), while also incorporating elements of established ideas—for example, paternalism and educational advancement—in its own theoretical discourse, applying these principles to the working class.

Several figures stand out among the early socialist thinkers that helped to shape socialist thought. These 'utopian' socialists (so-called by Karl Marx to differentiate their idealism from his attempt at application) set out the basic principles of the socialist critique of contemporary capitalist society and reflected a growing realization of the need for action to alleviate an expanding social crisis. French thinker Charles Fourier (1772–1837), for example, placed blame for contemporary social problems directly on capitalism and other social institutions. These, he claimed, ran counter to nature. The way to achieve harmony was through an understanding and recognition of the laws of the universe. Fourier emphasized not absolute equality but natural harmony so that individual needs were satisfied, and argued for the inevitable achievement of this harmonious society. It would be accomplished, he asserted, through small local communities (*phalanxes*) organized on a cooperative basis. Fourier's explanation for social crisis was not economic inequality but rather a lack of understanding of the constraints that acted on the human personality in society (Pilbeam, pp. 14–16). Thus, Fourier envisioned a society without the institutions that restricted human passions, a society where such passions were understood and embraced for the greater good of the individual and the community. Rejecting revolution, Fourier embraced the need for gradual social reforms that would move society toward his vision of universal harmony. Although his followers found it difficult to implement his utopian ideals, Fourier did establish the notion that the socialist society was based on historical laws and the inevitable progress of humankind.

Claude Henri de Saint-Simon (1760–1825), in contrast, saw social problems as a result of poor management of the economy, which was controlled by elites with little sense of the needs of ordinary people. He believed that society was engaged in a struggle between the lazy and the industrious, with the elites on one side and the entrepreneurs and workers on the other. While not supporting a wholesale redistribution of property, he proposed a radical restructuring of the balance of power among different social classes that would privilege intelligence and creativity while rescuing the poor from their misery and humiliation. Indeed, he stressed that workers would recognize the beneficial aspects of rational hierarchies of production if elites recognized their own responsibilities. Saint-Simon embraced industrial progress, technological innovation and capitalist growth, but linked them with social responsibility. He also stressed planning as a crucial element of a well-ordered society.

British industrialist Robert Owen (1771–1858) provides an example of the impact of the Industrial Revolution on socialist development. A self-educated, middle-class, successful entrepreneur, Owen attempted to combine social responsibility for his workers with ideas of rationality and economic production. Asserting that increased productivity and greater profits were not the best ways to achieve happiness, he established a model community at his textile factory in Lanark, England, that sought to provide improved working and living conditions for his employees. Owen attempted to prove that worker exploitation was not necessary for business success. He believed that environment formed the human character and that the only source of evil was ignorance. He also advocated the creation of settlements for the unemployed that would offer good living conditions, work, and educational opportunities, and supported the establishment of cooperatives and exchanges that would help communities and individuals trade goods. By pursuing these policies, Owen sought to create a company town in which workers could be treated with respect and have a decent standard of living while still maintaining a profitable capitalist enterprise.

In France, the ideas of Etienne Cabet (1788–1856) inspired popular support. He emphasized that private property caused working-class woes and proposed communism as the answer, envisioning a society of social harmony based on cooperation that was in many ways more backward-looking than that of Saint-Simon. Cabet was a pacifist and eschewed revolutionary violence. He remained attached to Christianity, emphasizing equality over productivity and the gradual creation of an ideal society without private property. His ideas appealed in particular to artisans, whose livelihoods were threatened by the advent of mechanized production and the abolition of guilds.

In contrast, Pierre-Joseph Proudhon (1809–1865) represents an alternative trend in the development of socialism. Known for arguing that 'property is theft', Proudhon condemned the absolute right to use property, not the individual ownership of goods. He asserted that only labour was productive, not the exploitation of it or profits derived from it; labour was the only real measure of value. He understood the source of inequality to be in the privileges of income not earned through labour and called for the abolition of such unearned income (Kolakowski, Vol. 1, p. 206). Proudhon distrusted state power and supported the middle-class small property owner. He also supported the idea of justice.

He understood the class struggle as taking place between the elites and big industrialists on one side and an alliance of workers and small bourgeoisie, or middle class, on the other. He also asserted the necessity to abolish the state in order to create a better society.

The ideas of Louis-Auguste Blanqui (1805–1881) reflect yet another early socialist approach, this time emphasizing the need for violent revolution. Middle-class and well educated, Blanqui had a strong faith in science, progress, and the improvement of the human spirit, although for Blanqui these were not necessarily synonymous with industrial development or economic productivity. Understanding socioeconomic relations as class warfare, Blanqui advocated the use of violence in plundering the rich. He believed the masses were inherently revolutionary but called for the seizure of power by an elite, conspiratorial leadership, a Parisian dictatorship, without necessarily obtaining popular support. Indeed, he emphasized the central importance of revolutionary organization and conspiracy. For his ideas, Blanqui spent a considerable amount of time in prison.

These thinkers represent some of the various approaches of early socialist thought. Each developed their own following as they sought to deal with the contradictions and disparities of wealth and poverty exacerbated by urbanized, industrialized society. The multiplicity of perspectives in early socialist thought ensured that as socialism developed during the nineteenth century in Europe its adherents would be able to choose from a variety of views, approaches and paths to achieving socialist goals. Early socialists were concerned with more than just political philosophy and economic issues. Believing that social reform needed to encompass all aspects of society, they often engaged in practical social reform efforts, joining campaigns against prostitution and venereal disease, studying poverty and seeking solutions to it as part of a moral crusade. Those who committed themselves to socialist ideas worked diligently to transform their societies. At the core of these efforts, however, was always a tension about how exactly such transformations would best be achieved—through reform of existing institutions or through revolution. This difference would eventually divide the movement and in some cases undermine its successes.

The particular conditions of European industrialization in the nineteenth century established the base of support for the nascent socialist movement. Innovations in agriculture enabled peasants to produce more with less labour, leading to rural overcrowding. At the same time, industrial development created opportunities for employment in Europe's growing cities. When migrants left the countryside for urban areas, they often found themselves at the mercy of the unpredictable economic forces of early capitalism. Demand for industrial goods varied, and when it was down, employers simply laid off workers, creating frequent periods of unemployment. When workers were employed, low wages, unskilled repetitive work, hazardous working conditions, and long hours strained their physical endurance and left them struggling to make ends meet. Housing shortages ensured that workers lived in cramped and often unsanitary conditions, and workers could rarely count on the system of extended family and community support they had known in the countryside. These trends left the worker increasingly isolated. As workers abandoned their rural mentalities, they came to see themselves as a separate group with interests different from those of factory owners and the middle class. They began to form workers' organizations and engaged in demonstrations that both encouraged governments to pass reform legislation addressing some worker demands and raised fears among the middle and upper classes regarding the unruly, unpredictable, violent and often poverty-stricken worker.

During the early nineteenth century, socialist thought and ideas began to appeal to the growing working class movement increasingly disillusioned with liberal efforts at reform. The early beginnings of a workers' 'class consciousness' can be seen in the efforts of the 1820s to organize labour. For instance, a so-called labour offensive resulted in the loosening of restrictive labour legislation in Britain in 1824 and increasing demands for expanded political rights for workers. The Chartist movement built on those demands, envisioning a more moral society without the privilege of wealth. Chartists called for the democratization of political life through universal male suffrage and greater access to political power for ordinary citizens, but had little success in achieving reforms of the British political system. Indeed, it seemed instead that legislation continued to privilege the wealthy at the expense of workers.

A Europe-wide depression in 1829–1832 helped to stimulate interest in labour unions. The difficulties and uncertainties the proletariat faced during this depression encouraged French workers to join with liberals in opposition to the monarchy. When Charles X dissolved the parliament, restricted the franchise, and instituted press censorship in July 1830, Parisian workers erected barricades throughout the city. Protests from French liberals forced the abdication of Charles X and the installation of Louis-Philippe, who agreed to establish a more liberal regime. Despite the sacrifices of the workers on the barricades for the new regime, called the July Monarchy, most of the reforms instituted by Louis-Philippe benefited middle-class professionals and capitalists. Angered by the lack of response to their demands, workers instigated riots in the early 1830s, resulting in more restrictions against worker organizations. Similar liberal revolutions and insurrections occurred throughout Europe during the 1830s and workers frequently participated in these efforts. Yet, as in France, their demands went unheeded. Out of these experiences, workers came to realize the validity of their own interests and the effectiveness of collective political action. They also began to understand that liberals were unwilling to promote or address worker concerns. Workers could not count on assistance from the liberal movement but rather needed to depend on themselves.

In early 1848, French workers again put up barricades, assisting in the overthrow of the monarchy and the establishment of the Second Republic. Enthusiasm for the events in France quickly spread, resulting in the creation of republican governments in much of continental Europe. A major cause of the 1848 revolutions was rising unemployment, the result of another economic downturn. In France, workers demanded government relief and the new Republic granted them their 'right to work' in the form of National Workhouses that provided jobs for the unemployed. When a workers' demonstration invaded the National Assembly and had to be subdued by force, however, the middle class abandoned its commitment to the workers. Fear of worker radicalism and violence, and an inability to meet the financial burden of maintaining the workhouses, caused government leaders to end the project, resulting in a massive worker revolt. Again, troops were called in to suppress the workers. The conservative backlash against the more liberal policies that resulted from the 1848 revolution led the middle class to discard the idea of the Republic and support the election of Louis Napoleon Bonaparte who, in due course, declared himself Emperor Napoleon III of France. Similar conservative reactions occurred throughout Europe, and within eighteen months all pre-revolutionary governments had been restored to power and had reasserted the status quo.

Although liberal governments emerged briefly as a result of the 1848 events, the revolutions were driven by the working class and their demands; workers manned the barricades. Despite their sacrifices, the gains of the 1848 revolution for the working class were limited and fleeting. Yet, the experience of 1848 helped solidify the workers' movement and provided a solid basis for the increasing influence of socialism among the working masses. On the one hand, workers came to realize the importance of permanent mass organizations for achieving their goals and representing and defending their interests. Indeed, in 1848 workers were only beginning to develop a sense of class consciousness and had few established organizations or leaders. The failures of 1848 thus stimulated the expansion of trade unions and other worker institutions that could serve as vehicles for expressing worker interests and political demands. On the other hand, workers came to realize that middle-class liberals made poor allies in their struggle for improved social and working conditions. Early successes that resulted from class cooperation melted away when middle-class fears led it to abandon the workers' cause. This rejection reinforced the need to pursue ruthless policies of class warfare to achieve the goals of a just society. It also reflected the failures of liberal reformers and the liberal movement in general to establish a society based on social justice and universal rights. These failures helped to spread the appeal of socialism among the masses as an alternative to the liberal vision of society, which did not seem to include the working class.

MARXISM AND MODERN SOCIALISM: FROM THE 1848 REVOLUTIONS TO THE PARIS COMMUNE

In 1862, in an effort to show goodwill toward the people, Emperor Napoleon III granted an elected delegation of French workers permission to travel to London to attend the International Exposition. Worker delegates met with their British counterparts and returned home to describe the better living standards of British workers and their greater rights to organize. Their reports inflamed opposition to Napoleon III's government among workers and suggested the importance of international worker cooperation to achieve social improvements and to ensure that the status and earning power of workers of one country were not undermined by the policies and practices of another. These first meetings led to the foundation of the International Workingmen's Association (the First International) in 1864 and stimulated the establishment of a new internationally minded labour movement. Karl Marx (1818–1883) stood at the forefront of the international orientation of labour organization. His leadership helped to raise worker awareness that their plight crossed national boundaries and that their solution rested in worldwide revolution. While international cooperation proved difficult to maintain due to the particular needs and dynamics of socialist parties within their national contexts, it played a key role in establishing the scope and direction of the modern socialist movement.

Karl Marx can be considered the founder of modern socialism. His ideas provided the basic form and structure for both the national and international socialist movement, and despite some challenges and adaptations his theories remain central to modern socialism. Marx was born in Trier, Germany, into a prosperous German-Jewish family that had converted to Christianity and he grew up in the Rhineland near the border with France. In 1835, he entered the University of Berlin to study philosophy, intending to go into academic teaching, but his increasingly radical ideas did not make him a suitable candidate so he turned instead to journalism. His sympathy for the masses forced him into exile in Paris in 1843. There, Marx was exposed to the leading thinkers of the day, who shaped his outlook and led him to embrace materialism, a doctrine established by German philosopher Ludwig Feuerbach that asserted that reality shapes ideas and ideas reflect material conditions (Landauer, Vol. 1, p. 101). At this time, he also developed a friendship with Friedrich Engels (1820–1895), whose wealthy family manufactured textiles and owned a cotton mill in Manchester, England, and who also sympathized with the plight of industrial workers. In exile, Marx continued to criticize the Prussian government. Under pressure, the French government expelled Marx in 1845 and he went to Brussels, Belgium, where he remained until 1848. The period in Brussels further shaped Marx's thinking and he began to define his socialism according to historical economic forces and class antagonisms rather than along the lines of the preindustrial sentimentality of the utopian socialists.

Marx's theories focused on the idea of historical materialism, an economic interpretation of history emphasizing that all social, political and cultural changes resulted from technological developments that shaped economic conditions. As Marx stated, 'It is always in the relationship between the owner of the instruments of production and the real producers... that we can find the inner secret, the hidden basis of the whole social structure' (Landauer, Vol. 1, p. 143). Marx argued that modern civilization had altered the nature of human productivity, alienating man from the means of production and leading to the exploitation of their labour. In contrast to the utopian socialists who focused on the alleviation of working-class poverty, Marx emphasized workers' dehumanization. He stressed that revolution would occur only when the proletariat gained consciousness of its total dehumanization (Kolakowski, Vol. 1, p. 222). Furthermore, Marx's theories included the idea that all change occurs because of tensions and imbalances. This notion of change and progress imbedded a revolutionary inevitability within Marx's philosophy, suggesting that reform, whether gradual or violent, was an inherent element of social progress. Marx also posited the existence of class struggle. To achieve socialism, he argued, a dictatorship of the proletariat would be necessary to lead the transition to a classless society (Landauer, Vol. 1, p. 169). Yet this goal could be realized only under the conditions of mature capitalism, when worker solidarity and class consciousness would enable the proletariat to win the support of the majority of the population.

Marx's greatest achievement was that he created a practical philosophical system for the labour movement. It provided evidence that more was at stake than a worker's personal advantage; it appealed to a sense of social justice and brotherhood among working people and emphasized strength through united action. Marx recognized and upheld the compatibility of labour and socialism and made workers conscious of this relationship, providing them with an historical destiny, a respect for science, and a sense of self-reliance (Landauer, Vol. 1, pp. 200–204). Marx's assurance that the achievement of socialism was inevitable gave workers a sense of purpose, hope and confidence in the validity of their cause.

In 1847, Marx and Engels were invited to write a new programme for the League of the Communists, published in early 1848 as the *Communist Manifesto*. The *Manifesto* set out the core elements of Marx's thoughts, laying out modern communist philosophy as well as a practical programme for achieving its goals. In many ways, the *Manifesto* both built on older socialist traditions and broke with them, establishing communism as a distinct political movement and setting out its revolutionary agenda. According to Marx and Engels, the aim of communism was to eliminate the exploitation of the proletariat by organizing workers into a distinct class that would seize power from the bourgeoisie. Basic communist principles and goals included the abolition of private property, the abolition of divisions of labour, the abolition of the exploitation of labour, the abolition of countries and nations and the abolition of the family. Marx and Engels asserted that the achievement of these goals would lead to a classless society where production and the use of the instruments of production would be in the interests of and for the good of the community, where goods would be commonly distributed, and where labour would enrich the lives of workers. These ideas were rooted in and dependent on a highly industrialized society that could produce goods in sufficient quantities to fulfil the needs of all people. The agenda the *Manifesto* set out for the communist movement focused attention on the destruction of capitalism at the hands of the proletariat and committed communists to working toward that revolution and the eventual creation of a new classless society free from capitalist exploitation (Sandle, pp. 37–42).

In February 1848, Marx returned to Paris to observe the effects of the revolution, but soon moved to Cologne, Germany, in anticipation of a similar German revolution. After the failures of the German and French revolutions, Marx relocated to London, England, where he lived with his family, often in desperate poverty, for the remainder of his life. In this setting, he produced his major work, *Das Kapital*, which refined many of the ideas set out in the *Communist Manifesto*. He argued that worker exploitation derived from the worker selling his labour-power and thus divesting himself of his own essence. In addition, he described the nature of capitalism as an effort to create something that man cannot consume, thus enslaving the entire community. For Marx, the alienation of labour led to the loss of human subjectivity and dehumanization, which formed a necessary precursor to creating the conditions for the establishment of a future society where men can control their own lives (Kolakowski, Vol. 1, p. 264). Nevertheless, Marx embraced an optimistic view of human nature, arguing that once the proletariat destroyed capitalist exploitation, all people would be able to live together in peace and harmony.

Marx and Engels also argued for the emancipation of women as part of their communist platform. They developed the idea of women's 'double oppression', that working women were oppressed both by the low wages that employers paid them for their labour as well as by the family structure that placed additional responsibilities on them (Sowerwine, p. 402). Marx and Engels stressed that women needed to obtain full political equality in order to fight together with men for socialism. For Marx and Engels, wage labour was the first step in the process for women to obtain economic independence, but women still needed equal political rights to help bring about the fulfilment of socialism's promises.

Along with his scholarly activity, Marx remained involved in practical work and the organization of the communist movement. The original League of Communists that had commissioned the *Communist Manifesto* had been dissolved in the aftermath of the 1848 revolutions, but Marx was asked to play a leading role in the establishment of a new organization, the International Workingmen's Association, or First International, in 1864. The First International emerged out of increasing worker activism, a desire among workers to advocate for their rights, and an emergent internationalist mind-set among political exiles like Marx and Engels. It was made up of English trade unionists interested in protecting their jobs from cheap foreign labour, as well as representatives from various other countries and socialist orientations. Marx delivered the inaugural address at its first meeting in Geneva, Switzerland, in 1864. In his address, Marx noted that significant developments had occurred in terms of worker organization and improved living conditions, but argued that international worker solidarity and cooperative labour could only be achieved by obtaining political power for workers (Sandle, p. 51). The constitution of the new organization, proposed by Marx, emphasized that the working class had to act to emancipate itself and called for the workers of the world to unite. Indeed, he stressed, only through international unity could workers prevail in their struggle against capitalism. By 1868 the First International began urging all workers to join unions. It gained prestige and visibility among workers by supporting strikes, raising funds for striking workers and hindering the use of strike-breakers. It also sought to prevent armed conflict among nations, emphasizing the importance of internationalism and solidarity among workers.

Within the newly emerging international socialist movement, however, differences of opinion and orientation appeared almost immediately. While Marx saw the International as a vehicle to increase the political strength of workers, to hone their revolutionary consciousness, and to work toward the eventual socialization of the means of production, supporters of Pierre-Joseph Proudhon stressed the necessity of promoting the spread of workers' cooperatives. This created a conflict within the international socialist movement regarding the nature of collective property ownership. Another challenge to Marx came from Mikhail Bakunin (1814–1876), a revolutionary considered the father of modern anarchism. Bakunin, like Marx, attacked the evils of private property and capital, but focused on the necessity of violent revolutionary upheaval to destroy all forms of authority. Only then could a new society based on worker cooperatives, 'without a state and without privileges', emerge spontaneously as 'the only mode of life compatible with human nature' (Kolakowski, Vol. 1, p. 252). Bakunin saw the state itself as the main source of evil, while Marx identified that evil in the division of labour, stressing the need to destroy capitalism first. Marx believed socialism could succeed only through the organization of workers, while Bakunin stressed spontaneity and local initiative, rejecting the notion that it was possible to reorganize social life based on ideas created by intellectuals. While Marx promoted worker leadership and cooperation with other worker movements, Bakunin emphasized the revolutionary potential of the oppressed masses. The conflict between Marx and Bakunin within the International was resolved at its 1872 Congress in The Hague when Marx's political approach gained predominance over Bakunin's 'autonomist' orientation. Marx's desire to protect the International from further anarchist influence led him to transfer its headquarters to the United States (Kilroy-Silk, pp. 25–30).

While Marx promoted the international workers' movement, socialism still developed in the national context. During Marx's absence from Germany, the workers' movement there continued to evolve. At the forefront of this effort was Ferdinand Lassalle (1825–1864). Lassalle was born in Breslau, Germany, to an affluent family. Although he became a dedicated socialist as early as 1843, Lassalle began to engage in politics only with the 1848 revolution, serving as a workers' representative for the democratic movement. By the 1860s he was a recognized advocate for the German workers, popularizing the notion that workers should have a voice in politics (Steenson, p. 9). German worker representatives travelled to the 1862 International Exhibition in London and were inspired in similar ways as the French, asserting that the workers needed to improve their living standards. In response, workers in Leipzig, Germany, sought to organize a general workers' congress and called upon Lassalle to provide his views. Lassalle argued that the working class needed to establish itself as an independent political party and demand universal suffrage as working class interests could only be satisfied through representation in existing legislative bodies (Landauer, Vol. 1, pp. 236–237). Acting on his own advice, in May 1863, Lassalle helped to found the Universal German Workingmen's Association, which he ran until his untimely death in a duel in 1864. The German Workingmen's Association promoted democratic civil liberties and the defence of the underprivileged. Although the Association grew slowly, Lassalle's ideas about the importance of worker organizations and engagement in the political process had begun to take root in Germany. Indeed, German socialists started to enjoy electoral successes. In 1867, Germany was the only country in Europe to have any socialist representatives in its parliament. Their influence, however, remained limited.

In France, socialism developed more slowly. Most of the rights workers had gained as a result of 1848, particularly the right to form trade associations, were erased when Napoleon III came to power. After re-establishing autocratic control, the Emperor sought to regain the support of workers. In 1859, he granted an amnesty to those exiled in the aftermath of 1848 and abolished the Le Chapelier Law of 1791 that forbade strikes and worker coalitions. In 1868, he lifted some restrictions on the freedom of the press and the right to assemble. Napoleon III also permitted workers to send elected representatives to the International Exposition in London in 1862, from which resulted the formation of the International Association of Workingmen. Some French socialists came to understand the importance of working-class activism and sought to channel such energies. For example, Henri Tolain (1828–1897) and his colleagues published the *Manifesto of the Sixty* in 1864, which set out their belief in the principles of democracy but argued that such goals could not be achieved through the traditional liberal approach alone. Tolain's *Manifesto* stressed the importance not only of political equality but also of social equality. It called for increased worker representation and a united effort between the working and middle classes to defend true democracy and abolish class distinctions. It stressed the importance of worker unions, but French law continued to prevent the formation of such organizations and severely penalized strikers (Landauer, Vol. 1, pp. 213–216). In addition, a class consciousness began to develop among French workers after 1848. Encouraged by Pierre-Joseph Proudhon and supported by educated workers who formed a working-class intelligentsia, this movement sought to instil a sense of 'separateness and autonomy' among the working class through the production of newspapers, plays, poems and organizations (Shafer, p. 14).

The French authorities continued to reach out to workers considered cooperative. Napoleon III again allowed the election of worker representatives to the Paris Exposition of 1867, but arrested French members of the First International, dissolving the organization in France. Workers' reports from the Paris Exposition reflected their opposition, and government support for workers' issues remained limited. Indeed, tensions rose when the French government used the military to suppress striking coal miners in 1869, resulting in 27 deaths (Shafer, p. 15). Another deadly confrontation between the military and striking miners occurred in early 1870. The government's defence of the capitalist system alienated workers, increasing their revolutionary fervour and radicalism, and leading to calls for a new republic.

Hoping to distract French society, Napoleon III sent troops marching against Prussia in July 1870. By autumn, the French defeat at German hands created a crisis within Paris that overthrew the emperor and instituted a republic. The new republic roused the patriotism of the people who tried to defend their new Government of National Defense against the Germans. Unwilling to make peace, the German military laid siege to Paris in September 1870. Parisians determined to resist and formed a new institution, the Paris Commune. Despite their efforts, Parisians were forced to surrender in January 1871 as the rest of France capitulated. Unwilling to allow a German occupation of their city, Parisians renewed their defensive preparations. This alarmed the French government, which sought to disarm Paris. Resistance to this disarmament resulted in a full-scale insurrection in mid-March 1871 that forced the French government to abandon Paris completely. In this revolutionary euphoria, the Paris Commune took charge, declaring on 28 March that it stood 'in the name of the people' and established itself as a rival for national authority (Shafer, pp. 69–72).

The Commune combined municipal autonomy and a socialist agenda with nationalist sentiment. As it set about governing Paris, the Commune sought to restructure society, altering the relationship between citizens and government and instituting a new set of values that understood 'freedom over one's destiny… as a liberating principle essential to society's achievement of a harmonious equilibrium' (Shafer, p. 132). Its leaders instituted policies to decentralize the government, giving greater power to local institutions. They also minimized the influence of the Catholic Church on Parisian society, separating church and state, eliminating public funding for religion, secularizing schools and nationalizing church property. In addition, the Commune's leaders established a Labor Exchange where workers could gather to learn about available jobs. They gave priority in awarding government contracts to workers' organizations, and even recognized women's unions, giving women a greater political role than in any previous revolutionary movement.

The Commune immediately found itself under attack by the French government and by early May it began to suffer defeats. On 20 May, the government initiated a massive bombardment of the capital and by the morning of 22 May had succeeded in retaking control of much of the city. Unable to muster much of a defence, the Communards barricaded the parts of the city they still controlled and set fire to a number of important civic buildings. By 28 May, the French government had regained control of the city. It instituted harsh measures of repression against the Commune's supporters, targeting for arrest and execution not only its leaders and those who manned the barricades but all those suspected of aiding the Communards. Those resisting the French government were dehumanized, labelled as obstacles to civilization, and subjected to harsh reprisals. Others were arrested, tried, and sentenced to hard labour or deported. Estimates of the number of victims of government repression during this 'Bloody Week' range from 17,000 to 30,000, with even more fleeing Paris for their lives (Shafer, pp. 95–98).

Despite its short existence, the Paris Commune made a significant impression on contemporary observers, creating fear among the upper classes and compassion among workers and socialists. Shortly after the Commune's collapse, Karl Marx called attention to it as a source of revolutionary inspiration that would provide the foundation for social and political change. He saw it as an example of working-class rule that suggested the need not just to seize political power but to smash it (Lindemann, p. 129). Marx placed the Commune within the context of class conflict and elevated its victims as martyrs for the future socialist revolution. Places of execution of Communards, such as Pere Lachaise Cemetery where 147 Communards were lined up along the cemetery wall and shot, became sites of pilgrimage for socialist and communist activists. Marx and the First International declared their solidarity with the Commune. This support drove European governments to consider the First International a dangerous organization and they began to take steps to destroy it as a 'center of conspiracy against the treasures of civilization' (Landauer, Vol. 1, p. 126). Under increasing external pressures and internal divisions, the First International formally dissolved in 1876. During its short existence, the First International served as a beacon for the socialist cause, a rallying point for workers' rights and political action, and an institution for the spread of socialist ideology on an international level. As an organization, it asserted the notion that there were no national boundaries among workers and it helped to establish a sense of internationalism and common bonds among workers' movements throughout Europe.

REVOLUTION OR REFORM: SOCIALISM IN PRACTICE, 1870–1914

Despite the setbacks suffered before 1870, the socialist movement emerged as a major force in European politics in the decades before World War I. Several factors contributed to the expanding influence and authority of socialists. A depression beginning in 1873 raised concerns about the potential radicalism of the working class. Continuing industrial investment, innovation, and expansion in the 1880s and 1890s, however, encouraged greater urban migration and increased the size of the industrial workforce. In addition, rising literacy rates and expanding franchise raised the visibility of the lower orders and gave them more influence in national political life. As liberals in governments instituted reforms that improved the living and working conditions, raised expectations encouraged workers to demand greater representation. Indeed, socialist parties seemed to grow in strength and influence during economic booms. In periods of widespread unemployment, workers could not afford to pay union dues or subscribe to socialist newspapers. Economic expansion, on the other hand, created human and financial resources socialists could harness for their cause. In this way, states created the conditions that allowed for the growth of socialist movements. Indeed, in many ways the pre-war period can be considered the 'classical age' for European socialism, as many socialists expressed optimism about the future, embraced their new status within governments, and committed themselves to working within the system to implement the changes and transformations necessary to establish a truly socialist society.

As in the previous periods, socialists pursued different agendas and embraced different opportunities according to the context of their national experience. Overlying national differences was the revitalization of the international socialist movement in the formation of the Second International in 1889. Despite the unity and solidarity the Second International promised, national contexts and national interests of socialists predominated, limiting the effectiveness of the international socialist movement. In most national contexts, socialism moved from an underground, revolutionary movement to become an accepted part of the parliamentary system through the creation of socialist political parties, and these parties sought to work within existing political structures to implement reforms. Often, the socialist cause was assisted by liberal reforms that continued to expand suffrage and to insist on representative institutions. To understand how this trend manifested itself in different ways according to unique national circumstances, it is worth exploring in more detail the national movements in this period. Developments in Russia, which took a different path from the rest of Europe, will be discussed separately below.

Germany developed the strongest socialist organizations in Europe before World War I. After the 1870 Franco-Prussian War, socialism seemed like a viable threat in Germany. German authorities understood that the socialist vision for the state, modelled on the Paris Commune, had no place for monarchy or feudal tradition. In addition, high levels of unemployment that accompanied the 1873 depression fuelled government fears that the working class would support a socialist attack on the capitalist order. This threat seemed more imminent when German socialists took steps to increase their influence among workers, meeting in Gotha in 1875 to establish a unified Socialist Labor Party (later renamed the Social Democratic Party of Germany, or SPD), the first national socialist party in Europe. The government focused on socialism as the cause of Germany's troubles, channelling middle-class dissatisfaction and discontent away from itself. After 1874, antisocialist measures increased, but it was the two attempts on the life of the emperor, William I, in 1878 that finally created the support necessary to enact anti-socialist legislation. The Anti-Socialist Law of 1878 and other emergency measures, repeatedly renewed until 1890, suppressed all socialist newspapers, dissolved socialist organizations, restricted the right to free assembly, subjected socialists to police surveillance, and curtailed activities of trade unions, effectively driving the German socialist movement underground. The German government also hoped to counter the growing popularity of the socialist movement by establishing a series of social welfare policies for workers that provided sickness insurance, worker's compensation and old age and disability insurance. Despite these measures, socialists continued to gain strength. When the emergency measures were not renewed in 1890, socialists re-established themselves politically and produced a new platform that called for the emancipation of the working class in Germany and all nations through worker organization and class consciousness, and called for political reforms including universal suffrage, increased representation and labour legislation. That year, the Social Democratic Party earned the most votes of any party in parliamentary elections (Landauer, Vol. 1, p. 270).

The SPD continued to increase its dominance in German political life. By 1893 it had obtained a plurality of the popular vote and by 1912 it was the strongest party in the German Reichstag, receiving over four million votes. At its core, the SPD committed itself to principles of democracy, asserting that all adult citizens should have a voice in their government (Steenson, pp. 41–42). Most socialist voters supported the party because they expected it to deliver concrete improvements for the working class. Indeed, workers who joined the party had the opportunity to become leaders within the organization and its core membership remained its working-class constituents. Socialist support developed in working-class neighbourhoods, promoted through personal ties and family relationships. In addition, the party promoted the creation of other proletarian activities and institutions to advocate for workers' interests and to provide outlets for worker aspirations. Workers formed trade unions and other worker clubs, societies, and associations that allowed them to gain access to the elements of 'civilization' that had previously been the sole purview of the middle class and the elites. These worker institutions strengthened the workers' movement and its ties to socialism as such organizations often presented a socialist vision of the future (Steenson, p. 143).

By 1903, gradualism had come to dominate the German socialist movement. Indeed, ideas promoted by the 'revisionist' Eduard Bernstein (1850–1932) challenged the philosophical basis of Marxism and its notion of inherent revolution. Bernstein argued that rather than dividing society, capitalism was becoming more stable and helping to improve the living conditions of all people. Socialism could therefore increase its influence through the growing political power of the proletariat, by embracing a strong moral standard, and by pursuing the gradual socialization of political institutions (Kilroy-Silk, pp. 41–45; Kolakowski, Vol. 2, p. 105; Muravchik, p. 106). To this end, German social democrats focused on promoting social reform through legal channels. Success in elections and the growing popularity of worker institutions helped to reinforce Bernstein's ideas and turn German socialism away from its revolutionary Marxist heritage. Political realities also forced German socialists to collaborate with other political parties, most notably the Catholic Center party and the liberal parties, to form coalitions. Indeed, socialists found it to their advantage to work with liberals in guiding German fiscal policy.

On the eve of World War I, the SPD had emerged as the strongest and best organized socialist party in Europe, yet it contained limitations. It remained primarily an urban workers' movement with little appeal to rural farmers or even the urban middle class. In addition, critics of Bernstein's revisionism and the party's approach continued to exist within its ranks. Rosa Luxemburg (1870–1919), for example, found fault with what she considered the relatively passive policies of the SPD, calling for a more active response to workers' unrest, increased use of mass strikes, and greater support for the spontaneous mass action of the inherently revolutionary proletariat. A major Marxist theorist known for her intellectual abilities, Luxemburg blamed party leadership for its lack of radical socialist action. She proved willing to act to advance her views, participating in an effort to push the German revolution of 1919 (see below) further than SPD leaders intended in what became known as the 'Sparticist Rising' (Steenson, pp. 214–221; Abraham, pp. 142–144). Her murder in January 1919 reflected the SPD's desire to marginalize radical socialists within the party and reinforced its embrace of the cautious, gradualist approach. Indeed, as Gary Steenson concludes, 'the reluctance of the (SPD) leadership to use more aggressive means to pressure for social and political reform severely restricted the ability of the movement to influence developments in Imperial Germany' (Steenson, p. 227).

The defeat of the Paris Commune in 1871 dealt a severe blow to socialism in France. While no laws were enacted specifically against socialists, most major cities in France remained under martial law and emergency measures prohibited socialists' public activities, as well as depriving the working class of its leadership. A smaller working class and stronger artisan culture meant that socialism found less support in France than in countries with a larger industrial working class such as Germany. Nevertheless, French workers held national congresses in 1876 and 1878 and called for an International Workers' Congress to be held during the 1878 International Exposition in Paris. A further workers' conference in 1879 resulted in the creation of a new political party with a revolutionary program—the Federation of Socialist Workingmen, or Parti Ouvrier Français, led by Jules Guesde (1845–1922)—and the rebirth of the socialist movement in France. The major feature of French socialism in this period, and one of its weaknesses, was its tendency to divide itself into rival sects that competed with other political parties for working-class support (Wunthrow, p. 426). Along with the Federation of Socialist Workingmen, French socialists formed the Socialist Revolutionary Labor party, the Possibilist party and the Socialist Revolutionary party, in addition to a group of Independent Socialists. The atmosphere of French politics in the Third Republic, a generally parliamentary system, enabled French socialists to put forth a great diversity of ideas, approaches and idealism. Indeed, it seemed more possible to achieve reforms by working through the system in France than in many other countries. The appeal of socialism in France extended beyond the working class as well. Difficult economic circumstances encouraged many property-owning peasants to share the ideas and attitudes of the working class (Judt, p. 149). Despite its lack of coordination and coherence, and because of its widespread appeal within French society, French socialism became an important element of French national politics and the international socialist movement by the 1890s.

In 1893, French socialists achieved significant electoral successes and found it essential to work together. Issuing a statement of common principles in 1896, French socialists embraced a gradualist approach that rejected violence and committed them to the principles of democracy. Yet this moment of unity was illusory and although socialist leaders became active participants in the French government, they were not able to count on widespread support for their policies and actions. Indeed, by 1902, French socialists had again divided into several opposing parties, clashing over the role that socialists should play within a bourgeois government. In 1905, French socialist parties again came together to form the Socialist party, French section, of the Workers' International, bringing some unity to the socialist movement in France. The new socialist party accepted principles of gradualism but remained hostile toward the liberal government, although some socialists continued to serve as government ministers. After 1910, socialist leaders came to realize the importance of cooperating with liberals to achieve the passage of beneficial legislation.

Even though the English working class was more developed, organized and conscious of its interests than in any other European country, the British socialist movement remained weaker than its continental counterparts. Widespread acceptance of the country's political institutions, consistent broadening of suffrage, and the belief that existing parties were capable of implementing meaningful social and economic reforms deprived the British socialist movement of its strongest arguments and support. For instance, the Fabian Society, established in 1884, pursued a gradual approach to achieving socialism, preferring to educate existing parties about social justice rather than engage in any revolutionary activity. Nevertheless, shifts in the orientation of established political parties created an opening for socialist political parties in England. In particular, by the 1880s the Liberal party began to orient itself toward the right and away from working-class interests. As a result, in 1883 British socialists formed the Social Democratic Federation, out of which emerged the Independent Labour Party in 1892. Despite the growing success and appeal of the Labour Party, limitations remained. Because of the strength of the Liberal Party, any parliamentary success depended on cooperation with other parties, preventing the Labour Party from aggressively pursuing the interests of the working class. Growing government-sponsored welfare programmes also undermined the appeal of socialism. As Robert Wunthrow concludes, socialism in Britain 'failed to flourish as a distinct ideology… but it did serve to strengthen the stability of the established state system and, indeed, legitimated an expansion of the state into a whole realm of welfare activities' (Wuthnow, p. 445).

In contrast, socialism developed a solid hold in northern continental Europe. Socialism in these regions was heavily influenced by their proximity to Germany. In Sweden, the Social Democratic Labor Party formed in 1889, emerging out of a union of various types of workers' organizations. These socialists sought a middle ground, recognizing the importance of class struggle without actually advocating revolution or rejecting the possibility of compromise with non-socialist parties. Their sponsorship in 1902 of a massive strike over the issue of suffrage involving workers from across the country reflected the Social Democratic Labor Party's leadership over the labour movement. The two-day strike resulted in the recognition of the principle of universal male suffrage and reinforced for Swedish socialists the effectiveness of moderate policies and peaceful protest. Another strike in 1909 to protest a worker lockout, however, had the opposite result. The strike stretched on for two months, paralyzing the country. In the end, workers lost middle-class support and failed to win concessions from employers. Nevertheless, Swedish Social Democrats continued to increase their parliamentary representation and engage in a practical and gradualist approach, promoting reforms to protect workers and establishing social welfare programmes.

Belgian workers faced the difficulties of industrialization sooner than their counterparts in other countries because of an unstable economy that depended on exports, yet a Belgian socialist movement did not fully emerge until the formation of the Belgian Socialist Workers' Union in 1877. Efforts to unify the movement resulted in the establishment of the Belgian Labor Party in 1885. Membership in the party was based through trade unions or cooperatives, creating an effective grassroots structure that drew workers into the party with little involvement from intellectuals. Participation in the effort to expand suffrage raised the political status of the socialist movement. When the 1893 Constituent Assembly rejected universal suffrage, the Belgian Labor Party proclaimed a general strike that paralyzed the country and resulted in a compromise measure that extended suffrage and ended the strike after one week. With its newfound authority, the Belgian Labor Party sought to appeal to the middle class as well as workers by focusing on creating 'a voluntary organization of education and welfare in the broadest possible sense' (Landauer, Vol. 1, p. 470). They also expressed a willingness to work with liberal parties and participate in a liberal-led government. The Belgian Labor Party continued to pursue the expansion of suffrage through the use of strikes, finally succeeding with a general strike in 1913, which seemed to confirm the power of the class-conscious worker to effect political change (Landauer, Vol. 1, p. 480). Socialist leaders learned that a general strike to expand democracy was more readily received than a strike against a democratic government, and that for a strike to be successful it had to be terminated at the right time, sometimes by being willing to accept partial successes.

Socialism in southern Europe remained more limited than in the more industrialized north. In Spain, socialists established a strong party with a clear Marxist vision in 1879, but failed to attract much support as decentralized power among elites and their exploitation of a weak state made it seem futile to engage in the parliamentary process. In contrast, in Italy socialists faced formidable opposition from a strong government that emerged during Italy's unification in the 1860s. An independent socialist movement was established with the creation of the Italian Socialist Party in 1895, led by Philippo Turati (1857–1932). Although the party maintained a Marxist orientation, it remained internally divided, weakening its position in the country. Liberal support against government repression encouraged Italian socialists to collaborate with liberal parties, yet strong government opposition to socialism made it more difficult for the movement to take hold.

The socialist movement also created opportunities for organizing women and sought to appeal to them. The platforms of most national socialist parties included calls for universal suffrage and the political, economic and social equality of women. The emancipation of women thus became part of the broader struggle for the emancipation of the proletariat. Theorists, too, addressed the issue of women in the socialist movement. August Bebel (1840–1913), a leader of the German socialist movement and Reichstag representative from 1871–1912, produced *Women and Socialism* in 1879, revised in 1891. In this work, Bebel took standard feminist demands for expanded educational, economic and political rights, but also added new elements, arguing that it was not women's 'natural calling' to raise families, and that women's oppression was rooted in history, not biology (Sowerwine, p. 403).

Socialists had the most success among working women in countries where socialist parties organized groups specifically for women. The work of Clara Zetkin (1857–1933) in the German SPD provides an example of the transformative effects of separate socialist women's organizations. Zetkin emphasized the importance of socialist support for the feminist movement and women's rights. Middle-class feminists, she argued, were correct to emphasize women's issues and to work for their resolution through increased political rights, but she also stressed that suffrage was only the first step toward emancipation for the female proletariat; class conflict also made up an important element of the struggle (Sowerwine, p. 407). Zetkin argued that only when women had the right of suffrage could they participate in the political struggle and support their own class interests. Postponing female suffrage only suggested that women had fewer rights than men. Zetkin also stressed the importance of women's economic independence, understanding that work broadened women's horizons and experiences and made them better mothers. She found that agitational and educational propaganda needed to be directed specifically toward working women so they could be organized separately from men, emphasizing that women knew best the needs and interests of other women. Separate women's organizations, she concluded, would enable women to learn to think for themselves (Honeycut, pp. 37–38). The SPD women's organizations had considerable success. By 1908, the women's newspaper of the SPD had a circulation of over 70,000 and by 1914 nearly 175,000 women had joined the party, making up over 16 per cent of the total SPD membership (Sowerwine, p. 409). In advocating for separate women's organizations, Zetkin fundamentally shaped the socialist response to the question of women's emancipation, as well as the attitudes of working women toward the socialist movement (Honeycut, p. 30).

In contrast to the German experience, the French Socialist Party did not form successful separate women's organizations, resulting in the smallest female proportion of party membership, at no more than 3 per cent (Sowerwine, p. 409). The French socialist women's movement also was hampered by its unwillingness to support the goals of the feminist movement. British socialists fared even worse in terms of recruiting women than did the French. An active and militant suffrage movement in England that effectively mobilized support among working women helped to minimize the attraction of socialist organizations.

By the 1880s, socialism had emerged in all major European countries and had gained political influence through elections. Socialist parties had proven their appeal among the working class and had, for the most part, committed themselves to working within existing parliamentary systems to achieve reform. Yet European socialism also contained an inherently internationalist component. Marxist ideology espoused worker solidarity across national boundaries, and for many leaders, the time seemed right to reconstitute the international element of the movement. On 14 July 1889, the 100th anniversary of the French Revolution, 400 delegates from socialist organizations around the world met in Paris, France, to form the Second International Workingmen's Association (Second International). The goals adopted by the delegates included preventing conflict by uniting workers, calling for improved working conditions, and promoting Marxist principles of class struggle and socialization. The Second International also incorporated women's rights into its platform, arguing for universal suffrage, stating that women should be allowed into the ranks of socialist parties, and accepting the ideas of equal pay for equal work and special protections for mothers. Because liberal democracy and parliamentary systems had become established across Europe by this time, most delegates favoured the gradualist approach of working through existing political institutions, and this promoted a national orientation within the international organization, giving the Second International a consultative function where ideas and experiences could be exchanged. Although resolutions of the Second International had strong moral authority, they were not binding on national parties; the International remained a supplementary organization, a loose confederation of like-minded socialist parties to coordinate national party policies and resolve internal party disputes, particularly the issue of revisionism. Nevertheless, some delegates remained committed to international worker solidarity and the revolutionary approach to change. These differences would create a break within the socialist movement between those promoting democratic socialism and those adhering to revolutionary communism (Sandle, pp. 52–53).

The most important actions of Second International were in its policies against war. The Second International Congress in Paris in 1900 proposed that socialists in national legislatures should always vote against appropriations for military forces and that the International should coordinate efforts of socialist parties to make them more effective at preserving peace. Debates at the congress at Stuttgart in 1907 over use of the general strike to prevent war concluded in asserting the role of the Second International to coordinate the efforts of the working class against war. The congress in Basel, Switzerland, in 1912 focused specifically on conflicts in the Balkans. With the threat of war imminent, the congress issued a resolution asserting that fear of the working class revolution that would result from World War was an essential guarantee of peace; it raised the potential danger of social revolution in event of war, but issued no specific commitment for strikes or protests in event of war.

Despite their common dedication to workers and social justice, international socialist leaders were unable to agree upon a unified approach.

While Marxism dominated socialist thought, most national organizations stressed gradualism over revolution. The lack of any rigid doctrine or coherent international policy, however, allowed the socialist movement to adapt to the unique circumstances of each national context and made it more likely that socialist leaders' first priority would be to their own nations. This was made clear in 1914 as the 'international solidarity of the proletariat' (Kolakowski, Vol. 2, p. 28) could not compete with widespread socialist support for the patriotic impulses at the start of World War I, causing the collapse of the Second International.

IMPLEMENTING REVOLUTION: SOCIALISM IN RUSSIA

In late 1825, Alexander I of Russia died without leaving an heir. Alexander I had defeated French Emperor Napoleon Bonaparte and in 1815 marched victoriously into Paris. Russian officers, exposed to Western ideas and political institutions in Paris, began to call for reforms at home to bring Russian political institutions up to the same level of civilization as her military might. Yet, opposition from the nobility limited Alexander I's ability to initiate domestic reforms. After Alexander I died, the officers saw an opportunity to demand constitutional reforms. Taking advantage of confusion over succession, they organized a rebellion in which they encouraged fellow officers and soldiers not to swear loyalty to the new tsar, to issue a manifesto announcing the overthrow of the monarchy, and to create a provisional government and a constitution. Some 3,000 men participated, but the majority of troops remained loyal and the new tsar, Nicholas I, resolved the crisis by ordering his soldiers to fire at the rebels, killing 70. Out of the 579 men to stand trial, five were given the death penalty; the 121 officers found guilty were sentenced to Siberian exile, while enlisted men ran the gauntlet and served terms of hard labour. The harsh treatment and severe repression of the Decembrists, as these rebels became known, created the first martyrs for the cause in Russia, helping to establish a revolutionary tradition that would inspire later radicals and opponents of the autocracy, including socialists.

While gradualism came to dominate socialist organizations throughout Europe, the radical revolutionary wing took hold in Russia and thus the Russian experience provides an alternative example of socialist development in modern Europe. The appeal of revolution over reform in Russia was due in part to Russia's political and economic climate. No representative institutions existed in Russia until the early twentieth century, and then those remained extremely limited. Strict censorship and strong adherence by Russia's rulers to principles of absolute autocracy meant that there were virtually no outlets for popular political participation. These constraints forced opponents of the tsarist regime to extreme, sometimes violent, measures that increased conflict with the authorities. The emergence of a revolutionary socialist movement in Russia was also shaped by economic conditions that separated it from the rest of Europe. While most of Europe industrialized during the nineteenth century, Russia remained primarily agrarian. The little industrial development that did occur was driven mainly by the state and its needs, so that by the end of the nineteenth century, Russia had a small urban population, a weak middle class, and only a nascent working class. In Russia, therefore, the driving force of the socialist movement came not from the proletariat but from the *intelligentsia*, a small segment of highly educated and socially conscious thinkers, like the Decembrists, who rebelled against tsarist autocracy and called for liberation in the name of the masses.

Russian socialism was shaped as well by the plight of the peasantry. Until 1861, nearly all peasants in Russia were serfs, bound to the land where they lived and obliged to contribute their labour or produce to their landlords. Understanding serfdom as immoral, fearing potential rebellion, and wary of increasing rural violence, tsar Alexander II emancipated the serfs in 1861. The emancipation granted land to the former serfs, basically through government purchase from landowners, but provided that peasants had to repay the government over a period of 49 years. The peasant commune (*mir*) was given control of the land to distribute to its members and responsibility for collecting redemption payments. These payments effectively saddled the newly freed peasants with a heavy tax burden, and many saw the emancipation as the imposition of a second serfdom.

Dismayed by the lack of significant change in peasant status and inspired by peasant protests over the terms of the emancipation, the *intelligentsia* began to focus on the peasantry as the source of revolutionary sentiment that would initiate more sweeping social and political reforms. Indeed, they understood peasant institutions such as the commune to be inherently socialist and believed the peasantry needed only to be made aware of its plight to stimulate an uprising that would overthrow the government and institute a new socialist order. This faith in the revolutionary potential of the peasantry was embodied in the Populist movement of the 1870s. In the summer of 1874, the Populists, a loose group of radical students and *intelligentsia*, sent thousands of representatives into the countryside to raise the peasants' awareness of their oppressed status and to agitate for revolution against the tsarist regime. The peasantry turned out to be much less revolutionary than the Populists expected. Despite their dissatisfaction, peasants generally supported the tsar and turned the Populists in to the police. Frustrated by police repression and the regime's resistance to any sort of social or political reforms, some Populists turned to terrorism to spread their revolutionary message, culminating with the assassination of Alexander II in 1881. This act was met with severe police repression against the conspirators that brought an end to the Populist movement and drove the Russian radical *intelligentsia* underground and abroad.

At the turn of the twentieth century, the Russian socialist movement revived. As it evolved, two basic trends emerged. The first took up where the Populists had left off, emphasizing the centrality of the Russian peasantry for the future socialist revolution. These agrarian socialists asserted that all toilers, whether in the factory or on the land, were exploited by bourgeois society. They believed that through patient agitation and propaganda, the peasantry would come to realize their oppressed status and rise up against the authorities. Because of the revolutionary potential and socialist orientation of the peasant masses, they argued, Russia could skip the horrors of Western industrial capitalism and proceed directly to socialism. The agrarian socialists developed a solid base of support among the peasants and in 1901 formed the Socialist Revolutionary Party (SRs). By World War I, the SRs had emerged as the most popular socialist party in Russia.

Other socialists took a more Marxist approach, focusing on the urban working class as the source of revolutionary potential. In the aftermath of the failure of Populism, the founder of Russian Marxism, Georgi Plekhanov (1856–1918), turned away from the idea of the peasantry as revolutionary. He argued instead that revolutionary initiative must come from the urban proletariat and the *intelligentsia*. Plekhanov stressed that Russia could not skip the capitalist phase of development, as the SRs asserted. Instead, he blamed the Russian autocracy and the vestiges of feudalism in Russian society for the slow pace of capitalist development. Once capitalism took off, according to Plekhanov, peasants would be transformed into a landless proletariat, thus creating the conditions for a true proletarian socialist revolution. He also called for the formation of a revolutionary party that could guide the proletariat and eventually seize power. Plekhanov's Marxism appealed to a new generation of Russian intellectuals frustrated at the lack of reform in Russian society and the failure of the Populist movement. Russian Marxists also were inspired by the growth of Russia's industrial base by the turn of the century. Agrarian reforms and economic policies that promoted industrial expansion encouraged peasants to migrate to the cities in search of new employment opportunities. Although workers still comprised only a small fraction of the total population, most of these were concentrated in large enterprises, often with over one thousand workers, located in major urban centres. Worker discontent over low wages and difficult living conditions stimulated massive strikes that had the potential to cripple the entire country. Russian Marxists sought to harness the revolutionary potential of this growing worker discontent to push for political transformation.

In 1898 several Marxist groups came together to establish the Russian Social Democratic Labor Party (RSDLP). One of the leading activists in the RSDLP was Vladimir Ilich Ulianov (Lenin) (1870–1924). Born in Simbirsk, a small city in central Russia, Lenin came under the influence of the Russian revolutionary tradition at an early age when his older brother was executed for taking part in a plot to assassinate tsar Alexander III. As a law school student, he became involved in radical circles and was expelled from Kazan University. Eventually, his efforts to disseminate revolutionary literature among striking workers earned him a four-year prison sentence, which he served from 1896 to 1900. After his release, Lenin went to Switzerland, where he joined Plekhanov's group of supporters and began publishing a popular Marxist journal, *Iskra* (*The Spark*). Lenin set out his revolutionary agenda in his 1902 pamphlet, 'What is to be Done?' in which he effectively reinterpreted Marxism, adapting it for Russian conditions. On the one hand, Lenin recognized that any successful proletarian revolution would need the support of Russia's large agrarian population. He argued, therefore, that the socialist revolution would involve an alliance between the peasantry and the proletariat. On the other hand, Lenin stressed that only a highly organized group of professional revolutionaries, the vanguard of the proletariat, could instigate and lead a successful revolution in an agrarian nation without waiting for full capitalist development.

In 1903, the RSDLP congress met in Brussels. At the congress, the RSDLP adopted a party program that sought to institute public ownership over the means of production, end class divisions in society, and eliminate oppression and exploitation by overthrowing the tsarist autocracy and establishing a democratic republic. While this programme was accepted with relatively little dispute, greater disagreement emerged over the definition of a RSDLP party member and thus the approach to revolutionary agitation. Plekhanov promoted a broad-based party of workers and intellectuals who could participate in decision-making, with activists focusing on agitation and education. This approach embodied democratic principles of mass self-determination, guided and shaped by socialist activists. In contrast, Lenin envisioned a narrow, highly disciplined and highly centralized leadership of professional revolutionaries who would direct the broader party membership in their actions and dictate policies for the party (Kolakowski, Vol. 2, p. 394). Lenin and his supporters held the minority position, but when a large group withdrew from the congress over a separate dispute, Lenin's faction suddenly became the majority. As a result, Lenin's group became known as the Bolsheviks (or majority group) while the others acquired the title Mensheviks (or minority group). Despite the terminology, Lenin's Bolsheviks never represented the opinion of the majority of Russian Marxists. Tensions remained within the RSDLP until it formally divided in 1912.

Turmoil within Russia in the early twentieth century caught the newly formed socialist parties off guard. Although workers were becoming more organized, they tended to act spontaneously in response to economic conditions, rather than as a result of any organized socialist agitational effort. This worker independence became clear in the events of the 1905 Revolution, which began on Sunday, 9 January 1905, when a peaceful procession of striking workers marched to the Winter Palace in St Petersburg to bring a petition of grievances to the tsar. Instead of receiving the petition, tsar Nicholas II ordered his troops to disperse the procession, resulting in the deaths of over one hundred unarmed workers. 'Bloody Sunday' eroded support for the tsar and set off a series of massive strikes, riots and protests. These disturbances culminated in a General Strike in October that paralyzed the country and forced the tsar to grant concessions, including the creation of a representative body with legislative authority (the Duma).

Although they had little to do with the worker disturbances in 1905 or the initiation of the General Strike, socialist activists quickly involved themselves in supporting the workers' initiative. Indeed, the General Strike seemed to confirm the importance of Plekhanov's vision of a mass party and the Mensheviks took the lead by helping to organize a strike committee, the St Petersburg Soviet of Workers' Deputies, to coordinate the strike and keep it going. This body played a key role in the success of the strike, but worker initiative and socialist party actions alone did not force the tsar to grant concessions; rather, widespread support for the workers from all levels of society convinced the government to implement changes. At the same time, the tsar pursued policies of harsh repression against the socialists, rounding up suspected trouble-makers and executing them. In response, some factions within the socialist parties initiated a campaign of terror against government officials. The violence on both sides made it impossible for even moderate socialists to see any hope of reconciliation with the government and reinforced the sense that the tsar did not intend to keep the promises he made.

The outbreak of World War I in 1914 altered Russian political dynamics. At the start of the war, the leaders of the Russian socialist movement were in exile in Europe. They espoused a wide range of opinions about the war. Plekhanov, for instance, supported it, believing that a Russian defeat would undermine the status of the proletariat. In contrast, Lenin deplored the war altogether as an imperialist venture in which socialists should play no part. He hoped the war would expose the fissures in the capitalist system and create an opportunity for socialist revolution. Nevertheless, most Russians, like their European counterparts, supported the war effort, at least in the early days of the fighting. As the war dragged on, however, the initial patriotic sentiment disappeared and opposition spread throughout Russian society. Confidence in the tsarist regime was undermined as well by incompetent administration of the war and the domestic front. In late February 1917, women workers demanding bread instigated a massive strike in Petrograd (as St Petersburg was renamed) and the troops ordered to disperse the strikers joined the protests instead. Amid the chaos, the tsar's advisers suggested that he step down. On 2 March 1917, Nicholas II abdicated the throne, bringing an end to the Russian autocracy.

As with the outbreak of the 1905 Revolution, socialist parties played a minor role in the events of February 1917. They did not instigate workers to strike or convince soldiers to mutiny. Once these events occurred, however, socialists acted quickly to support the popular movement. Mensheviks and SRs formed a Petrograd Soviet of Workers' and Soldiers' Deputies, modelled on the institution established in 1905. According to their interpretation of Marxist revolutionary theory, they considered the February events a 'bourgeois' revolution, the first step in the eventual progression toward socialism. Few socialists believed that Russia was ready for socialist revolution in 1917. Instead, they chose to support the revolutionary enthusiasm of the masses and serve as a 'watchdog' organization to ensure that the new Provisional Government, led by a coalition of moderate and liberal Duma members, honoured the democratic promises of the revolution. The Soviet received considerable support from workers and soldiers who saw it as the institution that best represented their needs and interests. While it refused to take on the responsibility of government, the Soviet had to approve the provisional Government's actions. Over the summer of 1917, however, Soviet leaders increasingly joined forces with the liberals in the Provisional Government, creating several coalition governments in an attempt to run the country more effectively.

One of the few socialist leaders who believed that the time was ripe for a socialist revolution in Russia was Vladimir Lenin. In exile in Switzerland in February, Lenin returned to Russia in early April 1917. His 'April Theses' proposed an immediate seizure of power and the establishment of a socialist 'dictatorship' of workers, peasants and soldiers. He called for direct opposition to the Provisional Government and an immediate end to the war. For most socialists and even most Bolsheviks, Lenin's views seemed out of touch with reality. The revolutionary euphoria of the time encouraged cooperation rather than opposition. Nevertheless, Lenin's 'April Theses' became the Bolshevik party platform. Ultimately, Lenin's radical stance, his decision to refrain from supporting the Provisional Government, and his refusal to participate in coalition governments positioned the Bolsheviks as a viable alternative to the moderate socialists in the Soviet, who increasingly were seen as having compromised their principles and ideals to work with the Provisional Government.

By the end of the summer, Lenin's oppositional stance began to pay off. The Bolsheviks had established themselves as staunch defenders of the revolution and their popularity had increased, along with support for their calls for 'Peace, Land and Bread' and 'All Power to the Soviets'. As a result, Bolshevik representatives began to participate in the Petrograd Soviet, taking over key positions in the Soviet and its militia, the Military Revolutionary Committee (MRC), which commanded the loyalty of troops stationed in Petrograd. In late October 1917, Lenin found an opportunity to seize power. Acting in response to the Provisional Government's closure of some Bolshevik printing presses, the Bolshevik-led MRC took control of most of Petrograd. The next day, Lenin proclaimed the overthrow of the Provisional Government and the transfer of power to the Petrograd Soviet's MRC. When the Second All-Russian Congress of Soviets of Workers', Soldiers' and Peasants' Deputies, a convention of representatives from soviets throughout the country, convened later that evening, power had already been transferred. Opposed to the undemocratic means through which this transfer of power had been achieved, Menshevik and SR representatives denounced the Bolsheviks and walked out of the congress. This action left the Bolsheviks with a clear majority and they immediately set about consolidating their control. Through his unilateral actions, Lenin had managed to take a relatively small political party and impose its leadership over the entire country. Yet, Bolshevik control was far from the broad socialist coalition government that most people envisioned when they supported the calls for 'All Power to the Soviets' and this gave rise to widespread opposition to the new government.

In addition to growing opposition to their control, the Bolsheviks had to address Russia's role in what had become a very unpopular World War. Lenin had always viewed the war as an imperialist venture that would undermine capitalism and create the conditions for socialist revolution. Once they came to power, the Bolsheviks found it essential to end Russia's participation in the war, both to fulfil their long-standing promises of peace and because they needed soldier support to consolidate power at home. On 24 February 1918, the Bolsheviks signed the Brest-Litovsk Peace Treaty with Germany, ending Russia's involvement in the fighting. The treaty's harsh measures horrified most Russians, including most Bolsheviks, but Lenin remained unconcerned. He believed the imminent socialist revolution in Germany and the rest of the capitalist world would make the peace treaty irrelevant (and indeed, Germany's eventual defeat in the war did result in the annulment of the treaty). Brest-Litovsk achieved Lenin's immediate objective: to get Russia out of the war. Nevertheless, dissatisfaction with the separate peace helped to solidify opposition to the Bolsheviks, ensuring that the path to secure complete Bolshevik control over Russia would only be achieved through a long, bloody and destructive Civil War.

The Russian Civil War pitted the Bolsheviks (Reds) against a loose coalition of anti-communist opponents, collectively referred to as Whites. The Whites had little to offer the population in terms of a vision for the future; their goal was to destroy the Bolsheviks, and many feared a restoration of the monarchy and an end to the gains of the revolution, especially the confiscation of land, if the Whites were victorious. In contrast, the Reds effectively branded their opponents as exploiting monarchists and capitalists, and appealed to the population's sense of social justice. While both sides treated their occupied areas harshly, employing indiscriminate violence and widespread grain requisitioning, local populations were more willing to put up with the Bolsheviks because the feared worse from the Whites. However, once the Whites were defeated, by 1920, a new opponent appeared—Greens, or peasant partisan bands—that sought to defend villages from Bolshevik policies of grain requisitioning and state control. The fighting between the Reds and Greens left much of central Russia devastated, destroying industry and agriculture, contributing to a massive famine in 1921, and resulting in the deaths and displacement of millions. By 1921, the Bolsheviks had emerged victorious in the Civil War, mostly because the entire country was exhausted and devastated from the fighting. No one remained to oppose Bolshevik control (Raleigh).

Despite the difficulties of the Civil War, the Bolsheviks lost no time in implementing revolutionary policies to transform Russia into a socialist state. These policies, known as War Communism, relied on central control of economic resources and the use of force to maintain that control, expressed through the confiscation of grain and through arrests, hostage-takings and executions of counterrevolutionaries or class enemies. The use of force extended to employment practices as well, as military discipline was imposed on workers to prevent them from leaving their jobs. At the same time, the Bolsheviks implemented social policies designed to reshape and transform Russian society by eliminating the sources of capitalist exploitation. These reforms included legal changes that altered family relationships by easing divorce and outlawing illegitimacy, among others. The Civil War thus provided the Bolsheviks with the opportunity to assert their vision of the new socialist society. What emerged—a state defined by centralized power and use of force—was created by the conditions and nature of the Civil War period. As some historians have argued, the Civil War was a formative experience for the Bolsheviks. It established the scope and direction of Bolshevik policy and fundamentally shaped the Bolshevik mentality by showing the Bolshevik leadership evidence of the widespread presence of class enemies and counterrevolutionaries and by providing a shared experience of fighting, loyalty and brotherhood among the rank and file (Fitzpatrick). These elements contributed in a fundamental way to the nature of the Soviet socialist system.

Even in victory, however, the Bolshevik leadership was not united in its vision of the direction economic policy should take. One group, known as the Workers' Opposition, argued that trade unions should direct economic activity, giving more control to workers. This approach conflicted with Lenin's interest in maintaining strong centralized state control. He sought to eradicate the possibility for further policy disagreements by proposing a ban on factions, to be implemented at the Tenth Party Congress in March 1921. Lenin stressed that the party had to present a united front. The ban on factions reasserted strict party discipline within the ranks and ensured tight central control over party and government actions. On the eve of the Congress, soldiers stationed at the Kronstadt naval base (an island in the Gulf of Finland near Petrograd) rioted, demanding an end to the Bolshevik dictatorship. Their demands reflected the deep dissatisfaction with Bolshevik rule that pervaded the country in 1921. Quickly branding the rebels as counterrevolutionaries, Bolshevik supporters launched a dramatic attack on the island and violently suppressed the revolt. The Kronstadt Rebellion again raised fears of counterrevolution among the Bolshevik leadership and helped to unite them around Lenin and his policies. Yet it also made clear that the current approach was not viable in the long term. Along with the ban on factions, the Tenth Party Congress initiated a new economic programme called the New Economic Policy (NEP). The NEP shifted economic policies away from the coercive and repressive features of War Communism to allow for economic recovery while still pursuing policies designed to transform Russia into a socialist state. The major feature of the NEP was the *smychka*, or alliance between the peasantry and the working class. It provided that once peasants had contributed a certain amount of grain to the state, they could trade or sell any surplus on the open market. While keeping state control of heavy and export industries, the NEP also allowed entrepreneurs and shop owners to own and operate small-scale industries and consumer production. These two innovations created space for economic recovery, provided food to cities and goods to purchase, and generated support for the Bolshevik regime, particularly among peasants who prospered under the NEP.

Although the NEP succeeded in stabilizing Russia's economy, many Bolsheviks remained uneasy with the policy, seeing it as allowing too many capitalist elements to exist within the socialist economy. Intraparty debates over the NEP created a power struggle within the Bolshevik, now Communist party, that allowed Joseph Dzhugashvili (Stalin) (1879–1953) to emerge as party leader. Born in the Georgian village of Gori, Stalin abandoned his seminary studies to become a revolutionary. He emerged as a leading member of the Bolshevik party during the Civil War, distinguishing himself in his ability to fulfil orders with ruthlessness and determination, no matter the cost. In 1922, Lenin appointed Stalin to the position of General Secretary, in charge of party personnel. From this position, Stalin established a group of supporters who owed their positions and their loyalty directly to him. Stalin also held important positions in the top party and government organizations, giving him unprecedented access to power and authority. When Lenin suffered a debilitating stroke in 1922 and died in 1924, Stalin was well positioned to take on the leadership position. The Communist Party was organized on the principle of collective leadership, yet even before Lenin died, its members began vying for control. In this contest, Stalin emerged victorious by using the same methods Lenin had employed to push his agenda, but with greater ruthlessness (Fitzpatrick, p. 110). Stalin scored a major victory when he advanced the slogan 'Socialism in One Country', stressing that the communist goal of world revolution could be relegated to the back burner temporarily while revolutionary gains were consolidated and secured in Russia. In other words, communism could succeed in Russia without a world proletariat revolution. Marxists hoped that the Russian 'revolutionary spark' would launch similar revolutions in Western Europe, where the foundations for such upheavals were far more developed (Lindemann, p. 206). Stalin's policy reflected political realism and appealed to the party rank and file eager to push forward with the socialist transformation of Russian society.

His leadership of the party was secured with the expulsion of his main rivals for power, Leon Trotsky, Lev Kamenev, and Grigory Zinoviev, at the Fifteenth Party Congress in late 1927.

Stalin, like many of his comrades, disliked the NEP with its capitalistic elements that seemed to privilege the peasantry at the expense of the urban proletariat. His vision of socialism was modelled on the Marxist understanding of the need for a highly industrialized society. In 1929, Stalin initiated his own revolution that sought to achieve that vision in Russia. The first element of this plan was agricultural collectivization. Although Lenin had promoted the alliance between the proletariat and the peasantry as the best way to promulgate revolution in Russia, Bolshevik experiences with grain requisitioning during the Civil War taught them that the peasantry could not be trusted. Stalin's collectivization policies brought the peasantry under the watchful eyes of the state by creating state-run collective farms to ensure the effective collection of agricultural produce. Collectivization made peasants into rural wage labourers, depriving them of the land they had so enthusiastically seized during the revolution. Those who resisted collectivization were labelled *kulaks* (rich peasants) or class enemies, and either executed or deported to forced labour camps, contributing to the creation of the Gulag, the massive labour camp system that engulfed millions during Stalin's rule. Widespread opposition to collectivization also resulted in a famine in 1932–33 that killed millions. Yet, by the early 1930s, Stalin's policies had been achieved and most peasants had joined collective farms, thus securing food supply for use by the government.

The core element of Stalin's revolution was the rapid industrialization of the country, achieved through a series of five-year plans in which the state took control of economic planning, distribution and trade. For many, centralized state control of the economy seemed like a positive step toward the achievement of socialism. The First Five-Year Plan (1929–1932) focused investment in heavy industry. The atmosphere of the time promoted the progressive drive toward socialism and over-achievement (indeed, the Five-Year Plan was declared fulfilled in four years). In this context, entire cities and industries sprang up where none had existed before and unemployment virtually disappeared. The commitment to heavy industry meant, however, that consumer needs often went unmet. Shortages of goods and housing abounded, and workers were asked to sacrifice personal comfort in favour of achieving long-term goals. Other problems accompanied rapid industrialization, including massive waste of both human and material resources. Nevertheless, the growth achieved in the early 1930s set the

Soviet economy on the road toward its goals, and established the base of industrial development that would enable it to outproduce Nazi Germany during World War II.

The Stalin Revolution sought to complete the transition to a socialist society. In doing so, it privileged the urban proletariat over all other social classes. Workers were given educational opportunities and promotions to leadership positions, often at the expense of those better skilled or qualified. Persons with the wrong social backgrounds—the bourgeoisie, many middle-class professionals, priests, and even some peasants—found themselves cut off from jobs and social advancement. The privileging of the proletariat created not the classless society envisioned by Marx, but rather a new social elite based on working-class background and dedication to the communist cause. The new cadres owed their success and their positions to Stalin, and gave him and the new regime their personal loyalty. They also participated in often ruthless policies of class warfare to eliminate undesirable groups from Soviet society, including those who voiced opposition to regime polices. This quest to remove potential class enemies led to repeated purges of both the Communist Party and society, creating an atmosphere of fear and mistrust that pervaded Soviet Russia by the mid-1930s and filled the Gulag with thousands of victims whose forced labour contributed to the exploitation of Russia's wildernesses, another inefficient use of resources.

Although purging continued for a few more years, the Stalin Revolution came to a conclusion with the issuing of a new constitution in 1936 that ended class warfare and declared the successful construction of socialism. The Russian Revolutions established the first socialist state, asserting the validity of the revolutionary approach and putting forth a new vision of what it meant to be communist. As historian Sheila Fitzpatrick notes, the revolutions 'established a definition of socialism that hinged on the seizure of state power and its use as an instrument of economic and social transformation' (Fitzpatrick, p. 171). For the Bolsheviks, socialism required the violent seizure of power. Lenin and Stalin reinterpreted Marxist ideology to fit Russian circumstances and conditions. They proved willing to employ coercive and often violent measures to achieve their goals and indeed believed such measures were necessary. Although other socialist revolutions were not forthcoming, the Bolsheviks never abandoned the principle of world revolution and remained committed to their vision of the ideal socialist state, based on the Soviet model that they hoped would emerge as a result of the destruction of capitalism in other nations. The violence of the Bolsheviks, however, made many socialists in Western Europe uncomfortable. As the repressive nature of the Soviet regime became clear, socialists in other parts of Europe sought to distance themselves from the Russian revolutionaries, reemphasizing the value of gradualism and further reinforcing the divisions between democratic socialism and revolutionary communism.

SOCIALISM UNDER ATTACK: INTERWAR DEVELOPMENTS IN WESTERN EUROPE

With the end of the war, European socialists sought to revive the international orientation of their movement. Some discussions about the role of socialism in promoting peace had occurred during the war in Zimmerwald, Switzerland, but most socialist parties had supported their national governments during the war. The achievement of peace, however, made it imperative to reassert socialist values and an International Socialist Conference was held in February 1919 in Berne, Switzerland. At the conference, socialists sought to move past issues of war guilt and responsibility to focus on new international institutions, such as the League of Nations, the question of reparations, and European reconstruction. The revived International, they believed, would provide unity and solidarity for the international socialist movement.

The Bolsheviks, fresh with the success of their revolution, tried to impose their leadership on this body, seeing it instead as a future league of Communist governments. They sponsored the First Congress of the Communist International in early March 1919. The delegates to the conference were carefully chosen by the Bolshevik Central Committee and despite its lack of representativeness, the Congress declared the founding of a new international socialist organization, the Third International, or Communist International (Comintern). They hoped this new organization would not fall victim to the nationalist elements within socialism that had contributed to the foundering of the First and Second Internationals. The Comintern limited membership to 'pure' communists and had a highly centralized structure that sought to impose its policies and objectives on its membership, recreating Bolshevik organizational principles in communist parties to awaken the masses to their interests and coordinate revolutionary activity throughout the world. By the end of 1921, Communist parties had been established in all but four European nations.

Few existing European socialist parties, however, were willing to accept the conditions the Bolsheviks placed on membership in the Comintern or the unquestioned leadership of the Russian communists. Instead, some formed a separate organization, the International

Working Union, or Vienna International, in 1921, in an attempt to restore international unity in the socialist movement. In addition, the restrictions of the Comintern helped to revive the Socialist International. Once the leaders of the Vienna International realized that compromise with the Bolsheviks was impossible, they joined forces with the Socialist International in 1923. Over the next decade, the Socialist International acted as the dominant international socialist institution in Western Europe dedicated to issues of European reconstruction, while the Comintern promoted worldwide communist revolution.

The success of the Bolshevik Revolution divided the European socialist world both nationally and internationally. National communist parties now received direction directly from Moscow through the Comintern and pursued policies of violent revolution on the Soviet model. In contrast, socialist parties continued to work for reforms within existing governmental structures. The fundamental conflicts between communists and socialists made compromise and cooperation difficult within the socialist movement. At the same time, these divisions made it easier for socialism's enemies to launch attacks, as they could easily lump socialists together with the more radical communists. In the interwar period, the disagreements between socialists and communists thus undermined what had been a successful, vibrant, and powerful movement throughout much of Europe.

German socialists achieved the most political power of any socialist organization in Europe, and also experienced the greatest fall. During the war, patriotism and the desire for German victory united the German people and the Social Democratic Party played an important role in mobilizing workers and helping to control strikes and opposition. Social Democrats acted out of patriotism and expected compensation for their efforts in an increase in political power at the end of the war. The events of 1917 in Russia inspired socialists in the rest of Europe and altered socialist expectations and hopes for revolution even as they were repulsed by the Bolsheviks' repressive methods. It seemed possible in 1918 that Germany would soon follow the Bolshevik path. In January 1918, German workers went on strike to demand a negotiated peace without annexations or indemnities. By that autumn, with the entry of the United States in the war, the situation began to look grim for the German military. In early October 1918, the German military leadership requested an armistice and peace negotiations. The sudden possibility of German defeat undermined support for and the authority of the military and the German monarchy. Yet, German socialists still sought to work within existing political structures to achieve their goals, increasingly committing themselves to compromise with the old order rather than rejection of it. Protests of soldiers, sailors and workers, however, drove revolutionary events. Calls for peace in Bavaria in early November resulted in the establishment there of a socialist-led republic. In Berlin, Social Democrats, seeking to guide events, began to disassociate themselves from the German government and call for the Kaiser's abdication. Acknowledging the Social Democrats as their leaders, workers participated in massive demonstrations on 11 November, the day the armistice went into effect, and when soldiers stationed in Berlin refused to fire on the crowds, the Kaiser finally agreed to abdicate the throne.

In contrast to the February 1917 Revolution in Russia, in the German revolution Social Democrats took the lead in establishing a new republican government, but that leadership was driven nevertheless by recognition of the power and authority of workers' and soldiers' Soviets that sprang up throughout the country. Conditions in Germany in 1918, however, ensured that Germany would not see a completely Bolshevik-style revolution. For one, German Social Democrats were committed to principles of democracy and unwilling to resort to the dictatorial and repressive measures embraced by the Bolsheviks. Indeed, most German socialists were not ready for socialist revolution. They hesitated to take on the responsibility for rebuilding a devastated Germany after the war, asserting instead the need for cooperation with the bourgeoisie to sustain the economy. In addition, alignment with Soviet Russia would have increased hostility with the West and a possible renewal of war at a time when, fearing starvation, German leaders hoped to obtain grain supplies from the West (Landauer, Vol. 1, pp. 810–812). Instead, the German Social Democrats refused to claim greater authority than their mandate and formed a democratic republic.

Elections to the new representative government took place in early 1919, with moderate socialists gaining the most seats of any party in the parliament. Radical socialists and communists refused to participate in the elections. The new National Assembly convened in Weimar, Germany, on 6 February. Although the SPD was the largest party, the socialists lacked an outright majority and formed a coalition government with the centre and liberal parties. In this way, moderate socialists could influence policy, but Weimar would not become a purely socialist government. Indeed, the new government sought to preserve traditional institutions of power. The failure to implement a true socialist government ensured radical socialist opposition to the new leadership. In Berlin, this took the form of violent street fighting in March 1919. In Bavaria, the centre of revolution in 1918, it led to a second revolution as moderate socialists and conservatives won elections in January 1919. When Kurt Eisner, the leader of the revolutionary government, was assassinated by a monarchist in February 1919, radical socialists attempted to seize control of the government, proclaiming the establishment of the Bavarian Soviet Republic. Conservative forces rallied troops and retook the city, arresting and executing those who resisted. With the collapse of the Bavarian Soviet Republic, German communists lost their chance to overthrow the Weimar system.

Concerns over a possible Communist takeover continued to haunt the Weimar government. Fear of communism and the expanded power of the working class turned middle-class public opinion increasingly against the government, which they held responsible for their difficulties. A wave of strikes in early 1920 further exacerbated the situation. Reactions against protesting workers led to a crackdown on radical socialists and communists that shut down their newspapers and prevented agitation in workplaces. In March 1920, several thousand disgruntled soldiers marched on Berlin and occupied government buildings, taking control of some aspects of the government. Within days, however, the insurrection had collapsed, although strikes and disorder continued for several more weeks. Despite the failure of the coup attempt, the episode further undermined worker and middle-class faith in the government. Elections in May 1920 reflected these changes. Although moderate socialists remained the strongest party, their influence was reduced, showing widespread disillusionment with the party in power. Instead, rightist nationalist parties made the largest gains. These defeats signalled the beginning of the decline of socialist influence and control in Weimar Germany.

Throughout this period, Comintern members in Germany worked underground with the hopes of fomenting further revolution. In March 1921 widespread unrest in Central Germany encouraged communist leaders to call a general strike, but lack of response caused the insurrection to be quelled within weeks, revealing that the German proletariat showed little interest in seizing power. The Communist defeat in March 1921 led to increasing control and direction of the German communist movement from Moscow through the Comintern, and unwillingness among Social Democrats to work with the radicals. Frustration at the activities of the Comintern and its Moscow-driven agenda also led some socialist leaders, including Clara Zetkin, to sever relations with the communists. Nevertheless, these actions drew a sharp dividing line between socialists committed to working through government channels to achieve reforms and communists who chose extra-legal actions to stimulate revolution.

The rise of German nationalism increased the precarious position of the socialists. Adolf Hitler and his National Socialist (Nazi) party posed a growing threat. The nationalist cause received a boost with the French occupation of the Ruhr Valley in early 1923. The German government advocated passive resistance (refusing to aid the French efforts to extract resources from the region), yet this course of action seemed to have little effect. Worsening economic circumstances and frustration at the violation of national sovereignty encouraged popular opinion to turn against the socialists, who were perceived to be in control of the government. The Nazi party exploited these sentiments by appealing to the middle class and their resentment of perceived worker privilege. The May 1924 elections reflected these frustrations and established German Nationalists as the strongest party, repositioning the SPD as an opposition party.

Social Democrats still played an important role in the German government, particularly in passing legislative measures opposed by German Nationalists, making significant contributions to the social welfare of the German population. By the late 1920s, Weimar Germany had established state-funded mandatory health insurance, old-age and disability insurance and unemployment insurance. It also had a system for resolving workplace disputes through arbitration, supported by both employers and trade unions. Social Democrats pushed for increased public ownership of industries and enterprises, but in the interest of protecting consumers and integrating Germany into the world economy, socialists often defended liberal policies on industrial organization and foreign trade (Landauer, Vol. 1, p. 1306). Through their participation in the exercise of executive power, Social Democrats increasingly linked themselves to policies that, dictated by difficult financial circumstances, placed additional burdens on the working class. The dire financial situation and the need for foreign investment prompted socialists to accept policies that in other circumstances they would have rejected as too burdensome to the masses. They defended laissez-faire economics and hesitated to support social services if they might lead to deficit spending. Their compromises stimulated disappointment and disillusionment among their working-class supporters.

The depression in Germany in the late 1920s altered the political dynamics of the country, bringing widespread discontent and economic hardship. Growing unemployment reduced working-class standards of living and placed an extreme burden of unemployment relief obligations on the federal government. These economic difficulties benefited the Communist Party and they, along with the Nazis, supported often violent demonstrations against the government and the Social Democrats. For example, the authorities' attempts to disperse demonstrators on May Day, a traditional socialist holiday, further undermined support among workers for the socialist-led government and the Social Democrats. By September 1930, discontent with the government was such that while the SPD remained the largest political party in the government, both the Communists and the Nazi Party emerged with significantly increased representation.

Even before 1930, German Communists had found common ground with the Nazi Party in their opposition to the government and their expression of it through violent protests. After 1931, Communists focused on the Social Democrats as their main enemy. The Comintern ordered German Communists to refuse to cooperate with or support socialists, seeing their welfare programmes as undermining the notion that a proletarian dictatorship was essential to improving the living conditions of the working class. Communists even expressed a willingness to work with the Nazis to some extent to achieve their common goals. Indeed, Communists argued that Nazism was 'a prelude to communism and must therefore not be prevented from coming to power' (Landauer, Vol. 2, p. 1388). Yet, increasing Nazi influence in German society and government spelled disaster for both branches of the socialist movement. As they gained power, the Nazis set about dismantling the welfare state socialists had so painstakingly constructed; they removed socialists from government positions and attacked Communists as disruptive to public order and safety. Indeed, violent clashes between Communists and Nazis increased, and the Nazis used the chaos to bolster their base of support.

Hitler's appointment as Chancellor signalled the end for both socialism and communism in Germany. Hitler blamed the Reichstag fire of 27 February 1933 on the Communists, creating public hysteria and fears of mass violence and a possible 'Bolshevik' revolution. He also placed responsibility for the difficulties of the German economy with all socialists. In addition to arresting leading Communists and closing down newspapers, Hitler suspended all activities of the SPD and arrested some of its leaders. The Hitler government also issued an emergency decree that suspended constitutional guarantees of personal liberty. The Nazis brought labour and trade unions under their control and seized all property of the SPD. Fear of arrest drove many SPD leaders into exile. Morale among socialists worsened, and as defeatism spread within the party, it lost more and more of its membership. By June 1933, all SPD activities were prohibited and the party was regarded as hostile to the state. These actions effectively ended the socialist movement in Germany.

French socialists remained less willing to engage in the political process than their German counterparts. At the end of the war, French workers began to turn to the left. Inspired by the Russian Revolution, radicalism increased, as did union membership. In May and June 1919, strikes swept across France, urging labour law reform and an end to aid to the anti-Bolshevik forces. In February 1920, strikes again threatened the country, but government use of troops to perform vital services undermined the strike effort. The failure of the strike turned many against radicalism and back toward reformism. Yet it was only after the Ruhr intervention in 1923 that the French socialist party obtained any influence in French politics. Despite their increasing presence in French society, socialists remained hesitant to participate in government, fearing a disruption of party unity and expressing an unwillingness to cooperate with non-socialists parties. As an opposition party, French socialists believed they would be more effective. It was only after 1933, as the threat of fascism increased in Europe that some French socialists began to collaborate with Communists and other radical groups. Others sought to broaden their base of support beyond the working class by abandoning some Marxist elements of their programme and emphasizing universal human values of ethics and social justice.

In northern Europe, socialism remained moderate. In Britain after the war, the Labour Party adopted a socialist platform, believing that government control of the economy would be beneficial to the interests of the working class and that government control would lead to increased wages, lower unemployment and broader measures of social welfare. Labour Party membership grew, and by 1922 it was the second largest political party, undermining the strength of the traditional Liberal Party. The Labour Party formed the government in 1924 and again in 1929, but the impact of worldwide depression and high unemployment prevented it from enacting socialist policies. It took the blame for the continuing crisis and by 1931 had been voted out of power.

Socialist parties also came to power in Sweden at end of war. Unlike in other countries, Swedish socialists willingly assumed governmental responsibility, understanding this involvement as a step that would enable them to implement meaningful social and political reforms. Social democrats emphasized central planning as a key role of socialism and established a programme directed at socializing the economy. They managed to implement policies that abolished property qualifications for elections, granted women the vote, established an eight-hour day and promoted arbitration in labour disputes. In the wake of the depression of the late 1920s, Swedish Social Democrats made impressive electoral gains, achieving a position of strength and leadership in the 1932 elections. They formed a government coalition with the Farmers' Party that served, in the 1930s, to prevent the rise of fascism in Sweden. Solid fiscal policies and investment in public works led Sweden out of depression, decreased unemployment and secured Social Democratic leadership. As Landauer concludes, 'Swedish Social Democrats demonstrated that moderation may be born of wisdom and not of weakness. Believers in human freedom the world over were able to draw from... Swedish developments the conclusion that the great crisis of the capitalist system would not necessarily lead to a victory for fascism or communism' (Landauer, Vol. 2, pp. 1553–1554).

Similarly, Danish socialists in power remained moderate. Socialists increased their electoral victories and in 1924 a socialist became prime minister of Denmark. By 1929, Social Democrats had gained considerable strength and built on that strength by obtaining worker support in defending wages during the difficult economic times of the depression. Danish socialists maintained a balanced and highly regulated economy that, as in Sweden, effectively prevented the rise of fascism among peasants and communism among workers.

Italian socialists, in contrast, faced formidable opposition in the emergence of an Italian nationalist movement after the war. Socialists had opposed Italy's participation in World War I and benefited from their staunch opposition after the war ended, winning control of many local governments and becoming a significant presence in the national government in 1919. Many Italian socialists looked to the example of Soviet Russia and petitioned to join the Comintern. There was even an attempt to assert worker control over the means of production when in August 1920 workers in Milan refused to leave their shops to prevent a lockout. The 'factory occupation' movement quickly became an attempt to socialize the workplace, yet without capital the workers found it difficult to continue production. By the beginning of September, it was clear that the factory occupation movement would not succeed. The settlement that resolved the dispute recognized the rights and authority of factory committees but rising anti-labour sentiment turned popular opinion away from socialism. Elections in May 1921 reflected this trend, reducing the proportion of socialist seats in the national legislature.

Rising Italian nationalism and the emergence of Benito Mussolini's fascist movement further undermined the position of socialism in Italy. In the wake of the failed factory occupation movement, Mussolini presented himself as the defender of the status quo. In the 1921 elections, nationalist parties, including fascists, emerged victorious. In response, socialists and fascists entered into a pacification agreement intended to stop mutual violence, thereby legitimizing Mussolini's group and eliminating the strongest arguments for forming coalitions against it—its widespread use of violence. Indeed, Italian socialists remained reluctant to join with any type of 'bourgeois' government, even to counter the threat of the fascists. In the spring of 1922, Mussolini used workers' strikes as an excuse to initiate a crackdown on socialist and labour organizations. With support from the middle class, fascists attacked anyone and anything with a socialist or communist affiliation, seizing control of local governments that had remained in socialist hands. Thus, socialists provided the scapegoat for Mussolini to attack the workings of government power in his quest to create a fascist state. By November 1926, all non-fascist parties, including socialists and communists, were outlawed in Italy.

As national socialist movements faced growing opposition, particularly in countries with strong nationalist and fascist parties, and communist efforts failed to produce proletarian revolutions in Europe, the international communist movement began to look beyond Europe, critiquing imperialism and colonialism as a way to undermine world capitalist systems and promote world revolution. Asserting that colonial exploitation could occur only under capitalism (a point the Soviet Union itself would soon render invalid), Comintern leaders aided local revolutionary efforts against imperialist regimes, regardless of their political orientation. In his 1920 'Theses on the National and Colonial Questions', Lenin argued that communists should work to support local anti-imperialist efforts to promote world proletarian revolution. His theses served as a basis for guiding Comintern work under colonial regimes. In engaging with the issue of colonial oppression, the international communist movement expanded its reach and influence beyond the borders of Europe, pursuing its agenda of world revolution, giving activists disillusioned with failures in Europe hope for success, and raising awareness of the capitalist exploitation of the Third World.

CONCLUSION

Socialism played a significant role in European politics during the period between 1850 and 1940. As an ideology, it provided an alternative to liberalism and capitalism, advocating the pursuit of social justice for those who often lacked a voice in government. Socialists committed themselves to improving the living conditions and political influence of the working class, either through revolution or gradual reform. They took advantage of the expansion of suffrage and the growth of liberal democratic institutions throughout Europe, using them to pursue their agendas and gain political power. Government fears of working-class radicalism also helped socialists establish the basic parameters of the welfare states that continue to exist in Europe today, instituting programs that protected workers and provided them with a social safety net. Yet, there were limits to the socialist embrace of the status quo. Often, socialists refused to cooperate with liberal or conservative parties. When they did, their working-class supporters accused them of abandoning their ideals. Socialists therefore had to balance their desire for social reform and political legitimacy with their status as an oppositional alternative to mainstream politics.

Karl Marx was not the first socialist, but his thinking fundamentally shaped the nature and scope of modern socialism. He emphasized the idea of revolutionary inevitability, arguing that the proletariat would rise up and seize power when capitalism had fully developed and the working class had gained consciousness of their oppressed status. Marx also stressed the importance of international worker solidarity. Only with worldwide revolution, he asserted, would the proletariat succeed in overthrowing the old system and instituting a true socialist society. Indeed, socialism became the only major European political movement to have an international organization and an international orientation. Marx's ideology did not look toward an imagined future but rather promoted change in existing society. In doing so, Marx provided hope that social improvement and social justice could be achieved. European socialists, reacting to their various national contexts, interpreted Marx's ideology according to their own needs and circumstances, creating a significant variety of opinion within the international socialist community. This lack of unity allowed socialism to adapt to particular national situations but these disagreements also made the movement more vulnerable to its enemies.

The 1917 Russian Revolution provided an example of a successful proletarian revolution (although not exactly along the lines envisioned by Marx) that inspired and energized the European socialist movement. The nature of the regime that emerged and the Bolshevik willingness to employ violence, coercion, and repression to achieve their goals, however, turned many socialists away from the idea of revolution and led them to reassert their commitment to gradualism and working within existing political structures. Except among small groups of communist revolutionaries dedicated to overthrowing the existing systems, gradualism came to define the socialist movement in early twentieth-century Europe. Socialists also tended to prioritize the national over the international, seeking to affect change through avenues available to them rather than promoting world revolution (although this remained a basic goal of the socialist movement). With the outbreak of World War II, socialists throughout Europe reasserted their national orientation, providing patriotic support for their nations. Even the Comintern shifted its stance when the Soviet Union entered the war, calling on the international communist community to defend Soviet socialism and encouraging national communist organizations to support their countries' war efforts.

The rise of fascism in Europe dealt a severe blow to socialism, particularly in Germany where it had the strongest political organization. Nevertheless, socialism re-emerged as a dominant force in European politics after the war. Western fears of the spread of Soviet-style communist governments helped to shape the Cold War and drove the United States' investment in rebuilding a devastated Europe. Socialists also played a leading role in the condemnation of imperialism and promotion of decolonization, another trend that shaped the second half of the twentieth century (Landauer, Vol. 2, p. 1600). Furthermore, welfare state governments, often with significant socialist party participation, re-established themselves throughout Europe, and socialist parties continue to be active members of the political establishment in many European countries, although they rarely challenge the basic structure and organization of capitalist society.

With the collapse of the Soviet Union and the end of the Cold War, fears of violent communist revolution in Europe have diminished. Indeed, at this point the prospects for a socialist revolution as envisioned by Marx seem remote, despite continued labour conflicts. As historian Tony Judt concludes, 'Once the capitalist forms of production are firmly established, the proletariat which appeared likely to threaten the very foundations of the system tends increasingly to become drawn into it—*not* losing its identity as a class, nor even its propensity for *economic* discontent, but losing both the will and the ability to replace the political realm with something different' (Judt, pp. 291–292). Socialism has remained an element of the political landscape in much of Europe. For the modern socialist movement, gradualism won out over revolution. Over the course of the nineteenth and twentieth centuries, the working class won rights of political representation, suffrage, and protective regulation. Modern European socialism, even without revolution, played a key role in the assertion of these principles of social justice.

Selected Bibliography

Essential Readings

Judt, Tony. *Socialism in Provence, 1871–1914: A Study in the Origins of the Modern French Left.* Cambridge: Cambridge University Press, 1979. A regional investigation of the development of socialism in France that argues significant support for the movement came from rural areas and the peasantry.

Hobsbawm, E. J. *The Age of Capital, 1848–1875*. New York: Charles Scribner's Sons, 1975. A survey of the mid-nineteenth century that provides context for the developments of socialism. Interested students should also refer to the author's other surveys of nineteenth-century Europe: *The Age of Revolution* and *The Age of Empire*.

Kilroy-Silk, Robert. *Socialism Since Marx*. London: Allen Lane The Penguin Press, 1972. This volume presents the basic ideas of Marxism, the challenges to it, and its development throughout the world during the twentieth century.

Kolakowski, Leszek. *Main Currents of Marxism: Its Rise, Growth, and Dissolution*. 3 volumes, Oxford: Clarendon Press, 1978. A detailed examination of the origins, emergence and impact of Marxist ideology in Europe that profiles the major theoreticians and their ideas, while also addressing the dynamics of Marxist socialist development.

Landauer, Carl. *European Socialism: A History of Ideas and Movements from the Industrial Revolution to Hitler's Seizure of Power*. 2 Vols. Berkeley and Los Angeles: University of California Press, 1959. A lengthy and detailed assessment of the emergence and development of socialism in Europe that is comprehensive in its scope although the author expresses a tendency to engage in speculation.

Lindemann, Albert S. *A History of European Socialism*. New Haven: Yale University Press, 1983. This volume presents a thorough and readable overview of the emergence and development of socialism in Europe, covering from its roots in ancient times to the post-World War II period.

Shafer, David E. *The Paris Commune: French Politics, Culture, and Society at the Crossroads of the Revolutionary Tradition and Revolutionary Socialism*. New York: Palgrave Macmillan, 2005. This short volume provides an assessment of the impact of the Paris Commune, presenting a variety of different interpretations of its existence and significance.

Sowerwine, Charles. "The Socialist Women's Movement from 1850 to 1940." In *Becoming Visible: Women in European History*, second edition, eds. Renate Bridenthal, Claudia Koonz, and Susan Stuard, 399–426. Boston: Houghton Mifflin Company, 1987. This chapter provides an overview of the socialist women's movement in Europe, arguing that independent socialist women's organizations were crucial for the successful recruitment and mobilization of working women.

Steenson, Gary P. *"Not One Man! Not One Penny!": German Social Democracy, 1868–1914*. Pittsburgh: University of Pittsburgh Press, 1981. A detailed analysis of the nature of the socialist movement in Germany in the years before World War I.

Wade, Rex. *The Russian Revolution, 1917*, 2nd ed. Cambridge: Cambridge University Press, 2005. A detailed and compelling overview of the events of 1917 in Russia.

Advanced Readings

Abraham, Richard. *Rosa Luxemburg: A Life for the International*. Oxford and New York: Berg, 1989. A biography of Rosa Luxemburg that assesses her life and her contributions to Marxist theory.

Boxer, Marilyn J and Jean H. Quataert, eds. *Socialist Women: European Socialist Feminism in the Nineteenth and Early Twentieth Centuries*. New York: Elsevier, 1978. A volume focusing on the efforts of feminist socialists and female revolutionaries in various European countries, including Germany, Austria, France, Italy and Russia.

Fitzpatrick, Sheila. "The Civil War as a Formative Experience," in *Bolshevik Culture: Experiment and Order in the Russian Revolution*, eds. Abbott Gleason, Peter Kenez, and Richard Stites. Bloomington: Indiana University Press, 1985. Illustrates the ways that the Civil War experience shaped the Bolshevik party and later Soviet life.

Geronimo, Dante. *Antonio Gramsci: Architect of a New Politics*. Baton Rouge: Louisiana State University Press, 1990. A biography of Antonio Gramsci (1891–1937), an important Italian socialist.

Haimson, Leopold. "Dual Polarization in Urban Russia, 1905–1917," *Slavic Review* Vol. 23, No. 4 (December 1964) and Vol. 24, No. 1 (March 1965). Explores the social dynamics that facilitated the collapse of the tsarist regime.

Hilton-Young, W. *The Italian Left: A Short History of Political Socialism in Italy*. Westport, Conn: Greenwood Press, 1975. An exploration of the socialist movement in Italy.

Honeycut, Karen, "Clara Zetkin: A Socialist Approach to the Problem of Women's Oppression," in *European Women on the Left*, eds. Slaughter and Kerns, 29–49. Westport, Conn: Greenwood Press, 1981. A short discussion of the background, ideas and work of Clara Zetkin.

Jarman, T. L. *Socialism in Britain: From the Industrial Revolution to the Present Day*. London: Victor Gollancz, Ltd., 1972. A detailed survey of the socialist movement in Great Britain.

Laybourn, Keith. *A Century of Labour: A History of the Labour Party, 1900–2000*. Gloucestershire, England: Sutton Publishers Limited, 2000. A history of the British Labour Party in the twentieth century.

McDermott, Kevin and Jeremy Agnew. *The Comintern: A History of International Communism from Lenin to Stalin*. New York: St. Martin's Press, 1997. An overview of the emergence, development and role of the Comintern and its influence on the international communist movement.

Moss, Bernard H. *The Origins of the French Labor Movement, 1830–1914: The Socialism of Skilled Workers*. Berkeley and Los Angeles: University of California Press, 1976. Describes the formation of the French socialist movement, the scope of its appeal and its activities.

Muravchik, Joshua. *Heaven on Earth: The Rise and Fall of Socialism*. San Francisco: Encounter Books, 2002. By providing descriptions of key episodes and players, including Babeuf, Bernstein and Lenin, among others, the author explores the development, successes and ultimate collapse of the socialist movement.

Naarden, Bruno. *Socialist Europe and Revolutionary Russia: Perception and Prejudice, 1848–1923*. Cambridge: Cambridge University Press, 1992. An assessment of the relationships among socialists in Western Europe and Russia.

Nollau, Gunther. *International Communism and World Revolution: History and Methods*. New York; Frederick A. Praeger, 1961. An assessment of the origins and efforts of the Comintern in the context of the notion of "proletarian internationalism."

Payne, Robert. *Marx*. New York: Simon and Schuster, 1968. A popular biography of Marx that details his life and lineage.

Pierson, Stanley. *British Socialists: The Journey from Fantasy to Politics*. Cambridge, MA: Harvard University Press, 1979. This work traces the emergence and development of socialism in Britain from the Victorian era to the eve of World War I, highlighting the rise of Fabianism, the movement for ethical socialism, and the triumph of the Labour Party.

Pilbeam, Pamela. *French Socialists Before Marx*. Montreal and Kingston: McGill-Queens University Press, 2000. Describes the socialist movement in France in the first part of the nineteenth century.

Raddatz, Fritz J., trans. Richard Barry. *Karl Marx: A Political Biography*. Boston: Little, Brown and Co., 1978. A biography of Marx that focuses on his personal circumstances and political involvement.

Raleigh, Donald J. *Experiencing Russia's Civil War: Politics, Society, and Revolutionary Culture in Saratov, 1917–1922*. Princeton: Princeton University Press, 2002. Focuses on the complex experience of the Civil War in Saratov Province, arguing that the Bolsheviks emerged victorious because they managed to survive the war better than their opponents.

Rees, Tim and Andrew Thorpe, eds. *International Communism and the Communist International, 1919–1943*. Manchester: Manchester University Press, 1998. A volume of articles tracing the history of the Communist International and its relationship with national communist parties between the Wars.

Rose, R. B. *Graccus Babeuf: The First Revolutionary Communist*. Stanford: Stanford University Press, 1978. A solid biography that recounts the major episodes, ideas and influences of Babeuf, as well as tracing his impact on the development of communism.

Sandle, Mark. *Communism*. Harlow, England: Pearson Longman, 2006. A short history of communism and its manifestations throughout the world.

Slaughter, Jane and Robert Kern, eds. *European Women on the Left: Socialism, Feminism, and the Problems Faced by Political Women, 1880 to the Present*.

Westport, Conn.: Greenwood Press, 1981. A volume of articles highlighting the lives and careers of various socialist or radical women, including, among others, Clara Zetkin, Alexandra Kollontai, Anna Kuliscioff and Angelica Balabanoff.

Stearn, Geoffrey. *The Rise and Decline of International Communism*. Aldershot, England: Edward Elgar, 1990. Discusses the emergence of the Communist International, its influence and decline.

Stearns, Peter N. *Revolutionary Syndicalism and French Labor: A Cause Without Rebels*. New Brunswick: Rutgers University Press, 1971. A short survey of French Syndicalism at the turn of the 20th century and worker responses to the movement. The volume includes statistics on workers' strikes and wages.

Wohl, Robert. *French Communism in the Making, 1914–1924*. Stanford: Stanford University Press, 1966. A study of the origins of communism in France that highlights the connections between French Communists and the Soviet Union.

Wrynn, J. F. *The Socialist International and the Politics of European Reconstruction, 1919–1930*. Uithoorn: Graduate Press, 1976. A dissertation on the role that the Socialist International played in the reconstruction of Europe after World War I.

Wuthnow, Robert. *Communities of Discourse: Ideology and Social Structure in the Reformation, the Enlightenment, and European Socialism*. Cambridge: Harvard University Press, 1989. A significant section of this work deals with the relationship between ideology and social context in European socialism between 1860 and 1914. The author stresses the importance of both industrialization and state structure in the growth of socialism in the Western European national contexts and emphasizes institutional structures and the development and success of socialist political parties.

7 *Industrialization and the Rise of Modern Class Society*

—Vijaya Rajni and
Shashi Bhushan Upadhyay

Industrialization is a general phenomenon whose existence can be traced in various epochs and under different forms of government and social organization. Industrialization, in howsoever different forms and limited scope, occurred in various societies since the beginning of civilization. To cater to the tastes of the privileged classes and to the requirements of wars and battles, so many goods were needed which needed certain forms of at least small-scale industries and some amount of industrial production. However, the development of industries in modern times has been exponential and it is manifestly linked with the growth of capitalism. In fact, the concept of economy was invented when the latter was already substantially capitalist in major European countries. Even within the process of capitalist development various levels of industrialization may be found in different countries. At a particular juncture in the development of capitalism the pace of industrialization became so fast and pronounced that it could be clearly recognized as a new stage of development encompassing all forms of life in certain areas of Europe and North America. Due to its relatively fast pace it has also been referred to as 'Industrial Revolution'. Many scholars regard it as the most important phenomenon affecting all aspects of human life since the origins of agriculture or the 'Neolithic Revolution'. In the period of the Neolithic Revolution, the human beings resorted to agriculture as the primary sustenance in place of hunting and gathering. This led to settled life and the beginnings of the early cities which could survive on the surplus generated by agriculture. Similarly, during the course of the 'Industrial Revolution', human beings experienced enormous changes in their economic and social life when, within about 100 years, the mode of life in European countries changed dramatically. The movement became faster, population increased rapidly and could be sustained by rising production, and there was a predominance of industry over agriculture. As modern industrialization advanced, most of European countries and North America underwent various changes during the nineteenth century. The new machines, factories and new industries replaced the crafts and agriculture based societies. The insatiable appetite for raw materials and unquenchable thirst for profit created big rivalry among the Western countries to secure all parts of the globe as markets for their manufactured goods and as suppliers of raw materials and food. It is with this phenomenon of rapidly developing and expanding capitalist industrialization that we are primarily concerned in this chapter. Our main focus will be on capitalist industrialization or industrial capitalism as it evolved and intensified in Europe from the mid-eighteenth to the beginning of the twentieth century.

In this period, the process of industrialization brought about revolutionary changes in Europe and radically transformed its relationship with the rest of the world. Till the beginning of the eighteenth century, Europe was one power—economic and political—among many others in the world. Economically, it was not noticeably superior compared to several countries in Asia, particularly China and India; some even argue that it was actually inferior. However, by the end of the nineteenth century, it had far surpassed all other regions of the world economically, except North America which experienced similar changes. Politically, it held the rest of the world in its thrall directly or indirectly controlling them. In this chapter, we begin by outlining the broad features of modern industrialization, followed by the background leading to relatively rapid industrialization. Then we will trace the development of industrialization in selected European countries and then its impact on the society and values. Finally, we deal with a very contentious issue whether this process, particularly in the nineteenth century may be termed as Industrial Revolution.

WHAT IS MODERN INDUSTRIALIZATION?

Modern industrialization which has also been often termed as the 'industrial revolution' is qualitatively different from all the earlier forms of industrializations because it heralded a decisive change in the mode of production. It was not an event or a short-term process with certain definite characteristics which occurred everywhere in the same way. In fact, it varied according to country and region, and took a rather long time to evolve fully. However, one may chart out certain features and related changes identified with modern industrialization as follows:

- A gradual shift from the use of animate to inanimate power. This implies increasingly extensive use of water, steam and, later, electrical energy in place of human and animal power.
- Significant technological changes, leading to increasing mechanization of production through displacement of human skills. This resulted in gradual devaluation of the traditional artisanal skills and emergence of a new class of technical persons qualified in dealing with new types of machineries.
- More and more production is geared towards market, both at the national and international levels. The earlier form of localized production for the family, village or a small locality is gradually abandoned.
- Extensive and systematic application of modern scientific and technological development for market-oriented production.
- The subsistence agriculture almost disappears over a period of time and is replaced by commercialized production of agricultural commodities.
- Development of modern industry centred on factory which represents a concentration of a large labouring population.
- Widespread movement of population from villages to the urban areas and transfer of labouring people from agriculture to industry.
- The unit of production gets much larger and impersonalized requiring greater outlays of capital.
- Emergence of new social and occupational classes such as the bourgeoisie, proletariat, middle classes, professional classes, engineers, etc.
- Generation of self-sustained growth assuring that the society does not slide back into the cycle of growth and decline. It ensured that the industrial and agricultural production remained at a level which could feed an ever increasing population.

- Creation of ever-expanding demand which would not only make available markets for industrial goods but would also support innovative potential leading to constant changes in technologies.

EUROPEAN BACKGROUND

The very fact that certain countries of Europe industrialized before the rest of the world constrains the historians to explain it. What kinds of conditions gave rise to this phenomenon and when the European path began to diverge are matters open to debate and no definitive answers can be provided. Historically, it may be said that the decline of feudalism in various parts of Europe between fourteenth and sixteenth centuries was the time when preliminary conditions of modernity began to be created. Some more enthusiastic scholars trace the origins of 'efficient institutions' to the tenth century on which the final structure of modern industrialization was erected. In this view, 'the medieval period was more dynamic than the three centuries from 1500 to 1800.' It was between 900 to 1300 that 'growth occurred on a pan-European scale, with strong population growth and long-term increases in real income per capita going hand in hand' (Zanden, 2009: p. 5). We may, however, reasonably say that it was since the sixteenth century that European activism began affecting the world in relatively decisive manner. There were thus several factors stretching back to many hundreds of years during which foundations for the modern growth were laid. Here we would try to outline some of the processes which set some European countries apart from the rest of the world in terms of modern industrialization.

1. In some European countries, there was concerted move towards ending the fragmentation of internal market. A unified market is necessary for speedy movement of goods and relatively low transport costs. Right since the seventeenth century, England, France, Sweden and some other countries took steps in this direction. Although the success was neither great nor universal in Europe but it initiated a policy which would ultimately help industrialization.
2. Some European countries moved decisively in the direction of providing protection to their industries against foreign manufactured goods. This policy was clearly evident with respect to the import of printed Indian cotton goods which arrived in European markets in increasing quantity in the second half of the seventeenth century. In Britain, the use of foreign 'printed, painted, stained and dyed calicoes' in any form was banned in 1722. In

France also, severe ban on such imports was imposed right since 1686 which decreed that such goods would be burned, and any contravention was punishable, sometimes with death. In Spain and Prussia also laws were promulgated to stop Indian imports (Rostow, 1975: pp. 61–66; also Rostow, 1973). Thus, an active policy by the state was initiated to cater to the domestic manufacturing lobby. Thus, in many respects the early modern European governments implemented policies which improved internal communication, erected trade barriers wherever required, helped in advancing industrial technologies, promoted exports, paid attention to agriculture to enhance supply of food to the urban areas and refined public administration. In effect, Rostow argues, in Europe, 'the preconditions for takeoff were slowly being built from the fifteenth to the eighteenth centuries' (Rostow, 1975: p. 103).

3. Increasingly, there was a shift away from the medieval style governance towards more efficient professional departments which proportioned the revenues for supporting different activities.
4. Agriculture was another area in which certain regions in Europe were moving steadily ahead. England, of course, was far advanced in this respect, but even France, Prussia, Russia, Spain and many other countries supported use of technology and innovations in agriculture.
5. Another great change was what has been termed as 'industrious revolution' by the Dutch historian Jan de Vries. He argues that people in Holland, south England and north Germany were buying goods and services from outside the families, and using their family labour in more concentrated and efficient way in particular trades. It further helped in developing a new sense of time discipline. Moreover, by creating demands for new consumer goods it also assisted in the process of industrialization.
6. There was an extraordinary growth of world trade due to European 'voyages of discovery' at the end of the fifteenth century and in the sixteenth century. Bartholomeu Diaz rounded the Cape of Good Hope in 1487; Christopher Columbus 'discovered' America in 1792; Vasco da Gama reached India in 1498. With these began the two motors of wealth accumulation for Europe—loot of gold, and international trade in commodities and humans. Initially, the Spanish and the Portuguese benefited, but later many other European countries, such as Holland, Britain and France joined in. In Americas, the greatest plunder of wealth and the greatest decimation of indigenous popula-

tion were effected. Between 1521 and 1660, according to official figures, 200 tons of gold and 18,000 tons of silver were transferred from America to Spain. Huge loss of human life occurred through killing, enslavement, forced labour and diseases. Almost 90 per cent of indigenous inhabitants died in Mexico and Peru, and elsewhere. As one author writes, 'Conquest, pillage, extermination: this is the reality out of which came the flow of precious metals to Europe in the sixteenth century' (Beaud, 2004: pp. 15–21). The import and, after modifications, re-export of tobacco, Indian calicoes and other manufactured exports increased substantially in the seventeenth century. The European penetration of Americas and the subsequent plunder of resources secured competitive advantage for the Europeans in the international trade. It also gave it access to massive resources which could be used for its various purposes, including that of industrialization. Moreover, the slave trade from Africa supplied labour to West Indian plantations. This forced, unpaid or extremely poorly paid labour from African slaves and captive American workers generated an enormous surplus value which was appropriated by European states. The related settlements created both the conditions for primitive accumulation and captive consumer base. Specialization in manufacture, creation of a broader consumer market in Europe, and influx of a large amount of bullion in international trade greatly increased European leverage vis-à-vis other parts of the world. Although some sort of 'industrious revolution' was witnessed in many other parts of the world, in north-western Europe this was embedded in multifarious processes of change which enhanced its transformatory potential manifold. Europe was also able to send its surplus population across to the Americas thereby reducing pressure on agriculture when it was not in a position to sustain large numbers. Moreover, from the Caribbean and Americas, foodstuffs such as sugar and fish were cheaply imported so that a growing urban population might be fed. (Bayly, 2004: pp. 49–60; Rostow, 1975, pp. 107–31). This great scaling up of the international trade immensely enriched the European states, and the commercial and banking bourgeoisie. It also fundamentally altered the European worldview on amassing wealth. What Calvin preached in the sixteenth century was a religious justification of the growing strength of the bourgeoisie. From the sixteenth to the early eighteenth centuries the bourgeois classes associated with banking and trade were enormously strengthened in many parts of Europe, particularly in Holland and England. Although the manufacturing bourgeoisie had also made its appearance, it had to wait for its ascendancy until the late eighteenth and nineteenth centuries. This wealth was not derived solely from colonial plunder, but substantially from the enhanced exploitation of the peasantry including through enclosures. Thus, these three centuries witnessed the rise of the bourgeoisie, creation of slave and other forms of captive labour, and the gradual movement towards a class of proletarianized workers.

7. European use of coal was also more efficient than the rest of the world. Certain modern technologies, first invented in Britain and then emulated in some other European countries, made the extraction of coal and its refinement much easier and cheaper. The energy from coal powered the early phase of industrialization.
8. The rise of modern science was probably the single greatest achievement which set off the conditions of modernity in Europe. It fundamentally altered the thought and belief of the European people over a period of time, changed the intellectual and social environment which facilitated the innovations and their acceptance. It is true that the critical inventions in the eighteenth century were not directly related to the contemporary scientific spirit. But it contributed to the growth of belief in 'useful knowledge' which was manifested in the possibility of technological innovations which decided the particular course of Western industrialization. It has also been argued that 'the particular path followed by technology leading to modern industrialized societies is typically western' and any non-Western form of industrialization, if it had occurred earlier would have been different (Mokyr, 2003). Thus, the quest for mastery over nature, a certain scientific rationality, and the intense competition for wealth and power seriously subverted the traditional ways of life and thought making change a positive value (Landes, 2003: p. 33).
9. The social and political conditions of Europe also accommodated the quest for industrialization. The regime of private property was better supported in European legal framework than anywhere else, and was less vulnerable to interventions by the state or dominant groups. Legal recognition of even intellectual property rights existed in certain advanced European countries such as Britain and France in the seventeenth century. This provided unparalleled space for private enterprise which not only helped dissolve the feudal land system but also financed the state. Moreover, the relative security of individual property cre-

ated environment for productive investment and accumulation of capital, which are indispensable conditions for capitalist industrialization. The process was initiated by the growth of rural manufactures. The conditions associated with private economic enterprise arose earlier in Western Europe than elsewhere, and it further developed with the growth of economy. Thus, we find records of various patents being registered in these countries. Such property regimes were not present in contemporary Asia, Africa and even in Eastern Europe. Even under those regimes, such as China and India, where powerful wealthy houses enjoyed certain rights, 'the rapid geographical relocation of political and commercial centres after 1680 meant that capital investment did not produce the same long-term cumulative rewards as it did in some parts of western Europe'. Secondly, the existence of relatively independent financial institutions, such as joint-stock companies and banks, afforded north-western Europe competitive advantages by maintaining commercial continuity. Since the city-states in Italy during the Renaissance, certain parts of Europe possessed a legal framework to avoid the risk of the intervention by the state and the failure of individual merchants. Finally, the bitter religious wars in seventeenth-century Europe were linked to new forms of finance. It also made the Europeans adept at devising war equipment. Moreover, their overseas expansion provided boost to ship-building activities enabling them to fight wars both at land and at sea. In effect, as C.A. Bayly comments, 'Europeans became much better at killing people' (Bayly, 2004: pp. 61–62). All these developments—sophisticated financial institutions to support long-distance shipping and to pay professional soldiers, innovations in lethal weaponry, and a private property oriented legal system—enabled the Europeans to capture the international trade in commodities and slaves, earning huge profits for them.

BRITISH SPECIFICITIES

Historically, the fact remains that it was in Britain that the modern industrialization first gained momentum in the last decades of the eighteenth century, and reached a high point by the middle of the nineteenth century. Britain was the 'First Industrial Nation' and remained so for some time. It was in this period that Britain made the final escape from the Malthusian trap of imbalance in production and population. It is for the first time during the nineteenth century that rapid increase in population was accompanied by rise in per capita income. For this period, as Eric Hobsbawm graphically stated, Britain was 'its only workshop, its only massive importer and exporter, its only carrier, its only imperialist, almost its only foreign investor... its only naval power and the only one which had a genuine world policy' (Hobsbawm, 1969: p. 13). Even though this description appears a little exaggerated, there is no doubting, the reality that modern industrialization propelled Britain to an unparalleled position of power in the world affairs, and this prompted or even forced other countries in Europe to industrialize as fast as they could. It was during this period that structure of economy changed, technological innovations took place and organization of the manufacturing industry, particularly in cotton and iron, was transformed. Now, we need to explore the reasons why Britain industrialized before anyone else. What were the factors which moved it ahead before its nearest rival, France?

If we look at various indicators, we find that France was not really behind Britain, and in certain areas it was actually ahead. France was the leading European power in the early eighteenth century, it was a unified political unit, and economically and socially it was quite a match to any other country in the world. So, a comparison with France will clear the picture about Britain's pioneering venture. Economic historians have taken varied and sometimes even opposing position on this issue. Thus, Tom Kemp emphasizes on 'the continued prevalence of traditional agrarian structures' in much of Europe, including France; E.E. Hagen thinks that 'the differences in personality rather than differential circumstances are the central explanation of Britain's primacy'; R.M. Hartwell argues that it was a long period of 'balanced growth' which was responsible for this phenomenon; M. Kranzberg criticizes the stress on single factor, and proposes multiple factors—economic, social, cultural, technological and political—for the success of modern industrialization in Britain; J.U. Nef emphasizes that 'the rate of industrial change from about 1735 to 1785 was no more rapid in Great Britain than in France, a far larger country with nearly three times as many people. What is striking... is less the contrasts than the resemblances between Great Britain and the Continent, both in the rate of economic development and in the directions that development was taking (Cited in Crafts, 1977: p. 438). Similarly, Peter Mathias argues that in France 'the record of scientific growth and invention in the eighteenth century was a formidable one' with more patents registered in France than in Britain. Moreover, as Rostow concedes that the French market was much larger both domestically and internationally to absorb industrial production. In such a situation, it becomes somewhat circular to argue that the take-off happened in Britain because the preconditions for it were present, and then guess that this was so because the modern industrialization first took off there.

Some of the recent opinion, therefore, point out that British success should not be projected in the past. The fact that Britain industrialized first did not mean that it was predetermined. The probability factor remained very strong until quite late. Crafts comments that 'The fact that Britain was "more advanced" in 1790 and had a much superior likelihood of further progress… than France does not of itself necessarily imply *ex ante* (in, say, 1740) Britain had the greater probability of achieving the first Industrial Revolution' (Crafts, 1977: p. 438). He suggests that instead of developing a fixed model of industrialization, it would be more appropriate to underline that 'economic development in general and technological progress in particular in eighteenth-century Europe should be regarded as stochastic processes' (Ibid., p. 431).

Yet there were some differences between Britain and the rest of Europe which laid the ground for initial advance in British economy leading to first burst of modern industrialization, or Industrial Revolution. The crucial differences which may be marked are as follows:

Agrarian Changes: Considerable degree of agrarian changes in Europe stimulated the process of industrialization. Normally, the traditional societies in Europe had produced only about 25 per cent agricultural surplus. Preceding the industrial innovations this surplus rose to about 50 per cent thereby passing the risk-of-famine limit. This increased surplus could provide food to a lot more people engaged in non-agricultural activities than was hitherto possible. In Britain, such changes have been termed as 'agricultural revolution', in view of the significant economic and social changes they brought in their wake. The transformation of agriculture took place in Britain considerably early than in France or anywhere else on the continent. The process started right from the middle of the fifteenth century when feudalism declined in Britain. It involved four important features—farming in bigger enclosed units replacing the medieval open-field system, absorption of common land for cultivation and promotion of livestock husbandry, ejection of peasantry from the land and their transformation into agricultural workers, and big increase in agricultural productivity. This was done by enclosing the land, introducing novel techniques of production, and adopting new ways of entrepreneurship (Deane, 1965: pp. 36–7). The process of enclosing the land in rural areas started early and, between 1455 and 1607, about 500,000 acres of land was enclosed. The number of people thrown out of employment amounted to about 40,000. The process continued with many breaks in between. In the eighteenth century, the enclosure movement acquired a new vigour. Helped by economic factors, force and new parliamentary laws, there was great concentration of land which proceeded throughout the eighteenth and early nineteenth centuries. Between 1727 and 1844, the British Parliament passed 4,000 acts to approve the enclosure of seven million acres of land. In the next 50 years, another 1,000 parliamentary acts were passed enclosing one million acres more (Wyatt III, 2009: p. 29). By 1790, about 75 per cent of the total cultivated land was in the hands of large farmers; small freeholders owned only about 15 per cent of the land, and the peasantry in the usual sense of the term had disappeared. This process, on the one hand, created a large mass of paupers some of whom could seek employment in the cities and provide cheap labour to the new industries, but many of them were forced to remain in the countryside surviving on dole and beggary. On the other hand, the large holdings which were, in many cases, in the hands of the agricultural entrepreneurs could facilitate experiment with new forms of agricultural techniques resulting in several productivity-enhancing changes. Introduction of new crops and continuous rotation of crops between the agricultural and pasture land, reclamation of marshy land, increasing use of horses in place of oxen for farm work, and introduction of new agricultural implements and improvement of the old ones were the changes which raised production. Between 1650 and 1800, about 30 per cent of total arable land in Britain was acquired through reclamation. The nature of land use changed, manures were used in increasing quantity, and the number of crops increased. The labour productivity in agriculture increased hugely. Between 1700 and 1800, the agricultural production per worker in England rose by about 100 per cent and between 1700 and 1850 'by a factor of 2.5–3' (Crouzet, 2001: p. 108). This led to proportionate decline in the ratio of agricultural workers to the total population. Thus, while, between 1700 and 1850, the population doubled, the number of workers in agriculture increased marginally from 2.78 million to 3.84 million. In mid-nineteenth-century Britain, agriculture used the lowest share of its total workforce than anywhere else in the world. (Wyatt, 2009: p. 35). In 1759, there were 46 per cent of English families with income from non-agricultural sources, and the share of agriculture in national income fell from more than 50 per cent in the late seventeenth century to just over 40 per cent in mid-eighteenth century (Crouzet, 2001: p. 112). This resulted in the increase in surplus food available for supply to the cities. In this period, Britain could be called the 'granary of Europe', as by 1750 it exported to the continent about 13 per cent of its own food consumption. However, the level of mechanization in agriculture was not large and the change basically came through the introduction of new nitrogenous crops such as legumes and root crops such as clover, alfalfa, sainfoin and turnips. The earlier method of crop rotation was abandoned, as these developments allowed constant cropping of land without fear of exhaustion. By the late eighteenth century, the British agriculture was largely capitalistic, oriented towards market and profit, employing wage workers on large farms (Deane, 1965: pp. 37–50).

As a result of these changes, significant amount of productive resources such as cheap labour were transferred from agriculture to the industry. The proportion of labour force in agriculture became much lower than in other countries. Secondly, the productivity in agriculture was quite higher than anywhere else. In fact, the productivity in agriculture was almost on par with the industrial productivity. And finally, the agricultural production could initially supply the demand for raw materials and food for the growing urban population.

Demographic Expansion: Population increase in Britain was related to industrialization both as a cause and effect. The expanding population supplied cheap and increased labour force to growing industry along with an enlarged market. On the other hand, the process of industrialization supported the growing population by increasing the income levels. In the eighteenth century, the initial spurt in population occurred during the 1740s. Such growth had occurred in earlier centuries also several times, but was cancelled due to increased death rates following soon after because of less food availability and epidemics. This time, however, no reverses occurred, and population grew steadily. During the 1740s, the rate of growth in population was about 3.5 per cent which went up in the succeeding decades reaching a peak of about 16 per cent during the 1810s. The number of people in England and Wales increased almost threefold from about 5.8 million in 1701 to about 14 million in 1831 (Deane, 1965: pp. 20–35; Deane and Cole, 1969; 103). The urban population also increased very rapidly in the eighteenth century and London around 1750 had about 750,000 people, which marked it as the largest city in Europe.

Availability of Crucial Natural Resources: The natural resources which were easily, and in large quantities, available in Britain, such as iron and coal, were suitable for the replacement of wood thereby enhancing the manufacturing process. Coal was the greatest support to early industrialization in most northern European countries, and Britain had it in huge quantity. This allowed it to mine an ever increasing quantity of coal: in 1700, 3 million tons a year; in 1800, 11 million tons; in 1830, 22 million tons; in 1845, 44 million tons and in 1870, more than 100 million tons. This was much more than in any other country, and it energized the initial expansion of new industries (Wyatt III, 2009: p. 41).

Structure of International Trade: In its trade with other countries, British exports were almost totally manufactured goods even when the economy was at a relatively low income level. Thus, the proportion of manufactures in export was far higher than in any other European country. The imports, on the other hand, consisted of food and raw materials when the process of industrialization was on its course. Britain thus possessed an already existing industrial base, consisting of pre-factory manufactures, spread primarily in rural areas. Cottage industries such as wool were an extremely thriving sector in the seventeenth and early eighteenth centuries. Such specialization gave boost to the already initiated process of modern industrialization. The increase in population and the removal of custom barriers created a sizeable market in many European countries. In British case, there were three important segments of the market—internal, European, and the colonial. The internal market was quite developed and had shed its barriers much before most European countries. It did not only have a market economy but a single national market which was sufficiently large and sturdy to provide cushion against the fluctuations caused by the American Revolution and the Napoleonic Wars. The colonial market, along with the European market, however, was much larger and ever expanding. Between 1700 and 1750, the output of the home-oriented industries increased by 7 per cent, while that of the export-oriented industries rose by 76 per cent; between 1750 and 1770 the respective figures were 7 per cent and 80 per cent. It was this overseas market to which the cotton industries—the pacemaker of the British industrialization—were linked. It imported most of its raw materials and exported most of its industrial products.

Better Transportation: The most important system of transport which boosted the British industrialization in initial period was based on canals. The cheapest method of carrying heavy goods was through water due to particularities of British geography. All regions of the country were within 70 miles from the sea. In the latter half of the eighteenth century, canal construction was hectically pursued and a lot of capital was invested in this. In 1790 alone, about 3 million pounds was invested for construction of canals. By 1800, there were 42 canals covering a length of 1,400 miles, and by 1858, about 4,250 miles of canals had been built in Britain. The total area of dockland also expanded significantly. Thus, the farthest part of interior was linked with the sea giving tremendous boost to trade (Deane, 1965: pp. 69–83; Wyatt III, 2009: p. 56).

Technological Efficiency: Britain was, as Joel Mokyr remarked, a 'technologically creative society'. It possessed a group of innovative craftsmen, particularly in mechanical crafts such as machine building, millwork and metalworking. It was already developing various labour-saving machines including the steam engine in its primitive form even before the mid-eighteenth century. British workmanship was highly praised. It was this group of innovative and risk-taking persons from the middle and artisanal classes who conceived the initial inventions which would ultimately lead to better forms later. Moreover, it could make more refined iron on a large scale which could be used to make big machinery. The technological innovations in textile industry, which was the pioneer industry of the industrial revolution, created the conditions for saving labour, producing faster and at cheaper rates. Hargreaves's jenny, Arkwright's water frame and Crompton's mule were the three extremely important inventions which transformed the spinning in British textile industry. Further strength was derived from the refinement and application of steam power in running the machines. Although the scientific knowledge was equally or even more advanced in certain European countries, in Britain there existed a higher level of technical skill, a greater interest in machines and keener desire to use the innovations in practical applications.

Role of Government: The role of the government was also very significant in creating an overall environment for entrepreneurship, investment and trade. The British government supported entrepreneurship at all levels, worked towards eliminating internal barriers, provided full parliamentary support for enclosure of land, kept the resentment of the dispossessed sufferers in check by maintaining strict law and order, and invested heavily in the pursuit of foreign and military policies. The striking growth of British navy, which was becoming increasingly capable of defeating its rivals and defending its international trade, helped in great measure the capital accumulation and expansion of overseas market. This was one of the most significant achievements of the government (O'Brien, 2006: pp. 16–20).

Availability of Capital: Sufficient supply of capital could be found in many European countries. Agriculture, trade in commodities and slaves and colonial plunder were the three methods through which the capital required for investment in industries was mobilized. Agriculture, as we have seen, concentrated the land in the hands of a few landowners opening the way for experiments and large profits. Colonial plunder and international trade generated enormous profits for the British merchants. But just the presence of capital was not enough; the existence of an entrepreneurial class interested in industrial investment was crucial. The spirit of commerce was deeply embedded in the British minds in eighteenth century. Even the members of British aristocracy were not averse to commercial activities and many of them engaged in mining and manufacturing operations. Similarly, although the banks and credit system were developed even in some other European countries, nowhere neither was the financial structure so advanced nor was anywhere else the people so accustomed to use paper instruments as in Britain. This was quite crucial in the initial period of industrialization because the enterprises were on small scale and short-period working capital was more required than long-period fixed capital (Landes, 2003: pp. 74–75; Wyatt III, 2009: p. 44).

However, it must be noted that the capital requirement in the initial period of industrialization was not large. It was not until the last two decades of the eighteenth century that capital formation increased appreciably and investment rate rose to about 1.5 per cent of national income. And it was only from the mid-1930s onwards when there was a general distribution of modern technology in most industries and the beginning of the railway construction that investment became around 2 per cent of national income (Crouzet, 1972: pp. 14–15). It was only when the industrialization process moved ahead that the requirement of capital increased, particularly as fixed capital in the machineries, factory-building, railways and intensive mining.

Thus, in the mid-eighteenth century, the British economy was relatively advanced compared even to the continental European economy. The generalized crisis of the European economy in the seventeenth century did not affect Britain so much, and since the 1660s the British economy forged ahead of its continental rivals. In the eighteenth century, it was the most commercialized, urbanized, monetized and, considering the spread of rural industries, industrialized in Europe. The most important factors which seem to set Britain apart from its continental rival were its highly productive agricultural sector, existence of a large foreign trade secured by state's investment in naval power, relatively easy availability of coal and iron in huge quantities, and technological innovations.

INDUSTRIALIZATION IN BRITAIN

As mentioned earlier, historians sometimes trace the background to industrialization as far back as tenth to thirteenth centuries which witnessed marked changes in economy, ideas and social structures accompanying the rise of urban communes in Italy, France and some other countries. The commercial revolution between 1400 and 1700 shattered the closed economies of medieval ages and promoted interaction at the economic, social and intellectual levels. Initially, southern Europe was commercially more advanced, but the severe crisis of the sixteenth and seventeenth centuries shifted the focus towards Holland, England and France. These countries could boast of significant mercantile groups possessing notable managerial abilities, economic power and political clout. They also had relatively large amount of capital, skilled manpower and high level of literacy. However, it was in Britain that the initial burst of industrialization occurred. By 1850, Britain had attained a position of unrivalled industrial and political supremacy in the world. It was also the wealthiest nation due to its industrial production centred on cotton textiles, iron and mining industries. The three factors basically associated with modern industrialization were technological innovations, structural changes in the economy and a noticeable shift in the organization of industry.

(a) Technological Innovations

J.A. Schumpeter distinguished between invention and innovation as two separate, though related, phenomena. While invention may be considered as an original discovery, innovation is the application of that discovery to practical use. It is innovation which, according to Schumpeter, is the basis of technological advancement. The use of invention in particular economic activities creates the conditions for incorporating it as the factor of production. All inventions are not applied immediately or sometimes ever for practical usage. On the other hand, all innovations are not the result of some original invention. It is the innovation or the practical use of some device for enhancing production which is of revolutionary consequence in the process of industrialization. Moreover, it was not the adoption of a single invention as innovation which formed part of the first wave of modern industrialization. Rather, the increasing adoption of a cluster of innovations which was decisive in radically transforming the economy of certain industries in late eighteenth and early nineteenth-century Britain. The inventions had been made earlier, some of them rather early before many of them were being used almost simultaneously for increasing production in some industries such as cotton textiles, iron and mining. They reinforced each other in significant ways to create conditions for cumulative growth (Deane, 1965: p. 95 and 103).

The late eighteenth-century Britain was one such period of innovations. As Dr Johnson wrote, 'The age is running mad after innovation. All the business of the world is to be done in a new way: men are to be hanged in a new way…' (Cited in Deane, 1965: p. 119). This fury of activity applied in the mechanization of certain industries resulted in a technological progress hitherto unknown. 'Technological progress', writes Joel Mokyr, 'is defined as the ability to extract more or better outputs from a given level of effort, equipment, fuel and other inputs. It is thus an improvement in the efficiency of our control of the physical environment, replacing known ways of putting food on the table and clothes on the body by better ones' (Mokyr, 1994: p. 12). It is, however, important to understand that much of the technology in the eighteenth century which heralded the modern industrialization was a completion of earlier developments rather than new departures. Moreover, many of the technologies in our present age were invented and applied after the conventional period of Industrial Revolution. But what is important is that in the late eighteenth and early nineteenth centuries a trend towards inventions was started on a hitherto unprecedented scale. The perfections of earlier techniques made them more potent and workable in the new developments in industrial organization. But these technological changes were not solely used by the new forms of industries such as the factory or the mill. Even the cottage industries made considerable use of them for increased productivity. For example, Kay's flying shuttle, invented in 1733, and the treddle hammer were as useful in household sector as it was in larger units. However, the trend was clearly towards technology-assisted concentration of workers in the factories under a single roof. The first industry to be mechanized was cotton textiles. Some of the important technological inventions employed here were as follows.

Spinning jenny, invented by James Hargreaves in 1764, was important in increasing the pace of spinning by mechanically twisting the spun yarn which was being done until now by human fingers. Any operative now could simultaneously spin a number of threads. In its earliest form it could hold 8 spindles, 16 spindles in 1770, 80 spindles by 1784 and by the end of the eighteenth century a large jenny operated with 120 spindles. Since one jenny containing many spindles could be operated by a single worker, the enormous expansion in productive capacity is quite evident. Another important invention was the water-frame by Richard Arkwright in 1769 which provided strength to the threads. Both these machines were combined in a most significant invention by Crompton in 1779. The Crompton's mule completely superseded the Indian technique of manual spinning by making it possible to spin finer and better yarns much faster and at extremely low costs. Combined with water and steam power, this great invention dominated the cotton industry for the next one century. Now, one hundred pounds of yarn could be spun in just 300 hours by using this machine in the 1790s, while earlier system of hand-spinning took 50,000 hours to do the same. One spinner in 1812 could produce as much yarn as 200 spinners before Hargreaves' jenny was put into use. This clearly shows how much difference this innovation made. The cost of production fell by more than 85 per cent between 1779 and 1812. The import of raw cotton rose eight times between 1780 and 1800. The cotton industry, from being one of the least important industries, rose to the heights of being the most important industry and the pacemaker of the 'Industrial Revolution'. About 100,000 workers were employed in spinning factories in 1812 and the weaving which was still manual provided employment to about 250,000. The share of cotton industry in the national income of the country rose to 7 or 8 per cent (Mokyr, 1994: pp. 19–20; Deane, 1965: pp. 84–89).

While spinning forged ahead, weaving lagged behind technologically. The massive production of yarn through revolutionized spinning process made available much cheaper yarn to weavers which enhanced their profits and increased their number. Already the use of fly-shuttle had increased the productive capacity of the hand-loom weavers to some extent. Thus, the handloom and household weavers experienced a golden age between 1780 and 1820. Powerlooms were introduced in the 1820s in a big way leading to concentration of production and decline of the artisanal production. Some technological changes were introduced in cotton ginning and carding sectors also. But production of cotton apparel and the cotton planting and picking remained completely manual processes.

There were important changes in energy sector also. Something closer to a steam engine was built by a Frenchman named Denis Papin in 1690, but the Englishman, Thomas Newcomen, built the first operational steam engine in 1712. It was basically used for pumping water from the mines. It was finally James Watt's invention, which used a separate condenser for cooling the steam that made possible the use of steam power in larger industrial operations. From 1765, when it was invented to 1800, there were about 2,500 steam engines used for various industrial purposes.

Iron was another industry to be technologically upgraded. The requirement of good quality iron for replacing wood in making machinery, ships, vehicles, buildings and drain-pipes is immense. Better quality iron is also needed in the extraction of coal. Two innovations transformed the iron industry in the eighteenth century—blast furnace by Abraham Darby in 1709 and puddling and rolling process by Henry Cort in 1784. The raw iron goes through two stages of refinement before it becomes useful. The raw ore is smelted in blast furnace to produce pig-iron and then the pig-iron is refined to make wrought-iron by removing the excessive carbon. It was wrought-iron which could be used in industries. Earlier, charcoal made from wood was used to smelt raw iron. The Darby's blast furnace made it possible to use coke made from coal. But there was a lot of carbon in the pig-iron which made it hard and brittle. Cort's method, by effectively removing impurities, could help in producing high-quality wrought-iron. The output of wrought-iron increased by about 500 per cent between 1788 and 1815 and the prices declined steeply. The production of pig-iron also rose from 25,000 tons during the 1720s to 2.7 million tons in 1852. Around 1750, Britain imported twice the amount of iron it produced; by 1814, however, it exported 57,000 tons of iron and by 1852, the amount of export rose to more than a million tons (Mokyr, 1994: pp. 25–26; Wyatt III, 2009: p. 53).

It has been argued that continuous technological inventions were made possible in Europe since the late eighteenth century because of a change in mentality, or more broadly, due to 'the culture that generated and diffused knowledge in Europe and the institutions that supported it, developed characteristics that allowed the epistemic bases of technology to become eventually ever wider in part as a result of the technique that it supported' (Mokyr, 2003: pp. 61–62). But this analysis does not fully explain why it was Britain where these inventions were most fruitfully applied. The incentive for innovations was derived from the possibility of profit. The remunerative opportunities for British innovators came from higher wages and cheaper energy than in other European countries. The possibility of replacing labour with capital and energy was at the root of technological adaptations by the British mechanics and entrepreneurs. Moreover, the opportunity for earning greater profits due to larger markets also stimulated quick innovations. Thus, the need to economically exclude Indian cotton goods from British markets might have been a factor in faster innovations in cotton industry. As one writer says, 'To an important extent, the industrial revolution was an exercise in import substitution' (Allen, 2006: p. 9).

(b) Factory System

These technological developments also created the conditions for transformative changes in the organization of the cotton industry. Water-frame, right from the beginning, was a factory machine to be operated by water or steam power. So was the mule. This resulted in the most revolutionary change in the structure of the industry by concentrating a large number of workers in a factory under a single roof. The factory which evolved from the manufactory system of production was another important characteristic which defined the era of modern industrialization. It was distinguished from the earlier system of manufacture by the crucial role which the newly innovated machines played in it. Initially, there was simple cooperation among workers assembled under one roof using a single source of energy for production. It was a revolutionary organization of labour process in which a large number of workers were congregated under one roof. Evolving out of the artisans' workshops or the merchant-controlled manufactories, the factories brought a sizable group of workers together to operate bigger machines under the vigilant eyes of the supervisors. Some of the new technological innovations, particularly in spinning such as water-frame and mule, were too large and expensive to be put in artisanal homes. They also required bigger power sources for operation. To be feasible and more profitable they had to be installed in the factories built around a central power source—initially water wheels and later large steam engines. The production was now broken into several routine operations performed by machines operated by workers. The system was geared to mass production and standardized articles. The artisanal skills became increasingly less important and the labour of the workers was closely supervised. In Britain the factory system became predominant in the cotton industry, particularly spinning, and later in weaving, between 1815 and the 1840s. Thus, the industrial capitalist in Britain, particularly in the zone of cotton industry such as Lancashire, was characterized by division of industrial population between capitalists and workers, production in factories and a profit-oriented economy.

But, it must be noted, that, however, this was a later picture. In the early period of industrialization in Britain, the factory system was rather archaic because it still incorporated within it the methods of craft unionism (Hobsbawm, 1969: p. 65). Moreover, in the initial period, most of the machines were rather rudimentary devices requiring vary small sum of money. A common jenny containing 40 spindles cost only about 6 pounds in 1792, a scribbling and carding machine cost one pound per inch of roller width, and a slubbing billy with 30 spindles could be bought with only about 10 pounds. Most of the factories in the late eighteenth century were 'no more than glorified workshops: a dozen workers or less; one or two jennies, perhaps, or mules; and a carding machine to prepare the rovings' Even the sources of power were still mostly manual and the places of operation were in many cases cottages or similarly small units. Even in 1850, most common cotton mills in Britain had only about 50 workers of which only a small number operated machinery. Much of industrial production was on a small scale owned and financed by family firms (Landes, 2003: pp. 64–65).

(c) Structural Changes

The gradual transformation of British economy from the agrarian to the industrial, the significant changes in income patterns, and emergence and growth of new social groups were parts of the overall structural changes materializing in the wake of industrialization. The crucial characteristic of modern industrialization was 'the fundamental redeployment of resources away from agriculture' (Mathias, 1983: p. 2; Mathias, 1990). In this respect, we find that Britain was far ahead of other European countries in the mid-nineteenth century. In 1840, at per capita income level equivalent of 550 US dollars at 1970 prices, Britain had 48.3 per cent urbanization, only 25 per cent of workforce in primary sector, only 28.6 per cent of male labour force in agriculture, and only 24.9 per cent of income from the primary sector; on the other hand, it had 47.3 per cent of workforce in industry, and 31.5 per cent of income from the industry (Crafts, 1990: table 3, p. 36). Considering the fact that the proportion of male labour force in industry was 23.8 per cent in 1759 and 29.5 per cent in 1801, this was really a major structural change. Thus, although the per capita income in Britain, between 1760 and 1840, rose relatively slowly compared to later development in industrialization in other European countries, the shift of labour from agriculture to industry had been enormously fast.

The boundaries of this first phase of industrialization were, however, quite limited. Except for cotton no other industry was fully mechanized by the 1840s, and even the wave of technological inventions seems to have exhausted itself without all of them being fully utilized in production. By the mid-nineteenth century, only 6 per cent of the total workforce was employed in the textile factories, the most mechanized sector of the economy. The majority of industrial workers still used hand implements. It was around this time, particularly in the latter half of the nineteenth century that a new phase of industrialization started.

SECOND PHASE OF BRITISH INDUSTRIALIZATION

From the 1840s onwards till the end of the nineteenth century, a new phase of industrialization occurred in Britain which was based on capital goods industries, iron and steel, and coal. It was also during this period that the factory production was generalized using new technological innovations across the industries. The onset of industrialization in Europe since the mid-nineteenth century, and in many other countries of the world in the late nineteenth century, created massive demand for British iron and steel, capital goods and capital investments. British exports increased enormously between 1840 and 1860, benefiting particularly the capital goods industry. This fuelled further industrialization in Britain which already had a base. Another important factor was the rapid building of railways from the 1830s onwards. From 1830 to 1850, around six thousand miles of railways were constructed in Britain, reaching into several remote areas hitherto unconnected with the cities. During the 1840s, some two hundred million pounds were invested in railways which employed around 200,000 workers in 1846–48. This led to enormous rise in production of iron, steel and coal. A lot of British capital was also invested abroad reaching a figure of 700 million pounds by 1870. Overall, during this period between the 1830s and the 1880s, the British economy achieved full industrialization expanding its industrial base from two or three pioneering industries such as cotton and coal to almost all industries (Hobsbawm, 1969: pp. 109–19).

But it also created competition for British cotton industry due to the rise of other industrial economies in Europe and America, leading to a 'depression' during the 1870s. The British agriculture also faced downturn because of the arrival of cheap grain from North America into the British markets. However, overall the British economy between 1850 and 1914 was on the upswing secure in its captive markets for consumer goods in its vast colonial territories, and its superiority in capital goods over its European and Japanese rivals.

INDUSTRIALIZATION IN OTHER EUROPEAN COUNTRIES

According to Rostow, the modern industrialization represented a total break from the past by ushering into an era of sustainable growth which began with a 'take-off' which signified a high level of savings and investment, a large number of people moving from agriculture to industry, development of factory system and rapid increase in urbanization. Britain was its first example which set a pattern for other countries to follow (Rostow, 1960). This thesis has been challenged by many, most famously by Alexander Gerschenkron who, in his *Economic Backwardness in Historical Perspective* (1962), argued that the process of industrialization in other European countries was not emulative but different.

Gerschenkron proposed a thesis about industrialization in backward economies according to which industrialization in relatively backward economies was accompanied by great surge in industrial output and by much more supportive role of the government and the banks. In fact, he argued that the more backward the economy, the government and the banks play more interventionist role. Both of these theses—Rostow's model of revolutionary 'take-off' as well as the imitative character of industrialization in the countries which arrive late, and Gerschenkron's model of industrialization in backward economies—have now been seriously questioned. It has been pointed out by many scholars that the British model, due to its pioneering nature, was 'unique, atypical, inimitable, non-reproducible, the exception rather than the norm.' Nevertheless, the fact of diffusion cannot be denied. There had been transfer of British technologies (even through industrial espionage in the early period when there was ban on such transfer), import of British machineries, and migration of engineers, skilled workers and entrepreneurs from Britain to the continent. At the same time, the progress of industrialization in countries like Belgium, France, Switzerland, Germany and other European countries adopted their respective models depending on their specificities. Thus, the diffusion was not an imitation of the British model but 'a complex process of creative adaptation' (Crouzet, 2001: p. 117). So, while the industrialization process in France radically differed from that of Britain that of Belgium and Germany displayed features closer to the British pattern. But even here, textiles were not as important as it had been in Britain. Rather, the heavy industries related to iron, coal and engineering were the leading sectors. In Switzerland, the capital-intensive and mechanized production as well as labour-intensive production centred on domestic or workshop manufacture was in evidence during the course of its industrialization. Sweden, Denmark and Norway represented a different pattern by importing primary products and exporting semi-finished goods after processing them. Italy and Spain, due to their environmental conditions, high transport cost due to difficult terrain and high cost of energy followed yet another pattern. This wide variety of national experiences of industrialization has led scholars like Sidney Pollard to question the very existence of a single industrialization in Europe and speak about different industrializations. On the other hand, some other scholars argue that 'Europe's industrialization was a single process that, like an epidemic, took little notice of national borders and crossed them with ease' (Crouzet, 2001: p. 119). In this section, we discuss industrialization in three big European countries—France, Germany and Russia—and see their similarities and differences with each other, as also with relation to the pioneering industrial country.

FRANCE

France was probably the only country where industrialization started almost simultaneously with Britain. Its income level was almost on par with Britain in the early eighteenth century; its pool of scientific resources was equal, if not superior, to Britain; and its population was about three times more numerous than its closest rival. Yet, it took much longer to industrialize and even by the late nineteenth century it was behind Britain. Meanwhile, other countries such as Belgium, United States and Germany had moved ahead. Thus, the French case was quite at variance with Britain due to the relatively much slower pace of its industrialization and the other features associated with it, viz., structural change, technological innovations and new industrial organization. The relatively fast pace of industrialization in Britain threatened the French market itself by producing low-priced manufactures. Moreover, the loss of the overseas colonies deprived the French manufacturers of captive markets. These conditions handicapped the French industrial entrepreneurs to a large extent. Many of them thus tried to move into areas of quality production, not mass production as done by the British manufacturers. By aiming at the high-end market both in Europe and world-wide, several French entrepreneurs focused on skilled craftsmanship rather than on machine technology. Even the machine-made textiles catered to refined tastes rather than the mass consumers.

According to one scholar, the 'agricultural revolution' in France began during 1750–60 (Bairoch, 1973: p. 460 and 470). However, the term 'revolution' for French agrarian changes is a bit of overstatement. According to most other accounts, overall stasis in agricultural growth was one of the stumbling blocks in French industrialization. Agriculture in France remained peasant-based and conservative in orientation. Most of its surplus in the pre-revolutionary period was siphoned off by the nobility, the Church and the state. The essentially feudal land tenure obstructed the economic growth because the peasant did not have any surplus to reinvest in the land and the lords were not interested in doing so. Whereas in Britain even the aristocracy was oriented towards commercial enterprises, in France an important section of the bourgeoisie remained interested in land and titles. Even when the state tried to induce the landlords towards improvement of land, it was never successful. Thus, in pre-revolutionary France, the agriculture basically remained backward and unfavourable for the growth of modern industry. The great French Revolution empowered the peasantry and further entrenched them in land by removing all feudal tenure. However, the techniques of production were not improved and an even larger number of peasants became tied to the land. Thus, as one scholar has argued, the 'continued predominance of agriculture in the economy and the weight of the peasantry in the agrarian system acted as a brake on industrialization' (Kemp, 1985: p. 57). On the other hand, this argument has been countered by the fact that there was a large migration of workers from the countryside to the cities. Between 1821 and 1871, 3.5 million people left the rural areas, although most of them had been in non-agricultural occupations. Moreover, there is no evidence of a shortage of labour for the modern industries. Thus, Crouzet argues that 'the situation of agriculture was not an insurmountable obstacle to French industrial growth.' What really affected the industries were the shortage of skilled labour and the unsuitability of the rural migrants for the factory work (Crouzet, 1996: p. 53).

Besides agriculture, the other factors which held it back on the path of modern industrial growth were (i) scarcity of coal and iron deposits crucial for establishing big factory-based industries in the early stages; (ii) lack of an emerging banking system and an organized credit network as it had existed in Britain in the eighteenth century. Despite the fact that a large amount of capital was raised by financiers, it did not go into industry but financed the wars or luxuries of the state; (iii) the cheap labour and restricted market made investment in industrial innovations unattractive; (iv) despite a large population base, the rate of demographic growth was much lower than in Britain; (v) relatively high cost of transport; (vi) limited internal market due to existence of a large mostly self-sufficient agricultural sector and (vii) a less enterprising bourgeois class which retained its interest in land as well as in bureaucratic positions.

Despite these handicaps, the French industrialization advanced and the economic growth became pronounced making it one of the few leading industrialized countries in the world. France had begun industrializing in the late eighteenth century, around the same time as Britain. The share of industry in national production gradually increased, there was proliferation of putting-out system in rural areas, and the increase in calico-printing works after 1759. To compete with the British goods, the French manufacturers adopted British innovations. The government was also quite supportive in this venture. The main industry in the initial stage, as in Britain, was cotton textiles. British innovations – spinning jenny, water frame, mule and carding machines—were obtained either through espionage or purchase for use in modern industries. Many of them were also being now made in France. Flying shuttle was introduced in weaving; steam engines were also introduced in some concerns. Even the British innovation in iron-making (puddling) was obtained and utilized. During the 1770s and 1780s, a few cotton mills were erected using jennies and water frames. However, it was a very limited effort and by 1790, there were only about 900 Jennies in the entire country. Similarly, although in 1785, the pioneering coke-smelting ironworks was set up at Le Creusot, it was not followed up. There were innovations in other areas also: soda-making began in 1791; and workshops for rolling copper sheets were established (Crouzet, 1996: p. 44; Landes, pp. 139–140). This constituted the initial phase of French industrialization which went on until the political Revolution occurred, and particularly until 1793, when the war with Britain began disrupting the transfer of technology.

The French Revolution and later the Napoleonic Empire, both covering the period from 1789 to 1814, had a dual impact on the pace of industrialization. On the one hand, it impeded the growth of industrialization due to loss of overseas markets, disruption in the import of machineries and technical expertise from Britain, and loss of life, including that of technical experts, scientists and inventors, in the course of the Revolution and the wars. On the other hand, it also created a favourable environment by wiping out the feudal relations, by opening up the continental markets for French traders and manufacturers, and by excluding the cheap British goods from European markets. The cotton-spinning industry received a big boost and the number of cotton mills increased from 37 in 1799 to 266 in 1810. In this period, the hand-spinning of cotton had almost ceased to exist, with cotton spinning almost wholly taken up by mechanized factory industry. However, other industries such as iron and coal did not register much progress. Overall, in the initial stages of French industrialization up to 1814, the rate of growth in the industrial production remained small at about 0.56 per cent per year between 1781–90 and 1803–12, compared to British rate of 2.1 per cent from 1780 to 1801 (Crouzet, 1996: pp. 44–46).

A new phase of industrialization started after 1815 which continued till the 1860s. This period witnessed the entrenchment of modern industries in France. After the end of Napoleon's continental system, the prohibition on British goods was lifted leading to large influx of cheap manufactures into European markets. Not only the consumption of French goods declined in the rest of Europe but even the French market was threatened with the prospect of being flooded by British goods. This prompted the Restoration regime to impose heavy duties on foreign manufactured goods. Even in the French colonies, trade with foreigners was banned. Such protectionist measures saved the French manufacturing industry but it also restricted its competitive edge. Cotton textile industry advanced but it specialized mainly in quality and luxury products geared to high-end markets. Nevertheless, after 1815, industrialization and economic growth accelerated due to peace, possibility of importing modern industrial technology from Britain, improved agricultural production, increased mobility of capital and improvement in transport. Cotton industry still remained in the forefront. The consumption of raw cotton rose five times between 1820 and 1860. In Alsace and Normandy, there was much increase in the number of mechanized cotton-spinning factories. In Alsace, the number of spindles rose from 500,000 in 1828 to 1,150,000 in 1847. The French spinners now began to produce finest quality yarn. The wool industry also grew with much more success in foreign markets.

Power looms were also extensively used in cotton weaving, particularly in Alsace from 1820s onwards. In other regions of France, it was used on a large scale only since the late 1840s. the number of power looms in cotton weaving in France increased from about 5,000 in 1834 to 31,000 in 1846 and 80,000 in 1866 (Crouzet, 1996: p. 48). Since the 1840s, France was decisively moving to capital-intensive production in cotton industry. During the 1850s, factory production in cotton hugely increased largely eliminating the handicrafts. By 1870, Alsace attained a comparable level of mechanization and sophistication to Lancashire in Britain. Coal production also increased massively: 5 million metric tons in 1853, and 13 million metric tons in 1869.

Another area, in which development occurred, though initially to a limited extent, was the iron industry. British technology and technicians were imported in the beginning. Coke-smelting and puddling and rolling technology was being introduced on increasing scale. In 1828, 32 per cent of iron produced in France was refined with coal in 1837 it was 50 per cent, 70 per cent in 1846 and 82 per cent in 1860. Consequently, the number of charcoal blast-furnace declined. By 1869, the iron industry in France underwent an almost total transformation becoming the largest producer of iron after Britain in Europe. Construction of railways on a huge scale after 1840s created big demand for the product of French iron industry. It was during this period that modern industrialization in France was accomplished (Crouzet, 1996: pp. 49–50).

France still did not quite fulfil the crucial indicators of a finished industrial revolution as compared with Britain. Even in 1870, more than 50 per cent of its male labour force remained in primary sector, while industry absorbed only about 29 per cent. Urbanization was only about 31 per cent, and the income from industry amounted to 36 per cent, almost on par with primary sector (34 per cent). However, compared to the continental European countries, France did not perform too badly even though its pace of industrialization was relatively slow. British case of fast structural transformation was unique which was not repeated anywhere else. The French case was also distinctive because it started rather early, almost simultaneously with Britain, and had the supporting indices such as income level and population similar to Britain. And yet it took a very long time to industrialize. It was only by 1911 that the industry overtook agriculture in terms of employment. Thus, French achievements in industrialization have been described as 'respectable but not outstanding' and 'not brilliant but quite creditable'. In 1860, per capita level of industrialization in France was fifth in the world after Britain, Belgium, Switzerland and the USA. This was not a small achievement by any standards.

GERMANY

German industrialization was another example of the different paths taken by various European countries on the highway of modern economic growth. Unlike France, where the process of industrial development were quite slow, Germany moved ahead fast towards advanced industrial base within a span of about 30 years. It was faster even compared to Britain. Instead of starting with the consumer industries, as was the case in Britain and France, Germany right from the beginning relied on heavy industries for the big push forward. The role of the state and big banks were particularly pronounced as was the entrenched feudal power, in the form of German *Junkers*, throughout the nineteenth century.

In contrast to France and Britain, which were compact political units, Germany was divided into several independent states until the unification of 1870. Even after 1815, there were more than thirty distinct political states with their own separate laws, administration, currencies, weights and measures, and customs barriers. In the late eighteenth and early nineteenth centuries, Germany was economically backward compared to its advanced neighbours. Labour mobility was extremely restricted due to prevalence of serfdom in some areas, and limited supply of capital. However, it was not an underdeveloped country in the sense of an ex-colonial country where the experience of colonization has created a huge economic and intellectual lag in comparison to the advanced countries. Germany instead was an equal participant in the economic, political and intellectual culture of Europe, including that of science and technology. Its educational institutions and the pool of intellectual resources were as, if not more, advanced as even the best. It had a credit network and early industrial tradition. Since the beginning of the nineteenth-century German nationalism was becoming strong and assertive. And it also possessed large chunk of raw material resources such as iron and coal needed in the early stages of modern industrialization.

The German industrialization went through three phases: (i) from the late eighteenth century until the 1830s was a period of early industrialization when industrial technologies were borrowed from other countries and institutional reforms were introduced, particularly in Prussia; (ii) huge spurt in industrialization since the late 1830s, initially driven by railway construction on a massive scale, accompanied by huge foreign and indigenous investment of capital, great mobility of labour into industries, significant rise in productivity and increase in per capita income and (iii) the phase of mature industrialization from 1870s to 1914 when Germany took a great leap forward on several fronts, becoming the second biggest industrialized country in Europe and the biggest on the continent.

Napoleon's victory over German armies in 1806 and subsequent French rule paved the way for several institutional changes conducive to the industrial growth. Agrarian reforms from 1807 to 1821 abolished the serfdom freeing the peasants and introducing individual property rights in land and labour. Although the process continued even in post-Napoleonic Germany, it had lost its revolutionary character. These reforms benefited the landowners and substantial peasants by linking their holdings to the market, creating differentiation among peasantry, and focusing on individual mobility. The common land and the pastures were divided and occupied by individual landowners. Since the peasants were required to pay the lords for securing their independence, a lot of money passed hands. It is estimated that between 1821 and 1850 there was a huge transfer of wealth to the landlords to the tune of about 327 million Marks or about 10 million Marks per year which was more than the annual net investment in Prussia's industrial sector during this period. The loss of common land, and payment to get freedom impoverished the small peasants further making them part of the rural labour force. It also afforded much disposable capital in the hands of the aristocratic estate owners whose position was further strengthened making them allies of the ascendant bourgeoisie. A surplus labour force was created which would move to the cities when opportunities presented. The guilds were abolished, removing the restriction on the mobility of labour and capital. All these measures created the conditions for capitalist industrialization. It is true that the impact of these measures was initially limited, but they did create an environment in which broader changes could be brought about.

Another important step in the direction of creating a common market was the creation of Prussian custom union in 1818, and finally the creation of the Zollverein or Customs Union among all German states in 1834. The establishment of a single free trade zone in most of Germany was a major factor in economic development. This also led to Prussia-controlled monetary integration making inter-state trade within Germany less costly. The political fragmentation was a big hurdle in the path towards industrialization. The free movement of goods in all parts of Germany would bring down the prices of commodities facilitating investment.

Now, an existence of a broad trading area inside German states necessitated the creation of a commensurate transport network. Although road construction had occurred significantly during the 1820s, long-distance travel by road was very expensive. River transportation on Rhine, supplemented by canals, had geographical limitations. The building of railways at this stage provided a great boost both to economical transportation as well as integration. It was also the prime mover in German industrialization. This was in contrast to Britain and France where the cotton textile industry was the pacemaker. Railway construction also led to the expansion of other heavy industries such as iron and coal as it required their availability in great quantities.

Since the 1840s the railway construction proceeded at a great pace. The length of railway network in Prussia increased from 1,600 km in 1844–45 to 20,700 km in 1879–81. In terms of investment, it absorbed a high amount of capital—88 million Marks in 1851–54 increasing to 503 million Marks in 1875–59. The proportion of the net investment in railways as compared to that of the entire economy was 11.9 per cent in 1851–54, rising to 25.8 per cent in 1875–59. This capital-intensive nature of this enterprise provided direct employment to a lot of workers and engineers, and created significant backward linkages. The iron and steel, and coal industries greatly benefited from it. Initially, capital was invested by foreign companies in the metal industry and coal mining. However, soon the German capital took over and the German businessmen became active in all these fields. Thus, while in the initial period of railway building in the early 1840s, iron rails were either imported or made with imported pig iron, by the 1850s Prussia started exporting iron-rails. Another sector of economy which was made immensely stronger by railway construction was banking. Huge sums of money needed for railways were mobilized by banks. Railways also brought to realization the hidden technological and organizational talent which was a result of the advanced German educational system. In a brief period, scientific and technical education at various levels poured out qualified individuals to work in most advanced industries. The German achievement has been so impressive that even before the unification in 1870 the German industrialization was proceeding rapidly. The economic prosperity was reflected in the increase in population which rose from 25 million in 1820 to 40 million in 1871 and 65 million in 1910. The real income rose (at dollar 1970) from 418 in 1850 to 602 in 1880.

Even after 1870, the rate of industrial growth continued at the same pace. Some important changes in the industrial organization and banking could be noted in the period between 1870 and 1914. Large-scale business enterprises came up in industries like steel, coal mining, chemicals and heavy engineering. Joint-stock companies increasingly replaced family firms. Thus, about 80 per cent of largest industrial enterprises in 1887 and 1907 were joint-stock companies which owned about 65 per cent of their total capital. German business was increasingly marked by concentration and oligopoly (market or industry dominated by a small number of sellers). It reduced competition through the formation of cartels which facilitated market-sharing agreements. This was also the period which witnessed the emergence of large joint-stock banks which almost fully replaced the earlier private banking system. Their size became so big that by 1913, the three largest German enterprises were banks. Among the 25 largest enterprises, 17 were banks. This shows the enormity of their capital and their role in German economy. Another feature was the role of the state in facilitating industrial growth in various manners. This included a guarantee on investment in railways, protectionist measures particularly after 1870 to secure German market for German goods and facilitating industrial and market expansion through aggressive foreign policy.

RUSSIA

By the mid-nineteenth century it was clear that Russia, one of the most powerful states in Europe, had slided into backwardness because the Western Europe had moved much ahead. This owed to the surge of modern industrialization in the latter area, whereas Russia still remained anchored in a pre-industrial economy. This weakness was revealed starkly in the Crimean War (1854–56) when it was defeated. It brought to the fore the fact that political and diplomatic power in a changed world would depend on modernization. And the latter involved, more than anything else, the growth of modern industry. However, the modern capitalist industrialization was a complex process depending upon many factors, the most important being a relative modernization of agriculture required to supply labour and primary produce to the growing industrial centres, the existence of an entrepreneurial bourgeoisie open to mobilize capital and take risks, and the growth of an educated middle class which could supply managerial cadres and technical personnel. And the later the industrial developments in a country, the more resources were needed to spur it on.

Russia in the nineteenth century faced tremendous obstacles to modern industrial development. It was one of the rare European countries which still had serfdom in the mid-nineteenth century; it was very large and unwieldy with great problems in communication; it suffered from extreme cold weather conditions when for a significant part of year agricultural activities were limited; its natural resources lay in the outlying areas which were difficult to reach due to poor transport; the internal market was limited due to the existence of village communes and poverty of the peasantry; the aristocratic landowners were averse to modern industrialization until the 1890s; and it had a very small middle class clearly inadequate to assume industrial leadership.

It was within this context of 'backwardness' that the industrialization in Russia occurred from the late nineteenth century to the beginning of the World War I. Alexander Gerschenkron gave an influential account of industrialization in backward countries in general, and in Russia in particular. According to this model, the more the economic backwardness at the beginning of industrialization in a country, the greater intervention is required in the market economy for mobilization of capital, the heavier is the emphasis on developing capital-goods industry than on the consumer goods industry, the higher is the speed with which the country attains a very high rate of manufacturing growth, the bigger are the industrial enterprises with much more labour concentration, the less is the role of the agricultural sector as a market for industrial product, the more is the coercive extraction from the population particularly lowering the consumption levels of the peasantry, and much greater is the involvement of state and the banks to procure capital for the fledgling industries.

This model has been criticized, but it has quite a bit of relevance in case of Russian industrialization. The state played far greater role in this case than in most other European countries. The main period of Russian industrialization falls between 1860 and 1914 and the highest growth is occurring during the 1890s. During this entire period, the role of the government remained quite prominent at various levels. In fact, the first big spurt in industrialization had occurred in the reign of Peter the Great (1700–1725) when important industries were established through mobilization of capital from internal resources, technological specialization from foreign countries and by creating some sort of industrial serfdom. This made Russia the largest producer of iron in the world until Britain took over in the late eighteenth century. However, this modernizing drive was abandoned after Peter's death. Peter's primary concern was to strengthen the state and the military, and not to boost industrial growth *per se*. For more than a century after Peter's death, the Russian rulers were not interested in this area. Whatever little industrialization occurred in the first half of the nineteenth century was due to the initiative of foreign businessmen, some members of the religious minorities in Russia, and even some serfs. It was only after 1860 that the government became actively interested in promoting industrialization, mainly to boost its declining military strength. The process began with the abolition of serfdom in 1861. A little earlier, however, the government started constructing railways, with the first major line linking Moscow and St Petersburg in 1852. But by 1860, only about 1,600 km of line was in operation. Even the great reform measure of ending the serfdom did not mobilize labour nor did it introduce private property in the land, also because these were not its main aims.

However, the construction of railways grew rapidly in subsequent decades expanding to 10,700 km in 1870, 50,000 km in 1880 and more than 70,000 km in 1914 (Grossman, 1973: pp. 488–491). This acted as a great stimulator of growth for both the industrial and agricultural sectors. Initially, private companies constructed and operated the railway lines, but after 1880 government actively took over, and bought most of the private companies while strictly controlling the remaining ones. This helped in achieving a remarkable rate of growth of about 5 per cent per year in the period between 1860 and 1913 for the industrial output, including manufacturing, mining, factory and artisan production as a whole. It was during this period that population also increased at the rate of 1.5 per cent per year. Thus, per capita increase in industrial production was on an average of 3.5 per cent per year. The rate of increase in agricultural output was about 1 per cent per person. Owing to the growth in population, the per capita increase in real national product was only about 1 per cent per year, which was well below the average of many other industrializing countries during this period. (Grossman, 1973: pp. 487–490).

Such fast industrial growth resulted in Russia becoming a major industrial power by 1914. Whereas in 1860, it was in the sixth position in total industrial output in the world (even behind China and India), in 1913 it occupied the fourth place (behind the USA, Germany and Britain). The growth of its modern industries had been quite remarkable.

Iron and steel, textiles, oil, electrical engineering, chemicals were the important modernized areas in which it had moved ahead. Thus, despite the tremendous rise in world's total manufacturing production between 1860 and 1913, Russia increased its share from 7 per cent in 1860 to 8.8 per cent in 1900 and 8.2 per cent in 1913 (Munting, 1996: p. 330).

In all these developments the role of the state had been quite important. Since the 1880s, when the government actively stepped in, the industrial growth rate became much faster. It was after this that it established a modern steel industry, engineering industry, and oil industry. The extremely important role of the state in the economic life of the country was unprecedented among European countries. The government was a very significant instrument of resource mobilization in terms of capital and foreign expertise, and it was also a major source of demand. Government purchases for railways and defence provided tremendous boost to engineering and metallurgical industries. The Ministry of Finance became one of the most important organs of the government. Although earlier Ministers of Finance such as Reutern (1862–78), Bunge (1881–87) and Vyshnegradsky (1887–91) also played important role in boosting industries, it was Sergei Witte (1891–1900) whose role was crucial in the great industrial surge during the 1890s. His policies of protectionism, encouragement to private entrepreneurs, direct state involvement in railway construction, placing Russia on the gold standard to encourage foreign investment, and preferential treatment of domestic industry for meeting the state's demands in railways and defence were crucial in propelling Russian economy on the highway of modern industrial growth.

Despite all this, however, Russian economic development remained lop-sided. Agriculture, despite some growth, remained basically underdeveloped; even by 1913, about 70 per cent of the population remained closely dependent on agricultural earnings; agricultural production per person and per acre remained quite low; despite Russia being the world's largest exporter of wheat, the condition of the peasantry remained precarious, dependent on the size of the harvest, and on the vagaries of climate; the consumption level of the peasantry fell because of high taxes to finance industrialization. Thus, the industrialization process intensified the dualism already existing between the industrial and financial sectors on the one hand, and agricultural sector on the other. Out of a population of 170 million, only about 20 million people in 1913 were dependent on the industrial sector. Out of the latter only about 3.1 million wage-earners were in factories and mines. In a vast ocean of peasantry, modern industrial working class represented a few isolated islands, generally concentrated around large plants. A small part of the national income was provided by the industrial sector, factory-based manufacture making only about 15 per cent of national income. Foreign capital predominated in the industries, French capital in metal and engineering industries, German capital in chemicals and electrical industries, and British capital in oil extraction. Its per capita income remained among the lowest in Europe.

A COMPARATIVE VIEW OF EUROPEAN INDUSTRIALIZATION

It was in the late nineteenth century that the full effects of the industrialization process were felt all over Europe. The construction of the Eiffel Tower in Paris in 1889, the high voltage electrical current over Germany in 1891 and the creation of modern automobile in Britain in 1895 heralded the era of what has also been called as the 'Second Industrial Revolution'. Increases in prices due to increased consumption and supply of gold from Africa and Alaska made the long-term investment attractive; transportation and communication facilities were improved by laying out huge railway lines, construction of inter-oceanic canals (Suez in 1856–69 and Panama in 1881–1914), and the inauguration of wireless communication between France and England in 1899. Steel parts produced by the new generation of machine tools made possible the creation of the internal combustion engine, the automobile and the aeroplane. Invention was now no longer left to individual initiatives; the large industrial enterprises used hired staff of inventors and scientists to research in assigned areas.

Britain was no longer the overall leader during this era. In 1913, it had about 27 per cent of Europe's manufacturing capacity, compared to 32 per cent for Germany; only about 10 per cent of world steel production, as against 24 per cent for Germany and 42 per cent for the United States; Germany had moved ahead in several new, high-tech industries such as chemicals, electrical engineering, and machinery-making; and by 1913, Germany supplied about 59 per cent of the coal output on European continent (Crouzet, 2001: pp. 134–36).

On the other hand, Europe also presented a picture of severe national disparities. While countries such as Belgium, France, Germany, Switzerland, Sweden and Netherlands progressed fast, the countries of eastern and southern Europe, particularly in the Balkans, lagged much behind. The countries such as Albania, Bulgaria, Serbia, Romania and Greece suffered from general economic backwardness, low literacy, small population, scanty natural resources and little proto-industrialization. Even somewhat bigger countries such as Spain and Portugal remained behind in the race to industrialization, despite an early start in colonization. This sluggishness to industrialize may be explained through various factors: low level of literacy leading to lack of human capital in technical, scientific and managerial fields; a very small middle class and bourgeoisie which was primarily responsible for taking a lead in the direction of industrial growth; overwhelming dependence on agriculture for income and employment; and lack of institutional reforms in legal, political and economic fields (Crouzet, 2001).

However, till the World War I, European countries as a whole remained much ahead of the rest of the world, except the United States. Europe's real GNP grew at a mean rate of 1.7 per cent annually between 1800 and 1913, its rate of industrial production from 1830 to 1913 was 2.6 per cent per year, and rate for agricultural output was 1 per cent. Europe's population rose from 180 million in 1800 to 450 million in 1914 when it constituted one quarter of the world's population. Europe in the nineteenth century became the banker of the world moving a large amount of capital both internally and to other continents (Crouzet, 2001: pp. 155–158). Thus, during the nineteenth century, Europe rose to a position of world eminence on the basis of its industrial growth.

IMPACT OF INDUSTRIALIZATION

The impact of industrialization was varied and complex. Industrialization in the initial period worked with the social structures which had been produced over a long span of time; some of the changes took place when the process was going on; and many of the changes which were noted later occurred after the economic processes related to the early phase of industrialization were more or less complete. In this section we will discuss some of the major impact it had on the life of the people and society.

Industrial Revolution reconstituted the society in some important ways, the most important being the growth of the new social classes intimately linked to its own success. The most crucial were the industrial bourgeoisie and the industrial working class. Some form of class society had always existed based on the appropriation of surplus by the dominant groups since the onset of the agricultural revolution about 10,000 years ago. However, it was different from the modern class society due to the extra-economic coercion applied to extract surplus from the labouring population of peasants, artisans and workers, and by defining the social relationship on the basis of status. The landowning nobility and gentry, the clergy, the peasants, the old mercantile groups, and the artisans and labourers in the rural and urban areas were the main classes whose position in the society were broadly decided on account of their birth. The modern class society differed from this pre-modern social structure in essential respects because it believed in social mobility at all levels and did not accord privileges on the basis of birth or previous status.

The rise of the industrial bourgeoisie testified to this new pattern. The older bourgeoisie, which emerged in Europe during the 11–14 centuries owing to urban revival and commercialization, consisted of four broad groups: the rentiers; the members of the learned professions, magistracy and administration; big merchants and bankers with large amount of money, and with significant influence on political power and the most numerous group of artisans, shopkeepers and small traders. Out of these groups, the first two had no collective role in modern industrialization. The third group of merchant and bankers, owing to their wealth, controlled main manufactories which played big role in the development of modern industrialism. And the fourth group, particularly artisans, could move both ways: they could either become rich masters and owner of a small manufactory or become a labourer if impoverished. However, none of the above groups transformed into industrial capitalists.

The industrial bourgeoisie which emerged did not collectively identify with either of the above groups. The manufactory-owning group of merchants and bankers also mostly kept to themselves distrusting the upstart industrialist, and had no association with them for many generations. The huge capital possessed by them was not invested in the industry for a long time. Thus, the emergence of the industrial capitalists was 'the quasi-spontaneous generation of a new group whose members came from every section of society. It was not birth, trade, or fortune that made the first industrialists, but initiative, ambition, and luck—if they succeeded, for the emergence of this new group was an affair for the fittest or luckiest; those who could not keep up helped to form the nucleus of the future pxproletariat' (Bergier, 1973: p. 408).

Since, in the initial phase of industrialization particularly in cotton industry, the capital requirement for setting up a spinning frame was small, almost anybody with some resources could become an industrialist. Thus, people from rural artisanate, farmers, shopkeepers, innkeepers started production by installing a few spinning Jennies. Thus, Richard Arkwright, the supposed inventor of water frame who later became a wealthy capitalist, was a barber. The grandfather of Robert Peel, the British Prime Minister in 1834–35 and 1841–46, was a farmer who became an industrialist. Similarly, William Radcliff, also a farmer, set up mills becoming one of the richest persons in early nineteenth-century Britain. Similarly, in France, many early industrialists arose from the ranks of humble artisans. However, as industrialization progressed, larger capital was needed to set up a plant. In this phase, the industrial bourgeoisie came more from the ranks of rich people such as erstwhile big merchants, bankers and even landed nobility (Bergier, 1973: pp. 409–411). The success of industrialization in most of European countries by the late nineteenth century attracted earlier wealthy groups which had kept away. Industry now became the pinnacle of achievement and the richest groups were in some form or other were now associated with industrial entrepreneurship.

While the story of industrial bourgeoisie was one of ascendance in wealth, influence and power, the story of the industrial worker was more complex. Even earlier, a large mass of proletariat, or manual workers without any means of production, existed in most European countries. The dependent artisans or journeymen in urban centres were present in significant numbers in all commercially advanced regions. The number of rural workers was also quite large. However, the modern industrial worker arose as a result of the increasing concentration of material and persons in limited geographic space. Increasing technological sophistication led to bigger machinery powered by mechanical energy. This resulted in gathering of more and more workers under one roof to operate relatively huge machinery. This novel organization of labour and production known as factory brought increasingly greater number of workers in close proximity. It increasingly dissociated the workers from their tools of production, de-skilled them, and subordinated them to the functioning of the machine. It also introduced a time-discipline which was quite unlike anything in the past. The concentration of mills in particular areas resulted in the concentration of workers in those particular localities giving rise to several industrial towns. At the same time, these developments created a relatively homogeneous working class, concentrated in a particular area, increasingly conscious of their own interests as well as their opposition to the employers, and the possibility of broader organization for struggle.

The workers, who inhabited these towns and worked in these mills or other concerns energized by the development of industrial capitalism, came from various sources. The villages were of course the main reservoir, but the journeymen, and artisans and other failed members of petty bourgeoisie also filled their ranks. In the initial period till the mid-nineteenth century, the proportion of factory workers to the total working population was extremely low: about 5 per cent in Britain, 3 per cent in France, 2 per cent in Prussia and 2 per cent in Switzerland. Since the process of mechanization was generally slow and varied, and was not concurrently applied to all industries, the working class was quite stratified. For example, in Britain, the weaving was mechanized much later than spinning. This led to the increase in number and prosperity of hand-weavers for many decades. However, about 50 years later than the spinners, the process of slow and painful elimination of hand-weavers began. Thus, for quite a long time, while the spinner was a factory worker operating a machine, the weaver remained a cottage worker working with hand, although both were contributing to the same industrial process. Similar situation could be found in many other countries, particularly in textiles. But the situation was not the same in all industries and in all countries. In the late-coming countries, the capital investment was large and the size of the mills was also larger. This resulted in greater concentration of workers. Thus, many concerns in Germany and Russia employed thousands of workers under the same roof.

The old social classes did not, however, disappear immediately. In many cases, they were further strengthened. Thus, in Britain, the aristocratic landowning class remained politically and socially predominant until quite late. In France, the peasantry survived strongly until the middle of the twentieth century. In Germany, the landed Junker class gained in wealth and power. In Russia, both the peasantry and landlords survived more or less unaltered the burst of industrialization during 1880–1913. Similarly, many of the old artisan groups survived the onslaught of industrialization through various manoeuvres. However, in most cases, all these older classes had to adjust with the new reality, sometimes profiting out of this, as in case of the British and German landlords, or in other cases declining, mostly slowly as in case of the handloom weavers in most countries.

The working and living conditions of workers in early period of industrialization were extremely bad in all respects. They had to work for very long hours (14–16 hours) under extremely trying conditions; the work was monotonous and hard with few leaves; and the life in the neighbourhood was miserable. Women and children were employed in large numbers working long hours. So far as the wages and the standard of living of the working classes were concerned, they are a matter of intense controversy. We briefly survey the debate before reaching any conclusion.

Long ago, in 1844, Friedrich Engels, in his *The Condition of the Working Class in England*, sketched a dismal picture of the lives of workers. Arnold Toynbee, in a similar indictment, held the industrialization responsible for the deteriorating moral and material conditions of the mass of workers. J.L. Hammond, in 1930, held the Industrial Revolution responsible for the 'extraordinary poverty' it created. 'What did Manchester or Leeds offer to the workman?' he asked. And his answer was that 'It had destroyed his contact with nature and turned him from a craftsman into a man serving the routine of a great industry.' It created a system in which 'For all workers alike there was the same want of beauty, the same want of playing fields or parks, the same want of pageants or festivals, the same speeding up of industry' (Hammond, 1930: pp. 223–224). Even though industrialization paid the mill worker a little more than other workers, yet 'the ugliness of the new life, with its growing slums, its lack of beautiful buildings, its destruction of nature and its disregard of man's deeper needs, affected not this or that class of workers only, but the entire working-class population' (ibid., p. 225). Hammond's critique, as with Toynbee, was based mostly on moral and romantic grounds in which a richer way of life was lost due to pursuit for money. But later historians disagreed sharply even on the issue of material living. Two views—optimist and pessimist—remain juxtaposed to each other. Thus, while Hartwell and Ashton thought that the material conditions of working classes improved, E.P. Thompson and Eric Hobsbawm argued that at least between 1780 and 1840, the supposed period of the Industrial Revolution, the workers were subjected to increased level of exploitation. Later Deane and Cole argued for substantial growth in the real income of the workers. However, figures given by Lindert and Williamson paint a rather dismal picture in which there was very little increase in the real wages and real personal consumption by workers. The estimates by Charles Feinstein also confirm the pessimistic view of relative stagnation. Revised estimates by Harley and Crafts generally support such conclusion of meagre growth between 1780 and 1820, the conventional period of Industrial Revolution (see Crafts, 1989). Broadly if we take the arguments by Crafts, who treads cautiously between the two polarized views, we get that the 'consumption growth (per capita) was indeed slow between 1770 and 1821', but 'by 1831 real per capita consumption expenditure exceeded eighteenth-century levels by a margin of 10 per cent or more.' Therefore, although the 'food consumption deteriorated during the early industrial revolution period', it is also true that 'consumption of other items was growing'. Most historians, however, hold that till the 1820s the real wages declined in Britain, but after that, particularly in the second half of the nineteenth century there was a rise in real wages (Crafts, 1985: pp. 89–113). Thus, it seems that the real wages of the working classes in Britain grew at a slower rate than the national income leading to increasing disparities. On the whole, 'there was a growth in inequality over most if not all of the Industrial Revolution period, caused by differential price changes. Only after 1860 or so was this reversed as food prices started to fall relative to other prices' (More, 2000: p. 147).

In other countries too, a similar trend may be noticed. On the whole, it may be said that low wages were making a decent living impossible. This resulted in a high rate of mortality and morbidity, particularly among the young. What was even more striking was the rapidly increasing hiatus between earnings of the rich and those of the poor. The sense of this rising inequality created more dissatisfaction in the minds of the dispossessed giving rise to strong working class movements particularly in association with socialist politics. Thus, the period witnessed increasing chasm between different social classes. Increasing landlessness, proletarianization, high prices, relative decline in the living standards of the workers and the restrictive laws against the poor created distrust and widened the differences between the poor and the rich. This was expressed in various ways. One was the dramatic rise in crime against property. Theft, poaching, forgery, embezzlement, smuggling and such other offences increased markedly. The opposition of the poor against the government and propertied classes resulted in various changes in the criminal-justice system with strong bias against the poor (Hudson, 1992: pp. 206–210).

The period also witnessed systematic dismantling of the old system of aristocratic paternalism which had some form of regulatory protection for the working classes. Instead, there was an increasing shift towards market economy. This gave rise to antagonism among the working classes against profit-seeking, laissez-faire ideology of capitalist industrialism. This also resulted in the increasing identity of interests among the working people based on institutions like co-operative societies, educational and religious movements, trade unions, and many other forms of organizations based on handloom weavers, cotton spinners, artisans, shoemakers, small shopkeepers and tradespeople, small masters, etc.

The labour movements which arose in many European countries generally went through three distinct phases: (i) workers' awareness of their own conditions as well as the rising profits and increasing wealth of the upper classes created a sense of dissatisfaction which was further enhanced by the critique of capitalism by several intellectuals and others. The early working class actions was expressed in the form of food-riots, absenteeism, foot dragging, and occasional violence against modern machineries, as expressed in the Luddite movement in England; (ii) workers' attention was now focused more on their collective strength towards finding a solution to their problems. During this phase, the workers also had the beginning of an early consciousness of class and (iii) the mature phase of labour movement through big organizations such as the Chartists, working class federations and the First International.

In their early realization about their situation and their antagonism to the property-owning classes, the workers were helped by members of the upper classes who were also critical of exploitation and oppression of the workers. The members of the nonconformist churches such as Quakers, Baptists, Presbyterians, Congregationalists, etc. were among the first people to criticize the industrialization and consequent social changes leading to new inequalities. Although their views were religious and their solution millenarian and impractical, they had substantial influence on working masses. But they attempted individual solution and their proposed reform measures did not go far in either pinpointing the cause of people's problem or in offering collective solution to their problem. The workers, however, expressed their dissatisfaction in many spontaneous actions. Some more organized form of protest as Luddism in England articulated the rebellious sentiments of the working masses. Similar instances of machine-breaking were evident in the early period of industrialization on the European continent also. In such actions, the participants were mostly the artisans and skilled workers who thought that the new machines were responsible for their plight. These actions were suppressed by various governments. In the initial period, only in Britain and France do we find even the preliminary form of class-conscious at the turn of the nineteenth century.

In Britain, soon after the demise of Luddism, we find the workers expressing their solidarity in other ways. Around 1815, in Britain, the more specific term 'working class' was being used in labour writings. In France, similar term was used around 1830. In Britain, attempts towards forging a broader solidarity by breaking sectional loyalties were made around 1818, and such a unity was successfully achieved in the powerful Chartist movement during the 1830s. Several contemporaries, such as Thomas Carlyle in 1826, noticed that the distance between the poor and the rich was increasing. Another contemporary, Peter Gaskell, bitterly commented in 1834 about the 'dense masses' concentrated in factories making it easier for unions to be formed and actions to be initiated with ease. He was alarmed that 'The organization of these working class societies is now so complete that they form an empire within an empire of the most obnoxious description. Labour and capital are coming into collision—the operative and the master are at issue, and the peace and well-being of the kingdom are at stake.' E.C. Tufnell, in 1834, also noticed this phenomenon of strong working class organizations and a 'complete separation of feeling... between masters and men', making them to look upon each other 'as an enemy' (cited in Hudson, 1992: p. 10).

In both Britain and France, the term 'socialism' in the context of working class movements was adopted since the 1820s. By 1830s, in Britain and France, consciousness of class among a substantial section of workers could be found. In some other European countries such as Belgium, Switzerland and Germany, this consciousness came during the latter half of the nineteenth century while in Russia such consciousness emerged only in the beginning of the twentieth century. Thus, working class consciousness broadly followed the graph of industrialization in various countries.

DEBATE ON INDUSTRIAL REVOLUTION

Modern industrialization, as we mentioned earlier, is also referred to as Industrial Revolution. The term 'revolution' implies a rapid process, an abruptness, a discontinuity, as happened in the case of the French Revolution, or the American Revolution, or later the Russian Revolution. This term was used to refer to the process of industrialization primarily in Britain from 1760 to 1840. Some influential writers such as Rostow, were more precise to compress the period between 1783 and 1802, but generally the proponents of 'revolution' thesis put the period relatively more broadly between 1780 and 1820, or even 1780 to 1840. Although it is clear to most users of the term that the process of industrialization was not exactly in the same league as some of the political transformations, the term was, and is, extensively used to refer to the process of industrial transformation in Britain and some other European countries.

Given the later emphasis on the relative slowness of the industrialization process, there has been a wide-ranging debate on the idea of Industrial Revolution. The basic issue is whether there is a continuity or discontinuity in the economic development during the late eighteenth and early nineteenth centuries in relation to the preceding period. The discontinuity view, which was the earlier one, emphasizes that the economic processes in the late eighteenth and early nineteenth-century Britain represented a break from the earlier period, and this had an impact on the society in general and livelihood of the working masses in particular. The continuity thesis, on the other hand, tends to emphasize that the processes of change were rather slow and generally represented continuity with the preceding era. They also discount the cataclysmic effect of these changes on the lives of the working people. They, therefore, also think that the term 'revolution' was not quite suitable for the changes taking place because they covered too long a period and affected only a few areas of the overall economy in the initial period. We here discuss various points related to this debate.

The term 'Industrial Revolution' was first used in France in 1799 by the French diplomat Louis Guillaume Otto (Crouzet, 1996: p. 45). During the 1820s, it was again found in records to denote economic changes in certain regions of the country as well as in Britain, and to compare it with the great political Revolution. In British case, the term was widely used during the 1840s and Friedrich Engels used it in his book on *The Condition of the Working Class in England* (1844). But, even before that, contemporary commentators indicated the process of rapid change. Thus, in 1814, Patrick Colquhoun wrote that 'It is impossible to contemplate the progress of manufactures in Great Britain within the last thirty years without wonder and astonishment. Its rapidity... exceeds all credibility.' (Hudson, 1992: pp. 9–10). And later, although Karl Marx never used the term, his description of the phenomenon was very close to the idea of a revolution. The term was popularized by Arnold Toynbee in his *Lectures on the Industrial Revolution* (1884) which perceived the period as when the old economy and society were 'suddenly broken in pieces by the mighty blows of the steam engine and the power loom.' Although these lectures were published later posthumously, the term got currency since then. Starting with Toynbee, the debate on this issue passed through broadly four phases. In the first phase, from 1880s to the 1920s, the discontinuity thesis was most marked. It also highlighted the negative social consequences of the rapid economic development, which it characterized as Industrial Revolution. During the second phase, from the mid-1920s to the early 1950s, the economic historians were divided into emphasizing continuity and in depicting downturns and cyclical patterns in the industrialization process. In the third phase, from the mid-1950s to the early 1970s, the economic historians, buoyed up by the post-war economic prosperity in Western countries, stressed on the nature of industrial revolution as a process of rapid economic growth as well as of increasing prosperity for all classes. Since the mid-1970s, however, the stories of economic growth do not look so much spectacular and progressive (Cannadine, 1984).

In Britain, during the 1880s, many commentators were much concerned about the 'association of poverty with progress', and spoke in favour of uniting 'social concern with economic conditions'. The persons most associated with sharply presenting this view, and in opposition to Marshallian unhistorical conception of economic development, were Arnold Toynbee, Beatrice and Sidney Webb, and the J.L. and Barbara Hammond. Their idea of industrialization was that it was fast, and with terrible consequences for the common people. The Hammonds, in several writings, attacked the exploitative landlords and greedy capitalists for impoverishing the rural workers and exploiting the workers in the cities. They also criticized the free-trade policies and professed an anti-capital view. Similarly, the Webbs argued for government intervention to ameliorate the conditions of the masses which was rendered intolerable due the fast-paced Industrial Revolution. Toynbee depicted it as cataclysmic in which the traditional system was completely overshadowed by new machines. This destroyed the old world and created a new one in its place. In a similar vein, a popular textbook in 1896 described the changes as 'sudden and violent' when 'the great inventions were all made in a comparatively short space of time' and simultaneously 'the modern factory system had begun'. The Webbs described the Industrial Revolution as 'wholesale adoption of power-driven machinery and the factory system' which was effected during the 1780s. Similarly, for the Hammonds, the initial period of modern industrialization was characterized by 'vast and rapid expansion' and it represented 'a departure in which man passed definitely from one world to another.' Besides its rapidity, or probably due to it, the Industrial Revolution was accompanied by terrible social consequences. It was 'a darker period', more 'disastrous and terrible' through which 'a nation ever passed'. Great poverty was witnessed along with enormous increase in wealth leading to growing chasm between classes which during this period of Industrial Revolution 'read like a history of civil war'. Toynbee pointed to a 'wide gulf' between the workers and the capitalists because the worker had become 'the living tool of the employer' both in industry and agriculture. Thus, 'an agrarian as well as in industrial revolution had taken place.' The Industrial Revolution gave rise to 'a profane and brutal system' which destroyed both the mind and body of people. It created a regime akin to slavery as was to be found in ancient Egypt, Roman Empire and American South. The standard of life of the workers declined, towns and cities became most squalid and congested, and the masses faced terrible agony as happens in the times of war. For them, the responsible agency for all this disorder and pain was uncontrolled capitalism, a regime of *laissez-faire* which had become the reigning ideology of the ruling classes. Thus, the Industrial Revolution was sudden and violent, and which descended like a thunderbolt, generated misery and horror unparalleled in British history (Cannadine, 1984: pp. 133–136; Cameron, 1982: p. 378; Teich and Porter, 1996: pp. 1–10).

This view of Industrial Revolution was opposed by J.H. Clapham, A. Redford, A.P. Usher, George Unwin and E. Lipson. They put forward a gradualist conception of industrialization occurring in the late eighteenth and early nineteenth centuries. George Unwin wrote in 1921 that 'when, on looking back we find that the revolution has been going on for two centuries and had been in preparation for two centuries before that ... we may begin to doubt whether the term... has not by this time served its turn' (cited in Cameron, 1982: p. 378). They argued that the economic changes were rather slow and even by the mid-nineteenth century most industries were not mechanized and before 1830 'no single British industry had passed through a complete technological revolution.' Even in the cotton industry the changes were less marked than was once thought, water power was still used at a large scale and the steam power was not universally used in British industries by the mid-nineteenth century. So far as the standard of living of the workers was concerned, they argued that it was steadily improving, and after 1790 the 'wages had risen markedly' for the industrial workers (Cannadine, 1984).

However, the main trend in economic history from the mid-1920s to early 1950s was somewhat similar pessimism which informed the early period. Now the pessimistic outlook concerning the future of capitalism became general after the World War I. The great crisis in the 1930s demoralized even those with great faith in the progressive march of capitalism, and the hardships of the World War II further dampened such spirits. The decline in international trade, restriction on international credit, cessation of international migrations, unprecedented degree of unemployment, and tremendous devaluing of currency created an anxiety which affected all thinkers. The cyclical nature of capitalist development became a much stressed topic. The search was now for the reasons of such cycles. Several economic historians and economists traced the origins of such cycles to the Industrial Revolution itself, and many thought that such cycles were integrally linked with the free market economy. The idea of cyclical fluctuations in industrial development was so common during this period that W.W. Rostow, the later proponent of progressive growth of industrialization towards self-sustenance, wrote his doctoral thesis on the cyclical fluctuations of the British economy during the late nineteenth century. In a later book, *British Economy in the Nineteenth Century* published in 1948, he provided a cyclical account of the Industrial Revolution arguing that the process was 'highly discontinuous' and occurred in 'major cycles'. The larger project of which Rostow was a part was published in 1953 in two volumes under the title *Growth and Fluctuations of the British Economy, 1790–1850*. It viewed the economic history of Britain from 'the perspective of business fluctuations'. Their conclusions differed from the continuity thesis of Clapham by concerning themselves predominantly with the cyclical view of capitalist industrialization. However, they did not quite support the Toynbee–Webbs–Hammonds thesis of decline in the standards of living of the people. Instead, their argument was that even though the population of Britain increased manifold, 'the masses were in a material sense better off' by the end of the nineteenth century than in the beginning. As a prelude to the new interpretation of the Industrial Revolution and its impact, T.S. Ashton wrote in his book *The Indusrital Revolution* (1948) that it was this phenomenon which rescued the mass of the people in European countries from the clutches of poverty, hunger and misery, and created the conditions for a permanent rise in the standard of living (Cannadine, 1984).

This optimistic view was to hold sway in the next two decades of interpretative exercises in the economics and impact of the Industrial Revolution. The change was most obvious when Rostow, who had earlier concerned himself with the cyclical nature of capitalist development, now unreservedly put forth the notion of 'take-off into self-sustained growth' in his most famous book, *The Stages of Economic Growth* (1960). Now the clear perception was that although the modern industrialization was revolutionary in the sense of its occurring within a short period, it was also much beneficial for the European economies which 'seemed to have learned the secret of eternal growth and prosperity'. Industrial Revolution was depicted as heralding 'a fundamental discontinuity in world economic development' resulting in 'a radical shift in the structure of the economy, in the composition of the total output, and in the distribution of employment, which gives concrete meaning to the idea of an Industrial Revolution.' The trade cycles and social consequences were brushed under the carpet and the model of continuous economic development became the reigning model of interpreting modern industrialization. This model of economic growth provided the framework according to which the facts of the period were selected and put forth. The modern industrialization in Britain was portrayed as paradigmatic, as a model to be followed by others, and as heralding a new era of revolutionary economic progress. There were equally vocal other proponents of a revolutionary change. Eric Hobsbawm started his famous book, *Industry and Empire*, with the assertion that 'The Industrial Revolution marks the most fundamental transformation of human life in the history of the world recorded in written documents' (Hobsbawm, 1969: p. 13). The Marxist historians generally regarded the modern industrialization as heralding a fundamental break from the past. E.P. Thompson, for example, regarded this period as signifying a formative era for working-class formation (Thompson, 1963). But even others such as Carlo M. Cipolla described this phenomenon in superlative terms as 'a far-reaching revolution, without precedent in the history of Mankind' and asserted that 'no revolution has been as dramatically revolutionary as the Industrial Revolution—except perhaps the Neolithic Revolution' (Cipolla, 1973: p. 7).

But this view of a fundamental discontinuity did not go unchallenged. Gradually, but inexorably, the continuity-oriented ideas were gaining momentum which would, in the course of time, radically questioned many of the basic notions of earlier paradigm. The main issue in this new interpretation were:

(a) The phenomenon known as Industrial Revolution was not exactly a revolution but a slow process which occurred over a very long period. And, as George Unwin had warned long ago, something which had taken so long to develop fully is difficult to designate as 'revolution'. Even those who had been using the term such as Ashton cautioned that 'The word "revolution" implies a suddenness of change that is not, in fact, characteristic of economic processes. The system of human relationships that is sometimes called capitalism had its origins long before 1760, and attained its full development long after 1830: there is a danger of overlooking the essential fact of continuity' (Cited in Cameron, 1982: p. 379). This understanding has become quite general since the 1970s. The downturn in economic growth since the mid-1970s has fostered this sentiment. Instead of being revolutionary, it is argued, 'Britain's transition to an industrial society was marked by admirably peaceful gradualism', that Britain 'has always been a slow growing economy', and, as A.E. Musson stated, that 'the general interpretation presented in most textbooks' about 'a sudden, cataclysmic transformation starting around 1760 (is) clearly no longer tenable.' He further emphasized this gradualist interpretation by asserting that 'Much of England of 1850 was not very strikingly different from that of 1750' (cited in Cannadine, 1984: pp. 164–165). Nick Harley, one of the strongest proponents of the continuity thesis has argued that 'Britain's industrial growth in the last decades of the eighteenth century and the first decades of the nineteenth century was about a third slower than currently available estimates indicate' (Harley, 1982: p. 267). He states that there has been too much focus on cotton, iron and steam. However, these constituted only about 25 per cent of total British manufacturing even in the 1840s. Thus, Harley argues, by giving disproportionate weight to these 'technological leaders', a wrong view of the industrialization process has been presented. Similarly, a general survey of the period argues that 'The British Industrial Revolution was a very modest affair which emerged slowly from the past as part of a long, evolutionary process, not as a sharp, instantly recognizable break from traditional experience: its technology was small-scale and comparatively primitive; it needed relatively little additional investment capital; its capacity for introducing labour-saving technology was circumscribed; and its pace was gradual and uncoordinated' (cited in Cannadine, 1984: p. 166).

(b) Another re-interpretation concerns the role of British industrialization as the model for other countries. Contrary to the earlier view, it is now argued that because it was the first industrial nation British case was unique rather than paradigmatic. It cannot act as a model for today's underdeveloped countries because in the mid-eighteenth century its situation was completely different as it had high levels of literacy, was rich in resources, had a well-developed market system, its population was not much and its agriculture was advanced. It took a relatively longer period to industrialize than many other countries which followed it. The state's role was much less and the capital outlay was much smaller. The growth occurred in a staggered manner and it was a limited and piecemeal process. The number of entrepreneurs who failed was much larger than those who succeeded. Many economic historians such as Knick Harley and N.F.R. Crafts strongly favour a gradualist version of industrialization.

(c) The period between mid-eighteenth to mid-nineteenth centuries, conventionally taken as the time of Industrial Revolution, is now seen in a different light. It is argued by Musson that 'If the Industrial Revolution is located in the period 1760–1830, as it frequently is, then there are good grounds for regarding it as the Age of Water Power' and not of steam power as commonly supposed. Steam power was used in very few industries, besides cotton. In fact, except cotton industry, particularly its spinning branch, hardly any other industry had been fully mechanized for a long time. Moreover, the mechanization had actually led to an increase in labour-intensive jobs. Even by the mid-nineteenth century, Britain 'had still an agricultural economy'. Considering all factors, it is argued that the period 1850–1914 was closer to an ideal of industrialization than the period 1760–1850.

In yet another view, the actuality of slow growth is accepted. But the fact of significant industrialization, almost amounting to industrial revolution, is not denied in the period between 1760 and 1820. The slow growth was rather due to expensive wars which Britain fought for 36 years out of these 60 years. This resulted in massive government debt, mobilization of potential labour for military purposes, high taxes reducing private savings, loss of European markets, and rise in the prices of imported agricultural and raw materials (Williamson, 1984).

In this way, the now prevailing trend of interpretation has almost completely overhauled the picture of the Industrial Revolution as conventionally conceived. Now the gradualist thesis seems to have been adopted by most economic historians. But the debate has not yet ended. The arguments for a break have been most strongly put forward by Maxine Berg and Pat Hudson who take into account many of the counter-arguments put forward by the other side. Even while accepting that not all sectors and all regions in Britain industrialized simultaneously and at the same pace, they assert that there were 'sectoral specialization of regions and the growth of regionally integrated economies some of which were clearly experiencing an industrial and social revolution... while others were deindustrialized' (Berg and Hudson, 1992: p. 44). According to them not only certain sectors such as cotton spinning experienced massive technological changes, there was also a significant impact of these developments on those sectors such as handloom-weaving which were not yet mechanized. This led to a 'considerable transformation even within the framework of the so-called traditional sector' (Berg and Hudson, 1992: p. 32). Analytically, no sharp divide can be posed between the modern and the traditional sectors as both were in different ways experiencing the impact of industrialization.

Overall, however, most historians now think that there was no sharp break in the middle of the eighteenth century, that during the conventional period of 'industrial revolution' between 1780 and 1820 most of the industries were not mechanized, that even by the mid-nineteenth-century Britain retained much of its traditional economy, and that industrialization was a rather lengthy process which carried on into the twentieth century in much of Europe.

CONCLUSION

Modern industrialization was the phenomenon which over a period of time introduced a transformation in the economy and society of Europe and North America in the beginning and later in many other parts of the world. In its developed form, it involved a shift from agriculture to industry, from handicrafts to mechanized manufacturing, from workshop to factory, and the transformation of a significant amount of population from peasants and artisans to proletarians. These changes were not effected in a few years. A comprehensive transformation of

European economy and society took almost two centuries from the middle of the eighteenth to the middle of the twentieth. Britain was the first to achieve a structural transformation of its economy and society, followed by Belgium, France, Switzerland, Germany, Russia, Italy and many other European countries. Both the economic and social changes were different in each country and took varying times and shapes. Nevertheless, by around 1914, much of Europe had experienced industrialization in various forms breaking the shackles imposed by traditional equation between population and production.

Essential Readings

Deane, Phyllis (1965), *The First Industrial Revolution*, Cambridge: Cambridge University Press. (One of the main authoritative study of industrialization in Britain, this books covers in detail various processes stimulating the British industrialization.)

Hobsbawm, E.J. (1969), *Industry and Empire: From 1750 to the Present Day*, Harmondsworth: Penguin Books. (An extremely readable book on British industrialization covering many aspects other than purely economic. It also deals with the second phase of British industrialization and the process of its becoming an imperial power.)

Crafts, N.F.R. (1985). *British Economic Growth during the Industrial Revolution*, Oxford: Clarendon Press. (A balanced survey of economic development during the British industrialization, this work takes into account the state of debate on various issues related to the British economic history of this period.)

Teich, Mikulas and Roy Porter (1996), *The Industrial Revolution in National Context: Europe and the USA*, Cambridge: Cambridge University Press. (An extremely important study covering industrialization in several European countries.)

Crouzet, Francois (2001), *A History of the European Economy, 1000–2000*, Charlottesville and London: University of Virginia Press. (A good, short survey of economic history of Europe; the pages 99–169 are important for the present topic.)

Kemp, Tom (1985), *Industrialization in Nineteenth-Century Europe, London & New York: Longman.* (An important text-book on industrialization in some European countries such as Britain, France, Germany, Italy and Russia. Its emphasis on agriculture in various European countries is particularly important.)

Cannadine, David (1984), 'The Present and the Past in the English Industrial Revolution 1880–1980', *Past and Present*, No. 103, May, pp. 131–172.

(A comprehensive and organized survey of debate on the issue of Industrial Revolution.)

Further Readings

Allen, Robert C. (2006), 'The British Industrial Revolution in Global Perspective: How Commerce Created the Industrial Revolution and Modern Economic Growth' at http://www.ehs.org.uk/ehs/conference2007/Assets/AllenIIA.pdf.

Ashton, T.S. (1968), *The Industrial Revolution 1760:1830*, Oxford: Oxford University Press (first published in 1948).

Bairoch, Paul (1973), 'Agriculture and the Industrial Revolution 1700–1914', in Carlo M. Cipolla (ed), *The Fontana Economic History of Europe: The Industrial Revolution*, Glasgow: Fontana Collins.

Bayly, C.A. (2004), *The Birth of the Modern World 1780–1914: Global Connections and Comparisons*, Oxford: Blackwell Publishing.

Beaud, Michel (2004), *A History of Capitalism 1500–2000*, Delhi: Aakar Books (first published in French in 1981, in English 1983).

Beaudoin, Steven M. (2000), 'Current Debates in the Study of the Industrial Revolution', *OAH Magazine of History*, Fall, pp. 7–13.

Berg, Maxine and Pat Hudson (1992), 'Rehabilitating the Industrial Revolution', *The Economic History Review*, New Series, Vol. 45, No. 1, pp. 24–50.

Bergier, J-F. (1973), 'The Industrial Bourgeoisie and the Rise of the Working Class 1700–1914', in Carlo M. Cipolla (ed), *The Fontana Economic History of Europe: The Industrial Revolution*, Glasgow: Fontana/Collins.

Cameron, Rondo (1982), 'The Industrial Revolution: A Misnomer', *The History Teacher*, Vol. 15, No. 3, pp. 377–384.

Cameron, Rondo (1985), 'A New View of European Industrialization', *The Economic History Review*, New Series, Vol. 18, No. 1, pp. 1–23.

Cannadine, David (1984), 'The Present and the Past in the English Industrial Revolution 1880–1980', *Past and Present*, No. 103, May, pp. 131–172.

Cipolla, Carlo M. (1973), 'Introduction', in Carlo M. Cipolla (ed), *The Fontana Economic History of Europe: The Industrial Revolution*, Glasgow: Fontana/Collins.

Crafts, N.F.R. (1984), 'Economic Growth in France and Britain, 1830–1910: A Review of the Evidence', *The Journal of Economic History*, Vol. 44, No. 1, pp. 49–67.

Crafts, N.F.R. (1985), *British Economic Growth during the Industrial Revolution*, Oxford: Clarendon Press.

Crafts, N.F.R. (1990), 'The New Economic History and the Industrial Revolution', in Peter Mathias and John A. Davis (eds.), *The First Industrial Revolutions*, Oxford: Basil Blackwell.

Crouzet, Francois (1972), *Capital Formation in the Industrial Revolution*, London: Methuen & Co. Ltd.

Crouzet, Francois (1996), 'France', in Mikulas Teich and Roy Porter (eds.), *The Industrial Revolution in National Context: Europe and the USA*, Cambridge: Cambridge University Press.

Crouzet, Francois (2001), A *History of the European Economy, 1000–2000*, Charlottesville and London: University of Virginia Press.

Deane, Phyllis (1965), *The First Industrial Revolution*, Cambridge: Cambridge University Press.

Deane, Phyllis and W.A. Cole (1969), *British Economic Growth, 1688–1959: Trends and Structure*, Cambridge: Cambridge University Press.

Grossman, Gregory (1973), 'Russia and the Soviet Union', in Carlo M. Cipolla (ed), *The Fontana Economic History of Europe: The Emergence of Industrial Societies-2*, Glasgow: Fontana/Collins.

Hammond, J.L. (1930), 'The Industrial Revolution and Discontent', *The Economic History Review*, Vol. 2, No. 2, pp. 215–28.

Harley, C. Knick (1982), 'British Industrialization before 1841: Evidence of Slower Growth during the Industrial Revolution', *The Journal of Economic History*, Vol. 42, No. 2 (June), pp. 267–289.

Hobsbawm, E.J. (1969), *Industry and Empire: From 1750 to the Present Day*, Harmondsworth: Penguin Books.

Hobsbawm, E.J. (1988), *The Age of Revolution: Europe 1789–1848* (first published in 1962 by Weidenfeld and Nocolson), London: Cardinal.

Hobsbawm, E.J. (1989), *The Age of Capital 1848–1875*(first published in 1975 by Weidenfeld and Nocolson), London: Cardinal.

Hobsbawm, E.J. (1989), *The Age of Empire 1875–1914* (first published in 1987 by Weidenfeld and Nocolson), London: Cardinal.

Hudson, Pat (1992), *The Industrial Revolution*, London: Hodder Arnold.

Kemp, Tom (1985), *Industrialization in Nineteenth-Century Europe*, London & New York: Longman.

Landes, David S. (2003), *The Unbound Prometheus: Technological Change and Industrial Development in Western Europe from 1750 to the Present*, Cambridge: Cambridge University Press.

Mathias, Peter (1983), The First Industrial Nation, London: Methuen.

Mathias, Peter (1990), 'The Industrial Revolution: Concept and Reality', in Peter Mathias and John A. Davis (eds.), *The First Industrial Revolutions*, Oxford: Basil Blackwell.

Mokyr, Joel (1994), 'Technological Change, 1700–1830', in Roderick Floud and Donald McCloskey (eds.), *The Economic History of Britain since 1700*, Cambridge: Cambridge University Press.

Mokyr, Joel (2003), 'Why was Industrial Revolution a European Phenomenon?', *Supreme Court Economic Review*, Vol. 10, pp. 27–63.

More, Charles (2000), *Understanding the Industrial Revolution*, London & New York: Routledge.

Munting, Roger (1996), 'Industrial Revolution in Russia', in Mikulas Teich and Roy Porter (eds.), *The Industrial Revolution in National Context: Europe and the USA*, Cambridge: Cambridge University Press.

O'Brien, Patrick (2006), 'Provincializing the First Industrial Revolution', Working *Papers of the Global Economic History Network*, No. 17/06.

Rostow, W.W. (1960), The *Stages of Economic Growth: A Non-Communist Manifesto*, Cambridge: Cambridge University Press.

Rostow, W.W. (1973), 'The Beginnings of Modern Growth in Europe: An Essay in Synthesis', *The Journal of Economic History*, Vol. 33, No. 3 (Sep.), pp. 547–580.

Rostow, W.W. (1975), *How it all Began: Origins of the Modern Economy*, London: Methuen & Co.

Teich, Mikulas and Roy Porter (1996), *The Industrial Revolution in National Context: Europe and the USA*, Cambridge: Cambridge University Press.

Tilly, Richard (1996), 'German Industrialization', in Mikulas Teich and Roy Porter (eds.), *The Industrial Revolution in National Context: Europe and the USA*, Cambridge: Cambridge University Press.

Thompson, E.P. (1963), *The Making of the English Working Class*, Harmondsworth: Penguin.

Williamson, Jeffrey G. (1984), 'Why was British Growth so slow during the Industrial Revolution', *The Journal of Economic History*, Vol. 44, No. 3, pp. 687–712.

Wyatt III, Lee T. (2009), *The Industrial Revolution*, London: Greenwood Press.

Zanden, Jan Luiten van (2009), *The Long Road to the Industrial Revolution: European economy in a Global Perspective 1000–1800*, Leiden, Boston: Brill.

8 Nationalism: Triumphs and Challenges in the Long Nineteenth Century and Beyond

—*Daniella Sarnoff*

Nationalism is an intrinsic part of what historians often refer to as the long nineteenth century (1789–1914). The story of nationalism also encompasses a grand swath of foundational European historical events—with its perceived origins in the new rhetoric and political claims to sovereignty residing in the nation during the French Revolution, through the birth of the nation state throughout much of Europe—notably the unification of Germany and Italy, the changing face of nationalist political affinities (from liberalism to conservatism) and the connection to late nineteenth and early twentieth-century imperialism, twentieth-century fascism, and its' change and endurance in late twentieth-century/early twenty-first-century Europe.

The endurance and 'success' of nationalism is readily apparent as most countries regard the nation-state as the most legitimate expression of a people and polity. The power of nationalist narratives, as well as the endurance of nationalist symbols (flags, anthems and national traditions), is further evidence of its ideological and organizing power. Nationalism, because of its impact in reframing much of nineteenth-century European cartography and political philosophy, has also been the topic of sustained academic analysis. There are numerous theories about the development of nationalism, as well as early scholarly creations and manipulation of history to help support the nationalist endeavour in new nations.

PRECURSORS TO NATIONALISM

As noted in the brief discussion of nationalism in Chapter 3 of the volume *Social Movements and Cultural Currents 1789–1945*, the idea of nationalism was a late eighteenth-century invention, but has some connections to earlier concepts of commitment and identification with a place, region, or ruler of an area. While the novelty, and many would argue the modernism, of nationalism is addressed later in the chapter, it is fitting to try and put this development into some context. The most significant context is the revolutionary rhetoric and fervour of the French Revolution, which is also addressed below. But it may be helpful to give some sense of identity to place before that period.

Today we may think that nations (that is, some coherent expression of a state as it relates to a population and geography) are the assumed arrangements of leadership, governments, culture and people, having the great legitimacy that they have. Further, we may extend that thinking to imagine that nations are timeless, that Germany or Italy has always existed. In fact, the notion of a nation being the most legitimate (or best) formulation of a state, rulers, people, etc. is a comparatively new idea. While one might argue that an idea of an English national identity has existed for centuries (perhaps to the Magna Carta of 1215) or that French National identity can be traced to the Frankish Kings or Joan of Arc, in fact, both British and French concepts of national identity belong more closely to later centuries—to the eras of the English Revolution and the French Revolution. Of course, for both countries the concept of the nation evolved over the course of the eighteenth and nineteenth centuries (and continues to evolve). And yet, as we look at the nineteenth-century Britain and France were two countries of Europe with the oldest and most pronounced sense of national identity. In many ways they were the exception.

To get a fuller understanding of the flux of the nineteenth century and to capture the novelty of national conceptions and identifications one might more aptly focus on Italy and Germany. The late nineteenth century saw the creation of Italy and Germany from principalities, separated by language, different forms of leadership, and economic development, into nations. This meant there was significant and immediate upheaval in those places; however, the actual process of creating the nation also included ongoing and long-term changes. And, while there are similarities in nation-state-building histories (including impacts on culture, region, religious identity, economic development, military structure and education), no nation shared the exact process with another.

The nationalism of the nineteenth century also helped to create a teleological view of the nation. That is, the idea that the nation was fated for certain greatness, that all that came before was to lead, inexorably, to the nation's great status and presumed superiority to others. The believed 'destiny' of a nation could be constructed—using history, folklore, culture, religion and language—which aided greatly in the necessary work of building a nation. National myths—often calling on ancient lore and stretched to reach its relevance to contemporary peoples and places—were powerful ways of asserting a national past, and hence the legitimacy or authenticity of a nation that had, perhaps, by 1900 only truly existed for 30 years.

Much of nineteenth- (and eighteenth-) century nationalism had what many would consider a liberal bent—that is, the belief that a nation was based on equals and that there could be a brotherhood of citizens across national lines and a potential inclusiveness of nationalism. Modern nationalism is generally dated to the French Revolution (1789–1801) because of the French revolutionaries' equation of nation, state, and territory and the assertion that sovereignty resided in the nation and the people, not the monarch. Most French revolutionary rhetoric and ideals were inspired by the Enlightenment: individualism (hence the call for individual (male) suffrage), freedom of the press and religious expression, increased secularism, the primacy of reason, economic rationalism and progress, the rule of law (not men) which was to be applied equally to all citizens. Nationalism inspired the hopes of a free citizenry who considered themselves instrumental to their own sovereignty and intent on an inclusive ideal of the brotherhood of nations who would all encourage free thought and open trade conducive to prosperity and progress. Of course, that Enlightenment rhetoric had never entirely born itself out. Women, non-Christians and non-whites had consistently been ignored in the extension of equal status in the nation, or, their access was continuously deferred.

However, by the end of the nineteenth century, and certainly by the time of overwhelming imperial competition between nations in the years leading up to World War I, that liberal view of nationalism was being replaced by a more competitive and exclusionary conception of nationalism. Further, as we see, the development of national identities was not so straightforward. Competing cultural and religious identities would have great meaning for people and would complicate the development of European nationalism.

THE FRENCH REVOLUTION: THE ORIGINS OF NATIONALISM

The details of the French Revolution are available in the first volume of the series. But a reminder of the main accomplishments and legacy are integral to understanding the spread and relative success of nationalism in the late nineteenth century. In addition, discussion of the theories of nationalism, which appear later in this chapter, rest on some understanding of the novelty of events, rhetoric and ideological significance of the French Revolution and its era. Without recounting the structure of pre-revolutionary France and its upheaval from the 1780s through the rise of Napoleon, a student of history might recall that the most significant accomplishment of the French Revolution is that it ended the absolute monarchy of the most powerful dynasty in Europe and brought a form of republican democracy to a major continental power of Europe. The French First Republic would be short lived, but the ideals and language of representative democracy, calling upon reason and the Enlightenment, would not be undone. Significantly, the language of that revolution, and the justification for such a momentous upheaval, would be the language of the nation—the first such invocation for ideological democracy. From that time forward, many would argue that the foundational concept of sovereignty—the right and a capacity to rule—resided with the people was a truism that was perpetually expressed and reaffirmed by the existence and functioning of a nation. For the first time, the power to rule would be seen as emanating from and being justly exercised by a wilful coming together of a people in a new form—a nation.

THE LEGACIES OF THE REVOLUTION: DOCUMENTS, SYMBOLS AND REALITIES

One of the symbols and political philosophical documents that emerged from the French Revolution was 'The Declaration of the Rights of Man and the Citizen.' This became the clearest expression of the philosophy of the Revolution. Adopted by the National Assembly in August 1789, it declared that 'the representatives of the French people have resolved to set forth the natural, inalienable and sacred rights of man. These rights were liberty, property, security, and resistance to oppression. Further, the source of all sovereignty resided essentially in the nation. The law became the expression of the general will and all citizens attained the right to participate personally, or through their representatives, in its formation.'

While it also established laws about search and seizure, arrest, freedom of expression and opinion (religion) the most significant accomplishment was that it placed the power to rule with the nation, as determined by 'the people'. The nation being presented in this document, in many ways the founding document of both the French nation and nationalist ideology, is a nation and nationalism based on inclusiveness, not exclusivity. This sentiment, of a free and equal people who come together as a nation and as such express their collective interests and assert their individual freedoms (at the same time!) will be the source of much nineteenth-century nationalist ideal. Nationalist leaders from the soon to exist Latin American nations to a nascent Italian nation will assert their individual rights to exist and come together as free people in a nation using language of government, law, and dream found in much of the revolutionary document production of the French Revolution.

While the 'Declaration of the Rights of Man' came from a specific moment in the French Revolution, its universality—its assertion that all men were equal in rights (not just French men) would become part of the spirit of nationalism. The limits of this universality should be noted. The author of 'Declaration of the Rights of Woman and the Female Citizen,' Olympe de Gouges, will not find such an enthusiastic audience. And, while slavery was abolished in France, it persisted in French territories (where there actually were slaves). On the one hand, nationalism seemed to emphasize specific place, people and community, yet the power of this early nationalism was its desire and ability to reach across and beyond nations (even those that do not yet exist!). The universality of expression, coupled with the specificity of national sovereignty claimed by nationalists across the globe, became the greatest legacy of the French Revolution.

Nationalists for centuries to come would be left with the core concepts and language of nationalism. The language of nationalism referred to a wide variety of symbols, ideas, memories and words that proved to be very powerful not only for France, but also for the development of nations in general. For example, what would be adopted as the national anthem, the *Marseillaise*, told the story of upheaval, bravery and bloodshed that brought about the French nation. And it did so using powerful symbols that would become 'standard' in nationalism. It recounted the idea of family, but the family made public. The family became the organic centre of human life, and the nation would be offered up as the family made public and writ large. The paternal ideal of the country (the king/father) was transformed in revolutionary nationalism into a brotherhood (Lynn Hunt, *The Family Romance of the French Revolution*, 1992). Certainly suffering and sacrifice would be a part of nationalist storytelling, and the French Revolution, a bloody one to be sure, set the language of that legacy.

The French Revolution, and the new French nation, also created the symbols of much political nationalism throughout the continent. The French tricolour flag (adopted to incorporate the white of the Bourbon dynasty with the red and blue of Paris) became the exemplar of a national flag (and rather specifically not the crest of a royal family). It was not by accident that the flags of new nations from Italy, Germany and Ireland were tricolours almost identical to the French flag. The political terminology of Left and Right came from the National Assembly debates in France—that is, the political ideology of representation was based on where representatives sat in relation to others (monarchist to the right, republican to the left).

The idea of accessibility and connection to the nation was a key component of French revolutionary nationalism and played itself out over and over again in different countries and would-be nations. The appeal of nationalist language (whether constitutions or anthems) was to citizens, not subjects. The new culture of France established by revolution (a calendar not connected to the Catholic/Christian Church, a metric system that decoupled measurements from royal history and asserted a rational approach of the Scientific Revolution and the Enlightenment) was also a show of the power of the nation separate, and potentially in opposition to, clergy and church. A requirement to tax all in the nation, not granting privilege to one citizen over another, including the nationalization of church-held lands, all indicated that the nation and its brotherhood took precedence over particulars. Clergy were to declare allegiance to the Nation (Civil Oath of Clergy). New myths and rituals of the nation replaced the old rituals and myths of the past (the Supreme Being, for the Biblical god, Temple to Reason for the Church or King, the Revolutionary Calendar, which was not based on old myths and rulers). Even educational reform, which was addressed more fully in nation-building, would come to be a nationalist cause, not just the province and privilege of the wealthy or under the auspices of religious orders.

NAPOLEONIC LEGACY

While within French and Revolutionary historiography the debate continues about whether Napoleon Bonaparte was a revolutionary in furthering the ideals of the French Revolution or its destroyer, there is little doubt that he was responsible for creating, and insisting upon, many of the conventions and apparatuses of a nation state. He established a certain degree of secularization within the country—essentially creating, maintaining and asserting state power over religious power. In its place came a range of political institutions—whether in the form of internal departments of the country (which itself had some predecessor) or new ministries that brought increased secularization of political institutions (France and European Continent). The reign of Napoleon (even as he turned the republic into an empire), further entrenched the concepts and functions of a nation into the consciousness and lives of those in France and the conquered territories. He created a new constitution, bureaucratic structures and a social hierarchy that was no longer dependent on birth (aristocracy) but on civil state service. Under Napoleon religion (Catholicism, Protestantism, Judaism) came under the purview of a new ministry. A network of state schools challenged previous Catholic near-monopoly over education. A system of meritocracy rewarded service to the nation-state (for example, the French Legion of Honor, established in 1802).

And, famously, the Napoleonic Code of 1804 established the laws of a land increasingly marked by the interest of a rising middle class. Property rights were strengthened in the new Code, the law code was made uniform throughout the territory of France, and the hierarchy of the family and property owners (and the power of both the male head-of-household and the property-owner) became as clear as the role of the state (workers unions were forbidden and women were legally dependent on male heads of households).

The massive and expanding army that was necessary to achieve the military victories of the Napoleonic armies created another vehicle to assert and reinforce the individual subordination to the state and nation. National conscription—required military service—was another way that the individual became linked more clearly to the state, and came to see the interests of the nation as their own.

As these ideas were carried into the territories that fell to the Napoleonic army there would be an interesting and transformative reception of the ideas. Many people, though not the displaced monarchs of these lands, would come to embrace this new approach of the supremacy of the nation over tradition, while, at the same time, they would bristle at the very soldiers and bureaucrats who were the messengers of these ideas. Many people became enamoured of the potentially liberating and democratizing ideas of nationalism, but sought its success in their own countries, free of French and Napoleonic occupation.

The crushing defeat of Napoleon (in Russian and then Waterloo) is a legend of military history. Less discussed is the impact that Napoleon's march had on individual countries long after Napoleon was imprisoned in Elba. While the monarchs of Europe tried to turn back the clock, to a pre-Napoleonic and pre-Revolutionary France, it simply was not possible. The revolution and Napoleon ushered in changes to the social, political and cultural world of Europe and all of those changes could in many ways stem from the very first nationalist rhetoric of the French Revolution. The nationalist discourse, and its attendant language and symbols, transformed Europe irrevocably into a continent of nations, and by extension, created a dominant world view that considered and considers nations and nationhood to be the most legitimate and recognized form of communal identity and existence.

RESTORATION EUROPE

With the defeat of Napoleon in 1815, the allies—Austria, Great Britain Prussia and Russia—set the terms of peace. Deciding on France's borders, undoing the Empire, and settling the accounts on the money that France was required to pay to conquered areas (indemnity) were certainly priorities for the powers. But perhaps the overarching concern was how to structure a peace, and a Europe that could withstand the corrosive force of a new ideology: revolutionary and liberal nationalism. The events of the French Revolution and the infectious ideas brought by revolutionary and Napoleonic armies—the ideas of creating nations and therefore undoing centuries old-dynastic monarchies made the monarchs and other conservative leaders of Europe very nervous. The worst case was that they might meet the same fate as Louis XVI (the guillotine, as you recall). But no better was the possibility of a constitutional monarchy which recognized the power and legitimacy of the people in ruling an area: a nation. There was no doubt that the French Revolution was a horrific warning to the crowned heads of Europe. In addition, the empire-building that Napoleon had undertaken was a threat to them all as well. This destabilizing force needed to be curbed. And as France had been responsible for both of them, she had to be controlled—for the sake of monarchies everywhere! In many ways the crowns of Europe met to try and turn back the revolutionary clock. When all is considered they did this with some short-term success.

To begin, they restored the Bourbon Family to the throne of France. Louis XVIII (the son of Louis XVII was passed over) became the King, though there was no question this was not undoing the work of the French Revolution. The absolute power of the French kings (as well as the power of the nobility) was not ultimately restored—nationalism and constitutionalism were too established. A certain 'Balance of Power' (associated with Prince Metternich of Austria) was created which featured an elaborate systems of alliances and treaties. To bind the fate of these monarchies together and in that keep them all in check seemed to offer the best hedge against the corrosive force of nationalism.

This system did not stem the tide of nationalist and democratic movements, but it did hamper European-wide war. The alliances created in 1815 would exist in some forms until 1914, but, in the meantime, the transitions, especially as it related to the idea of the nation, were incredibly dramatic. From economic ideology, cultural ideals and linguistic identity to claims for political rights, nationalism and nationalist rhetoric and action utterly transformed the world of the nineteenth century.

LIBERAL PHASE OF NATIONALISM

As one considers the landscape of Europe and nationalism in the middle decades of the nineteenth century, one is struck that nationalists could be found across the political spectrum. However, usually nationalists allied themselves with an ideology that was critical of conservatism and monarchy. After all, monarchy held together empires that gave no great concern to the ethnic, linguistic or cultural identity (or perceived difference) of the subjects of the land. Further, nationalists were most vocal when the cultural or linguistic identities of a group didn't align geographically with a state's boundaries. At that point nationalists rallied for control over that territory. Hence, nationalists posed a threat to monarchs who ruled that territory. In general, the nationalists of the nineteenth century considered themselves advocates for the masses and envisioned a place where the members of a new nation-state would be equal, or at least more equal than under a conservative monarchy.

Dramatic changes swept through Europe over the course of the nineteenth century. Industrialization, urbanization and the attendant conflicts they would cause—including the creation of a new social class of people (the industrial working class) would be some of the context of the waves of revolution in Europe in the 1830s and 1840s. The changed pace and structure of life—from agricultural work in a village replicating a life known to generations, to a life that would be increasingly centred on urban populations who had moved from the countryside for the economic opportunity of the new factory system, the overcrowding and poor public health connected to densely settled urban populations whose housing was quickly and cheaply constructed. The revolutions of 1830s and 1840s were the result of many different groups trying to address the problems of the industrial revolution. Inspired by ideologies that had been developing in post-French Revolution Europe, and sensitive to the evolving role of the government, as well as the great disparities of wealth evident in city life, many of the revolutions of the mid-nineteenth century were launched in the context of developing liberalism, socialism and nationalism. The full scope of ideologies cannot all be examined here, but it is worth noting that while liberals sought economic rights and freedom that would guarantee very little government intervention in economic matters (widely interpreted), and socialists argued that the very structure of the government and economy privileged the bourgeois over the workers, nationalists argued for rights and freedoms, often political autonomy, for certain groups based on shared linguistic or cultural identity. So, while 1830 would be a time of attempted (and failed) revolutions in Europe that sought to overthrow some of the dominant monarchies—and question the dominance of liberal economic rhetoric (which usually banned workers associations) it would also be era of nationalist movements, most notably by Polish, German, Italian and Irish nationalists. Nationalism was most complicated and fraught in the failing Austrian and Ottoman Empires as the territory encompassed so many different linguistic and cultural groups, each beginning to assert their desire for political autonomy. Across the empires many groups—Czechs, Slovaks, Croats, Poles, Italians, Magyars, Slovenes, Romanians and Serbs demanded recognition of their cultural, linguistic and religious identity, as well as connected political rights. Polish nationalists revolted against the dominance of Russia, as well as the Austrian Empire. Scholars and intellectuals created works in their mother tongue, not the language of Empire, and sought to kindle new interest in languages that had been subsumed by the language of the empire. Poles would find inspiration in new Polish poetry (notably Adam Mickiewicz, 1798–1855), who would in turn inspire Giuseppe Mazzini's (1805–1872) Young Italy nationalist movement, which would in turn inspire the Young Ireland of Irish nationalists. While there were many different forms of nationalists—some constructed in opposition to other nationalizing groups—there were also many shared intellectual origins and inspirations.

While this book focuses on Europe, it is worth noting that nationalist rhetoric and ideals inspired individuals and groups beyond Europe. In Latin America nationalist concepts were taken up by many who would go on to lead revolutionary independence movements. In 1822 Brazil successfully won its national autonomy from its imperial colonizer, Portugal. Similarly, in 1830 Venezuela would push for, and win, its independence from Spain. These are just two examples of the sweeping tide of nationalism that crossed the Atlantic and often met with greater success in Latin America than in Europe.

Nationalism also had a great impact beyond politics or the cartography of the globe. In art, music and other areas of culture the effect of nationalism was clear, often through the movement of Romanticism. Romanticism, also discussed in detail in the first volume, stressed sentiment over logic and nature over the technology of the period. Romantics were often seen as the 'antidote' or the cultural opposition to the overwhelming nineteenth-century changes of industrialization and urbanization. They stressed the mystical over the rational and created works that were often critical of the damage (or potential damage) of new nineteenth-century technology. For example, Mary Shelley's Frankenstein, written in 1818, presented the possibility of future men who were the monstrous botched constructions of modern technology. Eugene Delacroix (1798–1863) was a French painter of the Romantic school whose work can be seen as both a product of and a contributor to the nationalist dialogue of the period. Delacroix created paintings of historical scenes (real or imagined) that came to express the emotional appeal of nationalism as well as the sentimentality towards history. In these paintings the very history of the French nation was created. Delacroix's 'Marianne into Battle' created a nationalist icon in the figure of liberty leading the people into battle (an 1830 battle that would have been a 'failure', see below). The historical novels of Sir Walter Scott (1771–1832) are also examples of the connections of culture and nationalism, and especially the cultural undertaking of creating the nation through cultural works of the Romantics. Despite the lost battles of the mid-nineteenth century, the figures, stories, music and literature created by the Romantics of the period would be successful in creating the spirit of nationalist ideals of the period and would be essential to the myth-making of new and evolving nations.

REVOLUTIONARY ATTEMPTS OF THE 1830s AND 1840s

Is it too cynical to begin such a section on the note that, by and large, the attempted revolutions of the 1830s and 1840s were failures? If nothing else it may convey the frustrations felt by revolutionaries and nationalists of the period (not to mention the frustrations felt by those who study the period!).

Given the upheaval and long-term impact of the French Revolution it is unsurprising that the revolutions of 1830 and 1840s began in France and moved into other European countries. After the execution of Louis XVI and the rise and fall of Napoleon Bonaparte the Congress of Vienna installed a new Bourbon monarch, Louis XVIII, to the French throne. Louis XVIII ruled until 1824, and at his death Charles X was installed as King. Charles was intent on restoring the Bourbon monarchy to its fuller, pre-revolutionary power and over the years of his reign he became increasingly authoritarian, passing repressive laws. By 1830, Charles X had dissolved the legislature and passed extremely controlling censorship laws. The level of repression, and what seemed a betrayal of national ideals from the French Revolution, spurred many people to the 'barricades' (a reference that began to have shorthand meaning for revolutionary activity). The new and expanding working class, the poor, and students took to the streets to protest the repressive laws and to rally, in the name of the nation, for the expansion of national representation. There was some success at this stage of the 1830 revolution and Charles X fled France (for Britain) and in his place a 'bourgeois' king, Louis Philippe inherited the throne. Dressed in his 'banker' suits Louis Philippe made overtures to those who had protested his authoritarian predecessor, reversed some of the repressive legislation and increased the percentage of the population who were given the right to vote. While still well below even one tenth of the adults in the country, this move did quell the revolutionary fervour of some participants, but would not settle any national or political issues for the long term. It does, however, highlight the extent to which expanded suffrage was a common refrain throughout the century and was an argument argued in the name of nation. One of the great legacies of the French Revolution was the idea that the 'people' (not just aristocracy) should have the right to participate in the construction of the national legislature. That is, in a nation the right to govern should be granted by those who are governed. This basic ideal would be the core of national political discussions, the expansion of mass politics during the nineteenth century of nationalism, and the yardstick of national democracies as they began to expand throughout the world. Later, in the twentieth century, a version of this would also be the discussion around national self-determination for fledgling nations.

Among the nationalist successes of the 1830 uprisings one can count Belgium. Annexed to the Netherlands in 1815, the Belgians gained their independence from the Dutch a scant 15 years later, becoming one of the new nations of the nineteenth century and with a new king, Leopold. Both Louis Philippe and Leopold would bear new and telling monarchical titles, Louis Philippe as 'King of the French' and Leopold as 'King of the Belgians'. While this may seem a slight change from what would have been 'King of France' or 'King of Belgium' the titles do mark a shift in the conceptualization of the monarch—the king now ruled at the behest of the people, not simply over a territory. So, even within the persistent monarchies of Europe we see an acceptance and acquiescence to the significance of nationalism.

The revolutions of the 1840s brought together people across a spectrum of ideologies: liberals, socialist and nationalists in many countries began to rally against the persistent conservative monarchies. Many countries suffered persistent and mounting problems. The population of Europe was increasing and yet there had been food shortages going into the 1840s. Despite the ascendance of industrialization there was still pernicious underemployment. The potato blight which destroyed crops across Europe, impoverished farmers, and led to exorbitantly high food prices further exacerbated the suffering of the vast majority of people who still extracted their livelihood from the land. The problems created a situation in which former political sparring partners began to join together against a common foe. The blight and food shortages were felt sharply in Ireland, whose population had increased more relative to the rest of Europe, and which also relied heavily on potatoes for calorie intake. The hunger in Ireland, as elsewhere, added another dimension to the brewing political critiques of the status quo.

In France in 1848 revolutionary groups would be successful in establishing a Second Republic (harkening back to the First Republic established by the French Revolution). From February through the 'June Days' of 1848 workers, liberals, and socialist of France came together and demonstrated against the lack of government interest in addressing their economic and political concerns. Once again 'going to the barricades' the French revolutionaries were successful, to some extent, in the summer of 1848 in creating 'workshops' that provided government-funded work for many who needed it. However, the costly plans and the continued demands of those further on the left of the political spectrum began to alarm more centrist liberals and they turned their support to Louis Napoleon, a nephew of Napoleon Bonaparte. By 1852 Louis Napoleon had crowned himself Napoleon III and, like his uncle, turned the French Republic into an Empire (this time the 'Second Empire').

A similar uprising took place in Italy in 1848 with new focus on Italian unification, and a distinct whiff of nationalist rhetoric in the air. The nationalist movements of Giuseppe Garibaldi and Giuseppe Mazzini became more vocal in their demands to push the Austrian Hapsburgs out of Italy.

Similarly, in Vienna Magyar nationalists rioted in expressions of desired autonomy for Hungary—separate from Austrian rule. While some of these calls would be answered in the Austrian-ruled areas of the Balkans there would be a great deal of competition for national autonomy, and soon competing nationalisms would come to define the region. Many would call for the recognition of rights for ethnic minorities, but the claims to territory and territorial autonomy of some groups would (or could) come into conflict with the claimed rights and territories of other groups. In the mid-nineteenth century, those conflicts would be used by the multi-national empire of Austro-Hungary, who benefitted from the divisions amongst different minority groups.

While in the end the revolutions of 1848 were 'failed revolutions' the forces they unleashed had a huge impact on later generations and would not go away. To that extent the revolutions were a serious blow to the structure of the continent as set by the Concert of Europe in 1815. The revolutionary attempts of 1848 set the stage for the continued upheaval, arguments and expansion that would create new nations and that would eventually bring old and new nations into conflict.

NATION-BUILDING IN LATE NINETEENTH CENTURY

Throughout much of the nineteenth century, even after the failed revolutions of the 1830s and 1840s, nationalists in many countries advocated for the unification of their people and countries. Inspired by the ideals of the French Revolution and the Enlightenment, nationalists in Italy and Germany were responsible for a huge shift in European political and social history that had great repercussions for Europe and beyond, to this day. Italy and German were the largest European countries to unify into nation-states in the nineteenth century. While the details of national culture, identity and belonging may not have been immediately resolved, the mere fact of a unified military and state structure in a previously fragmented part of Europe would effect Europe, and the world, throughout the course of the late nineteenth and early-twentieth century and have a huge impact on the development of European imperialism and fascism.

ITALIAN UNIFICATION

In 1815, at the end of the Congress of Vienna, Italy was an association of seven regional kingdoms and duchies, much of it recognizable as the structural remains from hundreds of years earlier. In the south the Kingdom of the Two Sicilies (which included Naples and Sicily) dominated, in the north the Papal States (including Rome) and the Kingdom of Piedmont (which included Genoa and Turin) and Sardinia were the dominant powers. The fragmentation of what we refer to here as Italy had been the reality since the end of the Roman Empire in 476 C.E. We might pause and consider the difficulty of referring to an 'Italy' before the actual existence of what we can currently find on the map designated as such. As noted, it was a collection of states and principalities, ruled by different aristocratic dynasties, with different regional dialects, and different economies. Those fragmented states were bounded geographically by what we would recognize on the current map as Italy—the 'boot' jutting out into the Mediterranean. Much of Italy had been invaded, conquered, and ruled by the Napoleonic onslaught in Europe and there remained, in the North, some legacy of civil codes and rational administration brought by the conquering French.

The political fragmentation was joined by significant economic distinctions between the north and south. The north was much more prosperous than the south, with industrial development and developed trade and markets, compared to the south's overwhelmingly agricultural economy and a much more impoverished region. Other realities seemed to stand in the way of Italy's unification: The Austrian Hapsburgs continued to rule in Venetia (Venice) and Lombardy, the Pope had significant influence throughout all of the Italian states (but actual control over the Papal States), and the social structure of the south was apparent in its political structures where local elites held onto an old system of patronage. Certainly those who benefitted from a decentralized and archaic system would not be advocates of a new centralized system that would usurp their remaining power. And, in any case, there were competing nationalist ideals in Italy. And yet these issues would be overcome in 1870 and would produce the resurgence (Risorgimento) of Italy.

Harkening back to the 1830s and 1840s there were earlier nationalist movements in Italy. As noted, the 'Young Italy' of Giuseppe Mazzini (1805–1872), formed in 1833, had been part of the early wave of republican attempts at Italian unification. Mazzini was an outspoken advocate of chasing out Austrian control of key Italian areas (Venice, Parma) and a great exemplar of the liberal ideals of early nationalism, believing that Europe could be a brotherhood of democratic nations.

While the Mazzini-led uprisings (in 1834–1836 and 1844) ultimately failed, his legacy of liberal Italian nationalism was an important context both for the evolution of republican nationalism in Europe, as well as the eventual success of Italian unification. But Mazzini's republican nationalism was just one expression of Italian nationalist sentiment—and it would prove not to be the one that prevailed in the first Italian State. That accomplishment would be accomplished by uniting Piedmontese (northern) liberal aristocratic leadership with some (at least lip service to) more populist, ideals.

The lead characters in the Risorgimento (1815–1861) were King Victor Emmanuel II (ruled 1849–1878), Camillo di Cavour (1810–1861), and the ideals of Giuseppe Mazzini and Giuseppe Garibaldi (1807–1882). However, in the end, Italian nationalism and unification would prove to be a highly orchestrated manipulation by the political elite. This does not mean that there was not mass support for Italian unification, simply that the story of nationalism is a combination of popular action, demands for mass politics and the *realpolitik* of political elites.

Victor Emmanuel was the King of Piedmont-Sardinia, the most prosperous area of Italy, and the area most influenced ideologically by French Revolutionary and Napoleonic ideas (a legacy of their time under French rule). Victor Emmanuel hoped to expand the reach of Piedmont-Sardinia, and his personal realm, by the gradual expansion of Piemontese control. He may not have been up to the task by himself, but his newly appointed prime minister, Count Camillo di Cavour, was also keenly interested in seeing the expansion of Piedmontese control (including the liberal ideology of aristocrats like himself). By the time of his appointment as Prime Minister Cavour had shown himself to be solidly in the political centre (not a republican of the left, nor with the *ancien regime* right of nobility and church). He also embraced the importance of economic development (cultivated by his stint as minister of commerce and agriculture) and his ideas were clear expressions of the established nation-states of Britain and France: liberal secular values, a close eye towards increased trade and business developments for the small middle-class, a civil code that would apply to all and railway construction as a state investment (which could move consumer goods and conscripts). Clearly these policies put him solidly within the legacy of French national development and it did secure him a spot as a recognized proponent of Italian nationalism—beyond his Piedmontese roots and world. Cavour's constitutional monarchical nationalism still existed alongside Mazzini's more populist nationalist. Although Mazzini's more populist nationalism had, as noted above, been dealt a number of defeats over the preceding 15 years, his hopes of a republican Italy that was part of a brotherhood of democratic nations in Europe still held popular appeal. His belief, like others in the 'Young Europe' group of which 'Young Italy' was just one part, was that true nationalism originated with the people, not the rulers.

As these two strands of Italian nationalism and unification grew, and often conflicted with each other, the reality of the limits of both kinds of Italian nationalism was obvious as long as Austria/Hapsburg continued to rule important areas of northern and central Italy. In the end Cavour used a time-honoured approach: use one foreign power against another. Over a series of agreements and negotiations Cavour managed to use the French, under the leadership of Napoleon III, to help weaken, and ultimately dislodge, Austrian power in Italy. Cavour's manipulations would get some of the job done! The Crimean War, which the British and French had joined in 1853 in support of the Ottoman Empire against Russia (and which proved to be one of the few international European Wars to overtake Europe between the Concert of Vienna and World War I), provided Cavour with a diplomatic entry. He offered to have Piedmont-Sardinia join with French and British allies with the hope, if not promise, that this would give him some role in the peace process that was sure to come at war's end. On the other (French) side, there was interest in cultivating French presence in their neighbouring land's prosperous northern region—though they would not mind getting a region or two for France out of the deal (notably Nice and Savoy). In a formal agreement of 1859 France essentially promised support to Piedmont-Sardinian in any war against Austria that could prove useful diplomatically (which certainly included the benefit of two hoped-for regions). By the spring of that year Napoleon III led troops into northern Italy to help Piedmont fight Austria (ostensibly because of Austria's aggression and announcement that it would draft men from their Italian provinces into their imperial army). Austria's perceived aggression worked well for the larger European diplomatic structure as other powers, including Austria's usual allies the Prussians and other German states, refused to come to her side.

Defeat of the Austrian Hapsburgs meant that Piedmont had Lombardy, and by 1860 and the Treaty of Turin, Piedmont-Sardinia could add Modena, Parma and Bologna to the areas that were now unified and united in a constitutional monarchy. This is not quite the area we call Italy—but Cavour's form of nationalism could certainly claim great success in bringing together most of northern and central Italy.

The unification of southern Italy would fall to an inheritor of Mazzini's brand of nationalism. Giuseppe Garibaldi (1807–1882) had been part of the 'Young Italy' movement and had been active in the battles to push the Austrian Hapsburgs out of Lombardy and Rome in 1848 and 1849, and the more recent battles of 1859. Garibaldi wanted Italian unification to go even further and had visions of evicting the Austrians further, out of Venice, and eradicating French dominance in Rome. He raised a volunteer army with hopes of accomplishing this (something that Cavour, despite his rather different brand of nationalism, allowed in the hopes that it might annul France's diplomatic claims to Nice and Savoy). While Garibaldi's venture in Rome failed he soon used his army of volunteers in another nationalist attempt. In early April 1860, an uprising against the ruling monarch (Francis II) of the Kingdom of the Two Sicilies broke out (over high taxes of various kinds). Garibaldi (with secret encouragement by Cavour) landed in Sicily with his 'Red Shirts'. Garibaldi's 1,000 men (1,089 apparently!) were welcomed by many as nationalist liberators and his 'army' was successful in taking Palermo in May. By fall 1860 Garibaldi and his followers were successful in Naples and Garibaldi had claimed a right to rule on behalf on the Piedmont-Sardinia King Victor Emmanuel. The next logical step was for Garibaldi and his red shirts to march on Rome and evict the pope (potentially raising French ire, as French troops protected the pope) or marching on Venetia to evict the Austrians (potentially raising Prussian ire).

Cavour took this opportunity to send the Piedmontese army to Rome, in one fell swoop overcoming papal resistance to unifying Italy, and also asserting Piedmont-Sardinia's nationalist power over that of Garibaldi and his republican nationalists.

By November 1860, Victor Emmanuel of Piedmont Sardinia had joined Garibaldi in Naples (and had secured support from the major southern cities, as well as the Papal States) to have Italian unification under Piedmont-Sardinia continue. Victor Emmanuel of Piedmont-Sardinia became King Victor Emmanuel II of Italy (March 1861). Within five years Italy would also come to include Venetia (an outcome of Prussian and Austrian battle that had meant an Italian-Prussian alliance). Another battle involving Prussian troops (the Franco-Prussian War, which started in 1870) would provide Italy with the opportunity to bring Rome into the national fold. When French troops left Rome to fight the Prussians, Italian troops moved in. There was overwhelming Roman support to join Italy and, as it remains today, the temporal power of the pope was reduced to the Vatican, and Rome became the capital of the Italian state.

While the role of particular leaders and the political context of events, agreements and manipulations that led to Italian unification are essential parts of the Italian national story, it is not the whole story. The significant role played by the aristocracy and political elite should be balanced with a social analysis of the Italian story. As historian Lucy Riall points out, 'A non-political approach to the Risorgimento... allows us to broaden our investigation to include the slower, structural developments occurring alongside these more spectacular events; and it pays attention to those who were not leaders, or not even followers, and to their experience of historical change.' (Riall, *Risorgimento: The History of Italy from Napoleon to Nation State*, (2009, p. 72)

For example, what if we consider, as Riall does, the movement of Italian nationalism from the perspective of the Risorgimento as bourgeois revolution, an analysis that had traction even in the late nineteenth century—calling upon the historiographical argument that posited the French Revolution as a middle-class revolution of culture and economics? Riall argues that studies of the Italian middle-class make clear the difficulty of providing a definition of the middle-class in Italy and no consensus on whether this 'class' had any great investment in the ideals of Italian nationalist unification. Claiming that the Italian bourgeois was not so associated with industrialization (as the bourgeois of Europe supposedly were), Riall points out that well into the end of the nineteenth century, middle-class Italians invested in land (traditional economic power). Nor did they wrest political power away from the aristocracy.

In many ways the unified Italian nation remained quite conservative and there was no great push for change by a liberal middle-class (Riall, pp. 73–77). However, nationalizing Italy did create many new bureaucratic state structures (administrative, judicial and local) that offered employment to the university-educated sons of the bourgeoisie. Employment was available to non-nobles on the local, as opposed to central, level and would prove to be a significant force of social mobility (Riall, p. 78). In the South and in the North, the networks of power within newly created administrative arms of the state formed one part of new elites—an alternative to the family networks and land-based traditional aristocratic elites.

However, the new middle-class functionaries also had the opportunity to invest in the traditional expression of power and economic interest. Land sold from Church holdings or aristocratic families in decline found buyers in the middle class, thereby transforming the land-owning base of power, yet still evidence of the persistent traditional aspects of the Italian middle class. Land ownership and the networks of family relations became for the middle class the same essential sources of wealth and security that it had been for the aristocracy since the origins of dynastic order (Riall, pp. 79–81). It could also prove an enticement for middle-class support of nationalizing land.

The middle class would also participate in the secular cultural and intellectual worlds of the nascent nation, which in turn transformed the idea of the public sphere, itself a component of the nationalist revolutionary period. The cafés and clubs, scientific establishments and new journals of the period spread a new secular culture across class lines which in turn helped to create a new shared national culture.

Just as a consideration of the emergent bourgeoisie informs a view of the Risorgimento, a consideration of the lower urban and rural classes provides another lens through which to view an emergent Italy. There was anger on the part of the lower classes—they endured many hardships, did not manage to increase much land ownership, were first victims to periodic famines (and here in many ways we see linkages to the Irish national case and the impact of deeply uneven land ownership and cultivation). So, perhaps it is no surprise that when Garibaldi promised land to anyone that joined his army he found a great deal of support from southern peasants. However, others might point out that the Italian peasants, even those who supported the Risorgimento, were also deeply invested in the traditional structures of life—including the relationship, through land, of peasants and nobles and the significant support given to the (anti-nationalist) Catholic Church. While peasants offered up protest and resentment against some of the traditional structures of Italian life (bonded labour, lack of land ownership) that appeared to be on the chopping block under more liberal and nationalist plans, they also supported many traditional relationships and cultures (Church, language) (Riall, pp. 85–91). Pope Pius IX would pose a formidable challenge to the nationalist cause as he asked Italians to choose their loyalties: nation or Church. Given the assumption that these loyalties were incompatible perhaps it is amazing that one could have Catholic nationalists in Italy. But, of course, more accurately it illustrates the extent to which new identities could retain aspects of other identities and bring them into the fold of a new nation.

The story of Italian unification and nationalism is a stunning example of a combination of elite political will and popular actions which did not necessarily translate into a coherent idea of what Italy was or would be. The political reality of the unified nation was achieved, but the country itself remained deeply divided. The new myths of the nation (Mazzini's brotherhood, Garibaldi's redshirts and Piedmontese political leadership), as well as a new tricolour flag, of course, would be particularly important in a nation that had a huge gap in wealth from north to south. At the time of much of the unification in 1860 it is estimated that 98 per cent of Italians did not speak Italian, but a wide range of dialects. This tale begs the question of what did Italian nationalism mean to the newly minted 'Italians'? What made people draw together in this new creation, and fight dearly for this concept that must have still been murky, at best, to most people? In fact, many Italian historians would point out the great tensions of the new Italian state—that many were ambivalent at best about unifying national cultures and were deeply protective of regional and local culture and tradition. Others would point out that despite the focus on the potential liberalism (economic and political) of a unified Italian nation—that there was a tremendous continuity between the Italian nation of the late nineteenth century and the earlier 'Italy' of many duchies. Traditional economies and relationships endured, there was not massive economic change in most areas, conservatism and repression continued to exist, as well as evident political instability and the traditional power of the Church. These things themselves became part of the unifying culture of an imagined Italy.

GERMAN UNIFICATION

The process of German unification shares some characteristics with Italian unification, especially the use of foreign enemies (and battles) to help create national unity, and the work of political elites. At the end of the Congress of Vienna Germany was also an assortment of independently led principalities, divided by religion and regional politics. The dominant power among the others was the northern area of Prussia. As in Italy, there was general national sentiment, but also many obstacles to national unification. As in Italy, and other areas, that basic question when the idea of the German nation was pondered was what form a German nation would take. Who would or should be the unifying force? There was also, as there was throughout all of Europe where aristocracy and upper classes still enjoyed certain privileges, the fear that all citizens would be proclaimed equal.

Just as Piedmont-Sardinia seemed to offer the greatest potential for leadership in Italy, the German state of Prussia was poised to be the most effective force for German unification. It was the largest state in the German confederation and by many standards the most 'effective'. It had been run and administered for generations by the Hohenzollern family. It was a fairly homogenous area with a majority Protestant and German-speaking population. The Hohenzollerns and the state had the long-established support of powerful landed nobility—the Junkers. In contrast, other states in Germany were much more heterogeneous: having a multinational population (certainly many Austrians), as well as significant Catholic minorities. Prussia, like Piedmont Sardinia, had one of the strongest economies of the region, with early industrialization and tax systems that were fairly conducive to business and trade. And, it should be noted, Prussia had the largest army of the states and a famous officer corps staffed by those powerful nobility, the Junkers. Further, the revolutions that swept through German states in 1848 were thoroughly repressed, and many earlier advocates of German nationalism (especially the middle-class supporters) had left Germany out of fear of arrest and further repression. There seemed no doubt that the powerful Junkers of Prussia would never support a liberal nationalism that promised access to the masses. Some saw Prussian leadership, which they did not doubt would not be republican, as the only possible path to German unifications.

PRUSSIA: WILLIAM I AND BISMARCK

In 1861, William I was crowned King of Prussia. By that time he had ruled for three years for his brother Frederick, who had been deemed insane, and unfit to rule. Prussia had been deeply repressive towards nationalist of the republican stripe during the revolution of 1848 (which, as noted, utterly failed except in making the ruling class even more suspicious of any innovation or change that smelled of liberalism). Nonetheless, in 1849 Frederick had agreed to some constitutional controls over Prussian/Hohenzollern autocratic rule. William I indicated that he would actually honour those constitutional limits to power and be open to political expression beyond the reactionary conservatism of the Junkers. This had almost immediate implication for the Prussian parliamentary elections and, by extension, German nationalism. William's overtures to those outside the conservative status quo meant that a record number of voters voted in the 1858 elections (recall, William was ruling at that time for his brother) for the Prussian parliament. Liberals had a clear victory. Those liberals were men of some wealth (alas, they would not have been permitted to vote otherwise) but they were businessman, not just landed gentry, and they believed that the Prussian state had been helpful to their economic prosperity. Their nationalism was in part driven by a belief that German unification, especially under Prussian control, could be good for business. By this time much of Europe was observing the movements of Italian unification and many German nationalist were impressed with the Italian march to unification. While some Germans considered Austrian defeat at the hands of the Italians (and the manipulations of the French) as a blow to their ally in the German Confederation, others were buoyed by Austria's defeat and considered it one more step toward a Prussian-led German nationalist unification. German nationalism had another outlet: the various pan-German associations that were forming as an expression of greater German nationalism.

The other operating character in nineteenth-century German developments was the Prussian army. Having modernized over the course of the century—and burnishing its reputation after defeating Napoleon in the early part of the century—the Prussian army had established itself a major force in German politics (and, increasingly, as acting on behalf of a conservative government). There was, however, a mounting political crisis because liberals in the Parliament were beginning to assert control over the army's budget—and pointedly not giving the army all it requested. The army was also Junker dominated and many liberals wanted to see that change as well. With the hopes of finding a way to end the growing parliamentary opposition the King turned to Count Otto von Bismarck (1815–1898). Appointed Prime Minister in 1862 Bismarck would soon become synonymous with the new German nation-state and a new calculated international politics of the modern era. Bismarck went on to work on creating a unified Germany which he hoped (and planned) would still be marked by Prussian domination. The Bismarckian approach to German politics would be calculated for Prussian strength and highly bureaucratic and secular, especially important in a region that had seen sectarian violence between Catholics and

Protestants destroy the established political fabric over the course of the Protestant Reformation and Counter-Reformation (beginning in the sixteenth century). It would be an approach that weighed domestic and foreign policy against a larger calculus of German self-interest—based not on any religious or moral code, but an assessment of costs and consequences. There was also a certain disdain for political parties and liberalism. Having been brought in to address a parliamentary crisis Bismarck made use of party politics when necessary, but was not bound by them. He did not hesitate to operate the government without constitutional authority, and in his famous and infamous speech of 1862 proclaimed 'It is not through speeches and majority decisions that the great questions of the day are decided-that was the great mistake of 1848 and 1849-but through blood and iron.'

Blood and iron, and war proved to be an effective plan to achieve the unification of Germany. The two small territories of Schleswig and Holstein presented enough cause to go to war with Denmark (over whether the area and people would be ruled by Denmark even as they were part of the German Confederacy)—a war which the Prussian army, on behalf of the German Confederacy, handily won in the summer of 1864. This war, and victory, brought support from German nationalists of various stripes and would also provide a reason to battle Austria about what role they would play in the governing of the areas—themselves quite close to Austria. The Austro-Prussian War in 1866 also offered opportunity for numerous secret treaties and alliances between Prussian and France (promised territorial gains if they remained outside any Austro-Prussian conflict) and between Prussia and Italy (promising Italy territorial gains if they assisted Prussia in an Austrian defeat). And Bismarck also began to plan ahead towards further German unification and reached out to the German states. Surprisingly, Bismarck offered up a national parliament that would be elected by universal manhood suffrage, not something he had previously supported.

With claims that Austria was preparing its military to assault Prussia in the previously feuded over areas of Schleswig—Holstein Bismarck's Prussian army marched on Austria in Holstein. It was a swift victory for Prussia—achieved in three weeks—which meant the defeat of the smaller southern German Confederation states who had allied themselves with Austria (Saxony, Hanover). That defeat, against some German states and the Austrians, meant the further consolidation of Prussian rule in the North German Confederation, and a stopover for Bismarck on the way to full German unification.

War would prove such a useful device for German nationalism and strides towards unification that it would be put to such use again—in the Franco-Prussian War in 1870. France's loss in the war meant the gain of Alsace and Lorraine for Germany and the final consolidation of the territory of the German nation-state. While the German states lost some independence under the consolidations of the nationalist movements (as did all areas of newly formed larger nation-states) they also could see potential benefits, especially the economic 'pay off' for being part of a larger network of trade, access to funded infrastructure, and the power of a collective policy on trade. In this way it may also be useful to think of the parallel growths of liberal capitalism and nationalism in the nineteenth century. In fact, for many in the new Germany who took issue with much of the conservatism of the Bismarckian state, the bargain struck for liberals was that the material benefits it brought compensated for the on-going traditional structures which was the basis of a united Germany.

There was no massive populist nationalism in Germany at the time of unification, at least not the equal of a Garibaldi-led movement. It was very top-down enactment of national unification. This aspect of German history would be the focus of much discussion, especially with the turn towards exclusionary and aggressive nationalism in twentieth-century Germany. However, it should be pointed out that both Bismarck and Cavour are placed in the same 'realpolitik' camp of politicians. Both ended up being deft at manipulating larger forces (military, regional leaders, economic ideals) and using that to serve personal political gains—which left them, in the tales of nationalism, as those responsible for bringing the fated glory to nations that only needed to realize they were meant to be.

As in Italy many of the traditional structures of society remained. There was not, as a well-known German history book argues, a bourgeois revolution that was the bulwark of German nationalism. There was no equivalent of the French Revolution that overthrew the established structures and created a democratic ideal (Eley and Blackbourn, *The Peculiarities of German History,* 1984). On the other hand—as may be clear by now-there was and is no normal or peculiar path in the process to nationalism. Each nation had their own path—even if there were shared inspirations and some overlap in forms.

The new Germany also created and embraced new icons for the nation. The female allegorical figure of 'Germania'—harkening back to a perceived Greek and Roman past of Germanic people in the territories—became a new symbol for the nation. Her figure (like Marianne of French iconography) would be found on postage stamps soon after unification. The tricolour black-white-and-red flag, which had been used as the flag of the North German Federation (similar but not identical to the modern black-gold-and-red flag), was used as a symbol of a united nation. In Germany, as in other new nations, new symbols and rituals were fashioned, often based on familiar rituals and commemorations of a previous time, but reinforcing a new shared ideal and culture meant to refocus the populace—now citizens—on the greatness that was their new destiny.

NATIONALISM AND THE BALKANS: FOCUS ON SERBIA

While national identity may still be a complicated concept and not homogenous in Italy and Germany, they do not have the ongoing (or at least very recent) points of contention that are evident in the case of Irish and Balkan nationalism. Turning to those two examples will illustrate that while the nineteenth and early twentieth century was the 'height' of nationalist endeavours it did not mean that all national questions were neatly tied up by the post-World War II era. Much of this section on the Irish and Balkan 'questions' will consider the long nineteenth century, the ongoing conflicts over national sovereignty and identity, long-lasting conflict about who the nation truly represents and in what ways.

While Germany had unified under the new German confederacy by 1871, there were many neighbouring lands of Germany that were still part of a large Hapsburg Empire. Within the territorial boundaries of the Hapsburgs there were over 20 'nationalities' including the Magyars (Hungary), Czechs, Croats, Slovaks and Slovenes. This Empire, led by the long-established Hapsburg aristocratic family, was held together through military power and a German-speaking administrative bureaucracy in Vienna. The tide of nationalism felt throughout Europe was felt acutely within the Hapsburg Empire and there was the increasing threat that the multitude of nationalist groups operating (most secretly) would be more than the Hapsburg Empire could bear. Even the 1867 creation of a dual monarchy, Austria–Hungary, which gave some power to the expressions of Magyar nationalism (and yet hoped to contain it in the face of the weakening Hapsburgs) did not seem to offer a real solution.

The story of Balkan nationalism is a particularly complicated and fraught tale, involving the dissolution of two grand and large empires, a land filled with many different identities and national aspirations, and an area torn asunder by numerous invading armies and its own people.

The term Balkan, to apply to a particular area of Europe did not really even come into use until the late nineteenth century/early twentieth century. Yet, as historian Mark Mazower notes, 'At the end of the twentieth-century people spoke as if the Balkans had existed forever. However, two hundred years earlier they had not yet come into being.' (Mazower, location 811–920/2800).

For much of history the term Balkan had referred to the mountain range. This land that had been Roman and then conquered by the Ottomans was a pathway for many travellers to and through Ottoman lands and the term begins to appear in the nineteenth century (no surprise!) and was in use by diplomats and army officers who travelled through the lands. However, even though much of the nineteenth-century geographers still referred to the area as 'European Turkey', which conveys the 'neither here nor there' sense of the place. With so many of the nationalist stirrings in the nineteenth century, many claiming statehood from 'Turkey in Europe', and the rise of Greece, Bulgaria, Serbia and Romania there was the slow erosion of European Turkey. By 1912, and the end of Ottoman power in Europe, the term Balkan was evident and in use. 'In less than half a century, largely as a result of sudden military and diplomatic changes, a new geographical concept rooted itself in everyday parlance, "but", loaded with negative connotations.' (Mazower, location 5/2800).

In a period that saw the unification into large states of previously disunited smaller states (notably Italy and Germany, of course), the opposite happened in the Balkans. In that case a large state (though not necessarily one that had offered national self-determination) broke down into smaller fragments of a once greater unit. The dissolution of the Ottoman and Austro-Hungarian Empires would unleash new forms and variations of nationalist rhetoric and aspirations, ones whose impact would be seen and felt well into the twenty-first-century discussions of the Balkans (Mazower, location 53–97/2800).

As new as the term Balkan was in the nineteenth century, it did refer to a much older relationship amongst many people of different, though frequently linked, ethnic, linguistic and cultural practice. It also referred to a very old relationship between Muslims and Christians living in those areas. While the relationship between Muslims and Christians (and Jews) had been marked by a general Muslim toleration for non-Muslims, and a certain Christian respect for leaders of the Ottoman areas, by the late seventeenth century, Ottoman had become a shorthand in Europe for tyranny, despotism and fanaticism and what was mounting as a perceived clash of cultures between Islam and Christianity. Enlightenment work such as Montesquieu's *Persian Letters* provided the European view of the exotic 'Orient' to Europeans who would only be arm-chair travellers. By the nineteenth century that view had been thoroughly solidified in the imagination of the West.

Part of the complications of nationalism in the Balkans was that nationalist or linguistic categories and identities could prove less significant than religious identities. Over the course of centuries there had been Christian conversion to Islam in the Ottoman Empire; however, 80 per cent of Ottoman Europe remained Christian. As noted, there was generally greater Muslim tolerance for non-Muslims than there was Christian tolerance for non-Christians, but, in addition, because Christians and Jews within the Ottoman Empire paid higher tax, a type of payment for their religious prerogatives, there was not great imperial interest in seeing mass conversion, as it fed the coffers of the empire (Mazower, location 811–920/2800).

So, as the nineteenth century dawned, the division of people in these lands was far greater than the divisions encountered in a near-total Catholic Italy, or a Protestant and Catholic Germany which enjoyed significant linguistic cohesion. (Certainly Italy and Germany had Jewish minorities as well, but the percentage of the population was quite small in comparison to the percentage of various minorities in Balkan lands.)

Austria and the Hapsburgs had also long dominated some areas of the Balkans. While this may have served the German-speaking community well, there were many, especially the Magyars of the Hungarian areas, who resented the German domination of leadership and bureaucracy. To address these complaints, quell some discontent, but still hold the Empire together, in 1867 the Dual Austrian and Hungarian monarchies were created. The area of Hungary would be led by a King, but it would still fall under the larger province of the Austrian Empire.

Within the Balkans there were many different independent nationalist movements matched by an understanding that any great changes would require the support of the Great Powers (France, Great Britain, Russia, Germany and Austria). And, indeed, the nationalist movements within the Balkans, (German-speakers, Magyars, Croats, Serbs, Muslims, Orthodox Christians, Catholics) would draw on the interests and concerns of Russia, Germany, France and Italy.) Nothing would be simple.

There had been expressions of proto-nationalism among the different groups and ethnic identities in the Balkans. However, it would be between 1804 and 1878 that four independent states emerged from the Balkans: Serbia, Greece, Montenegro and Romania (and Bulgaria became an autonomous area). And so, as historians Charles and Barbara Jelavich note, 'the Balkan people were able, in a relatively short time, to regain control of their political destinies. (Charles and Barbara, and Jelavich, *The Establishment of the Balkan National States*,

1977, reprint 2000). However, both internal and external conditions (many of which led to the nationalist moment) would mean that Balkan nationalist developments would be marked by outside interests and pressures, as well as internal dissent.

While Serbia became a nation-state in 1878, it was marked a by a great deal of internal fighting and external pressures. By the early nineteenth-century, Serbia was already a place heavily marked by the competing forces of the Ottoman and Hapsburg Empires. Serbia (Belgrade) had been the site of many eighteenth-century battles between the Austrians and the Ottomans. Wars throughout the eighteenth century had made Hapsburg interest, and potential control, over the area clear. As the Jelavichs note: 'During the wars, the Hapsburg government was often in administrative control of Serbian lands. Despite the opposition of the population to Ottoman rule, Austrian dominance was not popular, largely because of the activities of the Catholic church.' 'As noted above, the Ottoman Empire had not actively sought to convert the Serbian population to Islam; however, the Catholic Church (supported by the Hapsburgs) was interested in conversion. Serbians would not find this an acceptable state as "the substitution of a Christian for a Muslim overlord was not attractive nor was it an aim that the Serbian population subsequently sought as a political alternative."' (Jelavich, p. 26). In the early-nineteenth century, during the Napoleonic invasions, there had been revolutionary activity, led by Karadjordje Petrovic. While that movement had not succeeded in breaking away from the Ottoman Empire, by 1817 Serbia, without settled borders within the Empire, had established a national-minded leadership and formulated a nationalist ideology. By 1830 Serbia had secured significant Russian support for Serbian autonomy and, under the leadership of Milos Obrenovic, Serbia had established a government with power over its own internal affairs. Further, 'Serbian officials administered the country, collected the taxes, and regulated church affairs and other major aspects of national life. Ottoman nationals were forbidden to live in the countryside. The Muslim population was concentrated in major fortress cities. Ottoman landed property was confiscated with the agreement made that the Porte would compensate the owners from Serbian tribute.' Within a few years of these changes the previous contested boundaries of Serbia were set and by the 1860s the Obrenovic family became the hereditary princely rulers of Serbia, though as a constitutional monarchy that recognized many civil rights and included 'statements on the equality of all citizens, property rights, freedom of speech, religion, and the press, and the right to petition.' By 1876, Serbia had achieved independence from the Ottoman Empire. (Jelavich, pp. 29–37, 53–67).

During this same period Greece had achieved full independence and by the late nineteenth century many Balkan territories would be pressing to follow the path to autonomy within the Empire, or full independence. The Ottoman Empire at this point in the late nineteenth and early twentieth century had a twofold problem: managing the empire in the face of internal revolt from different ethnic nationalist groups (further divided by religious identities) and withstanding the pressures of the European great powers 'who pressed to control, directly or indirectly, the decisions of the Ottoman state. The internal and external threats to Ottoman cohesion would prove fatal to the Ottoman and Austrian Empires.' (Jelavich, pp. 99–100).

As noted, the Great Powers were heavily involved in the internal affairs of the new states of the Balkans in the nineteenth century—Serbia is a grand example of the way that the development of nationalism could shift traditional loyalties and bring moments of opportunity, if not opportunism, to others. Russia believed that in the area in general they could lay claim to Slavic loyalties. Further, on the eve of World War I, there were many secret societies in Bosnia and Serbia and beyond who were against Austrian Hapsburg rule. A potentially strong Serbian state making overtures to Serb nationalist in other lands needed to be addressed by Austria in some way. With the infamous assassination of Archduke Franz Ferdinand (the inheritor of the Austrian Hapsburg throne) by a Serb nationalist the mode that Austria chose in dealing with it was a desire to destroy it. When Franz Ferdinand was assassinated in Sarajevo, Bosnia (an area annexed by the Hapsburgs) in June 1914, it caused a great crisis both within the Austro-Hungarian Empire and throughout Europe. This crisis, as is rather famously known, is part of what led to World War I, which, ironically or not, led to the end of both the Ottoman and Austrian Empires.

The two main issues, as the Hapsburg Empire considered the assassination, was whether the neighbouring and independent Serbian state had played a role in the assassination, and, further, what this action revealed about the Hapsburg fear of a pan-Slavic (Yugoslav) state. There is no evidence that the Serbian government supported the actions of or abetted Gavrilo Princip, the Serbian nationalist and Black Hand member who shot the Archduke. However, Austria was not convinced. 'The assassination presented the imperial leaders with the apparent necessity of making a clear choice, since they were convinced that Serbia was implicated in the plot. They could either destroy the Serbian state, which had been the center of continual anti-Hapsburg activities since 1903, or they could await the slow dissolution of the monarchy.' (Jelavich, pp. 263–264). Despite Serbia's acquiescence to all but one of the terms of

Austria's harsh ultimatum to Serbia (the one requiring Austrian officials to be part of the internal Serbian investigation into the assassination—a term that would have destroyed any believable claim to Serbian sovereignty), Austria did not accept, a decision that was, no doubt, informed by Germany's promised support.

'Once again... the great powers found themselves pulled into war over problems associated with the Eastern Question and the rise of the national movements in the Balkans.' (Jelavich, pp. 264–265). This war would destroy 'the empires that had ruled the Balkans, and much of Eastern Europe, for centuries.' (Mazower, location 1798/2800). It would also mean the end of the German Empire, as well as tsarist Russia.

Mark Mazower sums it up well when he notes that The First World War was the culmination of this entangling of Balkan liberation struggle with the European state system.' (location 1356) The post-World War II, world provided another answer for the fragmented reality of Balkan nationalism. In an attempt to gather these groups back together and insist on cohesion, Yugoslavia ruled the Balkans in the model of a twentieth-century nation, hiding (or stamping out with authoritarian insistence) the unsettled realities of the multi-ethnic empire lurking underneath. The end of the Cold War and of Soviet power holding the disparate parts of Yugoslavia together would mean that the unsettled nationalist particularities of the nineteenth century would come bubbling back to the surface. The conflicts of the 1990s would be a tragic replaying of the different strands of nationalism and ethnic and religious identity in the Balkans.

IRELAND

As in the Balkans, Irish nationalism laid claims to competing identities and roots extending back hundreds of years. While the events and political contests of the late nineteenth and early-twentieth century are indicative of the nationalist ferment of the period, Irish nationalism continued to evolve and pressure Great Britain for change well into the late twentieth century.

Ireland was very much an agricultural society in the nineteenth century (not unusual, of course), and the relationship of Irish nationalism to land would be deep and pronounced. Disputes over land were one of the main issues that led to increased pressure for recognition of Irish independence from Great Britain.

The Act of Union of 1801 had formalized an essentially colonial relationship between Britain and Ireland. The Act abolished the Irish

Parliament and created the United Kingdom of Great Britain, with British rule over Ireland. Catholics were discriminated against, and even after Catholic Emancipation was enacted in 1829 British Protestants continued to dominate politics and the economy.

As mentioned above, the potato blight that destroyed crops throughout Europe in the mid-nineteenth century was particularly destructive in Ireland. Over one million Irish died in the famine and over two million left Ireland between 1845 and 1855 (many settling in New York which became a site of Irish nationalist agitation). The aftermath of this huge movement of people meant the consolidation of land ownership and cultivation in Ireland. While there was some industrial development in Ireland (Dublin and Belfast), Ireland remained an economy defined by agriculture. So, just as in the Paris-based revolutionary attempts of 1848, nationalist protest and action was directed through and expressed by the economic dynamics of the time and place. French revolutionaries, based in an urban setting and representing a working class protested for workshops and worker banquets. In more agricultural Ireland the nationalist cause came in the form of land protest.

Further, as Catholicism had been a defining part of certain Irish identity (as distinct from Protestant British identity) there was a rising Catholic identity and an increased role of Catholic priests in the nationalist struggle. The rise of nationalism also meant the growth of political groups that were no longer content to push for full Irish inclusion within the British state, but insisted on separation and independence from Britain. The story of Irish nationalism is also (like the Balkans) an example of the impact of sectarian identity on national identity. Going back hundreds of years the struggle between Ireland and Britain had also been the struggle of the British/Anglican monarchy's attempts (and successes) in asserting control over the Catholic majority in Ireland.

By the 1850s the level of anger at British dominance was great enough that secret societies formed pledging their undoing of British rule. The Irish Republican Brotherhood, its precursor founded in 1858, was both secret and paramilitary and its goal was the establishment of an independent Irish Republic, using revolutionary means.

Throughout the nineteenth century, insistence on land reform and self-government would dominate Irish politics. As the key issue for Ireland, agrarian reform and tenant's rights guided Irish nationalism. Tenants rallied for fair rent, fixity of tenure (meaning that if you adhered to your contract and paid rent you could not be evicted) and the idea of 'free sale' (when a property is sold a tenant should be compensated for any improvements he made). For many, especially those in the tenant league that formed, there was a vital linkage between land and liberation in Ireland.

The peasant farmers in Ireland who rented from British landowners became increasingly agitated and affected by the land laws that recognized British owners' prerogatives as supreme. The renters continued to press Parliament for more protection from eviction from the land. The great depression of the 1870s hurt farmers across Europe and further reduced the price of agricultural products—making it even harder for farmers to pay their rent. The Irish Land League, formed in 1879, grew in response to this developing crisis. The Land League certainly pulled its membership from worried renter farmers, but it also pulled from the secret society of Irish Republican Brotherhood (also referred to as Fenians), which was deeply committed to Irish independence. Gaining support, both memberse phip and financial, in the United States the Fenians would eventually come to blows with those who did not want Irish independence: the Unionists who wanted to remain in the union with Great Britain.

By the mid-1860s, there were violent expressions of those political and nationalist clashes. For example, the 'smashing of the van' on 18 September 1867 was the first act of Irish revolutionary activity on British soil, when the rescue of two Fenian prisoners from a police van in Manchester led to the death of the police sergeant.

The British Prime Minister, Gladstone, tried to address some of the complaints in the hopes of undermining support for the Fenians. However, neither the 1869 'Church Disestablishment' (which ended the Irish Anglican Church) nor the Land Reform of 1870 and 1881 (which made overtures to Irish peasants and acknowledged their grievances and 'theoretical' rights on the land) quelled the ongoing agitation for Irish independence which was increasingly expressed as a call for 'Home Rule'.

The goal of those who called for 'Home Rule' was to create an Irish Parliament that would have control over Irish domestic affairs, but would still come under the ultimate control (on larger United Kingdom issues) of the British government. 'Home Rule' was offered up, and seen by many, as a compromise between the Unionist—who wanted to keep the base relation of the Union of 1801, and the militant Fenians who scared many with their revolutionary violence. Charles Stewart Parnell (1846–1891) would become the name most closely associated with nineteenth-century attempts at Irish Home Rule, though in his own time it would not be achieved.

The ongoing advocacy of Irish Home Rule became a deeply divisive issue in British Parliament. And it was not just men like Parnell who advocated for it. At Gladstone's return to Prime Minister in 1880 he also began to call for the necessity of Home Rule. His commitment to this eventually led to the split of his Liberal Party as well as the creation of the 'Unionists'. In this way the issue of Irish Home Rule created a restructuring of British political parties.

Eventually that realignment would mean that 'Home Rule' would pass, and in 1912 it was passed into law. A number of events would intervene that would stop this law from simply and quickly doing what it pledged and begin the steps towards what many imagined might soon be an independent Ireland. Firstly, those in Ireland opposed to this change—the Unionists—thousands of Ulster Protestants—pledged their support to insuring that this would never happen. Secondly, before Home Rule could be truly implemented World War I began. And so, as in the case of the Balkans, the forces of nationalism met opposition from within their own 'territory', and from without from a part of the Empire that they were pulling away from. But greater world forces (World War I) would also intervene. So, World War I would mean the suspension of Home Rule for the duration of the war, but it was clear in any case that those with a different sense of nationalism (the Ulster Unionists) would present a challenge to a unilateral nationalist vision, and certainly meant that Civil War hung on the horizon.

Home Rule would eventually come, just as the Austrian and Ottoman Empires would eventually fall. But, both Ireland and the Balkans would continue to have unresolved and violent nationalist movements which highlighted the contested nature of nation and identity in the regions.

NATION AND THE ABSTRACT: THE PROCESS AND THEORY

By the late nineteenth century there was a clear, and apparently permanent, shift to the primacy of the nation in domestic and international politics. Further, competition between powers (always an aspect of the world) became more clearly addressed through nationalist rhetoric of justifications for the good of a nation. And, of course, the nationalist competitions of Europe began to have an impact well beyond the continental borders, as imperial expansion—often framed with nationalist rhetoric—affected the lands and people of Africa and Asia.

Part of the challenge for new nations would be to get all of its inhabitants to 'buy into' the nationalist programme. This would prove to be a particular challenge in areas where ethnic minorities still felt marginalized by the dominant group, culture, language or religion of an area. This often posed a practical challenge to the government of new, emerging or established nations who had to quell minority unrest.

STATE-BUILDING

From the perspective of the government many of the concerns were quite practical: How to govern a people (and include the governed in some iteration of representative democracy) when they may be separated by historical, cultural, linguistic or religious differences? How to forge a coherent nation where there was not one before? While neither language, nor culture, nor religion nor economic homogeneity would be the thing that would define a nation, the government, as system of rule in the nation, did take those things into account.

As the job of a national government was to administer the inhabitants of a defined territory it meant that it had to pay increasing attention to the opinions of its citizens—as taxpayers, army conscripts, etc. And, as many observers of nationalism would note, there was increased interaction between citizens and members of a growing bureaucracy of the nation state. Over the course of the nineteenth century, the intervention of the state into the lives of individuals became routinized (see Eugen Weber, *Peasants into Frenchmen*, 1976). Unlike previous times, in the nineteenth century, one would have to be very isolated not to come into contact with some representative of national state (as opposed to a local official). Most citizens would expect to interact with a postman, police or gendarme, a school teacher, or railway worker (where it was public), no matter how distant they might be from the capital city.

In addition, the state began to keep more account and record of its subjects and citizens. While many previous governments (especially concerned, if not paranoid, monarchies) had created secret police forces and kept watch on individual they thought could be a threat to their rule, the actions of the state toward recordkeeping and tracking of citizens now became a matter of course (though certainly still of potential political use against those deemed suspicious). Nation-states began to conduct periodic census of its inhabitants, often becoming quite common and general by the late nineteenth century. Free and compulsory schools—at least at the primary level—became a standard component of nation states—as a means of spreading the national language (and, conversely, as a way to end the persistent use of dialects or language that were expressions of an allegiance to a group other than the dominant population). Military service was another vehicle of the inculcation of national languages and values, and, of course, the force that could wage national battles both on the continent and in the colonies which became a proxy battleground for European national rivalries.

States increasing provided (eventually insisted) a civil alternative to ecclesiastical celebration of certain rites and one would encounter state representatives at these moments in life. Not all such changes were orchestrated from above, though governments were plainly engaged in engineering this ideological shift and had a thorough interest in drawing citizens into a close relationship with (and defence of) the nation.

THEORY OF NATIONALISM

It is no surprise, given its import and locus of contention, that nationalism has been the topic of intense theoretical debate. Since the first modern use of the word nation there have been historians, political theorists and philosophers who have tried to address and understand the complicated dynamics of nationalist ideology and to understand the reasons the very concept of a nation has had such broad appeal.

The concept, meaning and import of nations and nationalism have been topics of great inquiry since even before the triumph of nationalism. One of the first theorists of nationalism was Ernst Renan (1823–1892). Considering what has already been written in this chapter on nationalism it is no surprise that Renan wrote during the latter part of the nineteenth century. In his oft-cited work, 'What is a Nation?' a lecture delivered at the Sorbonne in 1882, Renan commented on the abstraction of the nation as it operated in time and place, calling on the concept of a nation's soul and addressing the role of writing history in the national psyche. Renan felt history itself played a very important role in the concept of the nations and he wrote of two important aspects of the idea of the nations, a 'common rich legacy of remembering', and the 'actual consent, the desire to live together.' This idea—of the consent to live together—in conjunction with a shared remembering (or construction of national historical past) would have great influence over other theorists of nationalism, most notably Benedict Anderson, who will be addressed below.

Renan also pointed to other key characteristics of the individual and group relationship to the nation. For Renan, an idea, or shared memory of individual and group sacrifice was an important component of nationalism: 'A nation is a grand solidarity constituted by the sentiment of sacrifice which one has made and those that one is disposed to make again.' (Hutchinson and Smith, p. 17)

Writing in the nineteenth century, and having lived through the creation of Italy and Germany, Renan was straightforward about the constructed nature of nations. Although those that championed the creation of nations would call upon the idea of an eternal and organic national existence, Renan knew better, as he wrote, 'Nations are not something eternal. They have begun, they will end.' (Hutchinson and Smith, p. 17–18) Renan recognized his own time as a period of nationalism (and nationalization) and also forecast or envisioned a post-national world.

Other theorists of nationalism have focused on other aspects of the phenomena. Ernest Gellner (1925–1995) writing in the 1980s in his important work *Nations and Nationalism* (1983) argued that nationalism is the belief that 'the political and the national should be congruent.' Further, he specifically considered nationalism a modern phenomenon—a topic of significant discussion among nationalism theorists. Gellner argued that modernity—industrialization, mechanization, economic development—necessitated a certain level of education for a significant number of people in any place. Literacy was a precondition for the modern development of capitalism and nationalism. The developments of the modern era also created a great deal of competition for territory and economic expansion and this pushed governments to be a force for cultural standardization and literacy. In this scheme schools—as the site of cultural homogenization and mass literacy—were both vehicles for nationalism and products of it. Further, Gellner argued, to be a citizen meant understanding the language of legislation and to have the possibility of economic or social mobility. In the nineteenth century economic advancement and mobility would increasingly depend on the understanding of technological instructions and the ability to trade beyond the most local world of one's ancestral village. If literacy and technological competence were essential to that modern condition then, Gellner argued, only a 'nation-sized educational system can produce such full citizens.'

An education system, Gellner noted, and its medium or language created the confines of a nation and in most cases and places that medium stamps the parameters of the nation itself. Most people, he argued, function within their own educational and professional world, and in most cases that is congruent with their national world. In this way education has to be part of the nationalist project—to literally educate people in the language of their nation for professional and political comprehension, and at the same time, getting rid of the other identities that might be conveyed by dialect, which might only serve to break down national identity. Education is produced by the modern forces that also produce nationalism, but education systems also normalize nationalist politics and create partisans of the nation.

Gellner also argued for the rational embrace of nationalism, a point of some contention among nationalist theorists. 'Men do not in general become nationalists from sentiment or sentimentality, atavistic or not, well-based or myth-founded; they become nationalists through genuine, objective, practical necessity, however obscurely recognized.' (as cited in Hutchinson and Smith, p. 56).

While noting the power of national mythology (folklore, for example) Gellner believed that the reality of nationalism actually depended on the conscious 'artificiality' of these historical and cultural ideals. While the 'peasant' may be an icon of nationalist ideal Gellner, Nationalisn and Modernization, the actual peasant will not thrive or survive a nationalist world, nor will nationalist structures have truly set a foundation until the kin of the peasants have gone to school and learned the national language, new technology, and become part of new modern commerce. Such is Gellner's reliance on education and literacy to both transfer nationalist sentiment onto groups previously the repositories of particular, not national culture, but to also show the logic for individuals and groups to embrace nationalism. The end result for Gellner is that 'identification, loyalty and effective citizenship depends on literacy and education in the one favoured language.' (Gellner, Nationalisn and Modernization, p. 60). Gellner does give space for the reality of divisive nationalism (as would be seen in part of the Balkan story). He acknowledges that if language, or the acquisition of the dominant language, were the only issue in nationalism then there would be no cause for competing nationalisms. Gellner posited that this is in cases where it is difficult for certain individuals (because of the 'racial' or cultural constructions of the dominant nation) to enter into the larger, dominant nation. But in an optimistic spirit Gellner points out that just as industrialization (and modernization more generally) has not marched at a steady pace in all areas and times, so too the establishment of new nations, and the ability to enter their culture, happens in fits and starts.

Most theorists of nationalism, and all such theorists addressed in this chapter, considered nationalism a modern phenomenon. But they differ in their consideration of nationalism as a part of the process of modernization, whether nationalism was another manifestation of a modern world, or whether nationalism is the consequence of embracing certain modern cultures.

For example, Gellner openly critiques any notion that nationalism, and the subsequent creation of nations, was the clear destiny of previous political movements in certain areas. He clearly exposed as myth the idea that nations are in some way 'natural' ordained political destiny, or, as he notes, a 'God-given way of classifying men'. (Hutchinson and Smith, p. 63, citing Gellner, *Nations and Nationalism*, Blackwell: Oxford, 1983, pp. 48–49).

For Gellner it is nationalism which creates nations, and not nations which create nationalism (Hutchinson and Smith, p. 64 citing Gellner, *Nations and Nationalism*, Blackwell: Oxford, 1983, pp. 48–49) And, as this chapter has confirmed, one cannot comprehend the concept of nations outside the context of the period we call the 'Age of Nationalism'. This is because, Gellner wrote, that it is on this period that 'social conditions make for standardized, homogeneous, centrally sustained high cultures, pervading entire populations and not just elite minorities.' With that accomplishment, and the sharing of cultures across a social spectrum you have the creation of a 'unit' which many come to identify with and see as the valid and legitimate expression of their culture—a nation.

With this creation the culture can also be transformed, mythologies created, languages resurrected—and all presented as if this new nation was simply the destiny of long-held cultural practices; whereas, the practices are the nation's own invention (Hutchinson and Smith, p. 64 citing Gellner, Nations and Nationalism, Blackwell: Oxford, 1983, p. 65).

ANDERSON AND HOBSBAWM: IMAGINING AND INVENTING

One of the most-cited, and convincing, arguments made by recent scholars of nationalism is that, in the words of anthropologist Benedict Anderson, '[the nation] is an imagined political community and imagined as inherently limited and sovereign' (Benedict Anderson (1991), *Imagined Communities*, p.6). Anderson goes on to elaborate that we must conceive of this relationship in the nation as imagined because all the members of the nation will not meet or know each other, and yet each believes (or imagines) the connection of those in the community. He also elaborates what he means by limited—that no one believes they are part of a community that is the population of the planet. In the imagination of its partisans all nations do have some limits, they may change over time but there are boundaries, just as, coming out of the modern period, the nation is connected to the idea of sovereignty.

Anderson, while noting some connections to Gellner and his observation that nationalism invented nations, also points out what he sees as a flaw in Gellner's work. To Anderson, as to many, the fact that nations, like so many human propositions, are invented, does not make them 'false'. As Benedict argues, 'In fact all communities larger than primordial villages of face-to-face contact... are imagined. Communities are to be distinguished, not by their falsity/genuineness, but by the style in which they are imagined.' (Anderson, p. 6). What Anderson is also pointing out in this is the power of the abstraction of the nation. To know one's neighbours or some countrymen and to speak with them about their desires for a nation is one thing, to extend that concrete exchange of ideas into the sphere of millions of people one will never know, and imagine they share some of those some beliefs about a nation requires a leap into the unknown and into an abstraction from the specifics of a time and place to the general and unconfirmed—to the imagined. The power of this observation about the imagined nature of the nation is not to argue that it makes it inauthentic or fake, but simply to become conscious of the leap of abstraction that all members of a community make.

The work of the historian Eric Hobsbawm also operates within this framework: seeing the traditions and operations of the nation as purposely created, at a specific time and place (though necessarily evolving over time) in order to give some concrete practice to the imagined communities. Hobsbawm observes that many national traditions that claim to be old are actually very recent in their adoption and recently invented. Like Anderson, for Hobsbawm the claim that traditions are invented does not necessarily render them meaningless for their practitioners, but to make one conscious of the impetus for their original invention. Hobsbawm clearly sees the invented traditions, notable of the nineteenth and twentieth centuries, as one of the vehicles for transmitting national ideals—and hence creating nations themselves.

As he writes, '"Invented tradition" is taken to mean a set of practices, normally governed by overtly or tacitly accepted rules and of a ritual or symbolic nature, which seek to inculcate certain values and norms of behaviour by repetition, which automatically implies continuity with the past. In fact, where possible, they normally attempt to establish continuity with a suitable historic past.' (Hobsbawm and Ranger *The Invention of Tradition,* 2003. Page 1.) A suitable historic past is essential to the claims of nationalists—whether rallying for the recognition of their right to existence, or whether a more established nation appealing to its citizens for some sacrifice in the name of the nation. The lure of the past, as was noted above, was powerful to nationalist of all stripes. The presentation of a past history that legitimized a nation's existence, and argued its rightful place among other nations, or, indeed, to surpass them, was part of the lifeblood of nations. It legitimized them, allowed them to constantly renew connections to the people and made the abstract nation a concrete and felt practice in private homes and communities. Whether U.S. President Lincoln's creation of Thanksgiving, which constructed a shared past of sacrifice to help move past the more recent Civil War of the mid-nineteenth century, or the invention of the British monarch's Christmas Day address, created in 1932, the invention of these traditions reaffirmed the relationship of the state to subjects and citizens, and citizens to each other. To recognize that traditions we hold dear are invented (and some recently so) is not necessarily to diminish them, or, harkening back to Gellner and Anderson, to make them false. It is simple to realize that nations, and their 'national' languages, costumes, music, anthems, flags, foods and holidays were not handed down from the beginning of time, intact and ready to be received by an already accepting community, but simply the work of the nation itself, to reaffirm to itself what it is.

CONCLUSION

Nationalism has proven itself to be one of the most significant and enduring ideologies of the modern era. While the first seeds of nationalism were planted in the eighteenth century, by the end of that century, and the passing of the dramatic events and rhetoric of the French Revolution, the language, structures, arguments around and potential force of nationalism were already clear. As the eighteenth century ended, monarchs—the traditional and time-tested form of government and state—were on shakier ground than a half-century earlier. Though 'restored' in the second decade of the nineteenth century, the restoration would never be complete and by the mid-nineteenth century, the power of nationalist ideology, linked to reformists and liberals, in Europe was clear. The latter-half of the nineteenth century ushered in the 'heyday' of nationalist development and was the period of intense nationalist and state-making activity in many regions of Europe. The two grand examples—Italy and Germany—became nation-states by the last quarter of the nineteenth century—with many other examples throughout Europe and Latin America.

In the early nineteenth century, Napoleon brought reforms of state to the countries he conquered and the monarchies he ousted in his march (often to be replaced by rulers from his own family tree). Whether ending traditional privileges of the noble class or insisting on uniform law codes, creating administrative departments and expanding bureaucracies, Napoleons legacy vis-à-vis the trappings or practicalities of the modern nation state are evident throughout the nineteenth-century world. His defeat on the continent did not mean the end of the workings of the modern state, but simply a transformation. The wave of revolutions that swept through Europe in the 1830s and 18040s also provide some context for understanding the development of mass politics, the impact on nationalism, the demands of new citizens and the concerns and responses by those in power.

Italy's Risorgimento (1815–1870), 'Young Europe' movements, German unification, Irish claims for Home Rule and Balkan nationalism are all examples of the varied forms of new nationalist ideals.

Nationalism has had a huge impact in creating the accepted structures of global relationships. While in its history nationalism is being told in this chapter as a nineteenth-century story it has an impact well beyond that—both in temporality and in space. Indeed, as we consider the present day, for all the discussion of a post-national world, we still inhabit a globe that is structured according to nineteenth-century ideas of the nation as the most legitimate and recognized representation of people and states.

Parts of this chapter have tried to point out, particularly in a discussion on the theory of nationalism, that the very early work of a nation is to create founding myths, which are quickly held to be proof of the nation (and supporting state's) destiny and reason—or legitimization—for even existing. So, while urging students of history to be aware that history is the story that nation's tell themselves, the chapter has also indulged in pat of the process of maintaining national mythologies. Readers should understand that tales of Bismarck, Cavour and Parnell were essential to the cause of Italian, German and Irish nationalism respectively, but they are also part of the very invention of nationalist history that justifies the work of Bismarck, Cavour and Parnell.

As we look at our world today we see the continued presence and power of nationalism. While there has been much discussion in the last decades of living in a post-national world, it is equally clear that we continue to inhabit a globe that places the greatest recognizable legitimacy on the concept of the nation.

The symbols of a nation (flags, anthems and mythological or allegorical figures) still appear within the halls of government, industry and in private use to signify the belief in the cohesion and power of the nation. Nationalist ventures such as schools, national language (and even the debates around national language) and the army continue to be both expressions of a nation as well as a vehicle to acculturation within a nationalist framework. But, perhaps knowing the novelty of nationalism and the 'imagined' aspects of all nations can make us all more nuanced thinkers as we consider the course of a nationalist or post-nationalist world.

Essential Readings

Anderson, Benedict (1983), revised 1991. *Imagined Communities*. London and New York: Verso.

Breuilly, John (1996), *The Formation of the First German Nation-State 1800–1871*.

Foster, R.F. (1989), *Modern Ireland 1600–1972*. London and New York: Penguin.

Gellner, Ernest (1983, 2006), *Nations and Nationalism*. Ithaca, New York: Cornell University Press.

Hobsbawm, Eric and Terence Ranger (eds.) (2003), *The Invention of Tradition*. Cambridge: Cambridge University Press.

Jelavich, Charles and Barbara (1977), *The Establishment of the Balkan National States, 1804–1920*. Seattle and London: University of Washington Press.

Riall, Lucy (2009), *Risorgimento: The History of Italy from Napoleon to Nation State*. London: Palgrave Macmillan.

Further Readings

Theory

The following books are some of the key foundational texts of the discussion about the nature and dynamics of nationalism.

Breuilly, John (1982), *Nationalism and the State*. Manchester: Manchester University Press.

Calhoun, Craig (1997), *Nationalism*. Minneapolis: University of Minnesota Press.

Calhoun, Craig (2007), *Nations Matter: Culture, History, and the Cosmopolitan Dream*. London and New York: Routledge.

Chatterjee, Partha (1993), *The Nation and its Fragments*. Princeton: Princeton University Press.

Hobsbawm, Eric. *Nations and Nationalism*.

Kedourie, Elie (1960), *Nationalism*. London: Hutchinson.

Smith, Anthony (2010), *Nationalism*. Cambridge: Polity Press.

Edited Collections of Theory

Hutchinson, John and Anthony Smith (eds.) (1994), *Nationalism*. Oxford: Oxford University Press.

Woolf, Stuart (ed.) (1996), *Nationalism in Europe 1815 to the present: A Reader*. London and New York: Routledge.

National Examples

Each national story could be its own chapter in this textbook. The following provide both overviews of the national tale, as well as significant details of events over the course of the nineteenth and early twentieth century.

The Balkans

Dragostinova, Theodora (2011), *Between Two Motherlands: Nationalism and Emigration among the Greeks of Bulgaria* (1900–1949). Ithaca: Cornell University Press.

Mazower, Mark (2002), *The Balkans: A Short History*, Modern Library Chronicles, Kindle edition.

Germany

Breuilly, John (ed.) (1992), *The State of Germany: The National Idea in the Making, Unmaking and Remaking of a Modern Nation-State.*

Blackbourn, David and Geoff Eley (1984), *The Peculiarities of German History: Bourgeois Society and Politics in Nineteenth-Century German History.*

Smith, Helmut (1995), *German Nationalism and Religious Conflict: Culture Ideology, Politics, 1870–1914.*

Stern, Fritz (1977), *Gold and Iron: Bismarck, Bleichroeder, and the Building of the German Empire.*

Ireland

Garvin, Tom (1981), *The Evolution of Irish Nationalist Politics*. Dublin: Gill and Macmillan.

Townshend, Charles (1999), *Ireland: The 20th Century*. London: Arnold.

Townshend, Charles (1983), *Political Violence in Ireland: Government and resistance since 1848*. Oxford.

Italy

Banti, A.M. (2004), *Il Risorgimento Italiano*. Rome and Bari.

Beales, D. and E.F. Biagini. (2002), *The Risorgimento and the Unification of Italy*. London.

Davis, J.A. (ed). (2000), *Italy in the Nineteenth Century*. Oxford.

Hearder, H. (1983), *Italy in the Age of the Risorgimento*, London.

Index

S